THE
Herbalist
IN THE
Kitchen

THE
Herbalist
IN THE
Kitchen

GARY ALLEN

UNIVERSITY OF ILLINOIS PRESS
URBANA AND CHICAGO

Library of Congress
Cataloging-in-Publication Data

Allen, Gary (Gary J.)
The herbalist in the kitchen / Gary Allen.
p. cm. — (The food series)
Includes bibliographical references
and index.
ISBN-13: 978-0-252-03162-5
(cloth : alk. paper)
ISBN-10: 0-252-03162-8
(cloth : alk. paper)
1. Cookery (Herbs) 2. Herbs. I. Title.
TX819.H4A57   2007
641.3'57—dc22   2006100939

Contents

Illustrations

All illustrations are courtesy of the Missouri Botanical Garden, selected from volumes in its rare book collection. Titles of many of the old books are quite long, so they have been abbreviated in figure captions; complete information can be found in the bibliography.

Acknowledgments

A book like this is the product of the expertise and support of many people. All the credit for its strengths, and none of the blame for its weaknesses, goes to the folks below, and to countless others whose names should be here as well.

The collective culinary experience of my former colleagues at the Culinary Institute of America is probably unmatched anywhere. I thank especially Tony Colella, Bob Delgrosso, Jennifer Dunn, Markus Färbinger, Eve Felder, Steven Kolpan, Krishnendu Ray, David St. John-Grubb, Konstantin Sembos, Fritz Sonnenschmidt, Jonathan Zearfoss, and the late Karen Allison.

The librarians at the Conrad N. Hilton Library of the Culinary Institute of America, the Massachussetts Horticutural Society Library, the Sojourner Truth Library of the State University of New York at New Paltz, and the Vassar College Library were always helpful.

Carole Ford and Steve Lewis, of Empire State College, offered support, guidance, and endless good humor. I thank them for treating me like a fellow author, long before I was one.

Howie Michels and Francine Prose expressed an enthusiasm for cooking, gardening, and this project at its very inception and provided the necessary momentum at just the right time.

Suzanne Hamlin, food writer, gadfly, and culinary networker par excellence, is the sort of person who makes good food and wine books happen, all around her—and not just her own.

Carole Metsger and Debra Tobin Gray plied me with seeds and plants.

Bob Bragner, Joe Carlin, Armin Raab, Roger Whitehead, Richard Wright, and countless others contributed to the ongoing discussions at the rec.food .historic newsgroup.

Lisa Becker, Paul Canales, Daniela Cole, Mark Henry, Pete Minich, and Neal Swidler—former students at the Culinary Institute of America— exhibited an excitement and energy that fueled my work, and they never complained, at least to me, about being forced to hear, again and again, about this book.

Rachel Laudan, Harold McGee, Jacqueline Newman, Patricia Rain, and Paula Wolfert helped clarify my thinking and provided specific information I couldn't find anywhere else.

At the University of Illinois Press, Willis G. Regier, my editor and the Press director; Carol Betts, my copy editor; Copenhaver Cumpston, the book's designer; and the thoughtful, anonymous readers of my manuscript were incredibly attentive to detail, as was Andrew F. Smith, editor of the Food Series. They never lost the broad perspective needed to bring a project like this to completion.

Deborah Begley and Tamara Watson were always there when needed, usually with great food and wine, and always with great intelligence.

My parents, Jack and Billie, taught me that food is important, that wonderful dishes come from all over the world, and that those dishes needn't be expensive or difficult to prepare to be delicious.

My stepson, Aaron Rester, always the intellectual, is now beginning to show signs of becoming a good cook as well, thereby resolving (for me, at least) the ancient question about the relative importance of nature and nurture in a person's development.

And finally, I thank my wife—the saintly Karen Philipp—whose caring, knowledge, wisdom, practicality, and sense of humor (not to mention patience, forgiveness, and forbearance) make all things possible.

Introduction

This book is not a reissue of Nicholas Culpeper, even if his work has been the basis of most herbals written in English since the seventeenth century. His list of herbs—with many of the same recommendations for use—has been passed on, modified, and expanded. I hope that the present book is both larger and smaller in scope: larger, because my approach to herbs is not limited in the ways that an author from more than three centuries ago was limited; smaller, because household uses, including pharmacological uses, which were important in Culpeper's day, are not relevant to our purposes here.

Most herbs, at one time or another, have had claims made about their medical properties. Many books address these issues, but it is not within the scope of this book to do so. While I do not intend to list the real or imagined medical properties of each herb, however, it is worthwhile to acknowledge the subject in a general way.

In the interest of pharmacological correctness, let us examine the nature of traditional herbal remedies. There are two primary categories of herbal remedies: those that work and those that don't. Like most grand simplifications, this one overlooks the fact that specific examples may fall somewhere between these two extremes; but a simplistic assertion is sometimes useful as an explanatory tool, as long as we don't forget that it is only a tool.

Herbal remedies in the former category may have been discovered by careful research, trial and error, experience, or just plain dumb luck. The fact that they work is of great interest to scientists and physicians and certainly to people who may benefit by treatment with the herbs. Such plants contain compounds that have been used either directly as medicines or as sources of materials in the formulation of modern pharmaceuticals.

Among the ones that work, we may include those plants that are especially high in valuable nutrients. Some herbs, such as purslane and sorrel, do have substantial quantities of ingredients that are essential to our well-being. These two, because they are eaten in large enough quantities to provide a significant quantity of these nutrients, are exceptional. Most herbs, even though they are rich in vitamins and minerals, are used primarily as seasoning. One simply doesn't consume enough of the plant to make much difference in health.

The second category ("medicinal" plants that don't work as medicine) offers a number of intriguing areas for our scrutiny. If there is no scientific proof that an herb has curative properties, yet there is anecdotal evidence for its efficacy, we must look to other causes. Once again, there are two possibilities: the scientific basis has not yet been found (but if found, moves the herb into our original first category) or the herb has some placebo effect.

Mysticism and Culture

Placebos may work for many reasons, but they all depend on the belief of the individual taking "the cure." Beliefs are, by definition, not susceptible to proof by logical means. Some philosophers would argue that any subject that cannot be resolved by logical means is not worth discussion. This, however, is not a philosophical discussion. It is cultural. Herbs have been part of human culture for a long time. They have acquired a lot of cultural baggage along the way. It is this baggage that gives credence to the faith healers' claims.

The metaphors that are at the heart of these beliefs are also close to the associations we make when we eat. To say that taste resides in the tongue, with assistance from the nose, is to grossly oversimplify. We taste with our brains. Our palate resides there, making use of tongue and nose as tools—effective, but not exclusive, tools.

Everything we know—or think we know—affects our perceptions of food. When we taste the rosemary, sage, and thyme in the stuffing of a Thanksgiving turkey, we do not taste the sum of the ingredients alone. We taste all the collateral cultural associations as well. An ancient remembrance, pleasurable or not, can be relived through a single taste. Does anyone honestly believe that Proust's epiphany with his madeleine was accomplished by his tongue?

What does this mean for us, as herbalists in the kitchen? Whether we do or do not believe in herbal cures, the stories, metaphors, and allusions from which the placebos derive their power affect us as cooks and diners.

There may be some symbolism based on physical resemblances between the herb and the human body, or parts thereof. Plants that look like sexual organs are alleged to have aphrodisiacal properties. Hepatica is named for its leaves' supposed resemblance to the shape of the liver. The roots of mandrake and ginseng are thought to look like miniature human beings. Many cultures make medical use of these plants solely because of those resemblances. This form of analogous thought is known as "the doctrine of signatures."

A similar process, involving the physical appearance of herbs, is somewhat more removed. Sometimes visual features provide an herb with its name. If an herb is named after an animal, and the animal symbolizes certain strengths, the herb may be considered to share those traits. This could be called "the syllogistic method."

Closely related is what may be called "the assumptive method." The consumer of a certain plant *assumes,* or benefits from, the characteristics of the plant. Rosemary, having a long-lasting scent, is believed to help its users to recover their memories.

Sometimes herbs suggest their use as remedies by growing in proximity with other plants. Plants that grow near each other may be thought to either reinforce or counteract the properties of the other. Jewelweed grows near, but not right next to, poison ivy, so some people believe it to be a natural antidote for the itch of poison ivy. This belief process could be called "the proximate method." Whether or not jewelweed actually has the desired effect is outside of the scope of this book.

These quantum jumps of the imagination are exactly the kinds of creative association of ideas that are the foundation of poetry and other refined arts, including the culinary arts, and they may have led our ancestors to try herbal remedies that were, coincidentally, efficacious. Our logical selves may put them aside as insignificant, but we hold them carefully in reserve, knowing that we ultimately resort to them to create the metaphors we need to interpret our experiences.

Food Danger Issues

Beyond this passing notice of herbs as medicine, the subject is not covered in the herbal entries. The only exception to this rule is when the pharmacological properties of an herb may make its use dangerous. Some plants have chemical properties that cannot safely be ignored. It is possible to use some herbs in a dangerous or illegal manner. The fact that I do or do not mention such use should by no means imply that I recommend or condone such use.

I highly encourage *informed* use of any herb you intend to consume. It is not possible to take too many precautions. There are a number of types of concern.

I have listed several herbs for which one or more sources advise against excessive use. How much is too much? Alcohol, for example, has been used in almost every known culture. Yet everyone knows of problems related to excessive use. Almost everyone knows how difficult it is determine the threshold of danger for any particular individual. Why should the process be any easier with relatively obscure herbs?

Many plants, routinely used as foods, can be dangerous if used incorrectly. A potato, if allowed to become green or sprout eyes, can develop toxins. Our familiarity with potatoes preserves us from any inconvenience. Such familiarity will be just as beneficial to serious users of herbs.

It may sound obvious, but proper identification of herbs is essential. For example, many shrubs are called "laurel" in the United States. Almost every one of them is toxic, except for bay leaves. The leaves look the same. Only information about the source, or the plant itself, can properly identify a bay leaf.

I have tried to include warnings when dangerous confusions seem likely. I have also included some herbs, suitably noted, that are known to be toxic. I have done so because a reader of old herbal books or cookbooks may be misled by the multiple use of common names, or worse, by an ancient author's understandable lack of modern scientific information. In some cases, dangerous herbs have no known culinary purpose, but as their names may be found in old herbals or recipe books, they are included here—with appropriate warnings in the "Comments" section of the entries.

Once a reader ventures beyond the dozen or so common herbs, the literature tends to become somewhat more technical than most cooks would desire. I have tried to distill the relevant portions of this vast material to facts that might actually be of use in the kitchen. What might appear at first to be technical mumbo jumbo (e.g., the chemical names of the main flavorings contained in the herbs) could be useful to the cook. Suppose, for example, a recipe calls for za'atar, but your spice rack has none. Knowing that carvacrol and thymol are the most important flavoring components of za'atar can help in determining a last-minute substitution (in this case, thyme). Likewise, if you've also run out of thyme, wild bergamot, with its high carvacrol and thymol content, will do in a pinch. Such emergency substitutions bring along additional flavors and aromas as well. An alert cook will benefit from serendipitous juxtapositions of flavors, and new dishes will result.

Reading through the flavorings literature can offer some insights into areas beyond the kitchen. The history and geography of the herb and spice trade have been the subjects of several books already, but these subjects are more complex and fascinating than a reader might suspect. They cry out for a bigger, and fuller, understanding. They are far beyond the scope of this volume, but I would love to see a book on such topics. On a smaller scale, a fascinating book could be written on the history of adulteration of herbs and spices, alone. I allude occasionally, usually in the "Comments" section of the entries, to some of these illicit activities. To explore fully the mendacity of spice merchants through the centuries would provide a mesmerizing, if slightly depressing, look at humans' capacity for avarice.

Some Notes on Format and Conventions Used in the Text

Wherever possible, I have used *Hortus Third,* the third and most recent edition of L. H. Bailey and E. Z. Bailey's reference work, prepared by staff members at Cornell University's Liberty Hyde Bailey Hortorium, as the final arbiter in questions of scientific classification of herbs. There is an important limitation to the usefulness of *Hortus Third:* it addresses only plants known to be grown in North America at the time of its publication (1976). The list of plants cultivated in North America is increasing all the time. Some of the plants we use as herbs are not grown here, but may be soon. The last three decades have witnessed an unparalleled expansion in culinary and horticultural awareness. Perhaps the next edition of *Hortus* will address some of these new tastes. I don't envy its editors their task. The relentless increase in the assemblage of cultivated plants must produce some of the sensations felt by the sorcerer's apprentice.

Some plant names you may encounter are outside the scope of this book. Some herbs have no culinary use. I may include them, as limited entries, solely in the hope of eliminating some confusion due to multiple uses of matching or similar names.

A few words about words: if you spend much time reading through old books on herbs, you soon discover that spelling was not a high priority among early herbalists or, indeed, food writers. This is not entirely their fault; after all, there was no successful dictionary of the English language until Samuel Johnson saw the need for one in the eighteenth century. Because a reader might encounter any sort of unlikely spelling, I originally intended to include various unusual combinations of letters I encountered. In some cases, writers have dealt with foreign expressions phonetically. In others, it is hard to imagine *what* they were thinking. If the present book harbors any hope of untangling this messy subject, it must acknowledge the existence of some semantic snarls and bewildering lapses of lexical judgment. Viewed more positively, the misspelled words evoke the rustic charm of simpler times.

While not wishing to perpetuate these errors, I seemed to have little choice but to include them; however, for reasons of space, I have deleted many of the alternate names of plants that result from differing attempts at phonetic spelling.

Also, I did not wish to repeat, ad nauseam, that the Latin names used by apothecaries, pharmacists, and—to some extent even today—the flavorings industry do not correspond to scientific Latin binomials. They tended to use the common Latin name of the plant in combination with descriptors such as *cortex* (bark), *radix* (root), *flores* (flowers), *herbae* or *foliae* (leaves), and *semen* or *fructae* (seeds) to reflect only the part of the plant used.

Scientific naming of species grew out of that practice, but it imposes a rigorous set of rules, designed to eliminate the confusion of species by creating a unique hierarchy of groupings that define and locate the named species. In an ideal world, the system would work perfectly.

The real world, however, is a messy place, full of ambiguity. It is open to many varied, conflicting, and seemingly logical interpretations—simultaneously. As a result, even the highly rational science of taxonomy cannot resolve some confusions. Zoologists define species as a group of animals that, when mated, can produce viable, fertile offspring. If pressed, zoologists may grudgingly admit the existence of subspecies. Botanists, on the other hand, also allow "cultivars" and "varieties"; they even encourage hybrids of the most unlikely combinations of plants.

In zoological taxonomy, a genus (such as *Homo*) is capitalized, but the species (such as *sapiens*) is generally not capitalized. Botanists do allow for capitalization of species names, especially when the species name is derived from a proper noun, as in *Murraya Koenigii*. The scientific names are always listed in italic. There are, of course, exceptions. Subspecies and varieties simply add a third name in italic, preceded by the abbreviation "subs." or "var." in roman type. Cultivar names are also added after the species name; they are indicated either by preceding the cultivar's name with the abbreviation "cv," in roman type, or by enclosing the cultivar's name in single quotation marks, as in the present book. Cultivar names are never listed in italic. Readers who long to master this rather demanding—and sometimes arcane—system are encouraged to consult the *International Code of Nomenclature of Cultivated Plants* and *International Code of Botanical Nomenclature*. I should add that in the present book, names of botanical families or subfamilies are rendered without italic.

Not all the cookbooks and other sources I consulted in preparing this book have been taxonomically strict enough to satisfy the need for unequivocal information. In fact, some plants have eluded all efforts toward positive identification. Since it seems likely that readers will have encountered some of these naming nightmares, it seemed best to include all variations, even when they were known to be incorrect. This is not intended to condone sloppy scholarship, but to acknowledge the reality of the situation.

Since many users of this book are likely to be serious readers of obscure cookbooks, I have included the naming conventions of spices likely to be encountered. Spices, with some exceptions, are not herbs. The herb or spice name, even in the recipe context, may not be enough to categorize an unfamiliar term found in an old recipe.

This book is not intended to be a gardening book, although I suspect that some gardeners will find something of use in it. The origins of plants are included, out of general interest. Generally, a range is given for each herb, although most can be grown, with moderate care, in temperate areas everywhere.

A Few Words about Language and Ethnicity

It is obvious that national boundaries do not always define the ethnicity of the people living within them. Some countries are monolingual, but many of the most gastronomically interesting places have become so because of the history of interactions between their varied populations. These countries tend to embrace several languages. The same herb might have five or ten different names within a single country. Long, convoluted histories of conquest, trade, and migration are promising indicators of culinary diversity and richness. But this does not facilitate the task of cataloging the names of the herbs and spices used in such places.

For the most part, this book does not categorize herb names according to language, but by the countries in which those names are used. The decision to do so was based on the fact that most "ethnic" cookbooks are based on geography, not linguistics. While Ethiopian cookbooks may be difficult to find, an Amharic cookbook is impossible. Likewise, Indians speak dozens of languages, but cookbooks tend to be about "Indian" cuisine, not Assami, Hindi, Oriya, Punjabi, or Tamil. There are a few exceptions in this book. Swahili is a kind of lingua franca for much of Africa. It is not associated with any particular place, but recipes from many African cuisines may contain ingredients with Swahili names. Likewise, Arabic is the foundation for many of the languages of the Middle East and Africa, so Arabic herb and spice names are included as well. In fact, I use "Swahili" or "Arabic" instead of a country name in my lists of common, ethnic, or scientific names. Celtic and Gaelic names are included, not because they have the extensive influence we see for Arabic, but because one could conceivably encounter a Celtic or Gaelic cookbook.

I have tried to use current names for the geography of these fascinating places, even if it may sometimes be ethnically misleading. For example, an ingredient name that is used only by the people of Catalonia will be listed next to "Spain" under the heading "Other Common, Ethnic, or Scientific Names," even though the language and culture of the Catalonians is not Spanish. In some cases, ethnic tensions exist among some of the groups living within one political boundary. Armenians would probably, and justifiably, resent having their cuisine lumped under that of Turkey or Azerbijan. No ethnic, religious, or political slights are intended by this blanket approach to regionalism.

As a result of this consolidation, reflecting only today's sometimes illogical political boundaries, some herbs have a number of synonyms. When I see that a country has ten different names for one plant, I am intrigued, for it means that the plant is important enough in that culture to justify the subtle distinctions such naming requires. It also suggests the kind of cosmopolitan interaction that often leads to culinary eminence.

From Alchemy to Chemistry

When available, the chemical compounds responsible for an herb's taste and aroma are included in the entries. While most herbs contain many such compounds, for the sake of brevity I list only those substances that are present in significant quantities. When I've been able to determine the relative amounts of these compounds, I list them in descending order of concentration. When concentrations are not known, I list these chemicals in alphabetical order.

However, a few caveats should be noted.

Human senses, especially the sense of smell, are often much more sensitive than routine chemical analysis; a barely measurable trace of one substance can have a disproportionate effect on the way we perceive it. The compounds responsible for the fragrance of pandanus, for example, are present in amounts smaller than one part per billion.

While some compounds are extremely powerful, others require thousands of times the concentration just to be detectable. Consequently, mere quantitative analysis can be misleading.

Sometimes, the combination of hundreds of trace compounds is involved in our perception of the taste/scent profile of an herb or spice. Vanilla and ginger are perfect examples. The components of these taste/scent profiles are not equally volatile. When these plant materials dry or age, different compounds are lost at different rates, causing the herb or spice not merely to lose strength but to alter its taste/scent profile. Fresh tarragon, for instance, has an anise-like aroma that is almost imperceptible after drying, while a hay-like scent develops during the drying process.

Plants harvested at different stages of their development, or grown in different environments or in different years, often have significantly different taste/scent profiles. Wine tasters are well aware of differences in the scent of wines from different microclimates and *terroirs*—sometimes only a hundred yards apart. The same variability exists for herbs and spices. It is the reason why Tellicherry black pepper is often preferred over other sources of *Piper nigrum*. Chile peppers grown in the same garden will contain much greater levels of capsaicin if the plants are stressed by water shortages at certain stages of their growth.

Consequently, the chemical profiles I provide in this book should be used merely as starting points, not as definitive analyses. Wine experts spend their entire lives developing an understanding of the relationships between varietals, culture, climate, and soil for just one species: *Vitis vinifera*. Don't expect the study of the thousands of species of herbs and spices to be an easier task.

Measuring Conventions

The amounts of herbs and spices used in recipes are completely subjective. While the recipes in many cookbooks have been tested, flavors and the strengths of ingredients vary. Some herbs are quite intense in flavor; if you have any doubts regarding quantities, be conservative. You can always add more, if needed.

You must use common sense, and some trial and error, to resolve these questions. When you find a usable conversion for the units used by a particular author, by all means write it down. Keep your notes with the cookbook, for future reference. Usually, an author will use a measuring system consistently. Of course, if the author ransacked ("plagiarized" might be too strong a word; perhaps "consulted" is better?) a lot of other cookbooks, there may be no consistent approach. Watch for odd variations in things such as writing style or tense.

I have decided not to include recipes here. I love cookbooks and I have never been able to resist the temptation to add yet another one to an already too large collection. Even the very best cookbooks have fairly limited lifespans, however; they tend to be windows into particular moments in time. While tastes change, I would like this book to be useful long after any recipes that might be included are terribly, and inevitably, out of fashion. When was the last time you prepared beef Wellington or chicken à la king? The dishes are gone, yet all the components of these dishes are still with us.

This is a book about components.

Finally, it seems to me that there are only two kinds of books that should be written: books that no one else *can* write and books that no one else *will* write. This book, surely, belongs in the latter category.

1. Agavaceae: The Agave Family

Agave: *Agave americana*

OTHER COMMON, ETHNIC, OR SCIENTIFIC NAMES
American aloe, century plant, maguey
Germany: Amerikanische Agave
Mexico: Corteza de maguey, mixiote
Turkey: Sabirlik

CULTIVARS
'Marginata', 'Medio-picta', 'Striata', and 'Variegata'

RELATED SPECIES
Over three hundred species of agaves are found throughout the Americas.
Agave Parryi: Agave, century plant, mescal. Used to manufacture mescal
and tequila.

GROWTH HABITS
Perennial where native, rarely elsewhere
Origin: Mexico
Range: North and South America

CULINARY USES
Agave's main claim to fame, from my point of view, is its use in the production of alcoholic beverages. A sort of home brew called pulque is made from the sap, but the distilled products, tequila and mescal, are better known outside of Mexico. Tequila is made from a blue agave that grows only in the state of Jalisco. Mescal, a coarser quaff, is made from *Agave Parryi,* which grows in the area surrounding Oaxaca. One of these high-powered liquors is bottled with a maguey worm in every bottle. For a while, there was a macho craze for the ostentatious eating of these worms, a process that was eased considerably by ingesting the entire liquid content of the bottle beforehand. The reason these worms are placed in bottles of mescal is interesting, and not macho in the sense one might expect. The worms are a means of demonstrating the proof of the alcohol in the bottle. Since mescal that has been diluted below a certain level will not preserve the worm, a well-embalmed worm is an indicator of the bottle's bona fides.

"Worm salt" is a Mexican condiment made by frying maguey worms in oil until they are crunchy and friable. The worms are then ground together with coarse salt and dried chile peppers. The mixture is traditionally used to garnish the rims of glasses of tequila (perhaps this is the origin of the margarita?). Its flavor is, of course, salty, but it is also warm and musky, with an earthy quality that is reminiscent of tequila (without the heat of alcohol or the vanilla flavor of the wooden barrel).

Other agaves are used in several ways. Young flower stalks are baked as vegetables (the flavor has been described as sweet, something like pineapple and bananas). Nectar is sometimes reduced to a syrup. The enlarged base of the plant is sometimes roasted as a vegetable. A kind of vegetable parchment can be peeled from the leaves and used as a wrapper for foods, as corn husks are used for tamales.

COMMENTS

Some sources describe *Tequilana weber* as the species used to make tequila, but *Hortus Third* does not list the genus or species. *Hortus* does list *Agave Weberi* but describes it as being green, not blue.

Centaury, *Centaurium erythraea* (q.v.), is sometimes known as century herb, but it is not related to this species.

Tuberose: *Polianthes tuberosa*

OTHER COMMON, ETHNIC, OR SCIENTIFIC NAMES
France: Tubereuse
Germany: Nachthyazinthe
Italy: Tuberosa
Spain: Tuberosa

GROWTH HABITS
Perennial
Origin: Not found in the wild
Range: Commercially grown in France

CULINARY USES

Tuberose flowers are added to soups in Java. The thick Indonesian soy sauce–like *kecap* usually contains tuberose. The ketchup known in the United States is a rather innocuous descendant of kecap. Extracts of tuberose, with their powerfully floral scent, are used sparingly in the flavorings industry, especially in candies and soft drinks.

Tuberose contains eugenol, farnesol, geraniol, methyl anthranilate, methyl benzoate, and nerol.

OTHER USES

Used in the perfume industry, usually in combination with jasmine and rose. Tuberose extracts are very costly and tend to be used primarily in the most expensive perfumes.

2. Aizoaceae: The Carpetweed Family

Khadia: *Khadia acutipetala*

OTHER COMMON, ETHNIC, OR SCIENTIFIC NAMES
No common name in English

RELATED SPECIES
Glottiphyllum linguifore: Tongueleaf

GROWTH HABITS
Succulent perennial
Origin: South Africa
Range: Temperate regions

CULINARY USES
Khadi is a liquor made from the roots of *Khadia acutipetala,* and Kaffir beer is made from the roots of *Glottiphyllum linguifore* in the area once known as the Transvaal.

3. Alliaceae (Amaryllidaceae): The Onion Family

The *Allium* genus contains all the onions, leeks, and garlic.

Chive: *Allium schoenoprasum*

OTHER COMMON, ETHNIC, OR SCIENTIFIC NAMES
Chibbles, chiues, cive, grass onion. Chive is sometimes mistakenly listed as *Allium angustoprasum.*
China: Jiu cai, jiu tsai, gau choy fa, gau tsoi, kow choy
Denmark: Purløg, stikke med kniv
Esperanto: Senoprazo
Estonia: Murulauk
Finland: Ruoholaukka, ruohosipuli
France: Ail civitte, ciboulette, cives, civette, petit poureau
Gaelic: Feuran
Germany: Schnittlauch
Greece: Práso
Iceland: Graslaukur
Indonesia: Kucai

Iran: Tareh
Iraq: Kerrath
Israel: Eerit bazalit
Italy: Erba cipollina, porrini
Japan: Nira
Malaysia: Kucai
Netherlands: Bieslook, biezelok
Norway: Grasløk, gressøk
Philippines: Kutsay
Poland: Szcyzpiorek
Russia: Shnit-luk, luk-rezanets
Spain: Cebollana, cebolleta, ceballino ajopardo
Sweden: Gräslök
Thailand: Kui Chaai
Vietnam: He

RELATED SPECIES

Allium ascalonicum: Aka wakegi (Japan); ascalonia, chalota, escalma (Spain); Aschlauch, Eschlauch, Klöben, Schalotte (Germany); askalono (Esperanto); bawang merah (Indonesia and Malaysia); cebola roxa (Portugal); chota piaz (India); hanh huong (Vietnam); hom daeng, horm lek (Thailand); ciboule, échalote (France); ialottlauk (Estonia); khtim kraham (Cambodia); kitunguu kidogo sana (Swahili); kon tsung-tau (China); kyet-thun-ni (Burma/Myanmar); liis mean (East Timor); rathu-lunu (Sri Lanka); scalogna (Italy); schalottenlök (Sweden); sgalaid (Gaelic); shalottisipuli (Finland); sibuyas (Philippines); sjalot (Netherlands); sjalott-løk (Norway); skalotte løg (Denmark); eschallot, shallots, Spanish garlic. Gastronomic uses are well known for this bulb, which possesses the best traits of all the members of the Allium genus.

Allium cepa [as onion]: Ajuin, ui (Netherlands); atasuki, tama-negi, tamanegi, wakegi (Japan); batzal, yarok (Israel); basal (Arabic); bawang besar, bawang daun, daun bawang, bawang merah (Malaysia); bawang Bombay, bawang daun, daun bawang, bawang merah (Indonesia); cebola (Portugal); cebolla (Spain); cebollín (Mexico); cebula jadalna (Poland); chung, chung tau, cong, ts'ung, ts'ung tau, tsung-tau, yang-ts'ung (China); cipolla (Italy); hom yao (Thailand); dungari, dungli, irulli, kanda, nirulli, palandu, peyaz, piaja, pianj, piaz, piyaz, ponoru, vengayam (India); harilik sibul (Estonia); hua hom, ton hom (Thailand); kanda, lök, rödlök (Sweden); kepaløk (Norway); kesunni, kyet-thun-ni (Burma/Myanmar); khan kho (Vietnam); khtim kraham, khtim slek (Cambodia); liis Bombay (East Timor); luk (Russia); oignon (France); pias (Iran); ruokasipuli (Finland); piyaz, raripe, rat lunu (Sri Lanka); sibuyas (Philippines); sla (Morocco);

sibuyas (Philippines); Zwiebel (Germany); Egyptian walking onion, everready onion, onions, potato onion, winter onion

Allium cepa [as scallion]; Cebollita (Mexico); da cong or tai tsung (China); daun bawang (Indonesia); hari piaz (India); hanh la (Vietnam); lunu kolle (Sri Lanka); negi (Japan); sibuyas na mura (Philippines); ton hom (Thailand); multiplier onion, scallion, set onion, spring onion

Allium ceruum: Grassnut, lady's leek, nodding onion, wild onion

Allium Kunthii: Ajo, cibolla cimarron

Allium proliferum: Tree onions, Egyptian onions

Allium tuberosum (sometimes listed as *Allium odorum* or *Allium odoratum*): Bai kuichai, do kuichai, kuchai, tui chaai (Thailand); gau choy, gow choy, jui cai, kui choi (China); bawang kucai or ku cai (Malaysia); kucai (Indonesia); kuchai, kutsay (Philippines); la he, nentau, phi tu (Vietnam); liis tahan (East Timor); nira (Japan); garlic chive, Chinese leek, Chinese chive, Korean chive

GROWTH HABITS
Perennial
Origin: Europe and Asia
Range: Temperate regions

CULINARY USES
Chive is one of France's fines herbes, along with chervil, parsley, and tarragon. It has a definite onion presence but is decidedly more civilized. It is a classic component of the sauces and stocks of haute-cuisine. Use the leaves as a garnish or in salads or compound butters; with fish, meat, and poultry dressings; in soups (cauliflower, potato, dried mushroom) and stews, omelets, or vinaigrettes; or in anything calling for a delicate onion flavor.

Its lovely lavender-colored, globe-shaped flowers make elegant garnishes.

Many cheeses incorporate chives, either as a flavoring or as a decorative external coating. Saga is a Danish Brie-like cheese that is sometimes sold covered in chopped chives. In France, Boulette de Cambai is a fresh cheese containing parsley, pepper, tarragon, and chives. Boursin, the French triple-cream, available in little boxes everywhere, comes in several "flavors," one of which is largely garlic and chives. The Welsh have their Pant-Ys-Gawn (a Boursin-like fresh cheese, redolent of black pepper, chives, and garlic) and Llangloffan (which is flavored with chives and garlic). The English have Coverdale (which incorporates tiny bits of chives), Abreydale or Cotswold (a chive-flavored Double Gloucester), Wedmore (a Caerphilly layered with chives, from Somerset), Staffordshire Organic (a Cheddar that is occasionally made with garlic and chives), and Week-ender (flavored with chives, as well as garlic, lemon pepper, and parsley). County Limerick produces the Irish chive-flavored Cheddar called Ballintubber.

Leaves and unopened flower buds, but not bulbs, of *Allium tuberosum* are eaten in noodles, salads, and soups and as seasoning for meat-filled dumplings.

Chives are available fresh or freeze-dried and as chive-flavored salt.

All forms of onion are flavored primarily with a number of sulfur compounds (see Garlic). The compound responsible for our tears while cutting onions is either propenyl sulfenic acid or thiopropanal-s-oxide; these are chemically identical compounds whose molecular structures differ. The components of chive are similar to those of onion: dipropyl disulfide, methyl pentyl disulfide, penthanethiol, and *cis/trans*-3,5-diethyl-1,2,4-trithiolane

---

Garlic: *Allium sativum*

OTHER COMMON, ETHNIC, OR SCIENTIFIC NAMES
Poor man's treacle
Afghanistan: Seer
Arabic: Toom
Burma/Myanmar: Chyet-thon-phew, kesumphiu
Cambodia: Kthem
China: Suan, suen tao
Denmark: Hvidløg
East Timor: Liis asu, liis mutin
Estonia: Küüslauk
Ethiopia: Netch' shinkurt
Finland: Valkosipuli
France: Ail, thériaque des pauvres
Germany: Knoblauch
Greece: Skórdo
Hungary: Fokhagyma
Iceland: Hvítlaukur
India: Belluli, lasan, naharu, rasun, sudulunu, tellagadda, vellay
    poondoo, veluthulli
Indonesia: Bawang puteh, kesuna
Iran: Sir
Iraq: Thoum
Israel: Shum
Italy: Aglio
Japan: Nin-niku
Korea: Ma ni
Malaysia: Bawang puteh
Morocco: Tourma
Netherlands Antilles: Konofló
Netherlands: Knoflook
Norway: Hvitløk
Philippines: Bawang
Poland: Czosnek

Portugal: Alho
Romania: Usturoi
Russia: Chesnok, chyet-thon-phew
Spain: Ajo, all, baratzuri
Sri Lanka: Sudulunu
Surinam: Kunofroku
Swahili: Kitunguu saumu
Sweden: Vitlök
Thailand: Kratiem
Turkey: Sarimsak, sekhdor
Vietnam: Tai, toi

CULTIVARS
'Ophioscorodon' (rocambole or serpent garlic)

RELATED SPECIES
The Ampeloprasum group consists of great-headed garlic, Levant garlic (the bulbs are eaten), and kurrat, or salad leek, *Allium kurrat* (having small bulbs, the leaves are eaten).

Allium Ampeloprasum (sometimes listed as *Allium giganteum* and marketed as elephant garlic; also *Allium porrum* and *Allium ramosum*): Tai chung (China); krathiam tom (Thailand); kucai (Malaysia and Indonesia); kutsay (Philippines); poro negi (Japan); leeks, porro, wild leeks

Allium canadense: Meadow leek, rose leek, wild garlic, wild onion

Allium chinense: Jiao tou (China); rakkyo (Japan); Chinese chive. Often pickled with soy sauce and honey or sugar. The pickles are sold as "pickled scallions" or "rakkyo-zuke."

Allium fistulosum: Chang fa (China); negi (Japan); ciboule, Japanese bunching onion, Spanish onion, two-bladed onion, Welsh onion

Allium flavum subs. *tauricum:* Lauch (Germany); yabani sogon (Turkey); small yellow onion

Allium funceum subs. *tridentatum:* Lauch (Germany); yabani sogon (Turkey)

Allium myrianthum: Lauch (Germany); yabani sogon (Turkey)

Allium splendens: Chishima-rakkyo (Japan). Boiled or pickled in sake, shoyu, and rice vinegar.

Allium thunbergii: Yama-rakkyo (Japan). Leaves used cooked, pickled, or raw. Leaves sometimes stewed in oil or preserved in salt. The bulbs are sometimes preserved in sweetened and vinegared brine.

Allium tuberosum: Garlic chive, Chinese chive

Allium ursinum: Ail des ours, ail sauvage (France); Bärlauch, Ziguener Knoblauch (Germany); ceremsha (Russia); czosnek niedzwiedzi (Poland); daslook (Netherlands); garleag (Gaelic); karhunlaukka (Finland); karulauk (Estonia); ramslök (Sweden); teufelschnoblech (Switzerland); badger's garlic, bear's garlic, buckrams, gypsy's garlic, onion stinkers, snake's food, stinking Jenny, stinking lily, ramsons, wild garlic. Leaves used in Siberia. Very strong garlic odor when raw; tamed considerably by cooking. Green parts eaten with cheese in medieval England.

Allium vineale: Ail des vignes (France); crow garlic, field garlic, stag's garlic

GROWTH HABITS

Perennial

Origin: Asia (Mongolia)

Range: Temperate regions

CULINARY USES

Everyone knows the flavor and scent of garlic. The small cloves with pinkish-purple skin have the best flavor. The flavor of garlic goes with so many foods it seems unnecessary to list them all. A brief nod in that direction is required, however.

Use garlic with broiled fish and tomato-based fish soups, such as bouillabaisse or cioppino. Also in sausages consisting of beef, chicken, duck, goose, lamb, pork, and venison. It also belongs with the same varieties of roasted meats. Garlic and ginger are combined in a seasoned salt mixture that is delicious on roast lamb. It is also good in stews or mixed with soft cheeses for use in canapés.

Garlic and salads are natural allies. You can use garlic in the dressing or rubbed on the inside of the bowl, as in Caesar salad; or use the young leaves in the salad itself. Also use garlic in soups; aïgo-boulido is a French garlic-and-cabbage soup. Aïgo-saou is similar but adds fish and tomatoes.

Garlic, along with ginger and scallions, is the foundation of Chinese cooking, just as mirepoix is with French cooking. The young shoots of garlic, no more than 5⁄16 of an inch in diameter, cut 2 ½ inches long, are used like scallions in Szechuan stir-fried beef dishes.

The Guatemalan *recado,* like the *recaito* of Puerto Rico, is a garlic-laced sauce—almost a cooking medium—containing onions and various spices. Unlike recaito, the Guatemalan sauce includes tomatoes. Another tomato sauce laced with garlic, *chirmol,* is used everywhere in Guatemala. Sometimes it is customized with tomatillos and/or chiles, but it always there in some form.

Americans sometimes think Italian cooking is very garlic-intensive, but that's because many of the first immigrants from Italy came from Sicily. The tomato sauces of southern Italy do contain a lot of garlic, it's true, but most Italian cooking uses it more subtly. A northern exception to this rule is Piedmont's *bagna cauda,* a warm aioli-like dip enriched with white truffles and anchovies. Try replacing a dull macaroni salad with one using aioli and chopped toasted walnuts.

In Brazil, garlic is used in the Amazonian cassava-based condiment *tucupi.* The Thais make a kind of pickled garlic called *kratiem dong.* It is included in several Thai curry pastes. Ethiopians include garlic both in *berberé* and *niter kebbeh.*

Foudjou is a French goat cheese flavored with garlic and other ingredients, including eau-de-vie. Other garlicky goat cheeses include Norman Chevrette, and the richer Dauphiné Chevrette des Neiges, made with garlic and herbs. Gapron, Gaperon, or Le P'Ail are relatively low-fat cheeses made with cow's milk, garlic, and black pepper. The English have Week-ender, which is flavored with garlic, chives, lemon pepper, and parsley. Other English garlic-laced cheeses include Cumberland Farmhouse and Roubiliac. Beauchamp is a Leicester-like cheese flavored with garlic and assorted herbs. Loddiswell Banon sometimes contains garlic and parsley. Newbury is sometimes prepared with a layer of fresh garlic. Staffordshire Organic is a Cheddar that is occasionally dosed with garlic and chives, and sometimes smoked. Sussex Slipcote is a soft, Boursin-like cheese, sold in boxes and available flavored either with garlic, crushed black pepper, or a mixture of herbs. Many Irish cheeses incorporate garlic. Bay Lough, from County Tipparary, is a Cheshire-like cheese that is often flavored with garlic and herbs. Carrigaline, Coolea, and Roundtower (from County Cork), and Kilshanny (from County Clare) are garlic-laced Gouda-like cheeses. Kerry Farmhouse, from County Kerry, is a Cheddar-like cheese with a pronounced garlic presence. The Welsh produce Caethwas (a Cheddar-like cheese containing garlic and parsley), Pant-Ys-Gawn (a Boursin-like fresh cheese, redolent of black pepper, chives, and garlic) and Llangloffan (flavored with chives and garlic). Iraqis prepare some of their fresh sheep's milk cheese, Biza, with garlic. Some Goudas, in the Netherlands, are also garlic-enhanced.

Some pubs in Sweden flavor their beer with garlic. Garlic is not part of the brewing process but is added at service, much as lime is served with beer in Mexico.

A marinade of garlic, olive oil, and fresh thyme takes ordinary American "black ripe" olives from the pedestrian to the sublime.

Garlic's flavor and scent are the result of its allyl propyl disulfide, diallyl disulfide, and other sulfur compounds. Allicin, the characteristic raw garlic flavor, is produced when garlic is cut or chopped, that is, exposed to air and enzymes in the garlic cells. If garlic is cooked without being cut, allicin never develops. Slow cooking of whole cloves yields a milder, sweeter taste; roasting, as opposed to sautéing, gives garlic a rounder, less aggressive presence in a dish.

Bear's garlic contains several sulfur compounds that are characteristic of garlic: divinyl sulfide, dimethyl thiosulfonate and methyl cyctein sulfoxide. Methyl cyctein sulfoxide breaks down into methyl allyl thiosulfonate and methanethiol.

COMMENTS

Garlic is available in markets in a number of forms: fresh, fried flakes of garlic (sold in jars in some Asian markets and used as a garnish); dried garlic flakes; garlic powder; garlic oil; garlic salt; pickled; and chopped ("fresh") in jars. The last-mentioned form has been implicated in at least one case of botulism. Garlic's low acidity makes it a prime candidate for harboring *Clostridium botulinum* bacteria. While I do not use garlic in jars, I recognize its usefulness. For safety's sake use it only in dishes that will be thoroughly cooked after the garlic is added.

The wonderful hot garlicky flavor of allicin doesn't last long; it quickly degrades into diallyl disulfide, the foul-smelling compound associated with old garlic. Diallyl disulfide can be avoided by thoroughly cleaning all surfaces exposed to cut garlic immediately, or by not cutting the garlic until the enzymes that produce allicin are deactivated by cooking.

Ramps: *Allium tricoccum*

OTHER COMMON, ETHNIC, OR SCIENTIFIC NAMES
Bear's garlic, hill onion, wood leek. Sometimes listed as *Allium textile*.

GROWTH HABITS
Perennial
Origin: Eastern North America
Range: Eastern North America (harvested in the wild)

CULINARY USES
Use like leeks, only more sparingly; the garlic-onion flavor of ramps is more intense than that of leeks. Ramps can be blanched, baked, or broiled and served as a vegetable, with butter, hollandaise, or vinaigrette. Flavor soups and sauces with ramps when you would like a stronger onion presence than that offered by chives.

COMMENTS
The name "hill onion" is more commonly applied to a subspecies of onion known as *Allium cepa aggregatum*. The use of the common name for ramps is more suggestive of the place where they are found than the technique of their cultivation.

Society Garlic: *Tulbaghia violacea*

OTHER COMMON, ETHNIC, OR SCIENTIFIC NAMES
Has appeared in the literature with a typographical error as *Tulbhagia violacea*.

CULTIVAR
'Tricolor'

  Allium ledebourianum: Asatsuki (Japan)
  Tulbaghia alliaceae: Isikhwa (South Africa); wild garlic
  Tulbaghia fragrans: Sweet garlic, pink agapanthus

GROWTH HABITS
  Perennial
  Origin: South Africa
  Range: Temperate regions

CULINARY USES
  Use like chives (q.v.). Leaves of *Tulbaghia alliaceae* are eaten as potherb. Zulus make a condiment of chopped leaves and salt. Flowers are considered a delicacy.

COMMENTS
  "Wild garlic" is a common name associated with several different species.

4. Amaranthaceae: The Amaranth Family

Amaranth: *Amaranthus tricolor*

OTHER COMMON, ETHNIC, OR SCIENTIFIC NAMES
  Careless weed, Chinese spinach, Joseph's coat, fountain plant, pigweed, sag, spineless amaranth
  China: Hsien ts'ai, yin choy
  Colombia: Bledo
  Germany: Amarant, Tausendschön
  India: Marsa
  Japan: Hiyu, hiyuna
  Laos: Pak hom
  Malaysia: Bayam
  Mexico: Alegría, ataco, bledo, quelite de cuchi, quilites, quintoniles
  Panama: Bledo, calalu
  Philippines: Kulitis
  Sri Lanka: Thampala
  Thailand: Pak khom hat, pak khom suan
  Vietnam: Yan yang

CULTIVARS
  'Albus', 'Giganteus', 'Ruber', and 'Viridis'

Amaranthus cruentes: Quilites, quintoniles (Mexico); pigweed, wild amaranth

Amaranthus gangeticus: Bayam (East Timor, Indonesia); green amaranth, red amaranth

Amaranthus hybridus: Quintoniles (Mexico); green amaranth, pigweed, wild beet. Edible seeds. Cultivar: *Amaranthus hybridus* 'erythrostachys' or *Amaranthus hypochondriachus:* Amaranto (Mexico)

Amaranthus hypochindriacus: Quintonil (central and southern Mexico)

Amaranthus hypochondriacus: Amaranto, ficaria (Mexico); Pilewort

Amaranthus leucocarpus: Source of grain eaten in Latin America

Amaranthus palmeri: Quintonil (northeastern Mexico)

Amaranthus retroflexus: Quintonil (north-central Mexico)

Celosia argentea: Soko (South Africa); quailgrass. Used as a potherb, in soups, and as a source of edible oil.

GROWTH HABITS

Annual

Origin: Tropics

Range: Cultivated in Asia as a vegetable crop

CULINARY USES

Amaranth is used as potherb or greens in stir-fries. It can be eaten in salads or added to frittatas and omelets, curries, sauces, soups, and stews. It is a popular and important staple in the Caribbean, India, Indonesia, South America, and West Africa.

The *Amaranthus* genus contains at least twenty different edible species, with leaves available in several appetizing colors, from green to red to purple. The leaves of several species yield enough coloring matter to make them useful as food coloring. The corn-based beverage *chicha,* drunk in the Andes, is sometimes dyed red with amaranth, as is the Hopi tortilla-like bread *piki.* In New Guinea, jellies made from agar-agar are colored with *Iresine herbstii.* In China, amaranth leaves are used either fresh or canned (pickled in brine) and are marketed as red-in-snow. Quintoniles is a wild herb in Mexico. *Guisado,* a stew containing *charales* (a local fish), flavored with chipotles, is usually seasoned with the long, wrinkled leaves of quintoniles.

Many *Amaranthus* species provide valuable seeds, used as grains, especially in the Andes. The seeds are often eaten in sprouted form. The seeds also yield edible oils.

COMMENTS

Red-in-snow is also the name for chopped mustard greens (*Brassica juncea* subs. *multiceps*) pickled in brine. Red-in-snow may be different plants going by the same name; it all depends on which source you choose to believe. The ingredient listings on canned foods from so-called third world countries sometimes seem to be included for ambiance alone. Unadorned facts, if they even exist, are rarely permitted to sully the shopping or dining experience.

"Quilites" is also a Mexican name for *Chenopodium berlandieri* (q.v.).

Polpala: *Aerva lanata*

OTHER COMMON, ETHNIC, OR SCIENTIFIC NAMES
Lupungdare, pol-kudu-pala. Also listed botanically as *Aerva floribunda* and *Achyranthes lanata*.

GROWTH HABITS
Tropical perennial
Origin: Asia and Africa
Range: India

CULINARY USES
Leaves and stems are eaten in salads and sometimes added to curries. They were once used as tea in Sri Lanka.

COMMENTS
The genus is not listed among the genera under Amaranthaceae in *Hortus Third*.

5. Anacardiaceae: The Cashew Family

Ethiopian Pepper: *Xylopia aethiopica*

OTHER COMMON, ETHNIC, OR SCIENTIFIC NAMES
Guinea pepper, Kani pepper, Kimba pepper, Moor pepper, Negro pepper, Senegal pepper, spice tree
Colombia: Achon
Estonia: Etioopia ksüloopia
Ethiopia: Enge
France: Graines de Selim, piment noir de Guinée, poivre de Senegal
Germany: Kanipfeffer, Mohrenpfeffer, Negerpfeffer, Selimskörner, Senegalpfeffer
Nigeria: Alu, atta, eeru, egidije, kimba, uda

RELATED SPECIES
Xylopia aromatica: Burropfeffer (Germany); burro pepper
Xylopia frutescens: Malagueto chico, malagueto hembra (Panama)
Xylopia glabra: Bitterwood

Xylopia macrantha: Azotacaballo, malagueto (Colombia); coroba, rayado (Panama)

GROWTH HABITS
Tropical tree
Origin: Ethiopia
Range: Cultivated in West Africa

CULINARY USES
Fruit and seeds are used like pepper. Pods are broken to release the aromatic and pungent seeds inside, which are then crushed and added to pepper soups. The seeds have a mild peppery bite with a suggestion of nutmeg in the aroma. Used to flavor palm wine and coffee. Formerly popular in Europe, now used primarily in Senegal (see MELEGUETA PEPPER).

The main flavoring constituents of the fruit and seeds are tetracyclic diterpenes. The bark has a more diverse chemical makeup, containing α-pinene, myrtenol, *trans*-pinocarveol, and verbenone. The leaves contain β-carophyllene, cryptone, limonene, and spathulenol.

Xylopia undulata is a similar African species.

The seeds of *Xylopia frutescens* are used as a hot, aromatic pepper substitute in Brazil and Guyana. The wood, bark, and fruit of bitterwood, *Xylopia glabra,* which grows in Jamaica, are bitter and aromatic, a bit like the seeds of oranges. In Brazil, the seeds of *Xylopia sericea* are also used like pepper. The fruits have a similar flavor but are not as intense.

COMMENTS
The genus is not listed in *Hortus Third.*

Mango: *Mangifera indica*

OTHER COMMON, ETHNIC, OR SCIENTIFIC NAMES
Dried green mango, mango powder
Burma/Myanmar: Thayet
East Timor: Haas
Estonia: India mangopuu
Finland: Mango
France: Mangier
France: Mangue
Germany: Mango, Mangobaum, Mangopflanze
Greece: Mángo
Iceland: Mangó
India: Amchoor, amramu, etamba, ghariyam, mamagam, mamidi, mangay powder, mavadi kaya powder, mavinkai powder, mavu, wawashi

Indonesia: Mangaa
Italy: Mango
Netherlands: Mango
Norway: Mango
Russia: Mango
Spain: Mango, manguey
Swahili: Mwembe
Sweden: Mango
Thailand: Ma muang mun

RELATED SPECIES

Pistacia lentiscus: Mastixstrauch (Germany); sakizlak agaci (Turkey);
mastic tree
Pistacia terebinthus: Menengiç (Turkey); terebinth pistache (France);
Terpentin-pistazie (Germany); Cypress turpentine tree
Pistacia vera: Pistachio

GROWTH HABITS

Evergreen tree
Origin: India to Southeast Asia
Range: Tropics everywhere, cultivated in Southern California and
Florida

CULINARY USES

Powdered green mango, *aamchoor,* is used in Indian cooking. It imparts a
sour flavor, with some of the mango's resinous taste, to mixed pickles (*achars*)
and is used as a rub to tenderize meats. Aamchoor is sometimes served at the
table, as a condiment. The acidic green fruit is used to flavor dals (lentils)
and some vegetable dishes (see "verjuice," under CUCUMBER TREE, GRAPES).
Aamchoor is an ingredient in the Indian spice mixture *chaat masala,* along
with coriander seed, cumin seed, pepper, chiles mint, and dried ginger. The
mixture is used in salads. The sour green fruit is used in some Caribbean
chutneys, often in combination with tamarind.

Aside from its use as a fresh fruit, mango makes a delicious ice cream that
is often served after Indian meals. It has also been used to make wine.

Mangos, especially when still green, get their characteristically complex
flavor and scent from limonene, myrcene, and ocimene, along with aldehydes
and esters. Citric acid and other fruit acids provide the sour taste.

COMMENTS

The unripe fruits of the Cypress turpentine tree, *Pistacia terebinthus,* are
sometimes preserved in vinegar and salt. These savory little tidbits are served
with wines, as one would serve salty snacks with drinks. These pickles are
known as *atsjaar.* It is possible that the similarity of this name to achar is only
a coincidence. However, the eastern Mediterranean is midway along the old

trade routes that connected Europe with the lands where spices grew. Muslim traders may have introduced these pickled treats to the infidels along their route. They, in turn, combined the tasty snacks with wine drinking, a use no good Muslim would ever countenance.

The flavor is said to have a short shelf life. This may explain the relatively tasteless powder sometimes found at a local Indian grocery.

Maprong: *Bouea macrophylla*

OTHER COMMON, ETHNIC, OR SCIENTIFIC NAMES
Kundang

RELATED SPECIES
Bouea burmanica: Maprang
Bouea gandaria: Gandaria
Dracontomelon dao: Jên mien tzu, yun meen (China)

GROWTH HABITS
Tropical tree
Origin: Borneo
Range: Frost-free areas

CULINARY USES
Fruits are sweet and sour. Unripe or sour varieties are used, like lime juice, in cooking (see TAMARIND). The Malaysian desserts *asinan* and *rujak* are flavored with the sour juice. Fresh leaves are eaten with *sambal ontjom* in Indonesia.

Jên mien tzu, *Dracontomelon dao,* is used in curries (Singapore-style), with sweet-sour fruits simmered in soy sauce as a topping for rice, or with finely chopped pork. Leaves are eaten in the Philippines.

Pink Peppercorn: *Schinus terebinthifolius*

OTHER COMMON, ETHNIC, OR SCIENTIFIC NAMES
Brazilian pepper tree, Florida holly, pepper rosé
Brazil: Aroreira
France: Baies roses, molée des jardins, poivrier d'Amirique, poivre rosé,
    sorbier
Germany: Peruanischer Pfeffer, Rosé-Pfeffer, Weichpfeffer
Iceland: Rósapipar
Italy: Schino
Netherlands: Roze peper
Portugal: Pimenta-rosa
Réunion: Baies roses de Bourbon

Spain: Arveira, pimenta falsa, pirul
Sweden: Rosépeppar

RELATED SPECIES

Schinus molle: Pehme skiinus (Estonia); Peruaanse peperboom (Netherlands); piru, pirul (Mexico); Australian pepper, California pepper tree, false pepper, molle, pepper tree, Peruvian mastic tree, Peruvian pepper tree

GROWTH HABITS

Tree

Origin: Brazil

Range: Cultivated on the island of Réunion, in the Indian Ocean; naturalized in Florida and Hawaii

CULINARY USES

For a while, pink peppercorns were among the darlings of nouvelle cuisine. Not as hot as black pepper, chile pepper, or Szechuan pepper, they do have an interesting aromatic quality, and they do look beautiful sparsely scattered over poached salmon or grilled chicken. They are used, ground, as a spice, and whole, as a garnish. Pink peppercorns are fermented for vinegars, and an alcoholic beverage is made from them in Peru. The related species listed above are all used to make spicy brews in western South America (see MELEGUETA PEPPER for similar usage).

Schinus molle is used to flavor baked goods and candy. The berries are used in South America to make wines and nonalcoholic drinks known as *atoles* and *horchatas*. *Schinus molle* contains carvacrol, phellandrene, pinene, and thymol.

Pink peppercorns contain carvacrol, phellandrenes, α-pinene, and thymol. Their complex aroma is enhanced by α-cubebane, β-caryophyllene, β-cubebane, *cis*-sabinole, and hydroxymasticadienoic acid.

COMMENTS

Three entirely separate issues need to be addressed here. First, there is a concern about health. Pink peppercorns have been implicated in a number of minor poisonings, with symptoms like congestion, headaches, gastric problems, and—last but not least—hemorrhoids. The sale of pink peppercorns was at one time banned in the United States. The Food and Drug Administration later allowed them to be imported from Réunion, after the French government proved to the FDA's satisfaction that Réunion's pink peppercorns were safe to eat. Presumably, if you can afford to import the risk of hemorrhoids all the way from the Indian Ocean, you should be allowed to do so. Second, there is the tendency of the plant to become a pest. Much of southern Florida is overrun with pink peppercorns. The plants are almost as popular as kudzu. The third issue is unrelated to the first two, but it is made worse by the second. *Schinus* provides an alternate host to a black-scale disease that attacks orange trees. Obviously, *Schinus* species are not ideal plants to be planted in Florida.

Staghorn Sumac: *Rhus tryphina*

OTHER COMMON, ETHNIC, OR SCIENTIFIC NAMES

Hoghorn sumac, Indian lemonade, lemonade tree, mountain sumac, scarlet sumac, Sicilian sumac, velvet sumac, Virginian sumac

Arabic: Summag
Estonia: Sumahh
Finland: Sumakki
France: Sumac
Germany: Essigbaum, Färberbaum, Gerbersumach, Gewürzsumach, Hirschfarn, Sumach
India: Arkol, kankrasringi, titri
Iran: Somagh
Iraq: Simmak, summac
Italy: Sommacco
Netherlands: Zuurkruid
Russia: Sumakh
Spain: Zumaque
Turkey: Somak

CULTIVARS

'Dissecta', 'Laciniata'

RELATED SPECIES

Anacardium excelsum: Caracoli (Colombia); espavé (Panama); acajou, espavél, wild cashew. Edible nut, like cashew.

Anacardium occidentale: Acaju, marañon (Mexico); jambu meté (Indonesia); cajugaha, cashew, cashew nut. Tropical America to zone 10. Sometimes seen as *Semicarpus anacardium.*

Rhus aromatica: Agrillo, fragrant sumac, honeysuckle berry, lemon sumac, Indian lemonade, lemita, lemonade berry, polecat bush, quailbush, shoneehaw, skunk bush, squawberry, squawbush, stinkbush, stinking hazel, three-legged sumac

Rhus glabra: Sumaque (Mexico); bright sumac, dwarf sumac, Indian salt, mountain sumac, scarlet sumac, smooth sumac

Rhus integrifolia: Lemonade sumac

Rhus spp. (species formerly listed as *Toxicodendron*): Alicito (Costa Rica); alisito (Colombia); poison ivy, poison sumac, poison oak

Rhus trilobata: Fragrant sumac, squawbush

GROWTH HABITS

Small tree or shrub
Origin: Eastern North America
Range: Temperate regions

Berries, crushed and steeped, give up a good deal of malic acid, the main flavoring in green apples. The berries of all the edible sumacs can be used to make tart jellies and should make a good glaze for grilled meats. The extracted liquid is useful for marinating fish. It can also be emulsified with olive oil for use as a vinaigrette with no taste of vinegar or lemon. In Iran, sumac is used to season meats (especially kebabs), soups, and rice dishes. It is used as a spice in some Lebanese cooking. In Turkey, sumac and onions are used to season roast meats. In parts of the Middle East, the leaves are also used as a seasoning.

Sumac's tannins contribute more in the way of a dry mouthfeel than flavor. *Rhus coraria* is the sumac species most commonly used in the Middle East. A sweetened drink rather like lemonade can be made from the berries.

Anacardium occidentale yields the familiar cashew nut, but the fruit (cashew apple) is also edible. A kind of wine, called *kaju* (or *cajuado*), is made from the fruit in South America. In Brazil, *caju,* the fruit of the cashew tree, is used as a tart red addition to fruit compotes and salads (see Comments, below). Malaysians and Javanese serve raw young leaves as a garnish for rice.

OTHER USES

This is a wild plant, particularly lovely in fall, when its long, pointed leaves take on an unearthly luminosity that continues after the scattering of most

Staghorn Sumac
Rhus tryphina

From Jaume Saint-Hilaire,
Traité des arbrisseaux

other leaves. The nearly tropical appearance of the plant is quite different from the look of other autumn foliage. Sumac will grow almost anywhere, in the worst possible soils, along roadsides or in waste places, thriving even on rock piles.

COMMENTS

Zathar is a Middle Eastern spice mixture consisting of equal parts of thyme and sumac. I have also seen recipes that call for two parts of thyme for each part of sumac. Some recipes substitute *Origanum syriacum* for the thyme. Zathar is used to season soft cheeses. It is sometimes labeled "Za'atar" (q.v.), although it is not the same.

When infusing the sumac berries in water, it is best to use cold water. Hot temperatures release tannins in harsh quantities. To make hot drinks with sumac, steep cold until the desired strength is achieved, then strain the liquid before heating.

Do not touch any *Rhus*-like plant that has white berries. Six species are poisonous to the touch, among them: poison oak (*Rhus diversiloba*); poison ivy, Mercury, markry, cow itch (*Rhus radicans*); and poison sumac, swamp sumac, poison elder, poison dogwood (*Rhus Vernix*). I can't imagine the effect of eating them.

By the way, the pollen of these poisonous plants does not contain the irritating oil. Stories about people being poisoned by the very air near the plant are untrue, unless someone has been foolish enough to try to eradicate the plant by burning. The oils are not destroyed but are disseminated in the smoke.

Both species of *Anacardium* noted above have edible nuts, but they are poisonous until after they are roasted. As with burning of the *Rhus* species mentioned above, the vapor from the roasting nuts is extremely toxic. According to one source, severe allergic reactions and even blindness has been reported in people exposed to the fumes released during the processing of these plants.

6. Annonaceae:
The Annona (Custard-Apple) Family

African Nutmeg: *Monodora myristica*

OTHER COMMON, ETHNIC, OR SCIENTIFIC NAMES
Calabash nutmeg, false nutmeg, Jamaica nutmeg
Nigeria: Arigo, ariwo, ehuru, gujiya dan miya, iwo

RELATED SPECIES
Monodora tenuifolia: Striped calabash nutmeg, orchid flower tree

Shrub
Origin: Angola
Range: Sub-Saharan Africa

CULINARY USES

The seeds are roasted and ground for use in African cooking, especially with shrimp and in pepper soups. Aromatic seeds have been used as a nutmeg substitute. The seeds are also pressed to yield a cooking oil that tastes of nutmeg.

The seeds of *Monodora tenuifolia* are used in West Africa as a seasoning for soups. Both species have edible fruit.

Ear Flower: *Monodora myristica*

OTHER COMMON, ETHNIC, OR SCIENTIFIC NAMES

Mexico: Hueinacazatli, orichelas, xochinacaztl
Other botanical names have included *Porcelia cinnamonema, Unona penduliflora,* and *Uvaria penduliflora.*

GROWTH HABITS

Tree
Origin: Mexico
Range: High-altitude forests, from Mexico to Chile

CULINARY USES

The flowers add an aromatic perfumed quality, slightly reminiscent of anise, to hot chocolate beverages in Mexico. The dried petals are sold in small ceramic pots in Mexican markets.

COMMENTS

Ear flowers have been paired with chocolate in Mexico, along with vanilla, at least as far back as the time of the Aztecs, who believed them to have medicinal—and, especially, aphrodisiacal—properties, which may explain why such chocolate beverages were reserved for Montezuma.

Ylang-Ylang: *Cananga odorata*

OTHER COMMON, ETHNIC, OR SCIENTIFIC NAMES

Cananga flowers, ilang-ilang, perfume tree. Sometimes the name *Canangium odoratum* is seen in old field guides.

GROWTH HABITS

Tropical tree

Origin: Asia to northern Australia
Range: Asia and the Philippines

CULINARY USES

Extracts are used commercially to flavor baked goods and their icings, candy, and chewing gum. Ylang-ylang's sweet, flowery taste is a result of its geraniol and linalool content. Complexity is added by its benzoic acid, benzyl alcohol, cadinene, d-α-pinene, and eugenol.

OTHER USES

Used in manufacture of hair tonics, perfumes, and soaps.

COMMENTS

I have heard of another ylang-ylang, *Unona odoratissimus,* that is alleged to have a bittersweet taste. I have not found any other data that would either prove the separate identity of that plant or identify it as *Canaga odorata.*

7. Apiaceae (formerly Umbelliferae): The Parsley or Carrot Family

Ajowan: *Carum ajowan*

OTHER COMMON, ETHNIC, OR SCIENTIFIC NAMES

Ajava seed, ammi, ashweed, bishop's weed, goutweed, ground ash, ground elder, herb Gerard, javanee, tymolseeds. Ajowan has been listed botanically as *Ammi copticum, Carum copticum, Ptychotis ajowan, Trachysperma ammi,* and possibly *Ægopodium podagraria* or *Ammi majus.*

Arabic: Buranikataya, taleb el koubs
Estonia: Lõhnav karusköömen
Ethiopia: Netch azmud
France: Ajwain
Germany: Adiowan, Indischer Kümmel, Königs Kümmel
India: Ajamo, ajmodika, ajwain, assamodum, ayamodakam, brahmadarbha, carom, deepyaka, joni-guti, jowan, juani, omam, ugragandha, vayu, yamani, yavan, yavsaha
Iran: Nanavva, zinian
Italy: Ajwain
Netherlands: Ajwain
Spain: Ajwain

RELATED SPECIES

Ammi majus: Dis otu (Turkey); Große Knorpelmöhre (Germany); bishop's weed, false bishop's weed, Queen Anne's lace

Ammi visnaga (sometimes listed as *Ammi visnago*): Hiltan (Turkey); Knorpelmöhre (Germany); bisnaga

GROWTH HABITS
Perennial
Origin: Eurasia
Range: Naturalized in North America

CULINARY USES
Ajowan's leaves and young stems are eaten as salads. They can also be used as potherbs. *Grüne Suppe* is a German soup made from the leaves in the spring. Bishop's weed is used occasionally in a number of cuisines, but it is essential to the cooking of Ethiopia. It is used in *berberé* and *niter kebbeh* (see glossary), which are the foundation of the flavor principle—to use Elizabeth Rozin's term—that defines Ethiopian cuisine.

Seeds are used to flavor breads, *biryanis,* curries, and achars (Indian pickles).

Traditionally, spices like ajowan are fried in butterfat (ghee) to release their flavors. The scented butter, called *tadka,* is then poured over dals (pulses such as lentils or chickpeas) or vegetables.

Ajowan's scent resembles that of thyme (which makes sense, considering its high thymol content—as much as 60 percent of the essential oil), with a bit of anise. In addition to thymol, the seeds contain α-pinene, γ-terpinene, limonene, and p-cymene.

COMMENTS
Ajowan seeds (actually dried fruits, like caraway "seeds") are sometimes marketed as "lovage seed."

Ammi, or bishop's weed, *Carum ajowan,* may be the same species; it has also been listed as *Trachyspermum ammi.*

Bishop's weed, Queen Anne's lace, *Ammi majus,* may be yet another species, but it should certainly not be confused with the umbelliferous *Daucus carota.*

Alexanders: *Smyrnium olusatrum*

OTHER COMMON, ETHNIC, OR SCIENTIFIC NAMES
Alick, black lovage, black pot-herb, hellroot, horse parsley, megweed, skit, skeet, wild celery
France: Ombrelle jaune
Germany: Pfeerdeeppich
Italy: Macerone, smirnio

RELATED SPECIES
Smyrnium perfoliatum: Alexanders, perfoliate Alexanders

Zizya aurea: Golden Alexanders, golden parsnip, meadow parsnip, royal cowparsnip (formerly *Smyrnium aureum*)

Biennial
Origin: Mediterranean region
Range: Temperate regions

CULINARY USES
Coarse, dark, celery-like leaves and stems can be cooked. Younger leaves and flower buds can be used as garnishes for fish, in fritters, or in salads. Aromatic seeds are ground like pepper and used as a seasoning. Young stems are similar in taste (and cooking techniques) to asparagus. Roots are used as a vegetable, generally boiled and served with vinaigrette.

Smyrnium perfoliatum is a milder version of Alexanders.

OTHER USES
Seeds in potpourri

COMMENTS
Golden Alexanders may, like many other members of the Apiaceae, be poisonous (see Comments, under SKIRRET).

"Alexanders" is also used as a name for *Angelica atropurpurea* (see ANGELICA).

Angelica: *Angelica archangelica*

OTHER COMMON, ETHNIC, OR SCIENTIFIC NAMES
Angelica officinalis, archangel, Aunt Jericho, bellyache root, dead nettle, garden angelica, masterwort, seawatch, whiteroot, wild parsnip
France: Angélique
Germany: Angelika, Engelwurtz
Italy: Angelica, zavirna
Spain: Angélica

CULTIVARS AND RELATE SPECIES
'Sativa': (Angelica cultivar raised in France for same uses as the species)

RELATED SPECIES
Angelica atropurpurea: Alexanders, American angelica, great angelica, masterwort, purple angelica
Angelica sinensis: Dang gui, dong guei, dong quai, pai chi, tang kuei, tangkwei (China)
Angelica sylvestrus: Ground ash, holy ghost, wild angelica

Biennial, but can be kept going for up to four years by pinching back all new flower spikes.

Origin: Europe and Asia

Range: Temperate regions

CULINARY USES

Angelica has a sweet, aromatic flavor, a bit like anise, but with spicy undertones that suggest celery, iris blossoms, and musk. The seed has the same complex of flavors as anise, but adds an aromatic, slightly balsamic scent. Tender stems and roots are eaten raw and sometimes candied. The candied stems are usually dyed a pale green. They are used as a garnish in much the same way as candied violets.

The seeds are used as a flavoring for cordials and liqueurs such as absinthe, altvater, amaretto, anisette, Campari, both green and yellow Chartreuse, Fernet Branca, Grand Marnier, Pernod, as well as bitters, vermouth, and some gins and Rhine wines. The dried root is supposedly one of the secret ingredients in Benedictine. Krambambuli is a German angelica-based liqueur that is also flavored with violets. Gorny doubnyak is a Russian bitter liqueur flavored with angelica and other ingredients (see glossary). Raspail, a French liqueur, contains angelica, calamus root, and myrrh.

Golpar is an Iranian spice consisting of powdered angelica seeds.

Angelica sweetens acid fruits when you don't want to add extra sugar. Teas are brewed from dried and fresh leaves, roots, and seeds. Leaves are used to flavor jams and jellies. They can be cooked as a vegetable and are also part of the formulation of hop bitters. Scandinavians use both the roots and stems as a cooked vegetable, also adding chopped roots to bread. Blanched, the stems can be added to salads. The young stems of *Angelica sylvestrus* are eaten raw by Russians along the lower reaches of the Volga. Italians soak the sheaves in water, then dip them in egg, and fry them as the fritters called *zavirne fritte*. The sheaths can also be grilled and dressed with a simple vinaigrette, for use in an antipasto.

The roots of angelica derive their taste and smell from a number of substances: β-thujene (6,900 ppm), α-pinene (1,500 ppm), limonene (1,320 ppm), β-phellandrene (1,000 ppm), and p-cymene (980 ppm), among the two hundred or so ingredients commonly found in the plant. Bugleweed contains β-pinene (498 ppm), α-pinene (666 ppm), β-bourbonene (498 ppm), caryophyllene (80 ppm), and d-cadinene (40 ppm).

There does not seem to be an English name for dong quai, *Angelica sinensis*. Its dried roots, with a scent somewhere between that of celery and fenugreek, are used to flavor chicken soups. In Singapore, liquid chicken extracts flavored with *Angelica sinensis* are sold in small jars. In China, dong quai is traditionally paired with pigeon. It contains many of the same compounds as *Angelica archangelica* but substantially less essential oil.

As an ornamental, angelica is used horticulturally in perennial borders. Dried seed-heads are good in dried flower arrangements. Angelica is also used in the manufacture of perfumes.

COMMENTS

"Angelica" is also the name of *Guettarda speciosa,* a totally unrelated Brazilian fruit. It is a member of the Rubiaceae family.

Lovage (q.v.) is sometimes referred to as "wild angelica." "Archangel" is also a name for dead nettle (*Lamium purpurea*), bugleweed (*Lycopus virginicus*), and butterflyweed (*Asclepius tuberosa*).

The "alexanders" here is not the same as Alexanders (*Smyrnium olusatrum,* q.v.). This "masterwort" should not be confused with masterwort (*Astrantia* spp., q.v.) or masterwort (*Heracleum spondylium* subs. *montanum,* which is poisonous).

Angelica is susceptible to attacks by swallowtail butterflies, but in my own garden, cilantro, dill, and parsley have been the primary victims (see Comments, under DILL).

Anise: *Pimpinella anisum*

OTHER COMMON, ETHNIC, OR SCIENTIFIC NAMES
Fennel, sweet cumin, sweet fennel
Algeria: Habbet e'hlawoua, sanoudj
Arabic: Yanisum, yensoon
Brazil: Erva-doce
China: Huei-hsiang, pa chio, yan kok
Denmark: Grøn anis
Estonia: Harilik aniis
Ethiopia: Insilal
Finland: Anisruoho
France: Anis vert, boucage, grains d'anis noir
Germany: Anis, Anys
Greece: Anithos
Hungary: Anis
Iceland: Anís
Iran: Anisun
Iraq: Habbat hilwa, yansoon
India: Pedha jilkara, perumjeeragam, saunf, shatpushpa, shoap, sombu, sulpha
Indonesia: Jintan mani
Israel: Shamir
Italy: Anice, anice verde

Malta: Cumino dulce
Mexico: Anís, anís chico, pimpinela
Morocco: Habbt hlawa, nafaa
Netherlands: Anijs, groene anijs, nieszaad, wilde pimpernel
Norway: Anis
Philippines: Anis
Poland: Biedrzeniec anyz
Portugal: Anis, anis verde, erva foce
Romania: Anis
Russia: Anis
Spain: Anis, anís, matalahuga
Sweden: Anis
Turkey: Anason
Vietnam: Cay vi

GROWTH HABITS
Annual
Origin: Eastern Mediterranean
Range: Temperate regions

CULINARY USES
With their strong licorice flavor and scent, anise seeds (actually dried fruits) are a familiar spice. They are used in breads, cakes, cookies, and candies. They are good with cheeses, chutneys, curries, pickles, shellfish (such as crabs and shrimp), meats, poultry, soup, and stews.

Anethole is the essential oil that provides the main flavoring in anisette, arrack, Campari, Chartreuse, Kümmel, and Ricard. A drink related to Kümmel is the German Danzig Goldwasser. It is best known for the tiny flakes of gold leaf drifting dreamily in every bottle. In France and the Netherlands, there is an equivalent liqueur called Liqueur d'Or. Danzig Silberwasser has exactly the same formula as Goldwasser—except that it is garnished with silver leaf instead of gold.

Raki is a Turkish liqueur that is made from fermented dates, flavored with anise seeds and licorice. The Yugoslavian equivalent is called Rakiji. Both are similar to the Greek ouzo. Likewise, Spain has its Anis del Mono, from Barcelona, and Portugal its Escarchado. Ojen is a Spanish variation on French Pastis, or Libyan Kasra, that is available in sweet and dry forms. Russians also enjoy okhotnichya—hunter's brandy—a warming concoction consisting of alcohol, anise seeds, and other flavorings (see glossary). Sambuca, from the province of Lazio, Italy, contains a number of additional herbs and spices, including anise, elderberries, and vanilla. Other Italian liqueurs with similar flavors include Anisetta Stellata, from Pescara, and Elixir de China.

Before 1915, anise was widely used in absinthe, and it is still used in Spain, where absinthe was never banned. Ojen is a Spanish absinthe. In France, the void left by the departure of the green fairy, as absinthe was popularly known, has been filled in part by Pastis, Pernod, and lesser-known liqueurs such as Oxygenée and La Tintaine. The latter anise-flavored liqueur is sold with a flowering stalk of fennel inside every bottle. Greeks and Cypriots also make Mastic (Masticha or Mastika), a pungently sweet mixture of mastic gum and anise seed.

The seeds are often eaten at the end of Indian meals to cleanse the palate and sweeten the breath. As *erva-doce,* anise seeds are combined with lemon juice, olive oil, and white pepper in Brazil to make a dipping sauce for bread, just as is done by Italians and Palestinians.

Flowers can be used in fruit salads, especially with chestnuts, dates, or figs. Leaves are useful as a garnish or in salads, especially with carrots, cauliflower, cucumbers, and lettuce. Leaves and stems can be added to the cooking liquid when boiling shellfish, such as crabs, mussels, and shrimp. Leaves can be added to lamb or veal stews.

Anise derives its familiar flavor and scent almost entirely from anethole, but the scent is slightly altered by the presence of estragol, anise aldehyde, and other trace compounds.

OTHER USES

Anise seed appears in potpourri.

COMMENTS

Insilal is Ethiopian for "anise," but it is also the Ethiopian name for dill and fennel.

"Wild fennel" is also a name for nigella (q.v.).

These plants are eaten by swallowtail butterflies (see Comments, under DILL).

Asafoetida: *Ferula foetida*

OTHER COMMON, ETHNIC, OR SCIENTIFIC NAMES

Divel's dreck, food of the gods, hing, metath, stinking gum. It has been listed botanically as *Asafoetida nartex, Ferula asafoetida,* and *Narthex assafeotida.*

Burma/Myanmar: Sheingho
Estonia: Asaföötida
Germany: Asant, Stinkasant, Teufelsdreck
France: Asafetide, assa foetida, férule persique
Iceland: Asafoetida
India: Anjadana, inguva, hingu, kayam, perungayam, raamathan
Iran: Retshîna fena
Italy: Assafétida
Netherlands: Duivelsdrek, godenvoedsel
Norway: Dyvels drekk
Russia: Asafetida

Spain: Asafétida
Sri Lanka: Perunkayan
Swahili: Mvuje
Sweden: Dyvelsträck

RELATED SPECIES

Ferula communis: Common giant fennel. A weed indigenous to the eastern
Mediterranean area. This is not the familiar edible fennel (q.v.).
Ferula narthex: Asafoetita
Ferula gummosa: Asafoetita
Ferula scorodosoma: Asafoetita
Ferula galbaniflua: Galbanum; galbano (Italy and Spain)

GROWTH HABITS

Perennial
Origin: Afghanistan and Iraq
Range: Sandy deserts

CULINARY USES

Nasty-smelling almost beyond belief, asafoetida has somehow found its
way into a number of cuisines. Fortunately, it loses its pungency when cooked.
Like musk, it lends an intriguing, exotic quality to foods when used in small
amounts. The resin, made by drying the plant's milky sap, is used in India
and Iran to flavor curries, meatballs, and pickles. The achars, or mixed hot
pickles, of India are often laced with asafoetida. While the herb is popular
among Hindus in Kashmir, it is not used by Muslims.

Ferula foetida, Ferula narthex, Ferula narthex, and *Ferula scorodosoma* all yield
the commercial resin.

Asafoetida was used as a replacement for silphium—which was hunted to
extinction—in complex sauces in classical Rome; it may be that Worcestershire sauce is a descendent of those ancient concoctions.

Asafoetida's foul pungency results from diallyl aulfide and a number of
other sulfur compounds that are closely related to those responsible for garlic's antisocial behavior. The herb also contains α-pinene and phellandrene.
Galbanum yields a floral-scented oil that is used in baked goods, candies,
and ice creams. It contains myrcene, cadinene, d-α-pinene, β-pinene, and
several sesquiterpenes.

OTHER USES

People used to tie little bags of asafoetida around their necks to ward off
winter diseases. It is hard to imagine that in a time when running water was
unavailable, people sewed themselves into their long johns for the winter and
then adorned themselves with asafoetida. It probably worked, since the aroma
would effectively reduce the chances of exposure to communicable disease.

The resin, after a steam treatment to remove some of its more unsavory
aromas, is used as a fixing agent in perfumes.

Asafoetida
Ferula foetida

From Woodville,
Medical botany, vol. 1

COMMENTS

Save yourself a truly unpleasant experience: if you find a store that carries asafoetida, resist the temptation to smell it for yourself. Asafoetida was known to the ancients as *Stercus Diaboli,* the devil's own excrement. Enough said?

Other than *Ferula communis,* none of these species is listed as growing in North America, according to *Hortus Third.*

Caraway: *Carum carvi*

OTHER COMMON, ETHNIC, OR SCIENTIFIC NAMES

Foreign cumin, Vietnamese mint, wild cumin. Caraway has been listed in botanical texts as *Apium carvi* and *Seseli carvi.*

Algeria: Kerwia
Arabic: Karauya
China: Yuan-sui
Estonia: Harilik köömen
Finland: Kumina
France: Carvi, cumin, cumin des prés, graine de carvi
Gaelic: Carvie
Germany: Kümmel
Hungary: Kömény, köménymag
Iceland: Kmen

India: Gunyan, shah jeera, shia jeera
Italy: Carvi, comino, comino tedesco
Malaysia: Jemuju
Mexico: Alcarravea
Morocco: Karwiya
Netherlands: Karwij, romeinse komijn, wilde komijn
Norway: Karve
Poland: Kminek zwyczajny
Portugal: Alcaravia, comino
Romania: Cumin
Russia: Tmin
Spain: Alcaravea, carvi
Swahili: Kisibiti
Sweden: Kummin
Turkey: Kara kimyon, karaman kimyonu
Vietnam: Rau la tia to (leaves)

GROWTH HABITS
Biennial
Origin: Europe
Range: Temperate regions

CULINARY USES

The familiar seeds on rye breads are also a natural with apples and, of course, cabbage, as in cole slaws and sauerkraut. Caraway is useful with meats and poultry, in pickling, in salad dressings, and in soups and stuffings.

A candy is made by coating the seeds with a hard sugar shell.

Cheeses, such as the Gouda-like Walda of England or the Pompadour of the Netherlands, the Danbo (a Samsø-like cheese) of Denmark, the Kesti (a Tilsiter-like cheese) of Finland, the Norwegian Pultost, and the Spitzkäse and Stangenkäse of Germany, are often flavored with caraway. Italian caraway-flavored cheeses include a Mozzarella from Borelli, and from Trieste, Torta Gaudenzio, formed of layers of Gorgonzola and Mascarpone, the richness of which is sometimes relieved by the slightly uncouth urgency of caraway. In Hungary, Liptói, a soft cheese made from sheep's milk, is available with or without caraway seeds. This cheese is better known as Liptauer, but in Slovakia its name is Liptovká Bryndza. The Scottish Ballindalloch is a goat cheese made more pungent with caraway seeds or green peppercorns. The Scots also make a hard sheep's-milk cheese called St. Finan's that often contains the warm-flavored seeds. In the United States, Armenians sometimes add caraway seeds to their braided cheeses. Some Vermont Cheddars are flavored with caraway.

Caraway is the chief flavoring in akavit, Kümmel, and schnapps. Caraway oil is used in Chartreuse. The German Danzig Goldwasser and Silberwasser are flavored with caraway and anise seeds; French and Dutch equivalents to these liqueurs are known as Liqueur d'Or. In Denmark, there is caraway-and-cumin-flavored liqueur known simply as C.L.O.C., which stands for the Latin phrase *cumin liquidum optimum castelli.*

Young leaves can be added to salads and soups, such as cream of cauli-flower. The leaves can also be tossed into the cooking liquid for cabbage, cauliflower, potatoes, or turnips. Leaves are used like mint in Vietnamese salads (cold vegetable platters). Sprouted seeds of caraway, also called *rau la tia to,* or caraway mint, are used in Vietnamese cooking. Roots can be eaten like parsnips.

The flavor of caraway is primarily a result of the presence of the essential oils carvone and d-limonene. Caraway does, however, contain other flavor-ings, such as carveol and dipentene.

OTHER USES
Essential oil used in perfumes and soaps.

COMMENTS
Tia to is also the Vietnamese name for perilla (q.v.).

These plants are food for a number of swallowtail butterflies (see Comments, under DILL).

Carrot: *Daucus carota* subs. *sativus*

OTHER COMMON, ETHNIC, OR SCIENTIFIC NAMES
Bird's nest. Also known botanically as *Daucus sativus*
France: Carotte commun
Germany: Moehren
Italy: Carota
Mexico: Zanahoria
Russia: Morkov
Spain: Zanahoria
Sweden: Morot
Turkey: Havuç

RELATED SPECIES
Daucus broteri: Möhre (Germany); yabani havuç (Turkey)
Daucus carota: Markov (Russia); vildmort (Sweden); bird's nest, devil's plague, Queen Anne's lace, wild carrot
Pastinaca sativa: Chirivía (Spain); Pastinakwurzel (Germany); parsnip

GROWTH HABITS
Biennial
Origin: Eurasia
Range: Cool temperate regions. The wild version is a cosmopolitan weed.

Domestic, cultivated carrots are a subspecies of their wild counterparts (*Daucus carota*). Good breeding and careful gardening make much, but not all, of the difference.

Carrots, as a vegetable, are too well known to mention; however, they are used as a seasoning in a couple of ways. One of the most important is in mirepoix, the foundation of almost all French cuisine. Mirepoix is comprised of 25 percent carrots, 50 percent onions, and 25 percent celery. It flavors and colors countless soups, stocks, and sauces.

Less well known is the use of carrot seeds as a spice. This use should not be surprising, considering the carrot's close relatives among the Apiaceae: caraway, cardamom, coriander, and cumin. The seeds have a spicy aromatic quality resulting from butyric acid, carotol, limonene, and pinene. They have been used to flavor some liqueurs. The flowers have a caraway-like warmth, without the sweetness one might expect of carrots. The leaves of carrots contain many of the same compounds as the seeds and can be used (in small amounts) to add a slightly bitter, strongly aromatic garnish to couscous or roasted rich meats. They are added to soups and stews in Italy, and they flavor savory meat-filled pastries in Crete.

OTHER USES
Perfumes

COMMENTS
Most herbs are not bothered by insects. In fact, the intense aromatic qualities we desire in herbs probably evolved as defense mechanisms for the plants. Major exceptions are the Umbelliferous plants. Plants in the Apiaceae family are the preferred food of a number of swallowtail butterflies (see Comments, under DILL).

Celery: *Apium graveolens*

OTHER COMMON, ETHNIC, OR SCIENTIFIC NAMES
Ajomda (seed), celeriac, smallage
Algeria: Kharfez
China: Hon-Kun, k'an tsoi, kan-tsai, qin cai
Czech Republic: Celer
Denmark: Bladselleri, rodselleri, selleri
East Timor: Salsa
Estonia: Aedseller, seller
Finland: Ruokaselleri, selleri
France: Ache, céleri
Germany: Eppich, Sellerie

Greece: Sélino
Hungary: Zeller
Iceland: Sellerífrae, seljufrae
India: Ajmod, bariajmud, bodiajmoda, chiluri
Indonesia: Selderi, seledri
Iran: Karafs
Iraq: Krafs (seed)
Italy: Sedano, senani
Japan: Seri-na, serori
Malaysia: Daun seldri, daun sop, selderi
Netherlands: Bladselderij, eppe, juffrouwmerk, sèlder, selderie, selderij, sèldu, snijselderij, struikselderij
Norway: Selleri
Philippines: Kinchay, kintsay
Poland: Seler, selery zwyczajne
Portugal: Aipo, salsão
Russia: Syel'dyeryey
Singapore: Kin chye
Spain: Api, Apio
Sri Lanka: Salderi
Surinam: Supu'wiri
Sweden: Selleri
Thailand: Khen chaai, pak chi farang
Turkey: Kereviz

RELATED SPECIES
Apium prostratum: Sea celery, sea parsley, southern ocean (Australia)

CULTIVARS
'Dulce': Celery
'Rapaceum': Celeriac, turnip-rooted celery
'Secalinum': Céleri à couper (France); cutting celery, leaf celery, soup celery

GROWTH HABITS
Biennial
Origin: Americas, Eurasia, Australia, New Zealand
Range: Temperate regions

CULINARY USES
Carrots, onions, and celery together produce mirepoix, the foundation of good cooking of many kinds, but especially French.

Celery seeds are used in casseroles, curries, pickles, sauces, and soups, especially those containing fish and/or tomatoes. The seeds are also good in biscuits, breads, and potato salads. Stems appear in stir-fries ("chop suey" and "egg rolls" are usually little *but* celery). Seeds, stalks, and leaves are used to season fish (often added to the court bouillon used for poaching delicate fish), shellfish, stuffings for poultry and veal, salad dressings, sauces, sausages, soups (especially chowders and vegetable soups), and stews.

In Southeast Asia, the flavor of celery is much stronger than in temperate climates. Only the leaves are used there, as an herb, not as a vegetable.

Celery salt is a commercial blend of ground dried celery and salt. In the south of France, ground celery seed is used as a seasoning for fish, salads (especially those containing tomatoes), and salad dressings.

Among cheeses, the Gouda-like Pompadour of Holland is sometimes flavored with celery.

Celery seed's essential oil contains 3-n-butylphthalide (100,000 ppm), β-selinene (55,000 ppm), β-caryophyllene (up to 40,000 ppm), β-elemene (35,000 ppm), and *cis*-dihydro-Isocarvone (15,000 ppm), among many other compounds. Celery leaves contain many of the same compounds, but in much lower concentrations.

OTHER USES
The seeds, actually fruits, yield extracts used in the perfume industry.

COMMENTS
Sixteenth-century Italian apothecaries combined bugloss, endive, hops, and smallage (wild celery leaves) in a sugar syrup. A majolica jar in the Ringling Museum, in Sarasota, Florida, that once held this mixture is labeled *Sy Bisantinu,* which suggests that the recipe originated in ancient Byzantium; or perhaps that suggestion was only intended by the purveyors of this latter-day snake oil.

Chervil: *Anthriscus cerefolium*

OTHER COMMON, ETHNIC, OR SCIENTIFIC NAMES
French parsley, garden chervil, salad chervil, sweet chervil (sometimes incorrectly as sweet Cicely, q.v.), myrrhus. Sometimes listed botanically as *Cherifolium cerefolium.*

Arabic: Maqdunis afranji
China: San-lo-po
Denmark: Kørvel
Estonia: Aed-harakputk, harakputk
Finland: Maustekirveli
France: Cerfeuil
Germany: Französische Petersilie, Gartenkerbel, Kerbel
Iceland: Kerfill
Israel: Tamcha
Italy: Cerfoglio
Netherlands: Kervel

Norway: Hagekjørvel, kjørvel
Portugal: Cerfolho
Russia: Kervel
Spain: Cerafolio, perifolio
Sweden: Dansk körvel, körvel, trädgårdskörvel

RELATED SPECIES
Anthriscus sylvestris: Beaked parsley, cow parsley, woodland chervil

GROWTH HABITS
Annual
Origin: Mediterranean region
Range: Temperate regions

CULINARY USES
Chervil is one of France's fines herbes, along with parsley, tarragon, and chives (q.v.). It has a delicate, slightly bitter taste, with a hint of anise in the finish. It looks like a magically miniaturized parsley, only paler. It is a classic component of the sauces and stocks of haute-cuisine. It is essential to *sauce Béarnaise.* Chervil's delicate flavor is lost if cooked too long, so add the herb near the end of the cooking process. Similarly, drying destroys chervil's taste. Fortunately, it grows well in a pot on a sunny windowsill, so you can have fresh chervil year round.

Chervil is good with soft cheeses—even lowly cottage cheese—as well as with omelets, oysters, and sorrel soup. Use it with meats, in salads, in sauces, and steeped to create an herbal vinegar. Parsley is a cliché as a garnish, but chervil is always in style. *Kørvelsuppe* is a Danish chervil soup.

Beaked parsley, *Anthriscus sylvestris,* is used, fresh or dried, to season beans, potatoes, eggs, salads, and soups.

COMMENTS
Delicate chervil plants are no match for the appetites of swallowtail butterflies (see Comments, under DILL).

Cilantro: *Coriandrum sativum*

OTHER COMMON, ETHNIC, OR SCIENTIFIC NAMES
Arab parsley, coriander, Chinese parsley, cilantrillo, Indian parsley, Mexican parsley
Afghanistan: Gashneez
Algeria: Qasbour
Arabic: Kazbarah, kizbara, kuzbara (seed)
Brazil: Coentro
Burma/Myanmar: Nannambin (leaves); nan nan bin, nan nan zee or nannamzee, naunau (seed)

China: Fan yan sui, hu sui, xiang cai, yuen sai
Estonia: Aedkoriander
Ethiopia: Dimbilal
Finland: Korianteri
France: Persil arabe (leaves), coriandre, punaise mâle
Gaelic: Coireiman, lus a choire
Germany: Chinesische Petersilie, Indische Petersilie, Koriander
Greece: Koríadron
Iceland: Kóríander
India: Dhane, dhania, hara dhania, havija, kothambri soppu, kothamalli
    elai, kothamalli kooraku, kotthamallie (leaf); daniya kothambri,
    dhania, dhaniyaka, dhaniyalu, dahi, dhoney, kambari, kothimbir,
    kothamilee, kotimiri, kottamalli (seed)
Indonesia: Daun ketumbar (leaf), ketumbar (seed)
Iran: Gheshneez, gishniiz
Iraq: Kazbara, kizbarah
Italy: Coriandolo
Japan: Koendoro, koyendoro
Laos: Hap kom, phak hom pom, phak houa pom
Malaysia: Daun ketumbar (leaf), ketumbar (seed)
Mexico: Cilantro, culantro
Morocco: Kosbour (seeds)
Netherlands: Ketoembar, koriander
Norway: Koriander
Okinawa: Kushiba
Philippines: Ketumbar (leaf), kulantro, unsuy, wansuey, wansoy
Poland: Kolendra siewna
Portugal: Coentro
Puerto Rico: Culantro, culantro de monte, recao
Russia: Kinza, kishnets, koriandr
Spain: Coriandro, culantro
Sri Lanka: Kothamalli (seed), kothamalli kolle (leaf)
Swahili: Giligilani
Sweden: Koriander
Thailand: Mellet pak chi, pak chi bai (leaves), luk pak chee or pak chi
    met (seed), pak chi rahk (roots)
Tunisia: Tabil
Turkey: Kishnish, kisnis
Vietnam: Cay ngo, mui, ngo, rau mai, rau ngo

CULTIVARS

Several cultivars, and some varieties, are grown for seeds; others for foliage. If you're after long-lasting foliage, choose 'Bengal Giant', 'Kasturi
Sweet Scented', 'Large Leaved', and 'Santo', all developed for their foliage.

The Cook's Garden in Londonderry, Vermont, and other purveyors have carried a cultivar they call 'Slo Bolt'—which may be a trade name for one of the above—just what the cilantro lover requires. Burpee's herb seed 'Coriander' is a similar cultivar. In hot weather, it will still bolt, but it will provide more, and better-flavored, leaves before it surrenders to its procreative urges. 'Indian' and 'Moroccan' are grown specifically for their seeds; 'Indian' is the sweeter and more desirable of the two.

GROWTH HABITS

Annual

Origin: Mediterranean region

Range: Temperate regions

CULINARY USES

The leaves of cilantro are loved or hated, passionately.

The seeds are used in a wide range of foods: from baked goods to sugar-coated candies, to poultry dressings, to sausages (salt, garlic, and coriander are the main seasonings in bologna, hot dogs, and mortadella). They are good in pickles and in beet salads, with tomatoes, or as an interesting addition to ratatouille. Coriander seeds are combined with cumin seeds in many North African dishes.

The ground seeds are used, in combination with other spices and salt, in the French *sel épice,* which is used with meats, especially in the cured meats and sausages that constitute French charcuterie. They are good with rich roasted meats, such as pork, but they also serve in sauces and broths of other meats.

The seeds are supposedly among the secret ingredients in Benedictine, and they are also found in akavit, anisette, Fernet Branca, Kümmel, vermouth, and many gins. The seeds make an appearance in the recipe for Grand Marnier (and, presumably, Cointreau). They were used in absinthe. Oil derived from the seed is used in Chartreuse.

The fresh leaves are used in salads, sauces, and stews. They are essential to guacamole and other Southwestern or Mexican dishes. They are indispensable to the cuisines of Thailand, Laos, Vietnam, India, and parts of China.

They are widely used in Brazil, not surprising considering their popularity in Portugal. *Molho brasiliero,* "Brazilian sauce," is a kind of green salsa made with cilantro, lime juice, and other spices and herbs. African slaves certainly brought okra to the New World, where it appears in such dishes as shrimp gumbo. "Okra" derives from the Ashanti, West African, word *nkru;* "gumbo" comes from the Bantu, South African, word *Ngombo.* The Brazilian version of the same dish contains peanuts and cilantro.

The green seeds and flowers are a curiously hot blend of the musky cilantro taste with the sweet spiciness of dried coriander seed. In Southeast Asia, cilantro stems and roots are treated as distinct seasonings. They are used with beans and soups. The roots are chopped and included in some curries.

Cilantro leaves contain *trans*-2-trideceneal and decanal. Coriander seed contains α-terpinene, camphene, citral, coriandrol, limonene, and linalool.

OTHER USES
Coriander seeds are used in potpourri.

COMMENTS
Tabil, the Tunisian word for "coriander seed," also refers to a spice blend incoporating caraway seeds, coriander seeds, garlic, and chile.

Cilantro is quick to seed. A sure sign that this is about to happen: tall, stiff stems with finely divided leaves rise above the typical rounded parsley-like foliage. Once cut, cilantro does not keep well, though it will last longer if wrapped tightly in a damp paper towel and plastic wrap. The herb can be dried but loses its intense flavor and aroma.

Cilantro is fairly hardy—for an annual—but there is one disaster that it can encounter (other than bolting, of course): swallowtail butterflies. They love it, as we do. (See Comments, under DILL.)

Corkwing: *Glehnia littoralis*

OTHER COMMON, ETHNIC, OR SCIENTIFIC NAMES
Glehnia root. Also known scientifically as *Adenophora tetraphylla* and *Phelloptreus littoralis.*
China: Sang hu ts'ai
Japan: Hama-bofu

GROWTH HABITS
Perennial
Origin: Eastern Asia
Range: Sandy shorelines

CULINARY USES
The plant, said to resemble angelica and tarragon in flavor, is used to flavor the sweet rice wine called *toso.* Young leaves and stems are pickled and served with sushi and sashimi, or as a vinegared salad—*sunomono*—in Japan.

Culantro: *Eryngium foetidum*

OTHER COMMON, ETHNIC, OR SCIENTIFIC NAMES
Black Benny, broad-leafed cilantro, cilantrillo, false coriander, fit-weed, long coriander, Mexican coriander, Puerto Rican coriander, saw leaf herb, sawtooth coriander, stinkweed, thorny coriander
Caribbean: Culantro de burro, culantro de cimarron, culantro de coyote, culantro de monte

China: Jia yuan qian
Colombia: Cilantro
Germany: Langer Koriander, Méxicanischer Koriander
Jamaica: Fitweed, spiritweed
Laos: Hom tay
Malaysia: Ketumbar Java
Mexico: Perejil de tabasco
Netherlands: Stinkdistel
Spain: Racao, recao
Thailand: Pak chi farang
Trinidad: Shado béni
Vietnam: Cay muoy than, cay ngo tan, ngò ta
West Indies: Culantro de burro, culantro de Cimarron, culantro de
    coyote, culantro del monte

RELATED SPECIES

Eryngium carlinae: Hierba del sapo (Mexico); eryngo
Peperomia glaioides: Cuyanguilla, quereme (Colombia)
Peperomia pellucida: Hierba de sapo (Panama)
Peperomia quadrifolia: Retono (Spain)
Peperomia viridispica var. *Perjil:* Perejil (Colombia and Panama)

GROWTH HABITS

Annual or biennial
Origin: New World tropics
Range: Africa, Asia, Hawaii

CULINARY USES

Culantro is used all over the Caribbean region in marinades for fish and as an aromatic addition to the omnipresent meat patties. It is combined with tomatoes, garlic, and scotch bonnets in a Caribbean version of deviled crabs. People in Central America add it to beans, much as epazote is used in Mexico. It is an ingredient in *sofrito,* the seasoning paste used in Puerto Rican cooking.

Ngò gai, *Eryngium foetidum,* is used in sour soups in Vietnam and with fish dishes in Mexico. It is used in Thai cooking (such as *larp*—a raw beef salad—and *tom yam* soup). Thais use it to cut the effect of strong-smelling foods, which is why it is usually combined with the zest of Kaffir limes. The Thai name, *phak chee farang,* means "foreign coriander."

The herb's strong smell is the result of a number of aldehydes.

COMMENTS

This species is not listed in *Hortus Third.*

The unrelated "culantro de montana" is *Peperomia acuminata.* Both plants are used in the Caribbean and probably share the name because they are used in similar ways in cooking.

"Culantro" is a name used for cilantro at times, but in the Caribbean it usually refers to *Eryngium foetidum,* a plant that is closely related to sea holly (q.v.). "Culantro de monte" and "culantro de montana" (q.v.) may not be the same plant, but their uses are similar. I suspect that the two plants received nearly the same names because of their proximity and their usage. The two plants are used in the lands adjacent to the Gulf of Mexico. A number of different cultures coexist in that relatively small area, but most of them have been touched by the Spanish colonial presence. That may have been just enough to carry the names and uses, but not the plants themselves, from place to place.

Cumin: *Cuminum cyminum*

OTHER COMMON, ETHNIC, OR SCIENTIFIC NAMES
White cumin
Afghanistan: Zeera
Algeria: Kemmoun
Arabic: Kamoun
Burma/Myanmar: Ziya
Cambodia: Ma chin
China: Ma-ch'in, xiaohuixiang
Denmark: Kloeftsvoeb, spidskommen
Ethiopia: Kemun
Finland: Kumina, maustekumina
France: Cumin de Maroc, cumin officinal, faux anis
Germany: Kreuz Kümmel, Kumin, Mutter Kümmel, Römischer-
    Kümmel, Weißer Kreuz Kümmel
Greece: Kímino
Iceland: Kummin, ostakmen
India: Duru, cheeregum, jeera, shiragam, suduru, sugandhan, udgaar
    shodan
Indonesia: Djinten, jintan
Iran: Zireh
Iraq: Kammoon, kammun
Italy: Comino commune, comino romano, cumino, cumino bianco
Japan: Kumin
Malaysia: Jintan puteh
Malta: Cumino aigro
Mexico: Comino
Morocco: Kamoon
Netherlands: Komijn, komijne, spisskummen
Poland: Kminek
Portugal: Cominho

Russia: Tmin
South Africa: Gira (name used mainly by Cape Malays)
Spain: Comino, comino blanco, comino comun
Sri Lanka: Sududuru
Swahili: Jamda, jira, kisibiti
Sweden: Kummin, romersk kummin, spiskummin, vit kummin
Thailand: Yee raa
Tunisia: Khamoun
Turkey: Cemen, kimion, kimyon

CULTIVARS

In addition to the normal "white cumin" (which is actually tan), two other forms are available: the cultivars 'Lucknow' and 'Black'. The seeds of 'Lucknow' are pale green in color and are more curved than those of white cumin. Black cumin, also known as royal cumin, is sometimes listed as *Cuminum nigrum,* but—according to *Hortus Third*—there is really only one species in the genus. Black cumin is so highly prized that it has its own listing of names:

France: Cumin noir
Germany: Schwarzer Kreuz Kümmel
India: Chahi jeera, krishna jiira, kala jeera, kala zeera, kashmiri jeera, shahi jeera
Italy: Comino nero
Netherlands: Zwarte komijn
Spain: Comino negro

GROWTH HABITS

Annual
Origin: Mediterranean region
Range: Temperate to tropical regions

CULINARY USES

Cumin gets its warm flavor, in part, from carvone, the same essential oil found in caraway. Cumin has a sweeter, muskier, more exotic scent than caraway, and an appealing bitterness.

Caraway and cumin are used in similar ways, in similar cuisines, which makes sense since the seeds originated in the same region and migrated along the same routes. The difference in aromas has led to more uses for cumin. It is used in curries, with eggs, in pickling, and in soups and stews.

In Moroccan cooking, it is used with chicken and goat. A popular marinade called *chermoula* is essentially a vinaigrette of olive oil, lemon juice or vinegar, cumin, and an ever-changing list of herbs and spices. No Moroccan bean pot would be complete without cumin. The herb makes its presence known in salad dressings in Egypt. Cumin is commonly an ingredient in the Ethiopian seasoning paste called *berberé.* It is also used in the Turkish spice mixture *baharat.*

Cumin appears in many masalas and curries in India. In Mexican and Tex-Mex cuisines, it combines well with chiles and garlic (commercial "chili powder" blends these ingredients with oregano and, in some brands, coriander seed). The Portuguese use the seeds to flavor sausages. Cumin's warmth makes it an appealing addition to rich meats—sausage is a natural—but also to vegetables. Beans, especially chickpeas, are good when perfumed with garlic and cumin.

The foliage and stems are used as a seasoning in Vietnamese cooking. The seeds are used in Thai red curries and they are part of the Indian spice mixture called *panch phoron*. Vegetables, and any of a number of puréed legumes, called dals, are seasoned with panch phoron.

Cumin seed is used to flavor cheeses, such as the Leidse Kaas (Leiden or Leyden), some Edams, Nagelkaas (or Friese Nagelkaas), and Kuminost of Holland. Kilshanny, from County Clare in Ireland, is often flavored with cumin seed, garlic, pepper, and other ingredients. Mozzarellas made in Borelli, Italy, come in differently seasoned versions, one of which contains cumin.

Cumin seed contains, in addition to cuminaldehyde (up to 63 percent of the essential oil), α-pinene, β-pinene, *p*-cymene, and cuminyl alcohol.

COMMENTS

The French use "cumin" to mean either the cumin or caraway known in the United States. The seeds do appear very similar to the eye.

Many years ago, a friend asked me what was wrong with the rye bread he had just baked. It didn't seem to have the rye bread aroma he had expected. As soon as he sliced the still-warm loaf, it was obvious what had "gone wrong." He always bought his spices in bulk. This time he had labeled his cumin seed "caraway," based on its appearance. It was not the familiar deli rye bread he had planned, but it had its own, not at all unpleasant, taste—and it was great with Cheddar. My friend had discovered, by accident, what many cultures already knew: cumin-flavored breads are delicious.

Kala zeera and "black cumin" are often used as names for *Nigella sativa* (q.v.).

Cumin plants are often the target of swallowtail butterflies (see Comments, under DILL).

Dill: *Anethum graveolens*

OTHER COMMON, ETHNIC, OR SCIENTIFIC NAMES

Chinese adas, sweet adas. Former scientific names include *Anethum graveolus* and *Peucedanum graveolens*.

Afghanistan: Shabit
Arabic: Sjachet, sjamar, shibith

China: Shih-lo
Czech Republic: Kopr
Denmark: Dild
Estonia: Aedtill, till
Ethiopia: Insilal
Finland: Tilli
France: Aneth, fenouil bâtard
Gaelic: Dile
Germany: Gemeiner Dill, Gurkenkraut
Greece: Anitho, anithos
Hungary: Kapor
Iceland: Dill, sólselja
India: Anithi, enduru, sowa
Indonesia: Adas cina (leaf), adas manis
Iran: Sheveed, shiwit
Iraq: Shbent
Israel: Shamir, shevet rehanee
Italy: Aneto
Laos: Phak si
Mexico: Eneldo
Netherlands: Dille, stinkende vinke
Norway: Dill
Poland: Koper, koper ogrodowy
Portugal: Endro
Romania: Mărar
Russia: Ukrop
Spain: Abesón, aneldo, aneto, hinojo hediondo
Sri Lanka: Enduru
Sweden: Dill, dillsås
Thailand: Pak chee lao
Turkey: Dereotu, samit

CULTIVARS
'Dukat Dill' or 'Tetra-Dill'; 'Fern-leaf Dill'; 'Sowa' (Indian dill, satapashi)

GROWTH HABITS
Annual
Origin: Europe
Range: Temperate regions

CULINARY USES
Leaves and seed have a warm, aromatic scent. Fresh leaves have a more complex, more heated flavor than dried. Used in pickles and vinegars; with cucumbers (cooked or raw), it's a natural. The leaves are sometimes brewed as tea. Dill is used in soups, stews, and stuffings for poultry and fish.

Seeds are good with apples, cabbage, fish, and mushrooms. Try them in breads and soups. Sprouted seeds can be used in breads, salads, and soups.

The leaves make a significant contribution to sauces, especially emulsion-type sauces such as mayonnaise. They make a fine accompaniment to cold poached fish or chicken. Dill is good with soft cheeses, in compound butters, and in salad dressings. In England, Cumberland Farmhouse cheese is sometimes seasoned with dill. Perroche, a soft British cheese, is sometimes rolled in chopped dill weed. Some Goudas are flavored with dill in the Netherlands.

A dill vinaigrette is delightful on cold cooked asparagus, beets, or green beans.

Flowering tops of dill are good in meats and soups and go right in the jar with pickles and vinegars.

Dill is available, in season, fresh as "salad dill," but it is always available as dried dill weed or as dill seed. Several dill-flavored seasoning salts can be found, some in grocery stores and some in health food stores.

The main flavoring components of dill seed are carvone and limonene (with a small amount of carveol, d-limonene, phellandrene, α-pinene, and dipentene). Dill weed contains all of these, in somewhat reduced quantities—carvone levels are much lower in dill weed—plus dill apiole and myristicin. Dried dill weed is preferred over fresh in Turkish cooking.

Indian dill, *Anethum graveolens* Sowa, has a harsh caraway-like odor and taste. In India, the seeds (fruits) of this cultivar are preferred over those of *Anethum graveolens*. They are often an ingredient in curry powder, and in Indonesia they are also used in baking and to flavor some beverages.

COMMENTS

Insilal is Ethiopian for "dill" but also for "anise" and "fennel."

The intense aromatic qualities that we desire in herbs probably evolved as defense mechanisms for the plants, since most of them are not bothered by insects. A major exception is the parsley family. The caterpillars of some butterflies, especially the anise swallowtail, *Papilio zelicaon,* and the black swallowtail, *Papilio polyxenes asterius* (*ajax*), feed on the foliage of members of the Apiaceae. The larvae of black swallowtails are known as parsleyworms. In my own garden, I've found them to be especially fond of dill, eating the plants right to the ground.

Since you can't spray herbs, the best solution is to pick the large, brilliantly colored caterpillars off the plants yourself, dispatching them by whatever method you find least offensive. If you cannot bear to kill them, a gentler alternative would be to "transplant" them somewhere else—preferably, from their point of view, to the middle of a large patch of Queen Anne's lace. It shouldn't be too difficult to find such an area. Look along roadsides and the ever-popular waste places.

No doubt about it, butterflies are charming additions to an herb garden. That they choose to leave their offspring to eat our herbs, however, borders upon boorishness. Their beauty and grace almost excuse their inconsiderate haste to procreate on our turf.

Fennel: *Foeniculum vulgare*

OTHER COMMON, ETHNIC, OR SCIENTIFIC NAMES

Anise, bitter fennel, carosella, fenkel, Florence fennel, red-leaved fennel, sweet cumin, sweet fennel, wild fennel. Other scientific names, used in the past, include *Foeniculum capillaceum, Foeniculum dulce,* and *Foeniculum officinalis.*

Algeria: Zarr'at el besbess

Burma/Myanmar: Samong-saba, samouk-saba

China: Hui xiang, wooi heung

Estonia: Harilik apteegitill

Ethiopia: Insilal

Finland: Fenkoli, venkoli

France: Fenouil doux (*Foeniculum vulgare* 'dulce'); fenouil amer
    (*Foeniculum vulgare* 'amara'); aneth doux, fenouil, grains de fenouil

Gaelic: Lus an t'saiodh

Germany: Bitterer Fenchel (*Foeniculum vulgare* 'amara'), Heller Fenchel
    (*Foeniculum vulgare* 'dulce')

Greece: Márathon

Iceland: Fennikufrae

India: Badisep, badisopu, guamoori, madhurika, maduru, moti saunf,
    moti sonf, mouri, peddajilakaramu, saunf, shatpushpa, shauf,
    sohikirai, somp, vendhyam, wariari

Indonesia: Adas, jintan manis

Iraq: Habbet helwah, reznaya

Israel: Shumar

Italy: Finocchio selvatico, finocchio amaro (*Foeniculum vulgare* 'amara'),
    finocchio dolce (*Foeniculum vulgare* 'dulce')

Malaysia: Bunga adas (leaf or flower); biji adas (fresh seed); jintan manis

Mexico: Anizeto, hinojo

Netherlands: Venkel

Norway: Fennikel

Poland: Fenkul wloski, koper wloski

Portugal: Funcho

Russia: Aptechniy ukrop, fenkhel, sladkiy ukrop

South Africa: Berishap (name used mainly by Malaysian emigrés)

Spain: Hinojo amargo (*Foeniculum vulgare* 'amara'); Hinojo (*Foeniculum
    vulgare* 'dulce'); fonoll, hinojo

Sri Lanka: Maduru

Swahili: Shamari

Sweden: Fänkål
Thailand: Yira
Turkey: Rezene

CULTIVARS
'Amara': Common fennel
'Dulce': Florence fennel or *Foeniculum dulce, Foeniculum azoricum*

GROWTH HABITS
Perennial (cultivated as an annual)
Origin: Europe
Range: Temperate regions

CULINARY USES
Leaves and stalks are used raw, in salads, or cooked, in combination with beans, tomatoes, or chicken. Leaves are good in salads, soups, stews; with cooked vegetables; and with oily fish such as mackerel or salmon. The dried stalks are used in the Provençal *rouget flambé au fenouil*. Thick celery-like leaf bases are used as salad or cooked vegetable. Stalks can be placed under grilling fish, such as salmon.

Seeds season breads, fish, and tomato sauces. Sprouted seeds are eaten in salads. Fennel seed is the main flavoring in many Italian sausages, especially those from Umbria.

The seeds are part of the Indian spice mixture called *panch phoron,* which is used to season vegetables and any of a number of the puréed dals.

In England, Cumberland Farmhouse cheese is sometimes seasoned with fennel.

Fennel seed is an ingredient in Campari, Pernod, and vermouth, and it was in absinthe before that drink was banned by the French government in 1915.

Fennel gets its characteristic sweet licorice taste from anethole, an essential oil found in many, often unrelated, plants. Star anise, for example, is related to the magnolia family (Illiaceae), not the parsley family (Apiaceae), which contains most of the other anise-scented plants. Fennel also contains fenchone, which adds a bitter quality that makes it useful for savory purposes that might seem incompatible with its licorice-candy character. Florence fennel is sweeter than the fennel grown for seed because it contains less fenchone. Wild fennel contains so much fenchone that it is rarely used in cooking.

The essential oil content of fennel seeds is highly variable, but it is generally characterized by *trans*-anethol (up to 70,000 ppm), estragole (up to 64,000 ppm), α-pinene (up to 8,000 ppm), limonene (up to 9,000 ppm), isoleucine (7,000 ppm), and traces of many other compounds. The foliage contains much smaller amounts of these compounds than the fruits (seeds).

OTHER USES
Seeds are used in potpourri.

Insilal is the word used in Ethiopia for "fennel," but the term also applies to anise and dill.

If allowed to self-seed, fennel can become a weedy pest. Vacant lots in San Francisco are filled with fennel. Some gardeners have found fennel to be harmful to some garden plants. They recommend that it should not be planted near bush beans, caraway, kohlrabi, or tomatoes.

"Wild fennel" is also a name for nigella (q.v.).

Fennel, like other members of the Apiaceae, are often the objects of the appetites of parsleyworms (see Comments, under DILL).

Fo Ti Tieng: *Hydrocotyle asiatica* subs. *minor*

OTHER COMMON, ETHNIC, OR SCIENTIFIC NAMES

Asian marsh pennywort, bevilacqua, boilean, centella, Indian pennywort, Indian water navelwort, water pennywort. *Centella* is an alternate name for this genus. Also appears in older botanical texts as *Hydrocyle asiatica*.

Burma/Myanmar: Myin-kwa-ywet
China: Hang kor chow, ji xue cao
France: Hydrocotyle asiatique
Germany: Asiatisches Wassernabelkraut
Hawaii: Pohe kula
Japan: Tsubo-kusa
Malaysia: Daun pegaga
Philippines: Takip-kohol
Sri Lanka: Heen gotu kola
Thailand: Bai bobo, bua-bok
Vietnam: Nuoc rau ma

RELATED SPECIES

Hydrocotyle ranunculoides: Malacote (Mexico)

GROWTH HABITS

Perennial
Origin: India, Malaysia, Pakistan
Range: Sri Lanka, India, and Africa

CULINARY USES

Leaves are eaten in Sri Lanka, cooked in soups and stews, as a potherb, or raw in salads. Sweetened teas and other nonalcoholic beverages are made from the leaves in China, Thailand, and Vietnam. The leaves are slightly bitter and acrid as a result of their supply of tannins and essential oils. Malacote leaves are eaten raw, as salad, in Mexico.

Fo ti tieng is used in commercial flavorings, where it is known as gotu kola.

Purgative if eaten in quantity. Use cautiously, if at all.

There is an African seasoning referred to only as "musk" that is probably a piquant sort of kola nut (unrelated to gotu kola).

Do not confuse this plant with fo ti, *Polygonum multiflorum* (q.v.), or with true *Cola* spp. (q.v.), part of the *Sterculiaceae* family.

Pennywort is a common name applied also to species of the genus *Umbilicus*.

Fo ti tieng is a prime food for the larvae of swallowtail butterflies (see Comments, under DILL).

Imperatoria: *Peucedanum ostruthium*

OTHER COMMON, ETHNIC, OR SCIENTIFIC NAMES
Hog fennel, masterwort
France: Imperatoire, Peucedanum impératoire
Germany: Meisterwurz
Italy: Imperatoria
Spain: Imperatoria

RELATED SPECIES
Peucedanum officinale: Chucklusa, hog's fennel
Peucedanum palustre: Persil des marais (France); Sumpfsilge (Germany); brimstonewort, chucklusa, hoar strange, hoar strong, marsh hog's fennel, marsh parsley, marsh smallage, sow fennel, sulphurwort

GROWTH HABITS
Perennial
Origin: Europe
Range: Wild plant; not listed as cultivated plant in *Hortus Third*

CULINARY USES
The leaves have been used as a potherb.

The rhizomes yield a bitter tonic flavoring. Imperatoria is said to be an ingredient in Fernet Branca and some gins. It provides the slight bitter edge to Swiss cheese, as well as to some herbed cheeses.

The roots of marsh hog's fennel, *Peucedanum palustre,* have been used in Central Europe as a substitute for ginger.

COMMENTS
The FDA restricts use of imperatoria to alcoholic beverages.

Like other members of the parsley family, imperatoria is often attacked by the caterpillars of swallowtail butterflies (see Comments, under DILL).

Imperial Masterwort: *Astrantia* spp.

OTHER COMMON, ETHNIC, OR SCIENTIFIC NAMES
Masterwort; also known as *Imperatoria ostruthium.*

GROWTH HABITS
Biennial
Origin: Eurasia
Range: Moist, temperate woods

CULINARY USES
Masterwort has an aromatic hotness that is sour and tart. It contains imperatorin and ostenthin.

COMMENTS
This "masterwort" should not be confused with masterwort *Angelica atropurpurea*—q.v., under *Angelica*—or masterwort *Heracleum spondylium montanum,* which is poisonous.

The larvae of swallowtail butterflies love to eat imperial masterwort (see Comments, under DILL).

Korean Watercress: *Oenanthe stoloniferae*

OTHER COMMON, ETHNIC, OR SCIENTIFIC NAMES
Korea: Meenari

GROWTH HABITS
Perennial
Origin: Eastern Asia
Range: Wild plant in wet places within temperate range

CULINARY USES
The flavor of this plant is similar to that of the watercress *Nasturtium officinale,* familiar in the United States, but with more bite. Used as a potherb in Japan and Korea.

Lovage: *Levisticum officinale*

OTHER COMMON, ETHNIC, OR SCIENTIFIC NAMES
Bladder seed, Cornish lovage, garden lovage, Italian lovage, love parsley, Old English lovage, sirenas. An old scientific name is *Ligusticum Levisticum,* a name bestowed by Linnaeus himself.
Denmark: Loevstikke
Estonia: Harilik leeskputk

Finland: Libbsticka, liperi
France: Ache de montagne, céleri perpétuel, gaya atige simple, livèche
Germany: Badekraut, Liebstock, Liebstöckel, Luststock, Maggikraut
Hungary: Lestyán
Iceland: Skessujurt
Italy: Levistico, ligustico, maggi, sedano di montagna, sedano di monte
Mexico: Levistico, zazlipatli
Netherlands: Maggiplant, mankracht, lavas, lubbestok
Norway: Løpstikke
Poland: Lubczyk ogrodowy
Romania: Leustean
Russia: Goritsvet, guljavitsa, krovavnik, ljubistok, zorja
Spain: Apio de montaña, ligstico, levistico
Sweden: Libsticka
Turkey: Selam otu

RELATED SPECIES

Ligusticum monnieri: Giêng sàng or xà sàng (Vietnam)
Ligusticum porteri: Chuchupate, oshá (Mexico); lovage, masterwort,
    Porter's lovage
Ligusticum scoticum: Scotch Lovage

GROWTH HABITS

Perennial
Origin: Southern Europe
Range: Naturalized from Pennsylvania south to Virginia, and west as far
    as Montana and New Mexico

CULINARY USES

Seeds are used as flavoring for breads, cordials, potatoes, poultry dressings, rice, and salads. They appear in the recipes for some French liqueurs.
They are sometimes pickled in brine. Aromatic edible flowers are used in
confections, as are the crystallized stems.

Roots are sometimes brewed as tea or shredded for use in salads. They are
also preserved in honey.

In Turkey, a kind of meatloaf is made using allspice, garlic, and lovage
leaves in the forcemeat. It is served with yogurt and mint.

Leaves are used in cheeses, salads, and stews; with eggs; and in chicken
dishes. A small amount can be added to béchamel-based sauces, such as
Mornay, for use on baked fish. Lovage leaves can be used in any recipe that
calls for celery leaves; just use less, as lovage is about twice as strong in flavor. As always, don't take my word for it; taste your ingredients. Don't be an
unthinking slave to *anyone's* recipe.

Lovage tastes and smells of celery (because the two species both contain cedanolid), with a hint of yeast, but with a spicier, sweet-hot character

Lovage
Levisticum officinale

From Köhler, *Köhler's Medizinal-Pflanzen,* vol. 2

derived from coumarin (up to 43,000 ppm), hexanol (up to 600 ppm), co-paene (up to 300 ppm), β-phellandrene (up to 250 ppm), and α-pinene (up to 200 ppm). Its warmth is reminiscent of caraway, due to minute quantities of carvacrol and eugenol.

Scotch lovage, *Ligusticum scoticum,* is used like angelica (q.v.).

OTHER USES

Ornamental in herb gardens

COMMENTS

All of these lovages are targeted by parsleyworms (see Comments, under DILL).

Parsley: *Petroselinum crispum*

OTHER COMMON, ETHNIC, OR SCIENTIFIC NAMES

Garden parsley, parsley breakstone, persele, persely, rock parsley. Formerly known scientifically as *Petroselinum Hortense, Apium Petroselinum,* and *Petroselinum lativum.*

Arabic: Bakdounis, baqdunis

China: Heung choi, yang hu sui

Czech Republic: Petrzel

Denmark: Persille
Estonia: Aedpetersell, petersell
Finland: Persilja
France: Persil
Germany: Blattpetersilie, Petersilie
Greece: Maïdanós, maïntanos, makedonísi, petroselíno
Hungary: Petrezselyem
Iceland: Pétursselja, steinselja
Indonesia: Seledri
Iran: Ja'faree
Iraq: Maadanose
Italy: Prezzomolo
Japan: Paseri
Mexico: Perijil
Morocco: Madnouss (*Petroselinum crispum* 'neapolitanum')
Netherlands: Petersilie
Norway: Persille
Poland: Pietruszka
Portugal: Salsa, salsinha
Romania: Pătrunjel
Russia: Petrushka
Spain: Julivert, perejil
Sweden: Persilja
Thailand: Pak chi falaang
Turkey: Azadkegh, maydanoz
Vietnam: Rau mui tay

CULTIVARS
'Neapolitanum': Italian parsley
'Tuberosum': Heimischer (Germany); Dutch parsley, Hamburg parsley,
    parsley root, petroushka, rooted parsley, turnip rooted parsley.
    Formerly *Carum petroselinum* 'fusiformis'

RELATED SPECIES
Petroselinum vulgare: Seledri (Indonesia)

GROWTH HABITS
Biennial
Origin: Europe to Central Asia
Range: Temperate regions

CULINARY USES
Parsley is one of France's fines herbes, along with chervil, tarragon, and
chives. A few sprigs of parsley, some thyme, and a bay leaf constitute a bouquet garni, without which classic stocks and sauces are poor, insipid things.
Parsley has a delicate, yet definite taste, reminiscent of carrots (without the

sweetness) and fresh green scent. Parsley is good with fish, meats, poultry, salads, soups, and stews.

At one time, every pretentious plate in America was garnished with curly parsley. Considering the ennui of the cuisine of those gastronomically gray days, the parsley was probably the most flavorful item on the plate.

The flat-leaved or Italian varieties have more, and better, flavor than the more common curly parsley. They also lend themselves to more sophisticated garnishes: a leaf under glistening aspic or rolled between incredibly thin sheets of pasta.

Minced curly parsley can be used as a coating for soft cheeses. Boulette de Cambai is a fresh French cheese that contains parsley, pepper, tarragon, and chives. The Caethwas of Wales is a Cheddar-like cheese that is available with the combined tastes of parsley, pepper, garlic, and wine. The English have Wedmore, a Caerphilly layered with chives, from Somerset, and Week-ender, which is flavored with parsley, chives, garlic, and lemon pepper. Loddiswell Banon sometimes contains garlic and parsley. The Gouda-like Pompadour of Holland is sometimes flavored with parsley. Dauphin, or Thiérache, is an ancient cheese from Flanders that is seasoned with parsley, black pepper, cloves, and tarragon. *Persillé* is a generic name for any blue cheese in France—not because it contains parsley, but because of the supposed resemblance of the tiny flecks of blue-green mold to a garnish of minced parsley.

Combine minced parsley with nutmeg, salt, pepper, and butter for an instant "sauce" for potatoes or pasta. Cooks in the Lombardy region of Italy combine minced parsley, garlic, anchovies, and lemon zest to make *gremolata* (or *gremolada*), a great garnish for roasted lamb or veal or just a grilled tomato. This dish reflects the cooking of the south of France; no cuisine develops in isolation. A variation might replace the lemon zest with a tiny amount of fresh rosemary, the garlic with a bit of chervil or thyme.

Maître d'hôtel butter is flavored with lemon juice and minced parsley. Combine black pepper, oregano, parsley, scallions, and thyme as a rub for baked firm fish, such as grouper, mahimahi, or marlin.

"Italian Seasoning" is a name for several different mixtures of dried herbs and spices that are sold commercially. They often contain parsley.

Molho brasiliero, "Brazilian sauce," is a kind of green salsa made with parsley, lime juice, and other spices and herbs.

Parsley is available, fresh, everywhere. It is also available dried (see Comments, below) and as parsley-flavored salt. All parts of the parsley plant contain apiol, myristicin, and pinene.

COMMENTS

Don't waste a penny or a moment's consideration on the abomination that is dried parsley. It has all the flavor and charm of wood chips dyed green. That's unfair; one can easily find more interestingly flavored woods. Its sole redeeming feature is that is the cheapest item—other than salt—in the spice section of the market.

On a more serious note, dog parsley, dog poison, fool's parsley, lesser hemlock, smaller hemlock, *Anthriscus* or *aethusa cynapium,* has been mistaken for true parsley. It is a relative of chervil (q.v.), but it has an unpleasant odor and is, like many members of the Apiaceae, reputed to be poisonous. It cannot be said too often: if you are going to make use of wild plants as food, be certain of their identification.

These plants are gobbled by a number of swallowtail butterflies, called parsleyworms for good reason (see Comments, under DILL).

Pimpinella: *Pimpinella Saxifraga*

OTHER COMMON, ETHNIC, OR SCIENTIFIC NAMES
Bibenella, bibernel root, burnet saxifrage. Another name sometimes seen for this genus is *Anagallis.*
Germany: Bibernelle
Mexico: Anagalide, tlalocoxochitl

RELATED SPECIES
Pimpinella major: Greater burnet saxifrage

GROWTH HABITS
Annual
Origin: Eurasia and North Africa
Range: Temperate dry meadows

CULINARY USES
According to some authors, this plant has a biting, unpleasant taste. However, it is also said to taste like cucumber and to be used as salad burnet. This may be a confusion based on a similarity of names. The use of the plant as an alternative for hops in the brewing of beer would seem to lend some credence to the belief that it is quite bitter (also suggested by the alleged use of extracts of the roots in liqueurs). All the Pimpinellas seem to be used in the manufacture of liqueurs. Rumors of the use of the seeds as a sugarcoated candy only add to the confusion.

COMMENTS
The name "Pimpinella" has been given to a number of unrelated plants, ranging from the adder's eyes, bipinella, common pimpernel, poor man's weatherglass, shepherd's clock (*Anagallis arvensis*), the scarlet pimpernel of literary fame (a *Primula*), great burnet, and salad burnet (q.v.).

Pimpinella is often plagued by the larvae of swallowtail butterflies (see Comments, under DILL).

Samphire: *Crithmum maritimum*

OTHER COMMON, ETHNIC, OR SCIENTIFIC NAMES
Crest marine, glasswort, marsh samphire, rock samphire, sea pickle, sea bean, sampier, sea fennel, poussepied
France: Criste marine, Saint-Pierre
Germany: Meerfenchel
Greece: Krítamo
Italy: Finocchio di mare, finocchio marino, herba di San Pietra, Sanpetra
Spain: Fonoll marí

GROWTH HABITS
Perennial
Origin: Europe
Range: Temperate regions

CULINARY USES
Samphire is somewhat salty but crunchy and can be used as salad greens. Use as a garnish or as you would use kelp in a clam bake. The succulent leaves and seed pods are sometimes pickled. The pods are also used to season soups and sauces.

It is easy to confuse this with another samphire (also known as glasswort), *Salicornia europaea* (or *herbacea*), which has similar culinary applications. This species grows wild on West Coast beaches of the United States. Other names for this plant are chicken claws and pigeon foot.

Samphire contains cymol, phellandrene, pinene, and tertiary alcohols.

OTHER USES
Sometimes planted as an ornamental along sandy seashores.

COMMENTS
Avoid older plants. They are tough and prickly.

Samphire is not related to marsh samphire (q.v., under "Epazote"; see illustration, page 156), but both are used the same way. They have a crunchy, salty taste that makes them useful as snacks or in salads. The French lump them together with *Salsola kali* as *les salicornes*. Golden samphire, *Inula crithmoides*, is sometimes confused with this species (see ELECAMPANE).

Samphire is frequently eaten by parsleyworms (see Comments, under DILL).

Sea Holly: *Eryngium maritimum*

OTHER COMMON, ETHNIC, OR SCIENTIFIC NAMES
Eryngo, sea eryngium, sea eryngo, sea holm, sea hulver
France: Panicaut

Germany: Krausdistel, Stranddistel, Strandmannstreu
Italy: Eringo marino
Turkey: Çakir dikeni

RELATED SPECIES
Eryngium aquaticum: Button snakeroot, eryngo, rattlesnake master
Eryngium creticum: Eryngo
Eryngium foetidum: Ketumbar jawa (Malaysia); ngo gai (Vietnam); pak chee farang (Thailand); culantro, eryngo, foreign coriander, sawleaf, sawtooth herb

GROWTH HABITS
Perennial
Origin: Europe
Range: Coastlines of Europe, Eurasia, and North Africa

CULINARY USES
Roots can be used to flavor cooked vegetables. They are sometimes roasted and are said to taste like chestnuts. When they are candied, they are known as eryngoes. Marrowbone pie, a popular dish in Shakespeare's day, incorporated sea holly.

Very young shoots and leaves can be eaten, though they are alleged to be very bitter. *Eryngium creticum,* however, is said to be sweet-tasting. *Ngo gai* tastes like cilantro, but it is a bit more bitter and lacks cilantro's flowery overtones.

COMMENTS
Sea holly is frequently attacked by swallowtail butterfly larvae (see Comments, under DILL).

Skirret: *Sium sisarum*

OTHER COMMON, ETHNIC, OR SCIENTIFIC NAMES
Italy: Radice comestible, sisaro
Spain: Chirivia
France: Carotte blanche, chervy, girolle

RELATED SPECIES
Berula erecta: Berro de palmita (Mexico)
Sium decumbens: Jellico
Sium latifolium: Water parsnip
Sium suave: Water parsnip. Sometimes given as *Sium cicutifolium*

GROWTH HABITS
Perennial

Origin: Eastern Asia
Range: Temperate regions

CULINARY USES

Grown for its starchy, anise-scented, edible roots, which are eaten cooked or raw. The roots have also been dried, roasted, and ground for use as a substitute for coffee.

Berro de palmita is used in Mexico as watercress would be.

COMMENTS

Skirret is eaten by the caterpillars of swallowtail butterflies (see Comments, under DILL).

Water parsnip, *Sium latifolium,* has been reported to be poisonous to livestock.

A number of wild plants with similar names, sometimes planted in "wild" gardens (especially in wet or boggy areas), are certainly poisonous. You should avoid *Berula erecta,* commonly called water parsnip (also listed as *Berula pusuilla*), and *Cicuta maculata,* known commonly in Italy as cicuta and in the United States as beaver-poison, herb bennet, kex, kecksies, musquash poison, poison hemlock, poison parsley, spotted cowbane, and water hemlock. (The species is sometimes listed as *Conium maculata.*) This caveat is not something to be taken casually; make sure you know what you are eating. The active ingredient in these plants is the poison best known for its use in the execution of Socrates—and he's still dead after more than 2,400 years.

Spignel: *Meum athamanticum*

OTHER COMMON, ETHNIC, OR SCIENTIFIC NAMES
Baldmoney, bearswort
France: Meu

GROWTH HABITS
Perennial
Origin: European mountains
Range: Temperate meadows

CULINARY USES
The leaves of this mountain herb lend their aromatic sweetness to lamb and pork when used as a rub before roasting. The roots have a celery-like scent and a bitter-sweet taste. They are used as a cooked vegetable in Scotland.

OTHER USES
Ornamental

Sweet Cicely: *Myrrhis odorata*

OTHER COMMON, ETHNIC, OR SCIENTIFIC NAMES

Anise chervil, anis cicely, British myrrh, cicely, cow chervil, garden myrrh, great chervil, myrrh, anise, shepherd's needle, smooth cicely, smoother cicely, Spanish chervil, sweet bracken, sweet chervil, sweet cus, sweet humlock, sweet fern, sweets, sweet scented myrrh. Formerly known scientifically as *Scandix odorata.*

Denmark: Spansk Kørvel
Estonia: Mesiputk
Finland: Saksankirveli
France: Cerfeuil d'Espagne, cerfeuil musqué, cerfeuilmusqué, cerfeuil
    odorant
Gaelic: Cos uisge
Germany: Myrrhenkerbel, Spanischer Kerbel, Süssdolde (Süßdolde),
    Wohlriechende Süssdolde
Iceland: Spánarkerfill
Italy: Cerfoglio di Spagna, felce muschiata, finocchiella, finocchio dei
    boschi, mirride odorosa
Netherlands: Roomse kervel, vaste kervel
Norway: Spansk kjørvel
Poland: Marchewnik anyzowy
Sweden: Aniskål, spansk körvel

RELATED SPECIES

Osmorhiza aristata: Yabu ninjin
Osmorhiza Claytonii: Wooly sweet cicely, hairy sweet cicely, sweet jarvil,
    sweet javril
Osmorhiza longistylis: Aniseroot, North American sweet cicely, smooth
    sweet cicely, sweet myrrh
All of these *Osmorhiza* species have anise-scented roots. The last two grow wild in the eastern United States.

GROWTH HABITS

Perennial
Origin: Europe
Range: Temperate regions

CULINARY USES

Unripe seeds have a nutty, anise-like flavor that makes a good addition to apple pie, fruit salads, and ice cream. They are used to flavor some liqueurs. The ripe seeds are also used for flavoring, but they should be used in a sachet and discarded before service.

The leaves make a good garnish. They have a sweet, slightly anise-like flavor that is a fine addition to omelets, cabbage, salad dressings, soups, and sauces. The leaves are quite good combined with tart fruits, such as currants or gooseberries. Use only the fresh leaves, as the dried leaves lose almost all their scent.

Roots are eaten raw in salads or cooked as a vegetable. They are sometimes pickled.

The flavor and scent of sweet cicely are a result of anethol and methyl chavicol.

COMMENTS

Leaves are very similar to the leaves of poison hemlock (see Comments, under SKIRRET).

These anise-scented plants attract the larvae of swallowtail butterflies (see Comments, under DILL).

Trefoil: *Cryptotaenia japonica*

OTHER COMMON, ETHNIC, OR SCIENTIFIC NAMES
Honewort, Japanese honewort, Japanese parsley
Germany: Klee
Japan: Mitsuba

RELATED SPECIES
Cryptotaenia canadensis: San ip, san ye qin, ya er qin (China); mitsuba (Japan); mitsuba-zeri (Okinawa); honewort, Japanese parsley, Japanese wild chervil, Japanese honewort, white chervil, wild chervil

GROWTH HABITS
Perennial
Origin: Asia
Range: Temperate regions

CULINARY USES
With a taste something like celery and sorrel, this parsley- or cilantro-like species has been used raw and cooked, with eggs or in salads, sandwiches, and soups. It is also prepared by briefly boiling or frying. In Japan, it is used in *tempura,* or as an *aemono,* a cold salad of cooked greens, dressed with *shoyu* and *gomasio.*

The seeds of honewort, *Cryptotaenia canadensis,* are used to flavor baked goods. All parts of the plant have been used as salad, as potherb, pickled in vinegar, or as a cooked (fried) vegetable. The roots are always fried.

Trefoil is another name for buckbeans, *Menyanthes trifoliata* (q.v.). Like almost all members of the Apiaceae, trefoil is avidly consumed by caterpillars of the genus *Papilio* (see Comments, under Dill).

Yampah: *Perideridia Gairdneri*

OTHER COMMON, ETHNIC, OR SCIENTIFIC NAMES
Edible-rooted caraway, false caraway, ipo, squawroot

GROWTH HABITS
Perennial
Origin: Rocky Mountains
Range: Wild in temperate regions

CULINARY USES
Tuberous roots are used as a cooked starchy vegetable, eaten raw or dried, or made into a kind of flour used for baked goods.
The seeds, like caraway seeds, are used in baking and as a seasoning. They are also parched, like kasha (buckwheat groats), then boiled.

8. Apocynaceae: The Dogbane Family

Arabian Num-num: *Carissa edulis*

OTHER COMMON, ETHNIC, OR SCIENTIFIC NAMES
Chenille plant, Egyptian carissa

RELATED SPECIES
Carissa karandas: Christ's thorn, karanda
Carissa macrocarpa: Amatungula, natal plum. 'Fancy' is a cultivar grown in California.

GROWTH HABITS
Shrub
Origin: Tropical Africa
Range: Australia, Southern California

CULINARY USES
Fruits are used in jellies and vinegars or eaten fresh. Roots can be used to season fish. They have also been used, as bitters, in cocktails based on gin or rum.

Carissa karandas (sometimes listed as *Carissa congesta*) is an Asian species, used in baked goods, jellies, soft drinks, syrups, and wine. The tart jellies are often used as a glaze for grilled meats and fish. *Carissa macrocarpa,* a South African species, is used in similar ways. Its flavor is said to resemble that of cranberries.

Frangipani: *Plumeria rubra*

OTHER COMMON, ETHNIC, OR SCIENTIFIC NAMES
Nosegay

GROWTH HABITS
Deciduous tree (evergreen, except in times of drought)
Origin: Mexico to Panama
Range: Cultivated throughout Central America

CULINARY USES
The sweet flowers are used in commercial flavorings. Their flowery, pineapple-like scent is derived from p-methadien-1,4(8)-one. The almond-based pastry filling frangipane doesn't contain frangipani; it is named for its exotic, sweetly perfumed quality.

OTHER USES
Frangipani is used in perfumes.

Quebracho: *Aspidosperma quebracho-blanco*

OTHER COMMON, ETHNIC, OR SCIENTIFIC NAMES
Aspidosperma, quebracho bark, quebracho blanco. It is sometimes seen listed as *Aspidosperma quebracho-blanco.*
Italy: Quebraco

GROWTH HABITS
Tropical evergreen tree
Origin: South America
Range: South America, especially Argentina

CULINARY USES
Bitter, aromatic extracts are sometimes used to flavor ice cream and soft drinks. In South America, the ground bark is sometimes added to maté.

OTHER USES
Used as a dyestuff.

"Quebracho" is also a name for two other tropical trees, *Iodina rhombifolia* and *Schinopsis Lorenzii.*

9. Aquifoliaceae: The Holly Family

Maté: *Ilex paraguariensis*

OTHER COMMON, ETHNIC, OR SCIENTIFIC NAMES
Brazil tea, gón gouha, houx maté, ilex maté, Jesuit's tea, Paraguay tea, St. Bartholomew's tea, yerba-de-maté, yerba maté
France: Arbre à maté, thé du Paraguay
Germany: Matebaum, Paraguaytee
Italy: Maté

RELATED SPECIES
All the hollies, although only the following have any culinary interest:
Ilex cassine: Appalachian tea, cassine, Christmasberry, cussenca, dahoon, Henderson wood, inkberry, yaupon
Ilex guayusa: Guayasa, guayusa
Ilex latifolia: Holly tea, tara-yô (Japan)
Ilex verticillata: Black alder, dogberry, winterberry
Ilex vomitoria: Carolina tea, cassine, Christmasberry, dahoon, emetic holly, yaupon
Ilex glabra: Appalachian tea

GROWTH HABITS
Evergreen tree
Origin: Argentina, Brazil, Paraguay
Range: Frost-free areas

CULINARY USES
Maté, the famous tea of South America (especially the Argentinian Pampas), contains approximately the same amount of caffeine as coffee. It is available in the United States either green or roasted. It is generally consumed with lemon and/or caramelized sugar.

The dried leaves of both Appalachian tea, *Ilex cassine,* and Carolina tea, *Ilex vomitoria,* are used to make a bitter black tea called cassine. Leaves of holly tea, *Ilex latifolia,* are also brewed as tea, while its seeds are roasted and used as a coffee substitute.

Maté
Ilex paraguariensis

From Köhler, *Köhler's Medizinal-Pflanzen,* vol. 3

Maté contains, in addition to caffeine (up to 20,000 ppm), the caffeine-like theobromine (up to 5,000 ppm), and theophylline (up to 500 ppm), as much as 20,000 ppm of tannins, which provide the tea-like briskness.

OTHER USES

Guayasa, *Ilex guayusa,* has been used as snuff.

COMMENTS

Appalachian tea and inkberry are names also used for another plant, *Viburnum cassinoides,* which is sometimes called false Paraguay tea.

"Jesuit's tea," or *culen,* is also a name for the Chilean *Psoralea glandulosa,* a member of the Leguminosae family. It is used like maté, but it is also made into a carbonated soft drink.

Yaupon, *Ilex vomitoria,* is used as a narcotic, stimulant beverage in purification rites among some Native American tribes.

10. Araceae: The Arum Family

Arum Root: *Arum* spp.

OTHER COMMON, ETHNIC, OR SCIENTIFIC NAMES
Black callas, cuckoopint, lords and ladies, Solomon's lily

GROWTH HABITS
Tuberous perennial
Origin: Mediterranean region
Range: Temperate regions

CULINARY USES
The roots have a biting, peppery quality, but they have few culinary uses (see Comments, below).

COMMENTS
The leaves and roots are supposedly edible—if steeped in acids, such as vinegar, or thoroughly cooked. I have seen arum root mentioned only as a kind of survival food, but I have found no modern reference to its use as food.

Most arums are poisonous. They are included here, with the foregoing caveat, only because they appear in many old herbals, primarily as medicinal plants.

Calamus: *Acorus calamus*

OTHER COMMON, ETHNIC, OR SCIENTIFIC NAMES
Bitter pepper root, calomel root, citron grass, German ginger, flagroot, myrtle flag, myrtle sedge, poison flagroot, rat root, sweet cane, sweet cinnamon, sweet flag, sweet grass, sweet myrtle, sweet root, sweet rush root, sweet sedge
China: Shih ch'ang pu
France: Acore vrai
Germany: Kalamus, Rohrflöte, Schilfrohr
India: Bachh, racha
Italy: Calamo aromatico
Mexico: Acoro, calamo aromatico
Spain: Calamo

RELATED SPECIES
Acorus americanus: Bitter root, calamus, myrtle flag, sweet rush
Acorus gramineus: Grass-leaved sweet flag, sekishô (Japan)

Perennial
Origin: Northern Hemisphere
Range: Temperate regions

CULINARY USES

Calamus is used in teas. Largely in the form of extracted oils, it is part of the manufacture of such liqueurs as altvater, Benedictine, Campari, some gins, vermouth, and both yellow and green Chartreuse. It has an oddly sweet, camphoraceous scent and an acrid taste. Calamus roots and gentian provide the bitter taste in Stockton Bitters. Raspail is a French liqueur containing angelica, calamus root, and myrrh.

Tender inner parts of young shoots are used in salads.

The roots have been used as a substitute for ginger. They contain, among other compounds, β-asarone (48,000 ppm), eugenol (12,500 ppm), α-asarone (6,500 ppm), linalool (6,00 ppm), and methyl eugenol (3,950 ppm).

Acorus americanus leaves are sometimes placed in sugar, as a vanilla bean would be used. The rhizomes of *Acorus gramineus,* soaked in several changes of water and then fried, are eaten as a vegetable in Japan.

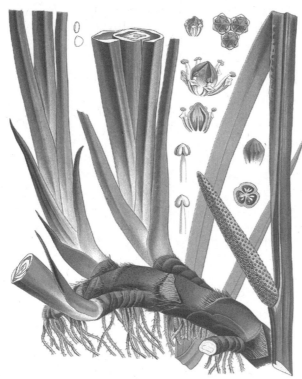

Calamus
Acorus calamus

From Köhler, *Köhler's Medizinal-Pflanzen,* vol. 1

Potpourri
Roots are chewed to sweeten the breath. Wee-kees is a snuff made from dried calamus root.

COMMENTS
Asarone and β-asarone are psychoactive compounds similar to, but not as strong as, mescaline.
The FDA does not permit the sale of any product containing calamus that may be considered as food or as an ingredient intended for use in foods.

Calaloo: *Colocasia antiquorum* subs. *illustris*

OTHER COMMON, ETHNIC, OR SCIENTIFIC NAMES
Arvi, elephant's ear, imperial taro, patra leaves, West Indian kale. Has been listed as *Colocasia artiquorum,* a perpetual typographical error.
Colombia: Mafafa, malangay

CULTIVAR
'Esculenta'

RELATED SPECIES
Colocasia esculenta (also known as *Caladium esculentum*): Khoai mon
    (Vietnam); dasheen, eddo, kalo, taro

GROWTH HABITS
Perennial
Origin: Tropical Asia
Range: Caribbean, Tropical Asia

CULINARY USES
Used as a potherb in Caribbean cooking. The plant produces edible shoots and tubers. The roots of taro, *Colocasia esculenta,* are a starchy staple in many tropical regions and are the main ingredient in the Hawaiian staple *poi.*

Tannia: *Xanthosoma sagittifolium*

OTHER COMMON, ETHNIC, OR SCIENTIFIC NAMES
Cocoyam, malanga, ocumo, tanier, tanyah

RELATED SPECIES
Xanthosoma caracu: Yautia, yautia horqueta (Spain)
Xanthosoma violaceum: Badu, coco, oto (Panama); rascadera (Colombia);
    primrose malanga

GROWTH HABITS
    Perennial
    Origin: West Indies
    Range: Widely grown in the tropics

CULINARY USES
Leaves of several species are popular potherbs in Central America, where they are seasoned with garlic and culantro. The starchy tubers are also edible.

11. Araliaceae: The Aralia or Ginseng Family

Acanthopanax: *Acanthopanax* spp.

OTHER COMMON, ETHNIC, OR SCIENTIFIC NAMES
    Genus also known as *Eleutherococcus*
    China: Wu jia pi

RELATED SPECIES
    Acanthopanax divaricus: Ô-ukogi (Japan)
    Acanthopanax seiboldianus: Ukogi, wu-chia (Japan)
    Acanthopanax sessiliflorus: Manshû-ukogi (Japan)

GROWTH HABITS
    Small shrub
    Origin: Japan (except *Acanthopanax sessiliflorus,* which comes from China)
    Range: Temperate regions

CULINARY USES
    The leaves of ô-ukogi are used to flavor rice wine in Japan, while the bark of manshû-ukogi is used to make wine in China. Tea and liquor are made from ukogi. The leaves of all these species are used as potherbs.

COMMENTS
    Some of these plants are grown in the United States, but male *Acanthopanax seiboldianus* are not planted there (see Comments, under MAIDENHAIR FERN).

Aralia: *Polyscias scutellarium*

OTHER COMMON, ETHNIC, OR SCIENTIFIC NAMES
    Cup leaf
    Indonesia: Daun mangkok, godong mangkokan

Aralia cordata: Japanese asparagus, tu-huo, udo
Aralia hispida: Bristly sarsaparilla, dwarf elder, sarsaparilla
Aralia nudicaulis: Aralia Manchurian (Russia); bamboo brier, country
    sarsaparilla or Indian sarsaparilla, false sarsaparilla, naked stem aralia,
    quay, quill, rabbit root, red sarsaparilla, sarsaparilla, shot bush, small
    spikenard, smilax sarsaparilla, spignet, spikenard, wild liquorice, wild
    sarsaparilla. Aromatic roots dug in autumn.
Aralia racemosa: Aralia Manchurian (Russia); espicanardo (Mexico);
    American spikenard, Indian root, Indian spikenard, like of man,
    old man's root, petty morrel, pettymorrel, spignet, spikenard, wild
    licorice

GROWTH HABITS
Perennial shrub
Origin: Indonesia
Range: Tropics or in greenhouses

CULINARY USES
Aromatic leaves are cooked as a vegetable, with coconut, in Indonesia.
Berries of *Aralia racemosa* are used in jellies and as an ingredient in root beer.
Aralia hispida is used as tea and as another ingredient in root beer. Udo is said
to have a lemony flavor. After the finely cut shoots are soaked in ice water,
they are served as a salad with vinaigrette dressing.

OTHER USES
The large leaves are used as serving dishes, much as banana leaves are used
in India. Other aralias are used as houseplants.

COMMENTS
"Wild licorice" is also a name for *Ononis spinosa* (see LICORICE).

Ginseng: *Panax quinquefolia*

OTHER COMMON, ETHNIC, OR SCIENTIFIC NAMES
American ginseng, Chinese ginseng, devil's walking stick, divine root, ga-
rantogen, grantogen, garantoquere, five fingers, korean ginseng, manroot,
ninsin, pannag, root of life, tartar root, redberry, sang. It is sometimes listed
botanically as *Panax quinquefolius*.
China: Jen-shun, yun sum
Korea: Insahm

RELATED SPECIES
Eleutherococus senticosus: Ci wu jia (China); eleuthero ginseng, Siberian
    ginseng. Origin in China and Siberia.

Panax pseudoginseng (sometimes listed as *Panax ginseng;* formerly classified as *Panax schinseng*): Chinese ginseng, Oriental ginseng. This is the real ginseng, in spite of its scientific name.

GROWTH HABITS
Perennial
Origin: Eastern United States
Range: Commercially cultivated in Wisconsin

CULINARY USES
Dried roots have an earthy, faintly licorice-like taste and are used to make an herbal tea. It is drunk for its reputed medical properties, rather than its gastronomic qualities. Ginseng is used as a seasoning for chicken soup in North Korea, especially in Kaesong, which is known for growing high-quality insahm.

Ginseng is available dried, in slices or whole; pickled; and in capsules (this last item is not exactly promising as a culinary commodity).

The dried roots are used to flavor the Chinese brandy called *kaoliang.* Flavored vodka, known as nastoika in Russian, sometimes contains ginseng along with chiles and various other aromatics.

Panax quinquefolia contains α-selinene, benzoic acid, β-elemene, caryophyllene and cinnamic acid, as well as ginsenin and several ginsenosides.

Ginseng
Panax quinquefolia

From Woodville, *Medical botany,* vol. 2

Oriental ginseng is used extensively in Chinese medicine. The roots' occasional resemblance to the human body has led to the belief that ginseng has medicinal qualities, not only in Chinese medicine but in Native American rituals as well.

I've seen a recipe for a French "love potion" in which ginseng, cinnamon, vanilla bean, and dried rhubarb are steeped for two weeks in white wine, then strained and served, but no mention of "dosage" or other instructions were included.

In the eighteenth century, American ginseng began to be sold in China at ridiculously high prices. A new industry sprouted among "mountain men," who gathered the wild, mandrake-like roots for export. The plant was driven nearly to extinction. The "wild" industry was replaced by the cultivation of ginseng, but even to this day, the wild plant is not very common.

Prickly Ash: *Aralia spinosa*

OTHER COMMON, ETHNIC, OR SCIENTIFIC NAMES

Angelica tree, devil's walking stick, Hercules club, toothache tree, prickly elder

GROWTH HABITS

Shrub or tree
Origin: Mid-Atlantic and southeastern United States
Range: Naturalized in New York and Connecticut

CULINARY USES

Bark is aromatic and bitter. It contains araliin.

COMMENTS

The common names and uses of plants named "ash" have led to some confusion (see also EUROPEAN MOUNTAIN ASH, *Sorbus aucuparia;* Ash, *Fraxinus excelsior;* and SZECHUAN PEPPER, *Zanthoxylum piperitum*).

12. Aristlochiaceae: The Birthwort Family

Colcameca Vine: *Aristolochia laxiflora*

OTHER COMMON, ETHNIC, OR SCIENTIFIC NAMES

Birthwort

Aristolochia arborescens: Mato (Colombia); Dutchman's pipe, snakeroot
Aristolochia maxima: Cuajilote (Costa Rica)

GROWTH HABITS
Tropical vine
Origin: South American rainforests
Range: Southern Florida

CULINARY USES
Leaves are used to flavor a chocolate drink.

Wild Ginger: *Asarum canadense*

OTHER COMMON, ETHNIC, OR SCIENTIFIC NAMES
Asarabacca, black snakeroot, broad-leaved asarabacca, Canada ginger,
Canada snakeroot, Canadian snakeroot, colic root, coltsfoot snakeroot,
false coltsfoot, hazelwort, heart snakcroot, Indian ginger, southern snake-
root, snakeroot, Vermont snakeroot, white snakeroot, wild nard
France: Serpentaire du Canada
Germany: Canadische Schlangenwurzel
Italy: Asaro
Russia: Kopiten
Spain: Asaro

RELATED SPECIES
Asarum arifolium: Heartleaf
Asarum europaeum: Hazlewort; wild ginger, the variety usually cultivated
    in shade gardens
Asarum sieboldii: Siebold's wild ginger

GROWTH HABITS
Perennial
Origin: Northeastern North America
Range: Wild within this area

CULINARY USES
Not surprisingly, wild ginger has been used as a substitute for "real" ginger, although it is much less powerful. It takes two to three times as much
Asarum to approximate the flavoring of true ginger. Wild ginger is a sweet,
spicy, aromatic addition to candies, condiments, and soft drinks. It is rumored to have been combined with chiles in the searing Russian vodka-
based drink called nastoika.

It has some value to the flavorings industry, because it contains α-pinene, α-
terpineol, bornyl acetate, geraniol, limonene, linalool, and other compounds.

European Wild Ginger
Asarum europaeum

From Woodville, *Medical botany,* vol. 2

Asarum sieboldii contains β-pinene, eucarvone, limonene, methyleugenol, and safrole.

COMMENTS

The European species, *Asarum europaeum,* is poisonous and should not be confused with the native wild ginger. This is an important distinction, because European wild ginger is a popular ground cover for shade gardens, where it helps relieve the monotony of ferns and hostas.

Virginia snakeroot (or serpentaria), *Aristolochia serpentaria,* is a well-known relative of this species. Its flavor is said to resemble that of cascarilla, quassia, and valerian; that is, it is bitter and aromatic. It is used only in some liqueurs.

OTHER USES

Asarum canadense is sometimes used, especially in combination with orris, in the manufacture of perfumes.

13. Asclepiadaceae: The Milkweed Family

Condurango: *Gonolobus Cundurango*

OTHER COMMON, ETHNIC, OR SCIENTIFIC NAMES

Condor vine, cundurango, eagle vine, mata-peroo. Has been listed botanically as *Marsdenia Condurango.*

GROWTH HABITS
  Liana vine
  Origin: Ecuador and Peru
  Range: South American tropical rainforests

CULINARY USES
  Condurango has a bitter-sweet, cinnamon-like quality that results from its condurangin content. It is used in the manufacture of some digestifs.

Mondia: *Mondia whitei*

OTHER COMMON, ETHNIC, OR SCIENTIFIC NAMES
  Mondia has been listed botanically as *Chlorocodon whitei.* It has also been included in the Periplocaceae family.

GROWTH HABITS
  Perennial vine
  Origin: Southern Africa
  Range: Côte d'Ivoire to South Africa

CULINARY USES
  Mondia gets its name from the Zulu word *e'mondi.* In parts of Africa, the tubers are used to make a beverage similar to ginger beer. The roots, supposedly tasting like vanilla, have been suggested as a flavoring for commercial soft drinks. The Tanzanian government is looking into the development of mondia as a starch- and oil-producing crop.

COMMENTS
  This genus and species do not appear in *Hortus.* The plant does not even have an English common name; "mondia" is used only for convenience.

14. Asteraceae (formerly Compositae): The Composite or Sunflower Family

---

Ambrosia: *Ambrosia maritima*

RELATED SPECIES
  Ambrosia artemisifolia: Ragweed

GROWTH HABITS
  Perennial

Origin: Mediterranean region, North Africa
Range: Temperate regions

CULINARY USES

Used to flavor some liqueurs. The leaves are used, at the table, to season soups.

Arnica: *Arnica montana*

OTHER COMMON, ETHNIC, OR SCIENTIFIC NAMES

Leopard's bane, mountain tobacco, wolf's bane
France: Arnique montagnard
Germany: Arnika Wohlverlei

RELATED SPECIES

Arnica cordifolia: Heartleaf arnica, leopard's bane. Native, wild species.
Arnica fulgens: Arnica
Arnica mollis: Arnica. Native, wild species.

Arnica
Arnica montana

From Woodville,
Medical botany, vol. 1

    Perennial
    Origin: Central Europe
    Range: Temperate regions

CULINARY USES

The only gastronomic use for arnica I've encountered has been in recipes for bitter liqueurs. Arnica blossoms are said to be among the many secret ingredients in Benedictine and both green and yellow Chartreuse (see Comments, below). If true, only small amounts are present in the famous cordials. The recipes date from the sixteenth century, a time when recipes composed of exotic and expensive ingredients—in large numbers, edible or not—were the norm.

Arnica has an aromatic, bitter taste and a scent that suggests chamomile and resembles that of celery, orris, and radish. These organoleptic properties result from arnicin (a bitter resin with a sweet, floral scent), inulin (a sugar-like substance), and mouth-puckering tannins. See Comments, below.

COMMENTS

At one time, arnica was used for treating bruises and sprains, but its application was strictly external. It has been implicated in cases of poisoning. The main culprit in arnica poisoning is choline, which affects the circulatory system. It can also cause acute gastric distress and muscular weakness, leading to death. It does contain some thujone, though the effects of the green fairy seem pretty insignificant by comparison with those of choline.

Bitter Leaf: *Veronia anyadalina*

OTHER COMMON, ETHNIC, OR SCIENTIFIC NAMES
    Ironweed. Bitter leaf is sometimes listed as *Veronia karaguensis.*
    Nigeria: Etido, ewuro

GROWTH HABITS
    Shrubby perennial
    Origin: West Africa
    Range: West Africa

CULINARY USES

The leaves are used, like filé (q.v.), to thicken soups and stews. Supposedly, filé was chosen in America by slaves from Africa to reproduce the effects provided by bitter leaf in the diet of their homelands (see also ANNATTO). In East Africa, utazi-zi, *Congronema ratifolia,* is used for the same purposes.

COMMENTS

Several *Veronia* species are listed on the USDA's Center for Food Safety and Applied Nutrition's "Poisonous Plant Database."

Blessed Thistle: *Cnicus benedictus*

OTHER COMMON, ETHNIC, OR SCIENTIFIC NAMES
Holy thistle, sacred thistle. The plant has been known scientifically as *Carbenia benedicta* and *Carduus benedictus.*
France: Chardon béni, chardon bénit
Germany: Benedicktenkraut, Bitterdistel
Italy: Cardo santo
Spain: Cardo benedito

RELATED SPECIES

Silybum marianum: Cardo espinoso, cardo santo, cardon morado (Colombia); Mariendistel (Germany); blessed thistle, holy thistle, Marian thistle, milk thistle, St. Mary's thistle (sometimes *Carduus Marianus*)

GROWTH HABITS

Annual
Origin: Mediterranean region
Range: Cultivated in Eurasia, naturalized in some parts of the United States

Blessed Thistle
Cnicus benedictus

From Köhler, *Köhler's Medizinal-Pflanzen,* vol. 1

Young stalks and roots of several species of *Cnicus* have been eaten as cooked, artichoke-like vegetables. Bitter extracts from the plant are used to produce herbal liqueurs (digestifs). Blessed thistle contains cnicin, sesquiterpenoid lactone, and tannins that give it a thujone-like flavor.

COMMENTS

Excessive use can cause burns in the mouth and diarrhea.

"Blessed thistle" is also a name for Mary thistle, *Silybum marianum* (q.v.).

Calendula: *Calendula officinalis*

OTHER COMMON, ETHNIC, OR SCIENTIFIC NAMES

Cowslip, golds, maravillosa, Mary gowles, Marygold, oculus christi, paggles, pot marigold, ruddes, solis sponsa, solesequia. Formerly known scientifically as *Caltha officinalis.* It has also been seen listed as *Calendula officinale,* which would seem to make more sense since the species and genus agree in gender. *Hortus Third,* however, prefers the masculine *officinalis.*

France: Souci

Germany: Dotterblume, Gartenringelblume, Ringelblume

Italy: Calendola, calendula, crisantemo, fiorrancio, fiore d'ogni mese

Mexico: Calendula, mariola

CULTIVAR

'Kablouna'

GROWTH HABITS

Annual

Origin: Southern Europe

Range: Temperate regions

CULINARY USES

Petals garnish soups and hors d'oeuvres. They also work well with butter, cakes, custards, eggs, light soups (especially milk-based soups), and rice dishes. Yellow rice is popular in many cultures; turmeric is used to create it in India, achiote (annatto) in Latin America, and, of course, saffron in the classic *paella* of Spain.

Leaves are used in salads, stews (braised beef or venison), and teas.

Calendula was at one time used to make cordials and a country wine.

OTHER USES

Potpourri and sachets

COMMENTS

Use only the petals, for other parts of the flower and plant are unpleasantly bitter. Use sparingly, as the flowers have the characteristic marigold smell. The aroma works at keeping insects from the garden, but it keeps me out too.

Petals are occasionally used as an adulterant in saffron. They have a light, tangy, bitter flavor that is nothing like the taste of real saffron, but they do have good coloring ability. They were once used as annatto is today, for coloring cheeses.

American cowslip, *Caltha palustris* (q.v.), is not related to this plant; it is a member of the Ranunculaceae.

Carolina Vanilla: *Carphephorus odoratissimus*

OTHER COMMON, ETHNIC, OR SCIENTIFIC NAMES
Deer tongue, dog's tongue, vanillaleaf, vanilla plant, wild vanilla. Also known botanically as *Chrysocoma odoratissima, Frasera speciose, Liatris amplexicaulis, Liatris odoratissima,* and *Trilisa odoratissima.*

GROWTH HABITS
Perennial
Origin: Southeastern United States
Range: Southeastern United States to middle of Florida

CULINARY USES
Dried leaves have a vanilla-like scent and have been used to flavor tobacco.

COMMENTS
Said to be toxic.

Chamomile: *Chamaemelum nobile*

OTHER COMMON, ETHNIC, OR SCIENTIFIC NAMES
Dog fennel, English chamomile, garden chamomile, goosegrass, ground apple, mayweed, maythen, pinheads, Roman chamomile, Russian chamomile. An earlier scientific name for this species is *Anthemis nobilis.*
Colombia: Manzanilla de castilla
France: Camomille, camomille romaine
Germany: Kamillenblutten, Römische Kamille
Italy: Camomilla romana
India: Babunah, babuni kephul
Mexico: Manzanilla
Russia: Damasky, romashka
Spain: Chamomilla, manzanilla
Turkey: Papatya

CULTIVARS

'Flore-plenum': Double-flowered chamomile
'Trenague': Trenague (nonflowering chamomile)

RELATED SPECIES

Anthemis Cotula: Dog fennel, mansanilla, mayweed
Chamaemelum mixta (sometimes listed as *Ormenis mixta*): Moroccan
chamomile
Matricaria chamomilla: Kamille (Germany); manzanilla (Mexico);
German camomile, wild camomile
Matricaria recutita: Manzanilla (Mexico); annual camomile, German
camomile, sweet false camomile

GROWTH HABITS

Perennial
Origin: Western Europe, northern Africa, Azores
Range: Temperate regions

CULINARY USES

Most commonly used in herbal teas. Try adding crushed dried chamomile
flowers and lemon zest to sugar cookies or shortbread.

Chamomile appears in some recipes for Benedictine, Fernet Branca, and
vermouth, and it was an ingredient in some formulations for absinthe. It has

Chamomile
Chamaemelum nobile

From Köhler, *Köhler's
Medizinal-Pflanzen,* vol. 1

been used as a source of bitterness in some beers, but it offers no real competition for hops. *Anthemis Cotula* is used in Peru as a seasoning; it is also made into teas.

Chamaemelum nobile contains esters of angelic acid and metacrylic acid, n-butyl isobutyrate, n-butyl alcohol, and isoamyl alcohol. *Matricaria chamomilla* contains chamazulene, caprinic acid, and sesquiterpenes. *Matricaria recutita* contains α-bisabolol, azulene, β-caryophyllene, β-damascenone, bisabolene, and several fruit acids. Bitterness is provided by quercetin, rutin, tannins, thujone, and other glucosides.

COMMENTS

Do not confuse with pineappleweed, or wild camomile, which are *Matricaria* spp.

The Spanish word *camomilla* is not specific to this herb alone. It also refers to feverfew and stichwort or chickweed. According to one source, it is this herb that is used in Spain for flavoring light sherry, but I have found no confirmation for this assertion. It may be the gastronomic equivalent of folk etymology.

"Goose grass" is a common name for a number of unrelated plants, but only one has any culinary use. *Triglochin maritima* seeds have been roasted and ground as a substitute for coffee.

OTHER USES

The apple-like scent of the dried leaves makes chamomile a welcome addition to potpourri.

Coltsfoot: *Tussilago farfara*

OTHER COMMON, ETHNIC, OR SCIENTIFIC NAMES

Ass's foot, bull's foot, coughwort, cowsfoot, donhove, fieldhove, foal's foot, foal's wort, ginger root, horse hoof

France: Pas d'ane
Germany: Hufflattich
Japan: Fuki-no-to
Mexico: Pata de mula, tunilago, una de gato
Russia: Mat i matcheha

RELATED SPECIES

Petasites japonicus var. *giganteus:* Akita-buki

GROWTH HABITS

Perennial
Origin: Eurasia
Range: Naturalized in North America, weedy in waste places, along highways

Herbal teas are made with coltsfoot, and the herb was once used to make a stick candy said to have had an anise-like flavor. Wines and teas are made from the blossoms, and unopened buds make a bitter garnish for Japanese soups.

COMMENTS

The plant seems to thrive in the salt-laced sand that snowplows spread beside highways all over the Northeast each winter. It is second only to the pussy willow as an early bloomer. The bright yellow, dandelion-like flowers appear on roadsides at the end of March, sometimes before the snow and ice have melted. It is a very welcome sign of spring's approach.

An unrelated plant, *Petasites japonicus,* is also known as coltsfoot. Its celery-like stalks are added to soups in Japan.

Common Dandelion: *Taraxacum officinale*

OTHER COMMON, ETHNIC, OR SCIENTIFIC NAMES

Blow ball, cankerwort, gray-haired grandmother, lion's tooth, priest's crown, wild endive
Colombia: Serraja
Costa Rica: Diente de Leon
France: Pissenlit
Germany: Löwenzahn
Greece: Radíkia
Italy: Radicchielle, tarassaco
Mexico: Amargon, diente de Leon, taraxaco
Russia: Oduvanchik, pushki
Spain: Diente de Leon, queixals de vella, xicoies

CULTIVAR

'Amelioré': a broad-leaved improvement of the wild dandelion

RELATED SPECIES

Taraxacum Kok-saghyz: Russian dandelion

GROWTH HABITS

Perennial
Origin: Europe and Asia
Range: Naturalized everywhere

CULINARY USES

Flowers are an ingredient in a homemade wine. Dandelions have been used, in place of hops, in herbal beers. In Canada, dandelion stout was popular. In England, the roots of dandelion and burdock flavor a root-beer-like soft drink called, not surprisingly, Dandelion and Burdock.

Young leaves are used in salads. Dutch salad is a Pennsylvania specialty, made with young spring dandelion leaves with a warm bacon dressing. Older leaves are cooked as a potherb, seasoned like spinach with nutmeg and lemon. Dried roots can be roasted and brewed like coffee. The roots have been used in some recipes for bitters.

Dandelions contain choline, inulin, levulin, and taraxasterol.

OTHER USES

Sixteenth-century Italian apothecaries combined bugloss, endive, hops, and smallage in a sugar syrup (see CELERY).

COMMENTS

Radíkia is also the Greek name for wild chicory. The word is used for weeds whose roots—especially bitter roots—are eaten and whose leaves provide early greens.

Common Sow Thistle: *Sonchus oleraceus*

RELATED SPECIES

Sonchus arvensis: Cerraja (Mexico); sow-field thistle

GROWTH HABITS

Perennial
Origin: Europe
Range: Weed of waste places

CULINARY USES

Young leaves can be eaten in salads, but they are better as a potherb, dressed with olive oil and lemon juice. They can be bitter, so they are often combined with milder-tasting greens.

COMMENTS

Not related to true thistles.

Plants of the *Sonchus* genus have been known to accumulate toxic levels of nitrates from the soil. Cooking in several changes of water (or limited consumption) can minimize any danger.

Costmary: *Chrysanthemum balsamita*

OTHER COMMON, ETHNIC, OR SCIENTIFIC NAMES

Herb Mary, Saint Mary's herb, mint geranium, alecost, bible leaf, balsam herb. *Balsamita major* and *Tanacetum balsamita* are two of costmary's former scientific names.

France: Herbe Sainte-Marie, tanaise balsamite

Germany: Marien Balsam
Italy: Balsamite
Spain: Balsamite

HYBRID

Chrysanthemum × morifolium: Florist's mum

GROWTH HABITS

Perennial

Origin: Europe and Western Asia

Range: Temperate regions

CULINARY USES

Fresh leaves have a somewhat mint-like aroma that becomes more akin to that of citrus as they dry. The taste of costmary is bitter, but the herb is often combined with bay leaves and sage to perfume roasted meats, especially beef, chicken, duck, and venison.

Leaves are used as garnishes, teas, and greens (edible chrysanthemum, actually several oriental varieties, though some people use ordinary florist's mums). The young leaves are used in sukiyaki, yosenabe, stir-fries, "chop suey greens," tempura, and various fritter-like dishes. The leaves of *Chrysanthemum coronarium* have the best flavor, completely without bitterness, for use fresh in salads. The flowers of some varieties are used as tea.

Petals can be used in salads, soups, and conserves. In Japan a pickle called *kikumi* is made from the petals.

Costmary seasons game, dressings for poultry, sauces, soups, and stews. It's a good match for carrots, peas, and potatoes. It was formerly used for clearing and flavoring ale.

Dried costmary can be used in potpourri.

Pyrethrum is a natural insecticide, preferred by many people because it is said to be relatively nontoxic to mammals and does not accumulate in the tissues of animals that consume it (see Comments, below). The plant was known as bible leaf because a sprig was often kept in the big books to discourage infestations of bookworms.

COMMENTS

"Natural" products are not necessarily safer than synthetic compounds. Even mildly toxic substances can have adverse effects when used in quantity, or in combination with similar substances, or by people who are sensitive to them. Pyrethrins in some of the chrysanthemums can cause allergic reactions in some people. Susceptible individuals should wear rubber gloves when handling the plants.

The FDA restricts the use of costmary to alcoholic beverages.

Curry Plant: *Helichrysum angustifolium*

OTHER COMMON, ETHNIC, OR SCIENTIFIC NAMES

Everlasting, immortelle, whiteleaf. *Helichrysum italicum* is a scientific name that is no longer in use.

France: Hélichrysum
Germany: Helichrysum
Italy: Elicriso, semprevivo
Spain: Perpetua amarilla

RELATED SPECIES

Helichrysum bracteatum: Strawflower
Helichrysum italicum: Curry plant
Helichrysum microphyllum: Dwarf curry plant
Helichrysum pamphylicum: Ölmez çiçegi (Turkey); Strohblume (Germany)
Helichrysum petiolatum: Licorice plant, silver licorice
Helichrysum serpyllifolium: Hottentot tea

GROWTH HABITS

Perennial
Origin: Mediterranean region

CULINARY USES

Leaves, fresh or dried, add a curry-like scent and flavor to eggs, pickles, rice dishes, soups, and stews. Flowering tops have a sweeter, fruity scent that is useful in candy, ice cream, and baked desserts. Flowers are used in herbal teas.

Helichrysum contains nerol, furfural, eugenol, valeric aldehyde, and d-pinene.

OTHER USES

Good in dried flower arrangements, potpourri. Essential oils from the flowers are used in the perfume industry.

COMMENTS

Do not confuse this plant with curry leaf, *Murraya Koenigii* (q.v.).

Davana: *Artemisia pallens*

GROWTH HABITS

Perennial
Origin: India
Range: Southern India

CULINARY USES

The leaves are delicately scented. The flowers yield a balsamic essential oil that has been used in baked goods, candy, chewing gum, ice cream, and soft drinks.

OTHER USES

Davana is used in the manufacture of perfumes.

Deer Tongue: *Liatris odoratissimus*

OTHER COMMON, ETHNIC, OR SCIENTIFIC NAMES

Wild vanilla, vanilla leaf. A former scientific name for this species is *Trilissia odorata*.

GROWTH HABITS

Perennial
Origin: North America
Range: Cultivated in England

CULINARY USES

Deer tongue has a scent that combines fresh-mown hay and vanilla, a result of its coumarin content. Used as a commercial flavoring.

OTHER USES

Used as a flavoring for tobacco.

Echinacea: *Echinacea angustifolia*

OTHER COMMON, ETHNIC, OR SCIENTIFIC NAMES

Purple coneflower, sampson

France: Rudbeckie à feuilles étroites
Germany: Kegelblume

GROWTH HABITS
Perennial
Origin: Midwestern United States and Canada
Range: Cool temperate regions

CULINARY USES
Earthy caramel flavor, with a hint of anise. Used in herbal tea blends.

OTHER USES
Various parts of the plant are used in medicines.

Elecampane: *Inula Helenium*

OTHER COMMON, ETHNIC, OR SCIENTIFIC NAMES
Allycupain, elfdock, elycompenny, horseheal, horseweed, inula, scabwort, velvet dock, wild sunflower, yellow starwort
Denmark: Elf-doc, elf-wort
France: Aunée, grande aunée
Germany: Alant, Alantwurzel, Echter Alant
Italy: Enula campana, inula
Mexico: Enula, enulacampana
Russia: Deviat sil, inula
Spain: Enula campana
Wales: Marchalan

RELATED SPECIES
Inula Conyza: Cinnamon root, clorn's hard, conyza squarrosa, great fleabane, horse heal, ploughman's spikenard
Inula crithmoides: Golden samphire
Inula viscosa: Alant (Germany); zimbit (Turkey); elecampane

GROWTH HABITS
Perennial
Origin: Eurasia
Range: Naturalized in Eastern United States

CULINARY USES
The dried roots smell like violets. They have a sharp, bitter taste, so they are often candied. They are also used in beers, bitters, liqueurs, and vermouth as well as in absinthes, from both France and Switzerland.

The leaves have been used to season sauces for fish. In ancient Rome, the leaves—too bitter for modern tastes—were used as a potherb.

Elecampane contains only traces of flavoring compounds, except for inulin, which can reach concentrations as high as 440,000 ppm.

OTHER USES

Seed heads are good in dried flower arrangements, petals in potpourri.

COMMENTS

The FDA restricts its use to alcoholic beverages.

Ploughman's spikenard, *Inula Conyza,* should not be confused with spikenard (which see, under ARALIA).

Feverfew: *Chrysanthemum parthenium*

OTHER COMMON, ETHNIC, OR SCIENTIFIC NAMES

Featherfoil, manzanilla. Sometimes listed as *Chrysanthemum indicum* and *Tanacetum parthenium.*

CULTIVARS

'Aureum', 'Roya'

GROWTH HABITS

Short-lived perennial
Origin: Southeastern Europe
Range: Cool temperate regions

CULINARY USES

The leaves add a bitter taste to salads. They have been used in some herbal liqueurs (digestifs).

Fleabane: *Erigeron* spp.

OTHER COMMON, ETHNIC, OR SCIENTIFIC NAMES

Butterweed, coltstail, fleawort, pridesweed
France: Erigeron
Germany: Erigeron, Flohkraut
Italy: Erigeron
Mexico: Hierba pulgera
Spain: Erigeron

GROWTH HABITS

Mostly perennial
Origin: Mostly North America, but also Europe, Africa, and Asia
Range: Weedy; never cultivated

Fleabane's slightly pungent scent and acrid taste are used to advantage in the commercial flavorings industry, mostly for candy, baked goods, and condiments. The plant contains d-limonene, *p*-cymene, dipentene, linalool, and cuminaldehyde.

OTHER USES

Fleabane is used in the perfume industry.

COMMENTS

The species *Erigeron canadensis* is listed in several reference books for the flavorings industry. It is not, however, listed in *Hortus Third,* and I have found no other positive identification.

French Scorzonera: *Reichardia picroides*

OTHER COMMON, ETHNIC, OR SCIENTIFIC NAMES

Also known botanically as *Reichardia macrophylla* and *Picridium vulgare.*

GROWTH HABITS

Perennial
Origin: Canary Islands to India
Range: Southern Europe

CULINARY USES

Young leaves are eaten in salads or cooked for use as a filling for savory pastries or ravioli.

Guascas: *Galinsoga parviflora*

OTHER COMMON, ETHNIC, OR SCIENTIFIC NAMES

Gallant soldier, quickweed
Colombia: Chipaca, guasca

GROWTH HABITS

Annual
Origin: South America
Range: Naturalized in United States

CULINARY USES

Flowers, leaves, and stems are eaten as vegetables. In Colombia, dried leaves are sold, already ground, for use as seasoning for soups and stews made with poultry.

Gynura: *Gynura aurantiaca*

OTHER COMMON, ETHNIC, OR SCIENTIFIC NAMES
Purple velvet plant, royal purple velvet plant, velvet plant

CULTIVARS
'Purple Passion', 'Purple Passion Vine'

GROWTH HABITS
Perennial
Origin: Java
Range: Naturalized in semitropical regions

CULINARY USES
Bremness says that the young leaves of gynura are eaten; but the same source warns that the flowers are "malodorous." *Hortus Third* is less dramatic but agrees that the flowers are "unpleasantly scented."

Iva: *Achillea moschata*

OTHER COMMON, ETHNIC, OR SCIENTIFIC NAMES
Musk yarrow. Iva is sometimes listed as *Achillea erb-rotta moschata*.
Colombia: Acapalti
France: Achillea musquée
Germany: Feldgarbe
Italy: Achillea muschiata
Spain: Achillea musgada

RELATED SPECIES
Achillea ageratum (sometimes listed as *Achillea decolorans*): English mace, mace plant, sweet yarrow
Achillea decolorans: Garden mace
Achillea herba-rota: Yarrow

GROWTH HABITS
Perennial
Origin: Europe
Range: Temperate regions

CULINARY USES
Iva has a warm bitter taste, something like that of hops. It is used in bitters (Iva Bitter is made in Switzerland) and some herbal liqueurs such as Benedictine, Esprit d'Iva, Chartreuse, and Iva liqueur.
Iva contains borneol, cineol, and ivain.

Iva is sometimes marketed as genepi (see MUGWORT).
The FDA restricts iva's use to alcoholic beverages.
Mace plant is not related to mace, *Myristica fragrans* (see under NUTMEG).

Mary Thistle: *Silybum marianum*

OTHER COMMON, ETHNIC, OR SCIENTIFIC NAMES
Blessed thistle, holy thistle, milk thistle, St. Mary's thistle. This species has also been known scientifically as *Carduus Marianus*.

GROWTH HABITS
Annual or biennial
Origin: Mediterranean region
Range: Naturalized, and weedy, in California

CULINARY USES
Used as a commercial flavoring

COMMENTS
"Blessed thistle" is also a name for *Cnicus benedictus* (q.v.).

Mexican Mint Marigold: *Tagetes lucida*

OTHER COMMON, ETHNIC, OR SCIENTIFIC NAMES
Mexican mint marigold, Mexican tarragon, Spanish tarragon, sweet mace, sweet marigold, sweet-scented marigold, winter tarragon
Germany: Samtblume, Winterestragon
Mexico: Anisillo, curucumín, hierba de Santa Maria, hierbanís, hierba anís, pericón, pericón amarillo, tzitziqi, yerba de nube; yahutli (ancient Aztec)
Spain: Pericón, yerba anís

RELATED SPECIES
Tagetes apetala: Ruda gallinoza, ruda silvestre de clavito (Colombia)
Tagetes erecta: Flor de mujerto, terciopelo amarillo (Colombia)
Tagetes minuta: Huacatay (Peru); Mexican marigold, Muster-John-Henry
Tagetes patula: Amapola, chinchimali, flor de muerto, terciopelo (Colombia); French marigold (see Comments, below)
Tagetes pusilla: Anisillo (Colombia)
Tagetes signata: Gem marigold. Varietals 'Golden Gem', 'Lemon Gem', and 'Tangerine Gem' have pleasantly scented and flavored petals. Use as garnishes, in salads, or in teas.

Tagetes tenuifolia: Dwarf marigold, lemon marigold, signet marigold
Tagetes terniflora: Ruda dulce (Colombia)
Tagetes zipaquirensis: Ruda de prados (Colombia)

GROWTH HABITS

Perennial, cultivated as an annual
Origin: Mexico, Guatemala
Range: Southern United States to Guatemala (more heat-tolerant than
true tarragon)

CULINARY USES

Marigolds, at least *Tagetes lucida* and *Tagetes signata,* are useful in soups and stews, adding golden color and a slight citrus tang. Leaves and flowers of *Tagetes lucida* are used as tarragon would be used: in compound butters, salad dressings, sauces, soups, and vinegars. They have also been used in herbal teas.

Like true tarragon, this herb, when fresh, has a pleasant anise flavor and scent.

COMMENTS

French marigold, *Tagetes patula,* and several other species of marigold are known in Mexico as *campoal, flor de muerto, hierba de las cinco llagas,* or *xochilt.*

Mugwort: *Artemisia vulgaris*

OTHER COMMON, ETHNIC, OR SCIENTIFIC NAMES

Cingulum sancti johannis, felon herb, motherwort, moxa herb, St. John's plant

China: Ai, ai ye, ngaai
Estonia: Harilik puju
Finland: Pujo
France: Armoise, ceinture de Saint-Jean
Gaelic: Liath lus
Germany: Beifuß, Gänsekraut, Vermut (wormwood)
India: Asfantin, vilayati asfantin (wormwood)
Iran: Berendjasef
Italy: Amarella, assenzio, artemisia, commune
Japan: Yomogi
Mexico: Alenjo (wormwood), artemisa, estafiate
Netherlands: Bijvoet, sintjansbrood
Philippines: Arbaaka, damong-maria, tinisas
Poland: Bylica pospolita
Russia: Chernobilik, polin obiknovennaya
Spain: Artemisia, asenzio (wormwood)
Sweden: Gråbo
Turkey: Pelinotu

Artemisia abrotanum: Aaprottimaruna (Finland); åbrodd (Sweden); abrodd (Norway); abròtano, erba reale (Italy); aurone, garde robe (France); boze drzewko, bylica boze drzewko (Polish); Eberraute, Eberries (German); kustarnikovaya polyn (Russia); sidrunpuju (Estonia); appleringie, boy's love, herb royale, kiss-me-quick-and-go, lad's love, maid's ruin, southernwood, old man

Artemisia absinthum: Absinthe, aluine, armoise amère, garde-robe, génépi (France); abrotano, ajenjo (Spain); ajenjo, assenzio (Italy); afsentin (Iran); absintalsem, averoom, citroenkruid, krampkruid, limoenkruid (Netherlands); ajenjo, aluinos (Mexico); buramaide, meath chaltuinn (Gaelic); bylica piolun, piolun (Poland); chernobyl (Russia); koirohi (Estonia); malört (Sweden); Wermut, Wurmkraut (Germany); common wormwood, devil's liquor, girdle of St. John, green ginger, green muse, old woman, wormwood

Artemisia genipi: Génepi (France); genepi nero (Italy); Schwarze Edelraute (Germany); black wormwood

Artemisia glacialis: Genepi, genépi des glaciers

Artemisia ludoviciana: Cudweed, estafiate, Louisiana wormwood, white prairie sage

Artemisia maritimum: Sea wormwood

Artemisia pontica: Petite absinthe, Roman wormwood. Used as a flavoring for Pontic vermouth and other cordials and aperitifs.

Artemisia princeps: Japanese mugwort, yomogi

Artemisia spp.: Shayban (Jordan); tree wormwood

Artemisia tridentata: Big sagebrush, common sagebrush, basin sagebrush (q.v.)

GROWTH HABITS

Shrubby perennial
Origin: Eurasia
Range: Naturalized in eastern United States

CULINARY USES

Most of the wormwoods are used in the manufacture of liqueurs having a bitter component. Vermouth uses both mugwort and alpine wormwood. These liqueurs stimulate the flow of gastric juices; hence they are served at the end of heavy meals and are known as digestifs. Green Chartreuse uses oil of wormwood; Campari uses the leaves. Benedictine, Fernet Branca, amaretto, altvater, and some gins contain mugwort (or sometimes oil of wormwood). Absinthe, of course, was the main use for wormwood (see Comments, below). Mugwort has been used, in place of hops (q.v.), in herbal beers.

Dried leaves make a bitter seasoning for poultry stuffing, especially for goose, and soups. They have also been used in teas. Fresh leaves are used as a flavoring for Japanese rice dumplings. They can also be rubbed on fatty meats before roasting to cut through their unctuousness.

Artemisia abrotanum is the sweetest artemisia. Its slight lemon scent makes it a natural choice for flavoring vinegars, herbal liqueurs, and, less obviously, some beers. It is used as a medicinal and culinary herb in Cambodia and Laos.

Artemisia absinthum is the famed ingredient in the forbidden liquor absinthe. Modern Pernod substitutes extra anise for the banished wormwood, even though the plant is, supposedly, still an ingredient in Benedictine.

Artemisia maritimum was used in England to flavor beers at the beginning of the eighteenth century. The introduction of hops (q.v.) in 1600 eventually eliminated all the older methods used by the British to add a bitter taste to beer.

Artemisia ludoviciana is used as a seasoning for sauces, as a garnish for pork or game, or in herbal teas.

Mugwort contains 1,8 cineol, camphor, linalool, thujone, and a host of other monoterpenes and sesquiterpenes. Its roots contain as much as 100,000 ppm of inulin. Wormwood, in addition to thujone, contains absinthin (a bitter glucoside), α-phellandrene, and other terpenoid compounds.

OTHER USES

Many artemisias make good foliage plants in perennial borders. They also discourage some of the insects that trouble vegetable gardens; they are especially useful around cabbage, carrots, and onions.

COMMENTS

Mugwort is used with what are described as "fatty" meats. Isn't it curious that "fatty" used to be referred to as "rich." Obviously, now that our diets are more enlightened (so to speak), we don't speak of fat with such affection, but our language hasn't caught up with our consciousness. We don't have acceptable terms for fat anymore. "Greasy" doesn't seem to be fair to those substances that served our less cardiovascularly aware selves so delectably.

"Herb royale" is another name for basil (q.v.).

Not only are many artemisias inappropriately called "sage," some of those so-called sages are also called "hyssop."

Common sagebrush, *Artemisia tridentata,* is not related to true sage and has no culinary use, but it does make a wonderfully aromatic—if quick-burning—fuel for a campfire.

Wormwood was unlikely to have been the sole cause of absinthe's bad reputation. Absinthe contains thujone, an essential oil that has been proven to cause symptoms similar to those of epilepsy; but arborvitae, hyssop, feverfew, and sage (q.v.) also contain thujone, and they are not banned. Many bottlers of absinthe adulterated the drink with antimony trichloride, a poison similar in its effects to arsenic. Other adulterants included aniline dyes, indigo, and copper sulfate.

Oddly enough, the symptoms allegedly triggered by wormwood's thujone can also be caused by strong doses of the other herbs generally included in bitter liqueurs: anise, hyssop, and sage. With all these strikes against absinthe, the final irony is that its alcohol content alone was more than sufficient to explain its powerful grip on the Parisian demi-monde. An *absintheur* could consume a lethal dose of thujone only by drinking many times the lethal dose of ethanol; which is to say, he would have had to continue knocking back many glasses after he had passed out from the alcohol. To be more exact, an average-sized man would have to drink fifty ounces of absinthe to risk a minimum toxic reaction to its thujone. Six ounces of ordinary alcohol of the same proof would render him legally drunk.

The FDA requires extracts of artemisias to be free of thujone ("free" being defined as "no more than one part per million").

Ox-tongue: *Picris echiodes*

OTHER COMMON, ETHNIC, OR SCIENTIFIC NAMES
Bitterweed, bristly oxtongue. Also known botanically as *Helminthia echiodes*.

RELATED SPECIES
Picris hierachiodes: Hawkweed oxtongue

GROWTH HABITS
Perennial
Origin: Mediterranean region
Range: Cosmopolitan weed

CULINARY USES
In France and Italy, the tender young leaves are added to soups. In England, the young leaves are eaten as potherbs.

Pápalo: *Porophyllum ruderale* 'macrocephalum'

OTHER COMMON, ETHNIC, OR SCIENTIFIC NAMES
Yerba porosa. Sometimes listed as *Porophyllum coloratum*.
Colombia: Chucha, gallenaza, ruda de gallina, venadillo
Mexico: Papaloquelite

RELATED SPECIES
Porophyllum nutans: Pápalo quelite de venado (Mexico)
Porophyllum macrocephalum: Chipaca, purranga, yerba de chulo (Colombia)
Porophyllum punctatum: Mata piojo (Mexico)

Porophyllum tagetoides (also known as *Porophyllum coloratum*): Chepiche, pepicha (Mexico)

GROWTH HABITS
Annual
Origin: Mexico
Range: New Mexico and Texas

CULINARY USES
Fresh pápalo is always used raw, on *cemitas* (sandwiches) or in salads. Occasionally it is an ingredient in guacamole. It is served with beans, soups, and stews and grilled meats, added as a garnish (like cilantro).

Pepicha has a powerful cilantro-like flavor that is commonly used in Mexican vegetable dishes, such as those containing corn or squash, or in salsas made with tomatillos.

Chepiche is a traditional Oaxacan herb, prized for its fresh scent. In the newer, more eclectic Mexican cuisine, it adds its pungent grassy flavor to salads containing mushrooms and watercress.

COMMENTS
Quelites is a generic term for "greens" in Mexico.

Pellitory of Spain: *Anacyclus pyrethrum*

OTHER COMMON, ETHNIC, OR SCIENTIFIC NAMES
Bastard pellitory, bertram, peleter, pellitory, piretre, pyrethrum, Roman pellitory, Spanish chamomile. Sometimes listed botanically as *Anthemis pyrethrum* or *Matricaria pyrethrum*.
Spain: Pelitre

GROWTH HABITS
Perennial
Origin: Mediterranean region
Range: Mediterranean region

CULINARY USES
Liqueurs and cordials make use of essential oils derived from pungent roots of *Anacyclus pyrethrum*.

COMMENTS
"Great pellitory of Spain" and "false pellitory of Spain" are also names for *Peucedanum ostruthium*. "Bastard pellitory" or "wild pellitory" are common names for *Achillea ptarmica*. The name "pellitory of the wall" is also used for *Parietarea officinalis*.

Stevia: *Stevia rebaudiana*

Sugar leaf, sweet herb of Paraguay

GROWTH HABITS
Perennial
Origin: Paraguay
Range: Brazil and Paraguay

CULINARY USES
Stevia contains stevioside, a compound that is three hundred times sweeter than an equivalent amount of table sugar (sucrose). It is sometimes used in commercial herbal teas to sweeten without adding sugar or calories.

Tansy: *Tanacetum vulgare*

OTHER COMMON, ETHNIC, OR SCIENTIFIC NAMES
Bitter buttons, buttons, common tansy, golden button, immortality
France: Tanaise
Germany: Rainfarn
Greece: Alhanasia
Italy: Tanaceto
Mexico: Hierba lonbriguera, tanaceto
Russia: Riabinka obiknovennaya, pishma
Spain: Tanaceto

CULTIVAR
'Crispum'

RELATED SPECIES
Carthamus tinctorus (sometimes listed as *Cartamus tinctorius*): Agnisikha, kardai, kusuma, kusumba, kusumphul, shinduram (India); azafrán (Mexico); alazor, cártamo (Spain); cartamo, falso zafferano (Italy); cártamo (Portugal); carthame, safran bâtard (France); casubha or kasubha (Philippines); Färberdistel, Färbersaflor, Méxicanischer Safran, Saflor (Germany); hong hua (China); krokosz barwierski (Poland); litunarkollur (Iceland); saffloer (Netherlands); safflor (Sweden); safflor (Denmark); saflor (Norway); saflor (Russia); usfur (Arabic); värisaflori (Finland); värvisafloor (Estonia); zardak (Iran); bastard saffron, Mexican saffron, safflower

GROWTH HABITS
Perennial

Origin: Europe and Asia
Range: Naturalized in North America

CULINARY USES

The minced leaves can be used in compound butters, teas (sometimes called "tansies"), and omelets. Flowers make good garnishes or additions to a mixed salad.

Cheeses are flavored and colored with an infusion of tansy, added before the rennet.

Tansy cakes were once used as Lenten fare, possibly in an allusion to the plant's earlier use as one of the bitter herbs of the Passover seder. In Denmark, the plant finds its way into other desserts, such as custards.

Safflower has been used as a poor replacement, or as an adulterant, for saffron (q.v.). The seeds, however, yield a good polyunsaturated oil.

Tansy has an aromatic, bitter, slightly lemony, wormwood-like taste that results from the presence of isothujone (up to 4,100 ppm), β-thujone (up to 3,500 ppm), camphor (up to 1,800 ppm), 1,8-cineole (up to 1,300 ppm), and tanacetol-B (up to 1,100 ppm).

OTHER USES

Medicines, especially carminatives. Flowers have been used to produce a yellow vegetable dye.

COMMENTS

Essential oils can be toxic in relatively small quantities (4 cc is considered a lethal dose). The FDA restricts the use of tansy extract to alcoholic beverages only, and then only if it is virtually free of thujone (see Comments, under MUGWORT).

Tarragon: *Artemisia Dracunculus* 'sativa'

OTHER COMMON, ETHNIC, OR SCIENTIFIC NAMES
French tarragon, German tarragon, little dragon, mugwort
Arabic: Tarkhun
China: Ai-hao
Denmark: Esdragon
Estonia: Estragonpuju
Finland: Rakuuna
France: Herbe au dragon, estragon
Germany: Bertram, Estragon
Hungary: Tárhonya
Iceland: Esdragon, fáfnisgras
Italy: Dragoncello, estragone, targoncello
Netherlands: Dragon, drakebloed, klapperkruid, slangekruid

Norway: Estragon
Poland: Bylica estragon, estragon
Portugal: Estragão
Russia: Estragon
Spain: Estrágon, tarragona
Sweden: Dragon
Turkey: Tarhun

RELATED SPECIES
Artemisia dracunculus: Russian tarragon. Sometimes seen as *Artemisia Redowskii*

GROWTH HABITS
Perennial
Origin: Mediterranean region
Range: Temperate regions everywhere

CULINARY USES
Tarragon is one of France's fines herbes, along with chervil, parsley, and chives (q.v.). When fresh, it has a delicate, sweet taste, with a lingering warmth—not heat, but a romantic coziness, reminiscent of dill and anise and fresh hay. Dried, the sweet perfume and hay-like qualities persist, but the warmth and magic disappear. Perhaps some essential oils (methyl chavicol and anethol) are lost through evaporation.

Tarragon is good in omelets, soups, and stews. Try adding chopped fresh tarragon to a lemon vinaigrette for use on a salad of watercress and oranges, or in a lime vinaigrette for a salad of julienned pears and jicama. A salad of tomatoes topped with tarragon is a popular if sometimes surprising side dish in Mexican meals.

Tarragon is a classic component of the sauces and stocks of haute-cuisine. Béarnaise is impossible without it. Tarragon is delicious in compound butters, served on fish, steaks, or chops. Use tarragon to scent a roast chicken, especially if it is intended to be served cold. Is there anything better than a picnic with such a roast, some watercress sandwiches on crusty French bread, and a bottle of white Graves or Entre-deux-Mers?

Tarragon appears in some herbal liqueurs. Tarragon vinegar is warm and redolent of anise; it should be a part of any well-stocked pantry. Mustard can also be enhanced by a little tarragon.

Several cheeses are associated with tarragon. England's Crusoe is a soft-ripened cheese flavored with tarragon and other herbs and spices. Perroche, British in spite of its Gallic name, is sometimes rolled in chopped tarragon. In France, Boulette de Cambai is a fresh cheese containing parsley, pepper, tarragon, and chives. Dauphin, or Thiérache, an ancient cheese from Flanders, is seasoned with tarragon, black pepper, cloves, and parsley.

Tarragon contains methyl chavicol (up to 75 percent of the essential oil), anethol (up to 10 percent of the essential oil), α-pinene, β-pinene and myrcene.

OTHER USES
Potpourri, sachets

COMMENTS
It is important that the culinary herbalist not be fooled by Russian tarragon (same species, but not the varietal, 'sativa'). Unlike French tarragon, it has little flavor or taste. It is commonly sold as "tarragon" but has no place in a kitchen garden. While it has little flavor, it is a popular ingredient, in dried form, in Turkish cooking. To be fair, Russian tarragon is winter hardy, which is probably why it is more widely available in nurseries than the more desirable *Artemisia Dracunculus* 'sativa'.

When buying any plant for an herb garden, let your nose and palate be the final arbiters. Just because an herb is listed in a book (yes, even this one) doesn't mean you should be growing it for use in *your* kitchen. (See *Thymus serpyllum* 'cimicinus', under THYME, and *Salvia Sclarea*, under SAGE.)

The name "mugwort" is shared by another member of the *Artemisia* genus (q.v.), though they are certainly not interchangeable in the kitchen.

Toothache Plant: *Spilanthes acmella*

OTHER COMMON, ETHNIC, OR SCIENTIFIC NAMES
Alphabet plant, Australian cress, paracress. Also known as *Bidens acmella*, *Bidens ocymifolia*, *Blainvillea acmella*, *Pyrethrum acmella*, *Spilanthes ocymifolia*, and *Verbesina acmella*.

RELATED SPECIES
Spilanthes americana: Botoncillo (Spain); boton de oro, botonsillo, chisaca, chisaca calentano, chisaca de cafetal, rizaca, Santa Maria, yuyo quemado (Colombia)

CULTIVAR
'Oleraceae' (sometimes listed as *Spilanthes oleraceae*): Brazil cress, pará cress

GROWTH HABITS
Perennial
Origin: African and South American tropics
Range: Southern Florida and California; grown as an annual in cooler climates

Pungent purple leaves of the cultivar 'Oleraceae' are used in mixed salads. The species is a bit harsh for that use, but leaves, cooked or raw, serve as an accompaniment to plain white rice.

Wild Chicory: *Cichorium intybus*

OTHER COMMON, ETHNIC, OR SCIENTIFIC NAMES

Barbe-de-capuchine, blue dandelion, blue daisy, blue sailors, coffeeweed, common chicory, endive, hendibeh, horseweed, ragged sailor, succory, wild succory, witloof
  Denmark: Julesalat
  France: Chicorée, endive
  Germany: Brüsseler Endivie, Kaffeezichorie, Zichorie
  Greece: Radíkia
  Italy: Ciccoria, indivia
  Mexico: Achicoria, chicoria
  Netherlands: Brussels lof (endive), witloof
  Poland: Cykoria
  Portugal: Chicória, endívía
  Russia: Tzicory
  Spain: Achicoria, endibia, escarola, xicoira
  Sweden: Endiv
  Turkey: Hindiba

RELATED SPECIES
  Chicorum endiva: Belgian endive, endive, radicchio
  Latuca sativa: Lettuces. This species consists of many cultivars, but they
    are divided into three main groups: the cob or romaine group, the
    curled group, and the headed group.
  Scorzonera hispanica: Salsifis (France); scorzanera (Italy); black oyster
    plant, black salsify
  Tragopogon porrifolius: Salsfis (France); scorzanera (Italy); oyster plant,
    salsify, vegetable oyster
  Tragopogon pratensis: goat's beard, Jack-go-to-bed-at-noon, John-go-to-
    bed-at-noon

GROWTH HABITS
  Perennial
  Origin: Mediterranean region
  Range: Cosmopolitan weed

Flowers are used in salads and as garnishes. Young leaves work well in salads. Dried roasted roots are added as an adulterant to coffee; some cultures have used them so long that coffee without the bitter presence of chicory tastes flat and lifeless. Chicory has made the leap from weed and economic necessity to cherished gourmet ingredient. The "heads" of chicory, better known as endive or Belgian endive, do indeed belong at the top of the gourmet's shopping list. The leaves add a bitter contrast to rich meats, whether used as a garnish, in an accompanying salad, or as a braised vegetable.

Tragopogon pratensis, said to be sweeter-tasting than chicory, is an ingredient in stews and in the savory meat-filled pastries of Greece and Italy.

COMMENTS

"Blue sailors" is also a name for cornflower, *Centaurea cyanus. Radíkia* is the Greek name for common dandelion, as well. That name is related to the Latin *radix,* meaning "root," many of these wild greens having large taproots.

Yarrow: *Achillea millefolium*

OTHER COMMON, ETHNIC, OR SCIENTIFIC NAMES

Bad man's plaything, bloodwort, carpenter's weed, devil's nettle, devil's plaything, herbe militaris, gearwe, gordolobo, knight's milfoil, milfoil, nose bleed, old man's pepper, sanguinary, soldier's woundwort, staunchweed, thousand weed, yarroway

Colombia: Colchon de pobre
France: Millefeuille
Germany: Schafgarbe
Italy: Achillea millefoglie
Mexico: Alcanforina, mil en rama, real de oro
Netherlands: Yerw
Russia: Krovavnik, tisiachelistnik
Spain: Abrofia
Sweden: Field hop

RELATED SPECIES

Achillea ageratum (sometimes listed as *Achillea decolorans*): English mace, mace plant, sweet yarrow
Achillea ligustica: Milfoil
Achillea moschata: Achillea, achillea musquée (France); achillea musgada (Spain); Feldgarbe, Moschus Schafgarbe (Germany), iva, musk yarrow
Achillea ptarmica: Sneezeweed, sneezewort

   Perennial
   Origin: Eurasia
   Range: Naturalized (and weedy) throughout North America

CULINARY USES

   The various species of *Achillea* have similar properties and are used the same ways.

   Leaves have an astringent, bitter, and peppery taste with a slight nutmeg scent. Minced leaves flavor some soft cheeses. They can also be added to salads. Leaves and flowers add bitter flavor to liqueurs, digestifs, and vermouth. Yarrow has been used in place of hops in herbal beers.

   Milfoil, *Achillea ligustica,* is used in the cordial Lovage, along with real lovage and tansy.

   Achillea moschata has an aromatic, bitter, and pungent taste. Dried leaves make a somewhat medicinal-tasting tea.

   Achillea millefolium contains over a hundred compounds that influence its flavor; tannins predominate (28,000 ppm), followed by camphor (1,780 ppm), sabinene (1,225 ppm), α-pinene (1,000 ppm), and 1,8-cineole (960 ppm).

OTHER USES

   Good choice for dried flower arrangements.

COMMENTS

   Excessive consumption may increase skin's sensitivity to light.

   The FDA restricts its use to beverages alone, and only if certified to be free of thujone.

   Mace plant is not related to mace, *Myristica fragrans* (which see, under NUTMEG).

Yerba de Conejo: *Tridax coronopiifolio*

OTHER COMMON, ETHNIC, OR SCIENTIFIC NAMES
   Rabbit grass

RELATED SPECIES
   Tridax procumbens: Botoncillo (Colombia)
   Tridax radialis: Arnica de monte (Colombia)

GROWTH HABITS
   Annual
   Origin: Mexico, Central America
   Range: Mexico, Central America

This grass-like plant is used in Oaxaca to add a tart flavor to bean dishes.

COMMENTS

The USDA lists at least one species of *Tridax* as "a noxious weed."

15. Berberidaceae: The Barberry Family

Barberry: *Berberis vulgaris*

OTHER COMMON, ETHNIC, OR SCIENTIFIC NAMES

Common barberry, jaundice berry, pipperidge bush, piprage
Bulgaria: Kisel trun
Finland: Happomarja
France: Épine-vinette
Germany: Brebesbeere
India: Chitra
Iran: Zereshk
Italy: Berbero, crespino
Japan: Megi
Mexico: Agracejo
Portugal: Uva-espim
Russia: Barbaris
Spain: Agracejo, bérbero
Turkey: Diken üzümü

RELATED SPECIES

Berberis aristata: Indian barberry
Berberis candensis: American barberry
Berberis haematocarpa: Red-fruited barberry
Berberis thunbergii: Megi (Japan)

GROWTH HABITS

Shrub
Origin: Europe
Range: Temperate regions

CULINARY USES

The dried berries appear in Persian cuisine, cooked in rice dishes or sprinkled on top as a garnish, like currants. Fresh, tart little fruits are used to make jellies and jam, such as *confiture d'épine-vinette*. They also add tartness to sauces for rich meats. The berries are sometimes pickled.

American barberry and red-fruited barberry are wild North American species that can be used interchangeably with the European species.

COMMENTS

Berberis vulgaris (and some other species of *Berberis*) is an alternate host for a rust disease that affects grains, including barley, oats, rye, and wheat. Major grain-producing states often have laws designed to eliminate these offenders. Similarly, gooseberries (*Ribes* spp.) harbor an insect that causes deformation of white pines (*Pinus Strobus*), and eastern red cedar (*Juniperus virginiana*) is an alternate host for apple rust.

16. Bignoniaceae: The Bignonia Family

Guajes Hauxya: *Parmentiera edulis*

OTHER COMMON, ETHNIC, OR SCIENTIFIC NAMES
Cuachilote, cuajes hauxya, guajilote

RELATED SPECIES
Parmentiera stenocarpa: Arbol de la jujias (Panama); palo vela (Colombia); candletree

GROWTH HABITS
Small spiny tree
Origin: Mexico and Guatemala
Range: Mexico and Guatemala

CULINARY USES
In Oaxaca and Puebla, the little lens-shaped seeds found in the four-to-eight-inch purple pods are a key seasoning for *guasmole,* a local dish of braised meat. The seeds have a distinctive garlic-like flavor.

Pau D'Arco: *Tabebuia impetiginosa*

OTHER COMMON, ETHNIC, OR SCIENTIFIC NAMES
Tahebo bark, trumpet tree
Colombia: Alumbre, arco, apamate, canaguate, chicala, coralibe, curari, curaride, garza, guayacan polvillo, lumbre, ocobo
Costa Rica: Cortes, cortes amarillo, palo de fierro, roble de sabana
Mexico: Maculiz, pau d'arco, roble de sabana
Panama: Guayacan negro, roble de sabana
Spain: Guayacan, roble

Tabebuia heptaphylla: Pau d'arco
Tabebuia pentaphylla: Ocobo (Colombia); roble, roble de la sabana (Costa Rica and Panama)
Tabebuia pallida: Pink tabebuia

GROWTH HABITS
Tropical tree
Origin: Mexico to Argentina
Range: Southern Florida

CULINARY USES
The inner bark or heartwood of both pau d'arco species is used in herbal teas, as are the leaves of pink tabebuia. The shredded bark can sometimes be found in health-food stores.
Tabebuia heptaphylla contains traces of β-carotene.

17. Bixaceae: The Bixa Family

Annatto: *Bixa orellana*

OTHER COMMON, ETHNIC, OR SCIENTIFIC NAMES
Lipstick tree
Brazil: Uruc, urucum
Colombia: Achihuite
Estonia: Värvibiksa
Finland: Annaatto
France: Achiote, rocou
French Guiana: Roucou
Germany: Orleanstrauch
Indonesia: Kesumba
Italy: Annatto, anotto
Malaysia: Jarak belanda, kesumba
Netherlands: Achiote, anatto, annotto, orleaan, rocou
Panama: Achote
Philippines: Achuete, asuete, achwete, echuete
Portugal: Annato
Spain: Achiote, achote, annato
Thailand: Kam tai
Vietnam: Hot dieu mau
West Indies: Roucou

GROWTH HABITS

    Small tropical tree or shrub
    Origin: Old World tropics
    Range: Naturalized in New World tropics, grown in southern United
       States

CULINARY USES

    Seeds are used in Latin American cooking, primarily as a colorant for cooking oils. They were originally intended to be used this way to produce a substitute for *dendê oil* (made from the seeds of the African oil palm, *Elaesis guineensis*), also known as Macaw fat or simply palm oil. Dendê is essential to the cooking of West Africa, Brazil, and Malaysia, but its saturated fat content is anathema to modern health-conscious dieters. Annatto-laced oil (known as *oleo do urucum* in Brazil) cannot duplicate the crisp-frying qualities of palm oil, but it does color and subtly flavor rice and, as in the Ecuadorian soup *locro,* potatoes.

    If authenticity outweighs health concerns, use palm oil for its authentic flavor. While you're at it, go back to using lard in Mexican dishes and coconut oil in Indonesian cooking—you only live once. Actually, annatto-

Annatto
Bixa orellana

From Jacquin, *Plantarum rariorum horti,* vol. 4

colored lard is available in markets catering to Latin American (especially Guatemalan) customers.

The seed, whole or ground, is used throughout the Caribbean, Central America, and South America. In the United States, the whole seeds can usually be found in Hispanic markets or in the Hispanic-foods section of large grocery stores. They can be ground in a pepper mill and added to chickens and salads. *Achiote* is a Mexican paste consisting of ground annatto seeds, black pepper, garlic, and Seville oranges. *Bijol* is a commercial paste of corn, flour, cumin, artificial yellow and red dyes, and annatto used in the preparation of yellow rice in the Caribbean and in the Yucatan.

Annatto is essential to Puerto Rican cooking. Combined with garlic, lemon juice, oregano, soy sauce, and rum, it makes a marinade for *pollo frito,* a favorite fried chicken recipe.

Annatto has uses as a dye, and the active principle in the dye is bixin, which is present in greater concentration in the aril surrounding the seeds than in the seeds themselves. The aril does not, however, have the flavor or aroma of the seeds. Annatto is used to color butter and cheeses, notably English Cheddars, "red" Cheshires, and Hereford Red, a deep orange Leicester-like cheese. The rinds of some other English cheeses, including Bedwardine and Cloisterers, are washed with annatto. In Scotland, two deep yellow Cheddars are colored with annatto: Dunlop and Mull of Kintyre. The Australian Moyarra has an annatto-colored stripe through the center of the cheese. The American Colby and Longhorn are pale (if deeply colored) imitations of these cheeses of British descent.

France has a number of deep yellow or orange cheeses that incorporate annatto. Saint-Albray has a rind rubbed with crushed annatto seeds. Langres, from Champagne, is merely rinsed with bixin-laced brine while it cures, as is Pierre-qui-Vire. The Burgundian La Boule de Moines is a fresh Pierre-qui-Vire, rolled in chopped herbs. The reddish Saint-Florentine is another annatto-colored Burgundian soft cheese. Germany's Steppenkäse is colored with annatto, while Dutch Leidens (or Leydens) have their rinds rubbed with the dark red seeds.

Aside from its use in the manufacture of cheeses, annatto was traditionally used to color the marinade for Chinese roast pork, although it would be unusual to find a Chinese charcuterie anywhere today that does not use artificial food coloring exclusively.

The subtle flavor of annatto is derived from annotta and arnotta.

OTHER USES

Cosmetics; South American Indians make red body paints from annatto.

COMMENTS

Annatto stains.

18. Bombacaceae: The Bombax Family

Baobab: *Adonsonia digitata*

OTHER COMMON, ETHNIC, OR SCIENTIFIC NAMES
Cream of tartar tree, dead rat tree, Ethiopian sour gourd, monkey bread

RELATED SPECIES
Adonsonia gregorii: Australian bottle tree

GROWTH HABITS
Deciduous tree
Origin: Tropical Africa
Range: Africa, Australia, Madagascar

CULINARY USES
Young leaves are eaten as a potherb. The dried leaves are also ground and used like filé (q.v.) to thicken soups. The seeds can be pressed to release fony, or reniala, oil. The ground seeds are used as a seasoning. The sprouted seeds are also eaten. Fruit pulp is used to make a sour beverage, something like lemonade. It is also used to curdle milk.

OTHER USES
The bark is a source of fibers. It is also used as a source of dyestuffs and glues.

19. Boraginaceae: The Borage Family

Alkanet: *Anchusa officinalis*

OTHER COMMON, ETHNIC, OR SCIENTIFIC NAMES
Bugloss, dyer's bugloss
Mexico: Buglosa

RELATED SPECIES
Anchusa azurea (sometimes listed as *Anchusa italica*): Italienische Ochsenzunge (Germany); sigir dili (Turkey); anchusa, large blue alkanet

GROWTH HABITS
Biennial or perennial

Origin: Asia Minor
Range: Cosmopolitan weed

CULINARY USES

Add young leaves and blossoms to salads. The blossoms have been made into conserves. Alkanet was once used, as annatto is today, to color cheeses, but alkanet-dyed cheeses have a much ruddier complexion.

The blossoms of anchusa are used, like alkanet and borage, to add a colorful note to salads, sometimes in combination with rose petals, the tiny blooms of rosemary, or the bright, crumpled-tissue-like flowers of nasturtium.

OTHER USES

The dried roots provide color for cosmetics and hair and vegetable dyes. The musk-like leaves can be used in potpourris and sachets.

Borage: *Borago officinalis*

OTHER COMMON, ETHNIC, OR SCIENTIFIC NAMES
Burrage, cool-tankard, star flower, talewort
Estonia: Harilik kurgirohi, kurgirohi
Finland: Purasruoho
France: Bourrache
Gaelic: Borrach, borraigh, borraist
Germany: Boretsch, Borretsch, Gurkenkraut, Natternkopf (Bugloss)
Greece: Borántsa
Italy: Borragine, borago
Mexico: Borraja
Poland: Ogorecznik lekarski
Spain: Borratja
Sweden: Gurkört

RELATED SPECIES
Includes a large number of familiar botanical favorites: heliotropes, forget-me-nots, *Pulmonaria* spp. (Jerusalem sage and Bethlehem sage are not related to true sage, which see), and blue-bells (*Mertensia virginica*).

GROWTH HABITS
Annual
Origin: Europe and North Africa
Range: Naturalized in many areas

CULINARY USES
Add chopped cucumber-flavored young leaves to compound butters, salads, and soft cheeses. Mixed with other mild herbs, such as chives and parsley, the leaves enhance omelettes. The leaves have a faintly fishy taste that,

strangely enough, is not offensive. They can be added to cooking liquid for beans, peas, or root vegetables like salsify. The leaves are sometimes dipped in batter and deep-fried.

Borage finds several uses in Italian cookery. It can also be cooked as a potherb, with or without other greens, or added to soups. *Preboggion* is a classic greens dish from Liguria. Cooked borage is used in a Genoese ravioli filling. The leaves' fishy flavor is undetectable when they are combined with shellfish or calamari.

Flowers, candied or fresh, make good garnishes in salads or floated on cider, lemonade, or punch. The flowers can also be used to flavor herbal vinegars or wine. They are an ingredient in the concoction known as Pimm's Cup. The candied flowers are used in baked goods. The flowers share the cucumber taste of the leaves, but they leave a lasting, implied sweetness—something like the after-effects of eating artichokes—as well as a mouthwatering freshness. This feeling of *bien-être* could be described as the exact opposite of the drying sensation produced by the tannins in a young Cabernet Sauvignon.

The leaves and flowers are used in herbal teas.

Borage leaves contain 2,6 nonadienal.

OTHER USES

In sixteenth-century Italy, apothecaries made *zucar borragiudt,* or borage sugar. It was supposed to dispel melancholy. They also combined "bugloss," endive, hops, and smallage in a sugar syrup (see CELERY).

Borage
Borago officinalis

From Woodville, *A supplement to Medical botany,* vol. 4

Use only young leaves as food (and sparingly, as they may be toxic in quantity). It is unlikely that you would want older leaves in a salad, anyway; they are disconcertingly hairy, even bristly.

When using borage flowers, be careful to remove the bitter green sepals from the base of the flowers.

Do not mistake the apothecary's name for this species, "bugloss," for another species, viper's bugloss (also known as blue weed or blue devil), *Echium vulgare*. Viper's bugloss, while it is a member of the Boraginaceae, is a pernicious weed that offers little to the culinary herbalist (except for occasional use as crystallized flowers). It does add long-lasting blue spikes of flowers that look good with the black-eyed Susans on roadsides in high summer.

Comfrey: *Symphytum officinale*

OTHER COMMON, ETHNIC, OR SCIENTIFIC NAMES
Ass ear, blackwort, boneset, bruisewort, common comfrey, consolida, consound, gum plant, healing herb, knitback, knitbone, nipbone, saracen's root, sippery root, yalluc
Germany: Beinwell
Mexico: Carqueja, consuela mayor, sinfito
Russia: Okopnik

GROWTH HABITS
Perennial
Origin: Eurasia
Range: Naturalized in North America

CULINARY USES
Young leaves can be used in salads, older leaves as a potherb. In Germany, *Schwartzwurz* is made, along the lines of a *chile relleno*, substituting a comfrey leaf for the chile. Dried leaves are used in herbal teas.

Flowers are eaten in salads.

Roots, like the roots of wild chicory, have been dried and roasted for use as coffee substitutes.

Comfrey contains tannin (up to 90,000 ppm), allantoin (up to 8,000 ppm), carotene (up to 6,300 ppm), and the comfrey-specific symphytine and symphytocynoglossin.

OTHER USES
Comfrey is considered primarily as part of the spectrum of herbal medications.

While comfrey has been used medicinally, it has been implicated in liver poisoning when taken over long periods.

Comfrey forms large, somewhat uncontrollable "colonies" of plants that, once established, do not discourage easily. Digging them up will work, if every bit of the roots are removed. A tiny fragment of root, left behind, is sufficient for comfrey to begin colonizing anew.

Lungwort: *Pulmonaria officinalis*

OTHER COMMON, ETHNIC, OR SCIENTIFIC NAMES
Jerusalem cowslip, Jerusalem sage

GROWTH HABITS
Perennial
Origin: Europe
Range: Temperate regions

CULINARY USES
The leaves are said to be among the ingredients in vermouth. They can be used in soups.

OTHER USES
An excellent plant for shade gardens.

20. Brassicaceae (formerly Cruciferae): The Mustard Family

Candytuft: *Iberis amara*

OTHER COMMON, ETHNIC, OR SCIENTIFIC NAMES
Rocket candytuft
Germany: Schleifenblume

GROWTH HABITS
Annual
Origin: Europe
Range: Temperate regions

CULINARY USES
Seeds are sometimes ground and used like mustard (q.v.). Edible flowers are used in salads and as garnishes.

Cress: *Lepidium sativum*

OTHER COMMON, ETHNIC, OR SCIENTIFIC NAMES
English cress, garden cress, land cress, pepper grass, pepperwort, tongue grass, upland cress

Burma/Myanmar: Mongnyin

Denmark: Karse

Estonia: Salatkress

Finland: Vihanneskrassi

France: Cresson alénois, passerage cultivée

Germany: Kresse

Iceland: Karsi

India: Adiyalu, aliv, allibija, asaliya, ativerai, chandrika, halim, halon, hidamba saga, kurthike, raktabija, tezak

Israel: Rashad

Italy: Agretto, crescione

Mexico: Lentijilla, mastuerzo

Netherlands: Mosterdkers, sterrekers, tuinkers

Norway: Karse, matkarse

Poland: Pieprzyca siewna

Portugal: Jambu

Russia: Kress-salat

Spain: Berro, lepido, mastuerzo

Sweden: Krasse, kryddkrassing

CULTIVARS
'Broadleaf Cress', 'Curly Cress'

RELATED SPECIES
Barbarea verna: American cress, Belle Isle cress, early winter cress, land winter cress, scurvy grass, upland cress, winter cress

Barbarea vulgaris: Creases, rocket, winter cress, yellow rocket

Cochlearia officinalis: Coclearia (Italy); cranson (France); Löffelkraut (Germany); scurvy grass, spoonwort

GROWTH HABITS
Annual

Origin: Middle East

Range: Wild in North America

CULINARY USES
Use as you would use mustard greens, nasturtiums, and watercress: as garnishes, in salads, and in compound butters. Cress can also be used in creamed soups and with vegetables, such as cauliflower, peas, and potatoes.

The leaves of *Barbarea vulgaris* were used raw, as food, and cooked, as medicine, by the Cherokees.

Cress can be used as a potherb, either alone or in combination with other greens, such as beet greens, chard, collards, kale, spinach, or turnip greens.

Cochlearia officinalis can be used like other mustard greens, but has a tarry flavor that some find objectionable.

Garden cress contains gluconasturtiin which, when acted upon by enzymes in the cells, forms phenylethylene isothiocyanate, a kind of mustard oil (see Comments, under MUSTARD).

Curly Sea Kale: *Crambe maritima*

OTHER COMMON, ETHNIC, OR SCIENTIFIC NAMES
Scurvy grass, sea kale

RELATED SPECIES
Crambe cordifolia: Colewort, tartar sea kale
Crambe orientalis: No common name found
Crambe tatarica: Tartar bread plant

GROWTH HABITS
Perennial
Origin: Eurasia
Range: Temperate regions

CULINARY USES
Young shoots can be blanched and eaten as a vegetable, either in salads or in Moroccan seafood stews. Curly sea kale is said to taste like slightly bitter hazelnuts. The plant was popular with the ancient Romans; indeed, it was commonly in use throughout coastal Europe during the nineteenth century.

Honey-scented flowers can be used as a garnish. The roots of *Crambe orientalis* used like horseradish. Flower stalks are eaten as a steamed vegetable. *Crambe tatarica*'s raw roots and blanched leaves are eaten in salads.

Garlic Mustard: *Sisymbrium allaria*

OTHER COMMON, ETHNIC, OR SCIENTIFIC NAMES
Garlic wort, hedge garlic, Jack-by-the-hedge, sauce alone. Garlic mustard was formerly known scientifically as *Alliaria officinalis* and *Alliaria petiolata*. It was previously considered to be a member of the genus *Erysimum*.
France: Alliaire
Germany: Lauchkraut, Sasskraut
Italy: Alliaria

Sisymbium officinale: Bank cress, crambling rocket, hedge mustard, Jim
  Hill mustard, Lucifer-matches, singer's plant, tansy mustard, tumbling
  mustard, tumbleweed
Sisymbrium canescens: Tansy mustard
Sisymbrium Sofia: Herb sophia

GROWTH HABITS
  Biennial
  Origin: Europe
  Range: Wild in temperate regions, weedy in waste places

CULINARY USES
  Both seeds and leaves are useful for their slightly bitter, mild garlic flavor.
An English condiment is made by combining minced garlic mustard with
mint. It is served with fat fish, lamb, and mutton. The seed pods can be sautéed and served as a vegetable. Use fresh leaves, blossoms, and immature seed
pods in salads, as potherb, or as a seasoning for meats, sauces, and vegetables.

Hairy Bitter Cress: *Cardamine hirsuta*

OTHER COMMON, ETHNIC, OR SCIENTIFIC NAMES
  Bitter cress

RELATED SPECIES
  Cardamine flexuosa: Wavy bitter cress

GROWTH HABITS
  Annual or biennial
  Origin: Europe
  Range: Naturalized from southeastern New York to Georgia, and west
    as far as Illinois

CULINARY USES
  Both hairy bitter cress and wavy bitter cress contain the same active principle (allyl isothiocyanate) that is found in watercress and radishes (q.v.).
They can be used in the same ways: as garnishes, in salads, on sandwiches,
and in soups.

Horseradish: *Armoracia rusticana*

OTHER COMMON, ETHNIC, OR SCIENTIFIC NAMES
  Great raifort, mountain radish, red cole. Former scientific names for the
plant include *Armoracia lapathifolium, Radicula Armoracia, Rorippa Armoracia,*
and *Cochlearia Armoracia.* Before Linnaeus created the systematic (binomial)

nomenclature in use today, horseradish was known as *Amoracia* or *Raphanus rusticanus.*

Denmark: Peberrod
Estonia: Aed-mädarõigas, mädarõigas
Finland: Piparjuuri
France: Cranson de Bretagne, moutarde de Allemands, raifort
Gaelic: Meacan-each
Germany: Kren, Meerrettich, Petersilienwurzel
Hungary: Torma
Iceland: Piparrót
Italy: Barbaforte, cren, rafano, rafano rusticano, ramolacchio
Mexico: Coclearia, mostaza de frailes
Netherlands: Boereradijs, mierik, meredik
Norway: Pepperrot
Poland: Chrzan
Portugal: Raiz-forte
Romania: Hrean
Russia: Khryen, hren
Spain: Rábano picante, rábano rústico
Swahili: Mronge
Sweden: Pepparrot

RELATED SPECIES
Rorippa amphibia: Yellow cress

GROWTH HABITS
Perennial
Origin: Eurasia
Range: Temperate regions

CULINARY USES
The root is grated with a little vinegar to produce the familiar bottled horseradish. It is sometimes colored with beet juice or flavored with cayenne and shallots. If mixed with an egg-based emulsion it is marketed as horse-radish sauce. Either way, the pungent flavor goes well with hearty dishes, such as braised or roast beef.

Use horseradish in unsweetened whipped cream as a condiment for delicate smoked fish (especially trout) or smoked meats. Use only fresh horse-radish (or reconstituted wasabi); the vinegar in prepared horseradish will curdle the cream.

Horseradish is used to flavor some cheeses as well. Tudor is a Welsh cheese that is available either enlivened by horseradish or smoked. The Alsatian fresh cheese known as Bibbelskäse contains herbs and horseradish. The mass-produced soft French cheese called Tartare is made near Périgord, either with horseradish or with a mixture of garlic and parsley.

Horseradish
Armoracia rusticana

From Woodville, *Medical botany*, vol. 1

In Scandinavian countries, horseradish is combined with cooked puréed apples, lemon juice, and sour cream to make a sauce to accompany rich meats, especially goose. It is also good in compound butters, served with fat fish such as salmon or bluefish.

Serve young leaves in salads or add a small amount of grated root to salad dressings. They can be used in stuffings for poultry.

Horseradish gets its zip from some of the same compounds that heat up mustard (q.v.): allyl isothiocyanate, allyl cyanide, and carbon disulfide.

COMMENTS

Excessive use may be dangerous to pregnant women or to people with kidney problems.

The mustard oil that gives horseradish its bite is powerful. It deserves respect. In the days before food processors there was only one way to get the job done: by grating the big ugly roots on a hand grater. Tears flowed freely at horseradish time. A covered blender or food processor spares us that sturm und drang. You *could* rediscover the experience for yourself by opening the top of a blender full of freshly grated horseradish and inhaling deeply through your nose, but I do not recommend it. Thrill-seeking has its limits.

Lady's Smock: *Cardamine praetensis*

OTHER COMMON, ETHNIC, OR SCIENTIFIC NAMES
Bitter cress, cuckoo flower, mayflower, meadow cress

GROWTH HABITS
Perennial
Origin: Northern Asia, Europe, and North America
Range: Cosmopolitan weed

CULINARY USES
Lady's smock suggests the typical peppery bite of other members of the Brassicaceae, although its effect is quite mild. It is used much as watercress is used: in salads, as garnishes for meats, or puréed in soups (especially cold soups, since allyl isothiocyanate loses its pungency when cooked). The delicately colored flowers also share the leaves' warmth. They make an excellent garnish, their pink to lilac color being better suited to fish than to red meats.

Mustard: *Brassica* spp.

OTHER COMMON, ETHNIC, OR SCIENTIFIC NAMES
The mustards were formerly classified scientifically as members of the genus *Sinapsis*.
China: Xue li hong
Denmark: Sennep
Ethiopia: Senafich
Finland: Sinappi
France: Moutarde
Germany: Mostrich, Senf
Greece: Mustardha
India: Kimcea, kudoo, rai, sarson
Indonesia: Biji sawi
Iraq: Khardal
Italy: Mostarda, senapa, senape
Japan: Karashi, serifong
Malaysia: Biji sawi
Mexico: Mostaza
Norway: Sennep
Portugal: Mostarda
Russia: Gorchitsa
Spain: Mostaza
Sri Lanka: Abba
Sweden: Senap

Brassica hirta (formerly listed as *Sinapis alba* and sometimes even *Sinaplis alba*; once known to apothecaries as *Semen erucae*): Gorczyca jasna (Poland); hvitsennep (Norway); keltasinappi (Finland); mostarda branca (Portugal); mostaza, mostaza amarilla (Mexico); mostaza silvestre (Spain); moutarde blanche (France); mustar (Romania); senape biancha (Italy); Senf, Weißer Senf (Germany); sinnepsfrae (Iceland); valge sinep (Estonia); vitsenap (Sweden); witte mosterd (Netherlands); white mustard

Brassica juncea (sometimes listed as *Brassica nigra;* an old pharmaceutical name is *Semen Sinapis*): Abba, haradali, lal sarsu, rai, senafich (India); biji savi (Malaysia); brunsenap, sareptasenap, svartsenap (Sweden); dul-kae (Korea); gorczyca czarna, kapusta czarna (Poland); junceamosterd, sareptamosterd, zwarte mosterd (Netherlands); Juncea-Senf, Moster, Rumänischer Braunsenf, Rutensenf, Sarepta-Senf, Schwarzer Senf (Germany); mostarda, mostarda preta (Portugal); mostaza de Indias, mostaza negra (Spain); mostaza negra (Mexico); moustárda, sinapósporos (Greece); moster, sawi hijau (Indonesia); moutarde de chine, moutarde noire, sénevé noir (France); must kapsasrohi, sarepta kapsasrohi (Estonia); mustár, mustárfû (Hungary); mustarda (East Timor); mustasinappi, sareptansinappi (Finland); senape nera (Italy); sennop (Denmark); spandaan (Iran); svartsennep (Norway); black mustard seed, brown mustard, Indian mustard, leaf mustard, mustard greens, Romanian brown mustard, sarepta mustard. Cultivars include 'Broad-leaved Mustard', 'crispifolia', 'Curled Mustard', 'foliosa', 'Ostrich-plume', 'Southern Curled Mustard'.

Brassica Kaber (formerly listed as *Sinapis arvensis*): Hardal (Turkey); Senf (Germany); California rape, charlock, wild mustard. The seeds, less pungent than those of *Brassica hirta* or *Brassica juncea,* are sometimes used to make mustard.

Brassica Napus: Charlock, colza, cress, field mustard, rape, wild mustard

Brassica nigra: Moutarde noire (France); black mustard

Brassica rapa 'chinensis': Petasi, sawi (Indonesia); pet sai (East Timor); Chinese mustard greens

Brassica rapa 'Nipposinica': Mizuna, kyona

Brassica rugosa: Osaka purple mustard

GROWTH HABITS

Annual

Origin: Europe and Asia

Range: Cultivated in Austria, England, France, Germany, Holland, Italy, India, North Africa, and the western United States

The Brassicaceae family contains a number of important food crops worldwide. Most are outside the range of this book. They include, but are not limited to, cabbages, kale, broccoli, cauliflower, brussel sprouts, rape (or broccoli rabe), turnips, collards, and kohlrabi. Rape seed is the source of canola oil.

The Brassicaceae provide most of the calcium in the diets of several Asian countries, where dairy products are seldom used. Popular Brassicas include bok choy (or pak choi, in the old transliteration), napa cabbage, and numerous greens that are virtually unknown in the West. Many of these plants are pickled, a perfect example being the kim chee of Korea. One of my favorites is a chopped mustard green pickled in brine, called "red-in-snow," *Brassica juncea multiceps* (see also AMARANTH).

Speaking of kim chee, a similar pickle from Guatemala contains nearly the same ingredients and is served with similar foods. It is called *chile con repollo*. The only difference is preparation time; while kim chee often ferments for months, the Guatemalan dish is used after only one day of marination.

Young leaves of mustard (older leaves become tough and *hot*) and flowers are eaten in salads. The small leaves of the curled mustard are especially lovely in a salad; the plant's hot, peppery flavor and dark, puckered foliage add contrast to the usual ingredients in a mixed green salad. The leaves are delicious in place of lettuce on sandwiches. They are also good in soups, though their heat breaks down upon cooking. The leaves of *Brassica hirta* and *Brassica Kaber* are often eaten in Arabic-speaking countries, as a potherb, as a cooked ingredient in salads, or added to eggs.

Seeds of black and white mustard are familiar spices. Oil from black mustard is a key ingredient in many hot pickles from India. The seeds are part of the Indian spice mixture called *panch phoron*. Vegetables, and any of a number of puréed legumes, called dals, are seasoned with panch phoron. In northern India, yogurt-based dishes, *ranas,* become *pachadis* when mustard seed is added. In southern India, the same dishes are made, substituting coconut milk for the yogurt. Also, in southern India, a *tadka*-like flavoring (see AJOWAN) is made from black mustard seeds. They are fried in hot ghee or coconut oil until they stop popping, and curry leaves are added at the last moment. The flavored fat is poured over separately cooked lentils or vegetables.

The ground seeds provide a bit of quick fire to make mayonnaise more than just another acid-oil emulsion. It is possible that the ground seeds offer a slight mechanical advantage during the production of that amazingly thick and creamy emulsion.

The cheese known as Liptauer is known in Slovakia as Liptovká Bryndza. It is often spiked with mustard seed. Some Goudas in the Netherlands also use the warmth of mustard.

Especially good prepared mustards come from Dijon, France, and Düsseldorf, Germany. Coleman's, from England, is the standard for high quality in dry, powdered mustards. Mustard-flavored oil is available in Indian markets. This is made from seeds of *Brassica hirta,* the same fiery pale mustard served in Chinese restaurants, but its intensity is controlled by dilution with more benign substances. Some Italian prepared mustards add the zest of oranges or lemons. In Italy, *mostarda di frutti di Cremona* is a preserve of candied fruits in honey and white wine, made piquant by the addition of mustard oil.

Mustard is particularly good when combined with sweet herbs like tarragon (q.v.) to make salad dressings that double as basting liquids for grilled fish or chicken. A small amount of mustard oil adds character to lime-juice vinaigrettes.

Mustard's pungency results from acrinyl isothiocyanate (in *Brassica hirta*) or allyl isothiocyanate (in *Brassica nigra* and *Brassica juncea*). These compounds don't actually exist in the seeds but are formed when the seeds are broken, releasing enzymes and other compounds within the seeds to combine in the presence of some form of moisture. The temperature of the liquid used to prepare the mustard, as well as its acidity, determines the heat of the mixture. Too high a temperature, or a pH that is too low, and the prepared mustard will not be hot. The enzymes responsible for the transformation are easily destroyed by heat; in commercial use, the seeds are ground in a way that prevents buildup of heat from friction. In many south Indian recipes, the whole seeds are fried in hot fat, which provides not additional spicy "heat" but a pleasant nutty flavor. If you want the heat of mustard in a cooked dish, allow these enzymes to react first and then add the empowered product to the dish to be cooked. Mustards also contain allyl cyanide and carbon disulfide.

COMMENTS

Mustard oil, especially in the seeds, can burn the skin. Rubber gloves can protect susceptible individuals.

If allowed to reseed themselves, the mustards will soon take over. I'm talking about not only your garden, but every piece of soil not regularly mown or already covered with buildings or pavement.

Pepperroot: *Dentaria laciniata*

OTHER COMMON, ETHNIC, OR SCIENTIFIC NAMES
Toothwort

GROWTH HABITS
Perennial
Origin: Eastern North America
Range: Wild in temperate moist woods

CULINARY USES
Use as you would use horseradish (q.v.).

Radish: *Raphanus sativus*

OTHER COMMON, ETHNIC, OR SCIENTIFIC NAMES
Burma/Myanmar: Mhon-la-u
China: Luobo, loh baak, loh bok
Costa Rica: Rábano
Denmark: Radise
Finland: Retiisi
France: Radis
Germany: Radieschen, Rettich
Greece: Rapanakia
India: Mooli or muli (Daikon)
Indonesia: Lobak (Daikon)
Italy: Ravanello
Japan: Daikon
Cambodia: Moeum spey sar
China: Loh-bak (Daikon)
Korea: Moo or muu (Daikon)
Malaysia: Lobak (Daikon)
Netherlands: Radijs
Norway: Reddik
Philippines: Labanos (Daikon)
Poland: Czarna rzepa (Black Radish), rzodkiewki
Portugal: Rabanette
Russia: Ryedis, ryediska
Sri Lanka: Rabu (daikon)
Sweden: Rädisa, rädisa rättika (black radish)
Thailand: Hua pak had, phakkat-hua (daikon)
Vietnam: Cu cai tau, cu cai trang (daikon)

CULTIVARS
'Black Spanish Radish', 'Icicle Radish', 'Violet de Gournay', 'Caudatus' (aerial radish, rat-tailed radish), 'Longipinnatus' (daikon, Chinese radish), and many others

RELATED SPECIES
Wasabia japonica (also known botanically as *Alliaria wasabi, Cochlearia wasabi, Eutrema wasabi,* and *Wasabia pungens*): Bergstockrose, Japanischer Kren (Germany); bergstokroos (Netherlands); japaninpiparjuuri (Finland); japansk pepparrot (Sweden); namida, wasabe, wasabi (Japan); raifort du Japon (France); shan yu cai (China); Japanese horseradish
Raphanus raphanistrum: Yabani turp (Turkey); wild radish

Annual
Origin: Europe, Southeast Asia
Range: Temperate regions

CULINARY USES

Roots are eaten raw in salads. Sprouts, called *kaiware* in Japan, offer heat and texture to salads. Cooked, they lose their fire and taste much like turnips. The young seed pods are good in sandwiches, salads, or as a mildly peppery garnish.

Radishes of many different colors, both skin and flesh, are popular in China. Green varieties tend to be sweeter.

The cuisines of China, Japan, and Korea make extensive use of radishes, as a medium for vegetable carving, and for pickles. The Korean *muu,* sometimes called Chinese radish, should not be confused with daikon, which is also known as Chinese radish. The roots are eaten raw or pickled, and the leaves are eaten cooked.

In Germany, the Bierrettich is a baseball-sized white radish—pungent, but nowhere near as intense as wasabi or horseradish—that is commonly eaten on sandwiches, to accompany serious beer drinking. The French eat a similar sandwich, but they prefer young pink radishes and sweet butter on a baguette.

In Turkey, the young leaves of *Raphanus raphanistrum* are shredded, sautéed, and used as a garnish for omelets.

An interesting garnish, from Japan, is made from daikon: first thread fresh red chiles, like *lardons,* through a daikon, then grate the radish to produce a speckled condiment. It is called *momiji-oroshi;* without the chile, this grated radish is known as *daikon-oroshi.*

Wasabi is bright green when freshly grated, but its color—and flavor—fades quickly. It is usually seen as a paste made from reconstituted dried powder (or, in a less satisfactory form, squeezed, ready made, from a tube). *Wasabi-zuke* is a pickle made from slices of the fresh root. *Tobikko,* flying fish roe used for sushi, comes in several colors in Japan, one of which is tinted and flavored with wasabi.

Wasabi contains allyl isothiocyanate, like other mustards and horseradish, but its heat and flavor are modified by small amounts of 6-methylthiohexyl isothiocyanate, 7-methylthioheptyl isothiocyanate and 8-methylthioocytl isothiocyanate.

COMMENTS

Wasabi's heat is created from the same enzymatic reaction that gives mustard (q.v.) its fiery bite. It is subject to the same conditions.

Most of the dried "wasabi" found in little cans is not true wasabi but a mixture of horseradish, mustard, and food coloring.

Rocket: *Eruca vesicaria subs. sativa*

OTHER COMMON, ETHNIC, OR SCIENTIFIC NAMES
Garden rocket, rocket cress, rocket salad. Occasionally listed under the old scientific name, *Eruca sativa*.
France: Roquelle, roquette
Germany: Raukenkohl
Italy: Arugala, ruchetta, rucola, rugala

RELATED SPECIES
Arugala Selvatica: Wild arugala
Diplotaxis erucoides: False arugala
Diplotaxis muralis: Wall arugala, wild rocket

GROWTH HABITS
Annual
Origin: Mediterranean region
Range: Temperate regions

CULINARY USES
The leaves, known as *misticanza* in Rome, are a popular cooked vegetable.

COMMENTS
Cut the growing plant frequently to encourage the production of new young leaves. As the leaves get older, they get tough and accumulate more and more mustard oil—in fact, too much.

I have seen listings for seeds of wild arugala, *Arugala Selvatica,* but have not found any reference to the genus in *Hortus Third*. This may be a misnomer, or the plant is new to North America.

The peppery leaves of the *Diplotaxis* genus are also known as rocket and are used in salads, like true rocket. They can also be cooked as a potherb, and as a garnish for bean dishes.

Shepherd's Purse: *Capsella bursa-pastoris*

OTHER COMMON, ETHNIC, OR SCIENTIFIC NAMES
Blind weed, case weed, case wort, Chinese cress, hen pepper, lady's purse, mother's heart, pepper and salt, pepperweed, pickoocker, pickpocket, pickpurse, poor man's parmacettie, rattle pouches, sanguinary, shepherd's bag, shepherd's script, shepherd's sprout, St. James' wort, water chestnut vegetable, witches' pouches. The "purse" nature of this plant's seed pod was more than sufficiently suggested by its old scientific name, *Bursa bursa-pastoris*.
France: Bourse de pasteur
Germany: Hirtentasche, Hirtentäschel

Ireland: Clappedepouch
Mexico: Bolsa de pastor
Russia: Pastushya sumka

RELATED SPECIES
Capsella gracilis: Slender shepherd's purse
Capsella rubella: Red shepherd's purse
Lepidium campestre: Cow cress, field cress, field peppergrass, field pepperweed
Lepidium sativum: Garden cress
Lepidium virginicum: Poor man's pepper, peppergrass, Virginia pepperweed
Thlaspi arvense (sometimes listed as *Thlaspi arvensis*): Bastard cress, devilweed, field pennycress, Frenchweed, fanweed, stinkweed, treacle-mustard, mithridate mustard, wild garlic
Thlaspi perfoliatum: Pennycress

GROWTH HABITS
Annual
Origin: Middle East
Range: Cosmopolitan weed

CULINARY USES
All parts of the plant contain mustard oil. The pungent, peppery leaves and flowers can be used to season soups and stews. Shepherd's purse is used in stir-fries and in dumplings. Roots have been preserved in syrup like ginger. They are a popular vegetable in Korea.

The seeds have been roasted and added to breads. Flowers and blanched leaves add a warming garnish to salads. Greens are added to thick soups and omelets in Italy.

COMMENTS
Shepherd's purse and the *Lepidiums,* listed above, have escaped to become weeds. They can be found on roadsides and waste places everywhere. While the Chinese cultivate this herb, there is no need to plant it; all you need to do is look down.

Sweet Rocket: *Hesperis matronalis*

OTHER COMMON, ETHNIC, OR SCIENTIFIC NAMES
Dame's rocket, dame's violet, purple rocket, rocket, roquette, rucchette, vesper flower, white rocket. Sweet rocket used to be known as *Eruca sativa* and *Hesperis nivea.*

    Biennial
    Origin: Central and southern Europe
    Range: Common escapee from gardens

CULINARY USES
    A few young leaves, chopped finely and added to salads, add a pleasant bitter quality, somewhat similar to true rocket or arugala (q.v.). Sprouted seeds used in salads. Sweet-smelling flowers are used in salads and as a garnish for desserts.

OTHER USES
    Seeds can be pressed to yield honesty oil, which is known as *huile de Julienne* in France, or *rotreps oel* in the Netherlands.

COMMENTS
    Often mistakenly identified as wild phlox. A simple rule: *Hesperis,* like all other members of the Brassicaceae, has four petals (the cross-shaped flowers are the reason the family used to be called Cruciferae); phlox has five petals.

Watercress: *Nasturtium officinalis*

OTHER COMMON, ETHNIC, OR SCIENTIFIC NAMES
    Watercress used to bear the botanical name *Rorippa Nasturtium-aquatica* or *Sisymbrium nasturtiumaquaticum.*
    Arabic: Barbeen
    Brazil: Agrião
    China: Sai-eng-chai, sai yeung choy, sai-yong choi, xi yang cai
    Colombia: Berro, mastuerzo
    Costa Rica: Berro de agua
    East Timor: Angriaun
    Estonia: Ürt-allikkerss
    Finland: Isovesikrassi
    France: Cresson de fontaine, vert-pré
    Gaelic: Biolair
    Germany: Brunnekresse, Brunnenkresse, Wasserkresse
    Iceland: Vaetukarsi
    India: Bilrai, chamsur, kakutupala
    Indonesia: Cencil, selada air
    Iran: Shahat
    Italy: Crescione, crescione d'acqua
    Japan: Uotakuresu

Malaysia: Selada ayer
Mexico: Berros, trebol de agua
Nepal: Chamsur
Netherlands: Echte waterkers, waterkers
Norway: Brønnkarse
Philippines: Lampaka
Portugal: Agrião
Russia: Kress vodjanoy, zheruha
Spain: Berro di agua, créixens, crenchas
Sweden: Källfräne
Thailand: Phakkat-nam
Vietnam: Xa lach son

RELATED SPECIES

Nasturtium microphyllum: a wild American species that forms hybrids with *Nasturtium officinalis*

Nasturtium palustre: Agrião (Brazil)

GROWTH HABITS

Perennial
Origin: Europe
Range: Temperate regions

Watercress
Nasturtium officinalis

From Rousseau, *Recueil de plantes*

Use watercress in salads, as garnishes, and, of course, on sandwiches. In Mexico, watercress salad is usually dressed with a lime vinaigrette. Both species (and all their hybrids) are gastronomically identical. Watercress is good with fish and meats, in poultry dressings, and in salads and sauces. In the summer, a cold purée is delightful under cold poached chicken, shrimp, or lobster.

Tortilla de berro is an omelet made with chopped watercress and onions in Guatemala. *Tortitas de berro* are fritters, similar to the above, but smaller and containing chopped tomatoes as well.

Potage au cresson is a creamy watercress soup. Like vichyssoise, it is equally good hot or cold.

Watercress is used in Chinese pork soup, along with jujubes. Jujube, *Zizuphus jujuba*, is sometimes known as Chinese red date, hung ho, or hung zao. It is usually available, dried, in United States markets (see also, MAUBI).

The peppery bite of watercress is supplied by phenylethylene isothiocyanate, which is formed when enzymes in the cells act on gluconasturtiin (see Comments under MUSTARD).

COMMENTS

Agrião do Para is not related to this Agrião. In Brazil, it is used in the Amazonian cassava-based condiment called *tucupi*.

21. Burseraceae (formerly Simaroubaceae): The Torchwood Family

Elemi: *Canarium commune*

OTHER COMMON, ETHNIC, OR SCIENTIFIC NAMES

Canari, Chinese olive, Java almond, kenari-nut tree, pokok kenari, wild almond
France: Elémi
Indonesia: Kanari
Malaysia: Kanari
Papua: Keanee
Philippines: Pili
Sri Lanka: Rata kekuna

RELATED SPECIES

Canarium album: Larm yin (China); canarium, olive nut
Canarium edule: Safu
Canarium ovatum: Pili nuts

GROWTH HABITS
Tree
Origin: Philippines
Range: Philippines

CULINARY USES
The fruits are pickled or dried. The sweet, almond-like nuts are fried and salted. In the Philippines and the Moluccas, halvah- or marzipan-like candies are made from the ground nuts.

The sap yields gums and oils that have a citric, balsamic scent. The resin, called brea or Manila elemi, is used in the commercial flavorings industry for candies, ice cream, and soft drinks. The oil is used as a cooking medium.

Elemi contains α-*d*-phellandrene, dipentene, and sesquiterpenes.

OTHER USES
Used in the manufacture of perfumes.

Frankincense: *Boswellia serrata*

OTHER COMMON, ETHNIC, OR SCIENTIFIC NAMES
Frankincense tree
France: Encens oliban
Germany: Olibanum, Weinrauch
Italy: Olibano
Spain: Olibano

RELATED SPECIES
Boswellia carterii: Olibanum

GROWTH HABITS
Shrubby tree
Origin: Somalia and Arabian peninsula
Range: Dry regions of east Africa to India

CULINARY USES
In India, soup has been made from the fruit, but it may have been "famine food," not necessarily a gourmet's delight.

The gum is made by cutting into the bark of living trees and allowing the released sap to harden into "tears." Frankincense has a lemony, resinous flavor that is a result of its camphene, dipentene, α-phellandrene, pinene, and olihyzol.

OTHER USES
Incense and perfumes

Myrrh: *Commiphora myrrha*

OTHER COMMON, ETHNIC, OR SCIENTIFIC NAMES

Myrrh is sometimes listed in older botanical texts as *Commiphora abyssinica*.
France: Myrrhe
Germany: Myrrhe
Italy: Mirra
Mexico: Mirra

RELATED SPECIES

Boswellia bhaw-dajiana: Frankincense
Boswellia carteri: Frankincense
Boswellia frereana: Frankincense
Bursera delpechiana: Linaloe (also other *Bursera* spp.)
Commifora erythraae var. *glabrescens:* Balm of Gilead
Commifora opobalsamum: Balm of Gilead

GROWTH HABITS

Deciduous tree
Origin: Middle East
Range: North Africa

CULINARY USES

Myrrh is said to be one of the secret ingredients in Benedictine. It was probably included only because it was rare and costly at the time the liqueur was first made (the sixteenth century); today it is a rather ordinary commodity. Myrrh is included in Fernet Branca and in Raspail, a French liqueur containing angelica, calamus root, and myrrh.

Myrrh's bitter and aromatic qualities are provided by bisabolene, cuminic aldehyde, eugenol, m-cresol, and pinene.

Linaloe's essential oil, not surprisingly, contains up to 75 percent linalool, plus geraniol, nerol, myrcene, and seveasrl sesquiterpenes. It is used in commercial flavorings for sweet items, such as candy and soft drinks.

OTHER USES

Used as a commercial scent in cosmetics, incense, and perfumes, and as a commercial flavoring in toothpaste and mouthwash.

Commiphora spp. typically contain dozens of flavoring compounds, among them α-bisobolene, cadinene, cinnmaldehyde, cuminaldehyde, and eugenol.

COMMENTS

Myrrh is sometimes adulterated with bisabol myrrh or sweet myrrh, *Opopanax chironium* (a member of the *Apiaceae*) or *Commifora erythraae* var. *glabrescens.*

Quassia: *Quassia amara*

OTHER COMMON, ETHNIC, OR SCIENTIFIC NAMES

Bitter ash, bitterwood, gumbo-limbo, gum elemi, Jamaica quassia, naked Indian, quassia wood, Surinam quassia, West Indian birch. Quassia was previously known scientifically as *Camarium lufonicum, Simaruba Amara,* and *Simaruba officinalis.*

Colombia: Acuasia, caratero, guettarda, hombre grande, humiriastrum, vitex

Costa Rica: Aceituno, carana, hombron

France: Bois amer de Surinam, simarouba

Germany: Bitterholz, Bitterholzbaum, Quassie, Ruhrinde

Italy: Simaruba

Mexico: Cuasia, hombre grande

Nicaragua: Aceituno negrito

Panama: Aceituno, almacigo, crucete, guavito amargo, hombre grande, puesilde

Spain: Quassia amarga, simaruba

RELATED SPECIES

Picraena excelsa: Jamaica quassia

Simarouba excelsa: Causia (Mexico); cuassia

Simarouba glauca: Aceituno (Panama); aceituno, olivo (Costa Rica); aceituno, simaruba (Colombia); paradise tree

GROWTH HABITS

Deciduous subtropical tree

Origin: South America

Range: Northern South America, Mexico, West Indies

CULINARY USES

Quassia has been used as a source of bitterness in some beers, but hops (q.v.) provides better flavor and body. Oil of quassia is used, according to Merory, in something he calls "Nagaika Vodka Aperitif" (Merory scrupulously avoids use of registered trademarks, which sometimes causes some confusion).

Quassia contains several compounds unique to the species, such as quassin (up to 2,000 ppm), quassinol, and quassol, plus a number of alkaloids.

Simaruba bark yields a similar bitter essence used as a commercial flavoring. It contains phellandrine, d-limonene, and simarubin.

COMMENTS

The bitter principle is also derived from bitter damson, *Simauruba amara,* and Jamaica quassia, *Picraena excelsa,* which are closely related. These essences are all sold as quassia. The FDA restricts quassia's use to alcoholic beverages.

22. Calycanthaceae: The Calycanthus Family

Sweet Shrub: *Calycanthus floridus*

OTHER COMMON, ETHNIC, OR SCIENTIFIC NAMES
Apple shrub, bubby bush, Carolina allspice, pimento, pineapple plant, pineapple shrub, spicebush, strawberry bush, strawberry shrub, sweet betsey, sweetbush, sweet shade, sweetshrub

CULTIVARS
'Purpureus' has purple leaves.

RELATED SPECIES
Calycanthus occidentalis: California allspice

GROWTH HABITS
Deciduous shrub
Origin: Florida to Virginia
Range: Mild temperate regions, eastern United States

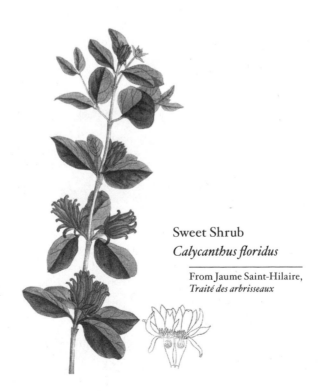

Sweet Shrub
Calycanthus floridus

From Jaume Saint-Hilaire,
Traité des arbrisseaux

Bark is said to resemble that of cinnamon in appearance and aroma. Young blossoms smell of cantaloupe and strawberries or pineapple, changing to apple as they age. The seeds reportedly have been used as a substitute for allspice.

OTHER USES

The bark, with its sweet aromatic scent, is a natural component of potpourris.

COMMENTS

Sometimes confused with spice bush, *Lindera benzoin* (q.v.).

23. Campanulaceae: The Bellflower Family

Rampion: *Campanula rapunculus*

OTHER COMMON, ETHNIC, OR SCIENTIFIC NAMES

Korean bellflower, ramps. Rampion has been known scientifically as *Platycodon glaucum.*
Germany: Rapunzel
Italy: Raperonzolo
Korea: Toraji

RELATED SPECIES

Campanula rotundifolia: Harebell, Scottish bluebell
Platycodon grandiflorum: Balloon flower, Chinese bell flower

GROWTH HABITS

Biennial
Origin: Eurasia
Range: Temperate regions

CULINARY USES

Lower leaves can be used as a salad green. First-year roots can be cut into fine julienne and added to salads. In Korea, the vegetable is garnished with fine shreds of dried hot red pepper (*silgochu*). Roots and young shoots can be eaten as cooked vegetables. The roots can be found in some Asian food markets in cellophane bags labeled "Dried Platycodon."

COMMENTS

The roots of these plants are poisonous until commercially treated. Since they are available safely in markets, there is no need to test fate with homemade versions.

German rampion, *Oenothera biennis,* is an evening primrose; that is, it is not related to the *Campanulas.* The uses of both plants in the kitchen, however, are similar. The seeds are used in breads and soups; the roots are eaten raw or cooked.

"Ramps" is better known as the name for a plant of the Allium family, *Allium tricoccum* (q.v.).

24. Cannabaceae: The Hemp Family

Hop: *Humulus lupulus*

OTHER COMMON, ETHNIC, OR SCIENTIFIC NAMES
Bine, common hop, European hop
Germany: Hopfen
Mexico: Flor de cervesa, flor de lupulo
Russia: Hmel

CULTIVARS
The hop species is available in dozens of cultivars.

Hop
Humulus lupulus

From Köhler, *Köhler's Medizinal-Pflanzen,* vol. 1

Perennial
Origin: Northern temperate regions
Range: Naturalized in many areas

CULINARY USES

The female flowers, or cones, of hops are the traditional flavoring for beers. One old-fashioned hop beer was made from hops, molasses, and dried ginger. Hops and other herbs are sometimes added to vodka. In Russia, these flavorings are known collectively as *zel'e*.

Hops have been used to flavor some bitters and tobaccos. Hops are used in small quantities in some herbal tea blends. Young shoots eaten as cooked vegetable in Belgium, France (where they are called *jet de houblon*), and Germany. They are also cooked and cooled for use in salads.

Hops contain caryophellene, geraniol, humulon (a bitter aromatic resin), myrcene, and terpene.

Marijuana: *Cannabis sativa*

OTHER COMMON, ETHNIC, OR SCIENTIFIC NAMES

Bhang, black Indian hemp, chanvre, charas, dagga, fimble, gallow grass, hanf, hashish, hemp, Indian hemp, kif, terouri, true hemp, soft hemp, and many, many more. Marijuana sometimes appears in old botanicals as *Apocynum cannabinum*.

China: Ma fèn or ta ma (ancient)
Colombia: Canamo
India: Vijaya (ancient)
Iraq: Quunabu (ancient Assyrian)
Jamaica: Canac, ganja
Mexico: Mariguana
Panama: Canyack
Russia: Kendir konoplevy

GROWTH HABITS
Annual
Origin: Central Asia
Range: Naturalized everywhere, much to the dismay of law-enforcement officials.

CULINARY USES

Everyone knows about the hashish-laced brownies of Alice B. Toklas. Cannabis does have some history as a foodstuff, besides that cultural icon. In Laos, for instance, it is used as a seasoning in soups and as a garnish. In Morocco, kif candy, or *majoun,* is made from hashish. It is a thick paste made of cannabis and dried fruits such as dates, figs, and raisins, seasoned with aniseed, cinnamon, ginger, honey, and ground nuts such as almonds or walnuts. It may also be perfumed with *zhaar* (see under BITTER ORANGE) and *ras el hanout*. Honey and hashish are combined in much the same way in Algeria, where the mixture is known as *madjound*.

Marijuana has been used in place of hops in beers known as Hi-Brew.

Mapouchari is a paste made with butter and marijuana in Egypt. *Mimea* or *momea* was a similar paste rumored to have been made in Tibet, allegedly with human fat.

In Japan, the seeds, known as *asanomi,* are used in vegetarian "burgers" made of bean curd, called *ganmo*. The seeds were also used, fried, as a dessert in ancient Scythia. They are parched and eaten in eastern Europe, especially Poland and Russia, where they are also pressed to yield cooking oil.

COMMENTS

It is not a good idea to plant this in your herb garden, for culinary or other experimentation (see Comments, under POPPY). However, there is substantial interest in the development of drug-free varieties of marijuana, usually referred to as "hemp." The seed has been used as a foodstuff, but the usefulness of the fiber is the primary economic incentive.

25. Cappardaceae (formerly Capparaceae): The Caper Family

Capers: *Capparis spinosa*

OTHER COMMON, ETHNIC, OR SCIENTIFIC NAMES
Caper bush
Denmark: Kapers
Estonia: Kappar
Finland: Kapris
France: Câpre, câprier épineux, tápana
Germany: Kaper
Greece: Káppari
Iceland: Kapers
India: Kabar, kokilakshmu, mullukattari
Iraq: Kubar
Italy: Cappero
Netherlands: Kappertjes
Norway: Kapers
Poland: Kaparki
Portugal: Alcaparra

Russia: Kapersy
Spain: Alcaparra, alcaparrón, caparra, tàpera
Swahili: Mchezo, mruko
Sweden: Kapris
Turkey: Gebere, kaper

GROWTH HABITS
Shrub
Origin: Mediterranean Region
Range: Can be grown as an annual (not winter hardy)

CULINARY USES
Buds are used as garnishes and as a flavoring for soups, vinaigrettes, and sauces, especially with tomatoes and olives. They appear in sauces for cold poached fish or cold roasted meats. Their tart, sour flavor is especially suited for stuffings, as it tempers the overly rich tendencies of fat meats, which makes it a logical inclusion on platters of antipasto.

Any dish labeled *à la Grenobloise* is sauced with a mixture of anchovies, capers, and lemon juice. *Remoulade* is a tartar-sauce-like mixture of mayonnaise and minced capers.

Buds are commonly found pickled in brine or packed in salt. The tiniest buds are marketed as *nonpareil*. These are supposed to be the best quality, but the larger (and less expensive) capers, especially those from Spain, often have more—and better—flavor. The larger, more open buds do absorb more brine, however, so give them a little squeeze before using and/or adjust the amount of salt used in the recipe.

In Slovakia, Liptovká Bryndza is a soft cheese that is often flavored with capers.

Caponata is a cooked Sicilian appetizer composed of eggplant, tomatoes, onions, and celery; it is flavored with capers, olives, and vinegar. In Finland, a sort of "Salisbury steak" called *lindströmin pihvi* is seasoned with pickled beets and capers. Capers are used in sauces for lamb in England, for veal in Italy, and for skate in France.

Capers get their unique bitter pungency from rutin and methyl isothiocyanate.

26. Caprifoliaceae: The Honeysuckle Family

European Elderberry: *Sambucus nigra*

OTHER COMMON, ETHNIC, OR SCIENTIFIC NAMES
Black elder, bore tree, bour tree, common elder, eldrum, ellhorn, European alder, hylantree, hylder, pipe tree

Arabic: Balasan
Bulgaria: Bez
Denmark: Hyld
France: Sureau
Germany: Hollunder
Greece: Sampoukou
Italy: Sambuco, zammucu
Japan: Niwatoko no mi
Mexico: Canilolerro; sauco (blossoms)
Norway: Svarthyll
Poland: Bez czarny
Russia: Buzina chornaya
Spain: Saco

RELATED SPECIES
Sambucus canadensis: American elder, black-berried elder, common elder, sweet elder
Sambucus cerulea: Blue elder
Sambucus mexicana: Mexican elder
Sambucus pubens: Red-fruited elder

CULTIVARS
'Albo-variegata', 'Argentea', 'Aurea', 'Aurea-variegata', 'Laciata', 'Variegata'

GROWTH HABITS
Deciduous shrub
Origin: North America
Range: Europe, North America, northern Africa, western Asia

CULINARY USES
The berries are, of course, used to make wine. The drink is actually fairly decent, with good red color and lots of tannin. It tastes a bit like Chianti, though it does have a slight mustiness that is unavoidable whenever you use elderberries. Elderberries were at one time known as "the English grape." The berries are used in the Italian liqueur Sambuca. An English Cheddar called Windsor Red is flavored, not with port, but with elderberry wine. The flowers, known as "blow," are also used to make wine, and they have been used in infused vinegars.

A pleasant country dessert is made by dipping the entire flower-head in batter and deep-frying to make a lacy, *crispelle*-like fritter. It is usually sprinkled with powdered sugar, and sometimes with orange juice, as well. In Italy the same dish, known there as *fritelle di fiori di Sambuca,* is made with a little grappa added to the batter. In the United States, a simpler dish is sometimes made by adding separated flowers to crêpe batter.

European Elderberry
Sambucus nigra

From Woodville, *Medical botany,* vol. 2

The sweetened juice of elderberries can be made into jellies, especially if given a little tannic "edge" with staghorn sumac (see Comments, under STAGHORN SUMAC) or lemon balm.

Sambucus nigra and *Sambucus canadensis* berries contain β-carotene, plus several fruit acids and sugars, quercitin, rutin, and tannin. Elderberry blossoms contain campherol, *p*-coumaric acid, rutin (up to 49,000 ppm), sambunigrin, and tannins.

OTHER USES

The stems have been made into spiles for tapping maple trees for their sap. The hardwood stalks have a large core of soft pith that is easily removed, and all of the bark and cambium is scraped off. The stalks have a relatively uniform diameter, making it a simple matter to drill holes of the correct size into the maple trees' trunks without constantly changing the bit.

Several parts of the plant have been used to produce vegetable dyestuffs. The berries were once used to adulterate wines, especially Port. Portugal banned the cultivation of elderberries in the eighteenth century, in an effort to protect the reputation of its wine industry.

COMMENTS

Red-fruited elder, *Sambucus pubens,* is poisonous. Even the edible species are not entirely benign; roots, stems, and unripe fruit should be avoided. The FDA restricts the use of elderberries to alcoholic beverages.

Some enzymes act on *Sambucus* berries, liberating prussic acid, a deadly poison. While this substance is eliminated by commercial processors, their safety measures are not readily available in the home.

Honeysuckle: *Lonicera* spp.

OTHER COMMON, ETHNIC, OR SCIENTIFIC NAMES
Germany: Geißblatt

RELATED SPECIES
Lonicera angustifolia: Narrow-leaved honeysuckle
Lonicera caprifolia: Common honeysuckle
Lonicera japonica: Japanese honeysuckle
Lonicera sempervirens: Trumpet honeysuckle

GROWTH HABITS
Vinous deciduous shrub
Origin: Northern Hemisphere
Range: Widespread

Honeysuckle
Lonicera caprifolia

From Jaume Saint-Hilaire,
Traité des arbrisseaux

Flowers (sucked by kids everywhere), fruit, and leaves of many of these species are edible, with the exceptions noted below. Flowers and fruits are used in jams and jellies. They are also used in some homemade soft drinks.

The berries of *Lonicera angustifolia* are eaten in northern India.

OTHER USES

Popular, sweet-scented ornamental

COMMENTS

The seeds of *Lonicera* species are poisonous and must be removed; this goes for berries and leaves of species such as the common red-flowered *Lonicera sempervirens.*

27. Caryophyllaceae: The Pink Family

Algerian Tea: *Paronychia argentea*

OTHER COMMON, ETHNIC, OR SCIENTIFIC NAMES

Chickweed, nailwort, whitlowort
Mexico: Alsine, hierba pajarera, pamplina

RELATED SPECIES

Paronychia capitata: Algerian tea

GROWTH HABITS

Evergreen perennial
Origin: Mediterranean region
Range: Cool, temperate regions

CULINARY USES

While annoying to gardeners, the plant is put to good use by Italian cooks as a salad green and as a potherb in thick soups.

COMMENTS

"Chickweed" is a name given to an unrelated but common and pernicious weed, *Stellaria media.*

Carnation: *Dianthus caryophyllus*

OTHER COMMON, ETHNIC, OR SCIENTIFIC NAMES

Clove gilliflower, clove pink, divine flower, pink, sops in wine, soupy wine

Germany: Fleischefarbe, Nelke
Mexico: Clavel

GROWTH HABITS
Perennial
Origin: Mediterranean Region
Range: Temperate regions

CULINARY USES
The edible, clove-scented flowers can be used in salads, in sandwiches, and as a flavoring for sugar, jams, vinegars, cordials, and wines. Make sure to remove the bitter white parts before using the flowers. Carnation petals are sometimes crystallized in sugar, for use as a sweet garnish.

Not surprisingly, carnation blossoms contain eugenol. They also contain benzyl benzoate, methyl salicilate, and phenyl ethyl alcohol.

OTHER USES
Perfumes, potpourri

28. Celastraceae: The Staff-Tree Family

Khat: *Catha edulis*

OTHER COMMON, ETHNIC, OR SCIENTIFIC NAMES
Abbysinian tea, Arabian tea, cafta, kat, qat, Somali tea

GROWTH HABITS
Small evergreen tree
Origin: Ethiopia
Range: Cultivated in Ethiopia, Somalia, Yemen, and Zambia

CULINARY USES
Khat has been used as a tea. The Ethiopian mead called *tej* is sometimes flavored with leaves of khat.

OTHER USES
Khat is best known as a popular stimulant used by Muslims in East Africa. During the hostilities in Somalia in the 1990s and after, the Western press made much of the fact that the Somalis were "on" the drug khat. The implication was that they were crazed and dangerous, as if khat were some kind of Islamic PCP. In fact, for most users of khat, the normal "dose" is roughly equivalent to a couple of cups of coffee (see GUARANÁ).

29. Chenopodiaceae:
The Goosefoot or Pigweed family

Epazote: *Chenopodium ambrosioides*

OTHER COMMON, ETHNIC, OR SCIENTIFIC NAMES

American wormseed, hedge mustard, hierba sancti mariae, Jerusalem oak, Jerusalem parsley, Jesuit's tea, Mexican tea, sweet pigweed, West Indian goosefoot, wormseed. Epazote has been known scientifically as *Chenopodium anthelminticum, Artemisia cina,* and *Teloxys ambrosiodes.*

Colombia: Cenizo
Estonia: Ürt-hanemalts
Finland: Saitruunasavikka
Germany: Jesuitentee, Karthäusertee, Méxicanisches Teekraut, Méxicanischer Traubentee, Wohlriechender Gänsefuß
India: Kadavoma, katuayamodakam
Italy: Allemand
Mexico: Ambrosia, apazote, epazote de comer, teloxya, yerba de Santa Maria
Netherlands: Amerikaans wormzaad, welriekende ganzenvoet, wormkruid
Norway: Sitronmelde
Panama: Paico
Poland: Komosa pizmowa
Portugal: Mastruz
Russia: Mar
Spain: Yerba de Santa Maria
Sweden: Citronmålla

RELATED SPECIES

Atriplex hortensis: Arroche, crimson plume, garden orach, mountain spinach, orache, red orach. Use as a garnish. Cultivars include 'Atrosanguinea', 'Cupreatorosea', 'Rosea', and 'Rubra' (may be the same species as *Atriplex angostipolia*).
Basella rubra: Ceylon spinach, Malabar nightshade, vine spinach
Chenopodium album: Quenòpode (Spain); seviche (Italy); vlíta (Greece); chenopodio, farinello bianco (Italy); quelite cenizo, quelites (Mexico); vromóchorto (Greece); bledes, fat hen, lamb's quarters, pigweed, white goosefoot, wild beets, wild spinach
Chenopodium berlandieri: Hojas de huazontle, huazontle, huauzontle, quelite cenizo, quelites (Mexico); lamb's quarters

Chenopodium bonus-henricus: Fette Henne (Germany); allgood, English mercury, Good King Henry, mercury, allgood, fat hen, goosefoot, mercury goosefoot, smearwort, tola bona, wild spinach

Chenopodium botrys: Ambrosia

Chenopodium graveolens (also listed as *Chenopodium foetidum*): Epazote de zorillo, wormseed

Chenopodium murale: Australian spinach

Chenopodium nuttaliae: Huazóntle (Mexico); lamb's quarters

Chenopodium quinoa: Quinua (Colombia); petty rice, quinoa

Salicornia europea: Almyrídes (Greece); salicorn (Spain); salicornia (Italy); chicken claws, glasswort, marsh samphire, pigeon foot

Suaeda torreyana: Romerito (Mexico)

GROWTH HABITS
Annual
Origin: Tropical Americas
Range: Cosmopolitan weed

CULINARY USES
Epazote is used in the southwestern United States and Mexico, dried and fresh, especially with beans. In Mexican markets, three forms are recognized: *el blanco, el epazote verde,* and *el morado.* The last named—the most aromatic—is preferred.

Freshwater snails, called *jutes,* are seasoned with epazote in Central America. Flower spikes can be steamed. Epazote was used as a tea in eighteenth-century Germany. Lamb's quarters and Good King Henry are eaten as cooked greens, used as stuffings, tossed in salads, and sometimes added to soups.

Glasswort, *Salicornia europea,* has been used like samphire, *Crithmum maritimum* (q.v.). It has a crunchy, salty taste that makes it useful as a snack or in salads. The French lump glasswort and samphire together with *Salsola kali* as *les salicornes.*

During Lent, in Mexico, the rosemary-like leaves of *Suaeda torreyana* are combined with dried chiles to flavor the broth for dumplings made of egg and dried shrimp, *tortas de camaron.* The tender shoots of *Chenopodium berlandieri* are sautéed with garlic and onions in Mexico, or deep-fried.

Chenopodium quinoa is the source of the Andean grain *quinoa* (small, round, brownish starch with a pleasant, slightly bitter, nutty flavor).

Epazote has a flavor that has been uncharitably likened to that of kerosene. No matter how described, that flavor results from the combination of α-pinene, d-camphor, cineole, *p*-cymene, l-limonene, and myrcene.

OTHER USES
Epazote is said to reduce the gas-producing qualities of beans. This flatulence is the result of fermentation of complex (indigestible) sugars in the

large intestine. It has been suggested that essential oils in a number of herbs and spices alter the chemical environment of the lower intestine, thereby inhibiting the fermentation of those polysaccharides. This hypothesis remains to be proved. However, science has developed two strategies to conquer the problem of this type of inflation. First, genetically redesign the bean to eliminate the complex sugars. That's the complicated method. A simpler technique is to precede the consumption of bean dishes with appropriate enzymes to break down the complex sugars in the upper part of the digestive system. It is the same approach used by lactose-intolerant people when they want to drink milk or eat cheese.

Virtually every culture that consumes large amounts of vegetables, especially gassy ones like beans or members of the cabbage family, has offered folk remedies for the age-old problem. The solutions range from varying cooking techniques (such as cooking in several changes of water, which serves only to reduce the quantity of water-soluble vitamins and minerals), to adding herbs and spices (it is interesting to note that the seasonings chosen are invariably the culture's favorites), to performing more arcane and mystical rituals. These approaches reveal an utterly charming optimism and trust in unverified anecdotal evidence. Until modern science masters this

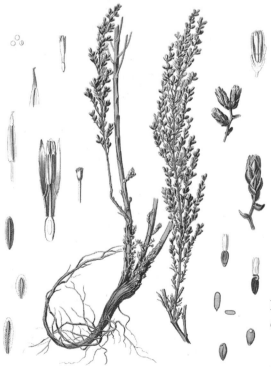

Epazote
Chenopodium ambrosioides

From Köhler, *Köhler's Medizinal-Pflanzen*, vol. 1

mephitic monster, it is best to follow the advice of Benjamin Franklin: "Fart Proudly."

Epazote is sometimes cultivated as a source of a medicinal oil, but most culinary epazote is harvested from wild plants (weeds). Epazote looks like lamb's quarters, but the edges of the leaves are toothed, not wavy.

COMMENTS

Epazote is a weed almost everywhere, although seeds are available from a number of commercial sources.

Caldo de huevo para la goma is a Guatemalan soup that is said to be an effective cure for a hangover. In addition to fresh epazote, it contains chiles, scallions, tomatoes, and poached eggs—not a thing I would care to experience first thing on the morning after. On the other hand, a good Bloody Mary has some of these ingredients, and that drink has been prescribed for this self-inflicted malady, so *¿quien sabe?*

According to one source, epazote is poisonous if consumed to excess. What defines "excess" is unclear. It has been used constantly in Tex-Mex cooking without reports of poisoning, so use your own judgment.

"Jesuit's tea" is also used as a name for maté, *Ilex paraguariensis,* and *Psoralea glandulosa* (see Comment, under MATÉ).

Quelite is also used as a name for *Amaranthus cruentes* (q.v.) and many other greens. Marsh samphire is not related to samphire (q.v.).

30. Cistaceae: The Rock Rose Family

Cistus: *Cistus incanus*

OTHER COMMON, ETHNIC, OR SCIENTIFIC NAMES
Pink rock rose, rockrose. The scientific name is sometimes listed as *Cistus creticus.*
Germany: Zistrose
Turkey: Girit ladeni

RELATED SPECIES
Cistus ladanifer (also known as *Cistus ladaniferus*): Labdano (Spain and
Italy); labdanum, ladanum (France and Germany); laudanum
Cistus villosus (formerly listed as *Cistus mas*): Shaggy rock rose

GROWTH HABITS
Evergreen shrub
Origin: Mediterranean region
Range: California and southern states

Used as a commercial flavoring for baked goods, candies, and soft drinks. *Cistus villosus* is brewed as herbal tea in Greece.

Cistus has an aromatic, balsamic, somewhat medicinal flavor and scent, somewhat musky. It contains terpenes, benzaldehyde, acetophenone, acetic acid, and eugenol.

OTHER USES

Cistus oil, with a scent that is reminiscent of chamomile, is used in perfumes.

COMMENTS

Laudanum, *Cistus ladanifer,* is not the same laudanum created by Paracelsus—and beloved by Thomas De Quincey. *That* laudanum was a mixture of gold, pearls, and opium, ground together and infused in alcohol. Since neither gold nor pearls are soluble in alcohol (unless the alcohol of choice is wine, which might have enough acid to react with the calcium carbonate of the pearls), the essential ingredient was obviously the opium.

31. Convolulaceae: The Morning Glory Family

Water Spinach: *Ipomoae aquatica*

OTHER COMMON, ETHNIC, OR SCIENTIFIC NAMES
Swamp cabbage
Philippines: Kang kong

RELATED SPECIES
Ipomoae Batatas: Sweet potato, sweet potato vine, yam

GROWTH HABITS
Annual or perennial
Origin: China and Southeast Asia
Range: China and Southeast Asia

CULINARY USES

In Vietnam, water spinach appears in soups, as a potherb. In China it is chopped and stir-fried, with a garlicky sauce containing a fermented element, either aged beancurd or shrimp paste. In the Philippines, it is usually accompanied by a pungently spicy sauce.

COMMENTS

True yams are members of the Dioscoreaceae family.

32. Crassulaceae: The Orpine Family

Hens and Chickens: *Sempervivum tectorum*

OTHER COMMON, ETHNIC, OR SCIENTIFIC NAMES
Common house leek, house leek, live forever, old man and woman, roof house leek. This species has also been known as *Sempervivum atropurpureum, Sempervivum atroviolaceum, Sempervivum cantalicum, Sempervivum juratense, Sempervivum LaHarpei, Sempervivum Lamottei, Sempervivum lesurinum, Sempervivum longobardum, Sempervivum Mettenianum, Sempervivum pallidum, Sempervivum Potsii, Sempervivum pyrenaicum, Sempervivum rhodanicum, Sempervivum royanum, Sempervivum robustum, Sempervivum rubrum, Sempervivum rupestre, Sempervivum speciosum, Sempervivum triste,* and *Sempervivum violescens.*
Netherlands: Donderbaard

CULTIVARS
'Atroviolaceum', 'Bicolor', 'Majus', 'Robustum', 'Rubrum', 'Violaceum'

GROWTH HABITS
Perennial
Origin: Europe
Range: Temperate regions

CULINARY USES
Succulent leaves are sometimes added to salads.

OTHER USES
Popular plant for small gardens

COMMENTS
This species is extremely variable, hence the long list of species names above.

Stonecrop: *Sedum acre*

OTHER COMMON, ETHNIC, OR SCIENTIFIC NAMES
Golden carpet, goldmoss, goldmoss stonecrop

GROWTH HABITS
Perennial
Origin: Mediterranean region
Range: Temperate regions

Stonecrop
Sedum acre

From Woodville,
*A supplement to
Medical botany,* vol. 4

CULINARY USES

The dried leaves can be used sparingly as a spice. They have a pungent, ginger-like taste.

COMMENTS

If used to excess, the leaves can be slightly toxic, acting as an emetic and as a laxative.

33. Cupressaceae: The Cypress Family

Juniper Berry: *Juniperus communis*

OTHER COMMON, ETHNIC, OR SCIENTIFIC NAMES

Common juniper
Estonia: Harilik kadakas
Finland: Kataja, kotikataja
Finland: Katajanmarja
France: Genièvre
Gaelic: Ailtinn
Germany: Kranawitt, Machandel, Wacholder
Greece: Árkevthos
Hungary: Boróka
Iceland: Einiber

Italy: Ginepro
Mexico: Enebro
Netherlands: Jeneverbes
Norway: Einer
Poland: Jalowiec pospolity
Russia: Mozhzhevelnik
Spain: Cedro, enebro, ginebró, junípero, nebrina
Swahili: Mreteni
Sweden: Enbär

RELATED SPECIES

Juniperus californica: California juniper

Juniperus lycia: Copal, incienso de iglesia (Mexico); frankincense, olibanum gum

Juniperus osteospermata (sometimes listed as *Juniperus utahensis*): Utah juniper

Juniperus Sabina: Savin, known in the flavorings industry as *Summatates sabinae,* contains citronellol, diacetyl, furfural, sabinol, and dihydrocumina alcohol.

Juniperus scopulorum: Rocky Mountain juniper

The genus contains many species, though only the above are used as food products. Other species include eastern red cedar, *Juniperus virginiana,* a source of cedar oil and wood for lining closets. The scent repels insects, especially clothes moths.

GROWTH HABITS

Small tree or shrub

Origin: North America and Eurasia

Range: Temperate regions

CULINARY USES

Dried berries are used in pâtés, marinades, and stuffings for pork and venison. They are also good with ham, sauces, and sauerkraut. The berries should be crushed lightly—just enough to break the skin—allowing their flavor to infuse cooking liquids. A conserve of juniper berries is a classic garnish for cold meats, especially German smoked meats. In at least one case, the berries are used not as a garnish, but as part of the cure; juniper ham (*Wacholder Schinken*) is a delicately flavored German ham that is cured and cooked before being lightly smoked.

The berries are the key flavoring ingredient in gin. Most gins are merely grain alcohol that has been flavored with juniper and other herbs and spices. Wachholder Kornbrannt, for instance, is a gin-like corn-based liquor that is only flavored by juniper. Steinhaeger, on the other hand, is a German gin that is actually made from fermented juniper berries. It is sometimes enhanced with an infusion of more juniper berries, after the brew is distilled.

Juniper Berry
Juniperus communis

From Jaume Saint-Hilaire,
Traité des arbres forestiers

Juniper's presence is less obvious in Pernod, but it is there. Juniper oil is included in the recipe for Chartreuse. Okhotnichya, the Russian "hunter's brandy"—an alcoholic beverage enhanced by juniper berries and a number of other warming spices—is designed to function as antifreeze for a polar populace (see glossary). The Finnish tapio, made with juniper berries and various herbs, serves a similar sympathetic purpose.

The berries are also used to flavor beer in Finland and Sweden. A French beer, Genevrette, is made with fermented juniper berries. Before 1516, when German laws banned several other additives as well, some German beers contained juniper berries.

In Norway, juniper berries lend their sweetly resinous scent and bitter taste to a Norwegian blue cheese called Gammelost.

Roasted berries have been used as a coffee substitute.

Juniper berries get their slightly bitter, peculiarly aromatic spiciness from α- and β-pinene (80 percent), α-terpineol (5 percent), and dozens of other mono- and sesquiterpenes. The best-quality berries come from Italy.

COMMENTS

Make sure that you use *Juniperus* species; yews, *Taxus* spp., are poisonous (compare illustrations here and on page 163).

Yew
Taxus brevifolia

From Jaume Saint-Hilaire,
Traité des arbres forestiers

34. Cyperaceae: The Sedge Family

Earth Almond: *Cyperus esculentus*

OTHER COMMON, ETHNIC, OR SCIENTIFIC NAMES
Chufa, flatsedge, nut sedge, nut grass, tiger nut, yellow nut grass, yellow nut sedge, Zulu nut
Mexico: Peonia
Morocco: Tara soudania

CULTIVAR
'Sativus': Chufa, earth almond, rush nut, tiger nut, Zulu nut

RELATED SPECIES
Cyperus longus: Galingale (see Comment, below)
Cyperus papyrus: Papyrus

GROWTH HABITS
Perennial

Origin: Western Asia and Africa
Range: Wild along riverbanks in southeastern United States

CULINARY USES

Said to have a perfume-like scent and chestnut taste, earth almonds were eaten in Egypt as early as 2400 BCE. They are included in some recipes for *ras el hanout,* the Moroccan spice blend.

Horchata is a Moroccan nonalcoholic drink flavored with earth almonds. *Horchata de chufas* is a similar Spanish drink, flavored with cinnamon, sugar, and vanilla. Atadwe milk is a popular sweetened drink made from flour, earth almonds, and water in Ghana. In Hungary, the tubers are dried, roasted, and ground for use as a substitute for coffee. In Turkey, sweet conserves are made from earth almonds.

COMMENTS

The plant easily becomes a weedy pest in the cultivated soil of a garden. The galingale listed above is not the familiar East Asian spice galingal (q.v.)

Earth Almond
Cyperus esculentus

From Host, *Icones et descriptiones,* vol. 3

35. Ericaceae: The Heath Family

Heather: *Calluna vulgaris*

OTHER COMMON, ETHNIC, OR SCIENTIFIC NAMES
Ling, Scots heather. Also known botanically as *Erica vulgaris*.

CULTIVARS
This is the only species within this genus, but there are a great many cultivars. *Hortus Third* lists thirty-six, broken down into a much larger number of varieties. Bremness says "there are more than a thousand cultivars."

GROWTH HABITS
Perennial
Origin: Europe and Asia Minor
Range: Escapee in North America

CULINARY USES
Heathers have been used in herbal teas. They have also added an astringent quality to beers.

Labrador Tea: *Ledum groenlandicum*

OTHER COMMON, ETHNIC, OR SCIENTIFIC NAMES
Continental tea, James tea, marsh tea, wild rosemary. Sometimes listed as *Ledum latifolium*.

RELATED SPECIES
Ledum glandulosum: Labrador tea

GROWTH HABITS
Evergreen shrub
Origin: Northern North America, Greenland
Range: Canada

CULINARY USES
Used as tea (see Comments, below).

COMMENTS
Labrador tea is said to be poisonous. It is recommended that the leaves should only be infused, not boiled, when brewing the tea. This reduces the chances of releasing possibly harmful alkaloids.

Labrador Tea
Ledum groenlandicum

From Meerburgh,
Plantarum selectarum

"Wild rosemary" is also used as a name for *Croton cascarilla* (q.v.) and *Ledum palustre* (q.v.).

Pipsissewa: *Chimaphila umbellata*

OTHER COMMON, ETHNIC, OR SCIENTIFIC NAMES
Bitter wintergreen, prince's pine
France: Herbe à pisser
Italy: Chimafila
Spain: Quimafila

RELATED SPECIES
Chimphia maculata: Spotted wintergreen

GROWTH HABITS
Evergreen subshrub
Origin: Western North America
Range: Europe and North America

CULINARY USES
Aromatic and tonic extracts from the leaves of pipsissewa are used in candies and soft drinks, such as root beer.

The Tepehuano Indians of northwestern Mexico brew *navaitai,* an alcoholic beverage made with corn and flavored with pipsissewa.

Spotted wintergreen, *Chimphia maculata,* is used in Mexico to make a fermented corn beverage called *tesguino.*

Wild Rosemary: *Ledum palustre*

OTHER COMMON, ETHNIC, OR SCIENTIFIC NAMES
Crystal tea
Germany: Porst, Sumpfporst

GROWTH HABITS
Evergreen shrub
Origin: Northern Eurasia
Range: Northern Eurasia

CULINARY USES
Germans and other northern Europeans used to add wild rosemary to beer to supply bitterness and increase its potency.

Wild rosemary contains a number of alkaloids and essential oils. The primary flavoring ingredients are myrcene, oxalic acid, quercetin, and tannins.

COMMENTS
Wild rosemary is an intoxicant that can, in large doses, cause gastric illnesses and miscarriage. Unlike melegueta pepper (q.v.), which only increased the apparent strength of the German brew by adding a hot taste, wild rosemary made a real difference. This so-called *Grutbier* has been linked to the savage fearlessness of the berserkers, much as marijuana is associated with the *hashshashin,* or assassins, who supposedly acquired their name and their courage from eating hashish.

"Wild rosemary" is also used as a name for *Croton cascarilla* (q.v.) and *Ledum groenlandicum* (q.v.).

Wintergreen: *Gaultheria humifusa*

OTHER COMMON, ETHNIC, OR SCIENTIFIC NAMES
Alpine wintergreen, creeping wintergreen
France: Gaultherie
Germany: Wintergrün
Italy: Gaulteria
Spain: Gaulteria

RELATED SPECIES
Gaultheria adenothrix: Aka-mono

Gaultheria ovatifolia: Salal

Gaultheria procumbens: Axocopaque, gaulteria (Mexico); thé du Canada (France); boxberry, checkerberry, chickenberry, chickerberry, deerberry, drunkard, ground holly, ground tea, grouseberry, hillberry, wintergreen teaberry, mountain tea, ivry-leaves

Gaultheria shallon: Salal, western wintergreen

GROWTH HABITS

Evergreen perennial

Origin: Rocky Mountains and east

Range: Cool, temperate regions; common wild plant in rich woods

CULINARY USES

Leaves are used in candies, chewing gums, preserves, soft drinks, and teas. Berries are also used for herbal teas and to make spicy jams, jellies, and baked desserts.

Root beer used to be flavored with the barks of sarsaparilla, sassafras, and wintergreen. *Gaultheria procumbens* is our wild wintergreen. It used to be a

Wintergreen
Gaultheria procumbens

From Köhler, *Köhler's Medizinal-Pflanzen,* vol. 3

source of oil of wintergreen, although *Gaultheria shallon* has the best wintergreen flavor. Both can be used to make a mild tea. Today, most root beer is made with synthetic methyl salicylate (which is exactly the same compound found in wild wintergreen) and anethole (either synthetic or derived from star anise), lemon oil, citral, ginger oil, oleoresin, something called oil of northern birch, and, finally, yucca sap.

OTHER USES

Wintergreen has been used by the perfume industry.

Oil of wintergreen, a valuable industrial flavoring, now produced synthetically or derived from cherry birch (also known as sweet birch, black birch, mountain mahogany), *Betula lenta*. If you like the flavor of wintergreen, you can tap these trees in the spring. The fragrant sap, combined with sufficient sugar and added yeast, ferments into birch wine or beer.

COMMENTS

Oil of wintergreen is toxic, so it is used in very small amounts as a commercial flavoring. It is employed in painkilling medications that are applied externally.

Boxberry is another name for partridgeberry, *Mitchella repens*.

36. Euphorbiaceae: The Spurge Family

Candlenut: *Aleurites moluccana*

OTHER COMMON, ETHNIC, OR SCIENTIFIC NAMES

Candlenut tree, candleberry tree, country walnut, Indian walnut, kukui, macadamia nut, otaheite walnut. Also known as *Macadamia ternifolia*.

Indonesia: Buah keras, kemiri

Spain: Nuez de India

RELATED SPECIES

Aleurites Fordii: China wood oil tree, tung oil tree

GROWTH HABITS

Tropical tree

Origin: Southeast Asia

Range: Cultivated commercially in China and in the Philippines

CULINARY USES

Inimona is a chile paste made with candlenuts in Hawaii. The ground nuts are used to thicken curries in Indonesia and Malaysia.

Aleurites Fordii is the source of tung oil, used in finishing hardwoods for items such as fine cabinetry and gun stocks.

COMMENTS

The roasted nuts are popular in Hawaii but eaten only in small quantities; people there are quite familiar with the laxative properties of the nuts if eaten to excess.

Cascarilla: *Croton eluteria*

OTHER COMMON, ETHNIC, OR SCIENTIFIC NAMES

Aromatic quinquina, Bahama cascarilla, eluthuria, false quinquina, sweet-wood bark. An outdated scientific name is *Clutia Elutaria.*
France: Cascarille
Germany: Kaskarillbaum

RELATED SPECIES

Croton alamosanus: Copalquin, ocotillo (Mexico); croton
Croton Cascarilla: Palo sarito (Mexico); wild rosemary—a bitter West
    Indian herb
Croton corymbulosus: Chaparral tea, encinilla, hierba loca
Croton incanus: Salvia real (Mexico); fragrant croton
Croton leocophyllus: Salvia de Castilla (Mexico); croton
Croton Malambo: Malambo bark, matias bark, winter's bark
Croton monanthogynus: Hierba del gato (Mexico); croton
Croton niveus: Copalchi (Mexico); croton
Croton reflexifolius: Copalchí, hoja amarga, sasafrás (Mexico); croton
Croton tiglium: Purging croton

GROWTH HABITS

Shrub
Origin: Caribbean and northern South America
Range: Tropics and subtropical regions

CULINARY USES

Bitter, warm, spicy (a bit like cinnamon, cloves, eucalyptus, and nutmeg), and slightly aromatic, cascarilla bark contains cascarillin, cymol, and eugenol. The extracted flavor (cascarilla oil) is used in amaretto, baked goods, candy, and ice cream.

Chaparral tea has been used as a tea or coffee substitute. Copalchí is used as a flavoring for rum in Central America.

COMMENTS

"Cascarilla" is used as a name for quina morada, *Pogonopus febrifugus,* a tree of the Rubiaceae family, the bark of which is used as a chinchona substitute in Argentina.

"Wild rosemary" is also a name for *Ledum palustre* (q.v.).

"Winter's bark" is more commonly used as the name for *Drimys winteri* (q.v.), a member of the Magnoliaceae family.

There is some confusion between this genus and the *Croton* of florists, which is actually a variegated laurel, *Codiaeum variegata.* The *Croton elutaria* listed above is not mentioned in *Hortus Third* and may in fact be a cultivar of *Codiaeum variegata.*

Chaya: *Cnidoscolus chayamansa*

OTHER COMMON, ETHNIC, OR SCIENTIFIC NAMES
Also known as *Jatropha urens* var. *inermis.*
Mexico: Chayacol, chayamansa, keki-chay

GROWTH HABITS
Perennial
Origin: Yucatan
Range: Mexico to Brazil

CULINARY USES
Used in traditional Mayan cookery, as well as in modern Mexican *aguas frescas, pipians,* and *tamales.*

37. Gentianaceae (formerly Menyanthanaceae): The Gentian Family

---

Buckbean: *Menyanthes trifoliata*

OTHER COMMON, ETHNIC, OR SCIENTIFIC NAMES
Bogbean, marsh trefoil
France: Ményanthe, trefle d'eau, trefle des marais
Germany: Bitterklee, Bocksbohne, Fieberklee, Scharbocks Klee, Sumpfklee
Netherlands: Bocks, boonan

Italy: Trifoglio fibrino
Spain: Trebol fibrino

GROWTH HABITS
Perennial
Origin: North America, Europe, and Asia
Range: Subarctic

CULINARY USES
The bitter, aromatic leaves of buckbeans are included in the recipes for altvater and Campari and have been used, in place of hops, in herbal beers. While most of the herbal substitutes for hops mentioned in this book are historical, buckbeans are still in commercial use in Sweden.

The dried leaves have been used as an herbal tea. The dried roots have been ground for use as flour by some Inuits in Canada.

Buckbean leaves contain only traces of the chemicals usually found in essential oils, but they derive their bitter astringency from small amount of rutin and plenty of tannin (up to 30,000 ppm).

COMMENTS
Trefoil is also a name for *Cryptotaenia japonica* and clover (q.v.).
The FDA restricts the use of buckbeans to alcoholic beverages.

Calumba: *Frasera carolinensis*

OTHER COMMON, ETHNIC, OR SCIENTIFIC NAMES
American calumba, faux colombo, green gentian. It has been known scientifically as *Cocculus Palmatus, Frasera Canadensis, Frasera Walteri,* and *Jateorhiza palmata.*
France: Colombo
Germany: Kolombo
Italy: Colombo

GROWTH HABITS
Shrubby perennial
Origin: East Africa
Range: Cultivated in East Indies

CULINARY USES
The original calumba root, *Jateorrhiza Columba,* from Mozambique, is used interchangeably with this American species. Columba is an ingredient in Fernet Branca. Its bitter, aromatic (somewhat medicinal) taste is an effect of columbannine, columbic acid, columbin, jateorrhizine, and palmatine.

The FDA restricts the use of calumba to alcoholic beverages.

This species is sometimes listed as a member of the Menispermaceae family.

Centaury: *Centaurium Erythraea*

OTHER COMMON, ETHNIC, OR SCIENTIFIC NAMES

Bitter bloom, bitter clover, common centaury, centaury gentian, century herb, red centaury, rose pink, Christ's ladder, feverwort, Russian centaury. Centaury used to be known botanically as *Centaurium erytraea* and *Sabbatia angularis.*

France: Petit centaurée
Gaelic: Ceud bhileach, teantguidh
Germany: Tausenguldenkraut
Italy: Centaurea minore
Scotland: Feverfoullie, gentian
Spain: Centauri menor

RELATED SPECIES

Centaurium umbellatum: Minor centaury

GROWTH HABITS

Biennial
Origin: Eurasia
Range: Temperate regions

CULINARY USES

Centaury is said to be one of the bitter ingredients in amaretto and Fernet Branca.

Its bitter, tonic, quality comes from erytaurin, erythrocentaurin, gentiopicrin, oleanoic acid, and valeric acid.

COMMENTS

The FDA restricts the use of centaury to alcoholic beverages.

Chiretta Root: *Swertia chirata*

OTHER COMMON, ETHNIC, OR SCIENTIFIC NAMES

Chirata, Indian balmony, Indian gentian
France: Chirette indien
Germany: Indische Chiretta

Annual
Origin: Northern India, Himalayas
Range: Cultivated in South Africa

CULINARY USES

Chiretta is extremely bitter. The only culinary use I have encountered was its inclusion in some recipes for bitters, herbal liqueurs, and vermouth, and even the references to this use were vague.

COMMENTS

The FDA restricts the use of chiretta root to alcoholic beverages.

Gentian: *Gentiana lutea*

OTHER COMMON, ETHNIC, OR SCIENTIFIC NAMES
Yellow gentian
France: Gentiane jaune
Germany: Gelber Enzian
Italy: Genziana
Mexico: Genciana
Spain: Génciana

RELATED SPECIES

Gentiana acaulis: Gentiane acaule (France); Grossblütiger Enzian (Germany); genzianella (Italy); génciana acaule (Spain); stemless gentian. Uses similar to those of *Gentiana lutea.*
Gentiana scabrae: Bitterwort, felswort, Japanese gentian, ryntem root
Gentianella campestris (formerly listed as *Gentiana campestris*): Gentian

GROWTH HABITS
Perennial
Origin: Europe and Asia Minor
Range: Cultivated in North America

CULINARY USES

Glucosides in gentian roots add to the bitter taste of amaretto, Angostura Bitters, Benedictine, Enzian Schnapps (from Bavaria), Edelenzian, Fernet Branca, Gentian Bitters, Gentian Brandy, Moxie, Stockton Bitters, and vermouth. Several other species of gentians are used interchangeably with this species in the production of these bitter drinks, including cross gentian, *Gentiana cruciata* or *Gentiana pannonica;* spotted gentian, *Gentiana punctata;* and purple gentian, *Gentiana purpurea.*

Gentian (both *Gentiana lutea* and *Gentianella campestris*) has been used as a source of bitterness in some beers (especially in Sweden), but hops have been preferred for some three centuries.

COMMENTS
"Bitterwort" and "felswort" are commonly used indiscriminately as names for all the gentians. *Fel* is Old English for "pill," indicating its flavor and usage. A bitter pill to swallow, indeed.

38. Geraniaceae: The Geranium Family

Rose Geranium: *Pelargonium graveolens*

OTHER COMMON, ETHNIC, OR SCIENTIFIC NAMES
Sweet-scented geranium, scented geranium. *Pelargonium terebinthaceum* was formerly used as a scientific name for the species.

France: Géranium
Germany: Geranie
Italy: Geranio

RELATED SPECIES
Pelargonium acetosum: Stork's bill
Pelargonium capitatum: Attar of roses (rose scented)
Pelargonium citronellum: Mabel Grey geranium
Pelargonium citrosum: Citrosa geranium
Pelargonium crispum: Lemon geranium (lemon scented)
Pelargonium denticulatum: Fernleaf geranium
Pelargonium fragrans: Nutmeg geranium
Pelargonium grossulariodes: Coconut-scented geranium
Pelargonium limoneum: English fingerbowl geranium (lemon scented)
Pelargonium odoratissimum: Apple geranium (source of geranium oil)
Pelargonium quercifolium: Gooseberry geranium, coconut geranium (pine or resin scented). Oak-leaved geranium, almond geranium, village-oak geranium (incense scented).
Pelargonium raden (sometimes *Pelargonium Radula*): Crowfoot (rose/lemon scented)
Pelargonium tomentosum: Chocolate mint geranium, herb-scented geranium, peppermint geranium (peppermint scented)

HYBRIDS
Pelargonium graveolens × *Pelargonium quercifolium:* 'Camphor Rose', 'Capri', 'Fragrantissimum', 'Granelous', 'Grey Lady Plymouth', 'Little Gem',

'Lady Plymouth', 'Logeei', 'Marginata', 'Minor', 'Mrs. Taylor', 'Red-Flowered Rose', 'Rollison's Unique', 'Variegatum' (mint scented), 'Prince Rupert' (lemon scented), 'Giganteum', 'Godfrey's Pride'

Pelargonium graveolens × Pelargonium tomentosum: Joy Lucille, Rober's Lemon Rose

Pelargonium × citrosum: Prince of Orange, orange geranium (orange scented)

Pelargonium × fragrans: Nutmeg geranium (nutmeg scented). Cultivars include 'Cody's Fragrans', 'Logee's', and 'Variegatum'.

Pelargonium × nervosum: Lime geranium (lime scented)

Pelargonium × rutaceum: No common name found; rue scented.

GROWTH HABITS
Perennial
Origin: Southern Africa
Range: In temperate regions, cultivated as annual or as houseplant

CULINARY USES
As with most herbs, the best-quality leaves are collected from plants that have not yet blossomed. Fresh leaves are used in baking; as a flavoring for wine and other beverages, jellies, sorbets, butters, syrups, vinegars; and in fruit salads. Use rose- or peppermint-scented varieties in tea or wine. Pine- and nutmeg-scented varieties can be used in pâtés. Apple-scented varieties make a good addition to baked fish. Add dried leaves to teas, or infuse chopped fresh leaves in hot liquid and strain.

The sour leaves and buds of *Pelargonium acetosum* are eaten in South Africa.

The plant is the source of several different geranium oils. Reunion geranium oil has a rose-mint scent. The oil from Algeria has a reduced mint presence, while the oil from Morocco (made from *Pelargonium roseum,* a species not listed in *Hortus Third*) substitutes herbaceous notes for the mint. All these oils have a bitter taste.

The leaves of scented geraniums contain geraniol, citronellol, diacetyl, dimethyl sulfide, and ethanol.

OTHER USES
Sachets and potpourri

Zdravets: *Geranium macrorhizum*

OTHER COMMON, ETHNIC, OR SCIENTIFIC NAMES
Cranesbill. Previously listed botanically as *Geranium japonicum.*

GROWTH HABITS
Perennial

Origin: Europe
Range: Temperate regions

CULINARY USES

Extracts of this plant are used in the flavorings industry. They contain azulen, hentriancontane, geraniol, and germacrol.

COMMENTS

The genus *Geranium* should not be confused with the plants commonly called "geraniums" (see ROSE GERANIUM). Most of those plants are actually part of the genus *Pelargonium*.

39. Guttiferae (Clusicaceae): The Garcinia Family

Asam Gelugor: *Garcinia atroviridis*

OTHER COMMON, ETHNIC, OR SCIENTIFIC NAMES
Indonesia: Asam gelugor
Malaysia: Asam gelugor, asam keping
Thailand: Som khaek, sommawon

RELATED SPECIES
Garcinia globulosa: Asam kandis (Indonesia)
Garcinia nigrolineata: Asam kandis (Indonesia)
Garcinia schomburgkiana: Madan (Thailand)

GROWTH HABITS
Tropical tree
Origin: Southeast Asia
Range: Not hardy outside the tropics

CULINARY USES

The fruits of the *Garcinia* species are used in Indonesia, Malaysia, and Thailand to add a sour tang to fish curries. The thinly sliced dried fruits are reconstituted in water before being used in much the same way as tamarind (q.v.) is used.

Fresh madan is occasionally used in Thai salads.

Kokum: *Garcinia indica*

OTHER COMMON, ETHNIC, OR SCIENTIFIC NAMES
Garcinia

Garcinia kola: Bitter kola, false kola, male kola
Garcinia mangostana: Manggis (Indonesia); mangosteen, mangus, mangus kai (Sri Lanka); mangkut (Thailand); mingut thi (Burma/Myanmar)

GROWTH HABITS
Tropical tree
Origin: Southwest India
Range: India

CULINARY USES
Dried fruits are used, like tamarind (q.v.), as a souring ingredient in Indian cooking. They flavor chutneys, curries, fish, marinades, pickles, and rice. Kokum is sometimes sold as "Garcinia Powder" or "Garcinia Cambogia Powder."
It gets its sourness from hydroxy citric acid.

OTHER USES
Garcinia kola is sometimes used as an adulterant to true kola (*Cola nitida*). While it does contain tannin, which provides some astringency, it lacks the alkaloids that give cola drinks their kick.
Gamboge, a muted yellow-orange pigment used in artist's watercolors, is derived from the sap of several species of *Garcinia.*

St. John's Wort: *Hypericum perforatum*

OTHER COMMON, ETHNIC, OR SCIENTIFIC NAMES
Hypericum, Klamath weed, the Lord God's wonder plant, tough and heal
France: Millepertuis officinal
Germany: Johanniskraut
Italy: Iperico
Mexico: Hierba de San Juan
Russia: Zveroboi
Spain: Hipericón
Turkey: Binbirdelik otu

GROWTH HABITS
Perennial
Origin: Europe
Range: Naturalized in North America

CULINARY USES
The only culinary citations I have found for St. John's wort refer to its use in flavoring beverages, such as teas, mead, and vermouth, and in a recipe for Fernet Branca.

The herb has a bitter, astringent quality derived from hypericin and an aromatic, balsamic scent from α-pinene.

OTHER USES
Used as a dye plant.

COMMENTS
Light-sensitive people sometimes have reactions after consuming St. John's wort. The herb contains hypericin, a powerful photosensitizer that may increase one's chance of becoming sunburned. Apparently, livestock can be affected more dramatically, which is a problem because St. John's wort can easily become a weedy pest in pastures.

The FDA restricts its use to alcoholic beverages.

40. Hydrophyllaceae: The Waterleaf Family

Yerba Santa: *Eriodictyon californicum*

OTHER COMMON, ETHNIC, OR SCIENTIFIC NAMES
Bear's weed, consumptive's weed, gum bush, gum leaves, gum plant, holy herb, holy weed, mountain balm, sacred weed, tarweed

France: Herbe sainte
Germany: Eriodictyon
Italy: Erba sante
Mexico: Hierba santa
Spain: Eriodicto
Yerba santa was formerly known scientifically as *Erdyction glutinosum*
(almost certainly a typographical error).

GROWTH HABITS
Evergreen shrub
Origin: Northern Mexico and southwest United States
Range: California and Oregon to Brazil

CULINARY USES
Leaves have an anise-like, balsamic flavor. They are used in Mexican and Tex-Mex cooking. Extracts are used commercially to flavor baked goods, candy, and ice cream. The leaves, dried or fresh, are used in herbal teas. Bees make an aromatic honey from the flowers.

Yerba santa contains achillein, tannins, and a number of other phenolic compounds, such as eriodictyol and eriodictyonone.

Yerba santa is smoked and chewed, like tobacco. It is used in medicines as an inert ingredient; its flavor disguises the unpleasant taste of the active ingredients.

41. Illiciaceae: The Illicium Family

Star Anise: *Illicium verum*

OTHER COMMON, ETHNIC, OR SCIENTIFIC NAMES
Chinese anise, Indian anise
China: Ba jiao, five fragrance, pak kok, peh kah
Denmark: Stjerneanis
Estonia: Harilik tähtaniisipuu
Finland: Tähtianis
France: Anis de la chine, anis étoilé, badiane
Germany: Badian, Sternani
Iceland: Stjörnuanís
India: Jaiphul, jathikka
Indonesia: Bunga lawang
Italy: Anice stellato
Malaysia: Bunga lawang
Mexico: Anís estrellado
Netherlands: Steranijs
Norway: Stjerneanis
Philippines: Anis, sangke
Portugal: Anis estrelado
Russia: Badjan
South Africa: Bahia (name used by the "Cape Malays")
Spain: Anís estrella, badiana
Sweden: Stjärnanis
Thailand: Poy kak bua
Vietnam: Hoi huong

RELATED SPECIES
Illicium anisatum (sometimes listed as *Illicium religiosum;* see Comments, below): Chinese anise, Japanese anise
Illicium floridanum: Florida anise, Florida anise-tree, poison bay, polecat tree, purple anise, stinkbush, sweet laurel, starbush

GROWTH HABITS
Evergreen tree

Origin: Southeast China and northern Vietnam
Range: East Asia

CULINARY USES

This herb delivers typical anise flavor in a charming chestnut-colored pod shaped like an eight-pointed star. It is often used in combination with Chinese five-spice powder (anise, cinnamon, cloves, fennel, and Szechuan pepper). This may seem like entirely too much licorice flavoring, but the sweet spices create a sort of bridge linking the salty taste of soy sauce, the pungency of ginger, the earthiness of garlic, and the fire of hot peppers. Done well, five-spice powder provides a balance among all the flavors of the dish, none dominant, none obscured. Done badly, it is like a childish nightmare, with too many sweets to be pleasurable.

Star anise is essential to red-cooked dishes, those rich dishes that are patiently simmered in soy sauce and spices until the toughest meats become succulent, the braising liquid gradually thickening into a velvety ambrosia that blurs the distinction between solid protein and mere broth. Chinese roast pork, barbecued spare ribs, and barbecued duck would be unimaginable, and certainly unimaginative, without the ethereal sweetness of star anise.

Star Anise
Illicium verum

From Köhler, *Köhler's Medizinal-Pflanzen,* vol. 2

Star anise is used, with a number of other herbs (including several licorice-flavored varieties), to produce absinthe, anisette, Kümmel, and Pernod.

Star anise contains *trans*-anethole (up to 45,000 ppm), methyl chavicol (up to 6,500 ppm), limonene (up to 5,200 ppm), caryophyllene (up to 3,600 ppm), 1,8-cineole (up to 3,500 ppm), and many other elements.

OTHER USES

The essential oil from star anise is cheaper and stronger than that in aniseed, so it is used in most commercial products that require that flavor. This includes items as diverse as candy and toothpaste.

The bark of *Illicium anisatum* is used as incense in Japanese Buddhist temples.

COMMENTS

The fruit of *Illicium anisatum* is supposedly poisonous. It is not likely that anyone would mistake it for an anise substitute; it smells like cardamom, not licorice. The leaves of both species are said to be toxic.

Star anise is not related to anise or fennel (q.v.).

42. Irideaceae: The Iris Family

Orris: *Iris Đ Germanica*

OTHER COMMON, ETHNIC, OR SCIENTIFIC NAMES

Flag. Sometimes listed using its old scientific name, *Iris germanica*.
France: Fleur-de-lis, iris
Germany: Iris, Schwertlilie
Italy: Giaggolo, iris
Mexico: Lirio
Morocco: Amber el door
Spain: Lirio

GROWTH HABITS

Perennial
Origin: Mediterranean region
Range: Temperate regions

CULINARY USES

The licorice-like flavor and violet scent of orris are extracted from the rhizomes. Orris is used to flavor altvater, anisette, Campari, vermouth, and some better-quality gins. Orris is used as a commercial flavoring for baked goods (usually in icings), candy, ice cream, and soft drinks. Orris contains

irone (up to 86 percent of the essential oil), plus various terpenes, sesquiterpenes, aldehydes, and esters.

OTHER USES
Used in the manufacture of perfumes.

Saffron: *Crocus sativus*

OTHER COMMON, ETHNIC, OR SCIENTIFIC NAMES
Kaisar, karcom, kesar, krokos, saffron crocus, zaffer
Afganistan: Zaffaron
Algeria: Za'afran
Arabic: Kurkum, za'faran
China: Fang-hung-hua
Estonia: Krookus, safrankrookus
Finland: Sahrami
France: Safran
Gaelic: Cròdh
Germany: Safran
Greece: Krókos, zaforá
Hungary: Füszersáfrány
Iceland: Saffran
India: Jafran, kashmiiran, kesar, kesari, kungumapu, kunkumapave,
    zaffran
Indonesia: Kunyit kering
Iran: Kurkum, zafraan
Iraq: Zaafaran
Italy: Zafferano
Japan: Safuran
Malaysia: Koma koma, kunyit kering
Morocco: Zafrane
Nepal: Kesari
Netherlands: Saffraan
Norway: Safran
Philippines: Kashubha
Poland: Szafran
Portugal: Açafrão
Romania: Safran
Russia: Shafran
Spain: Azafrán, safrà
Sweden: Safran
Thailand: Ya faran

Turkey: Safran
Vietnam: Nghe

RELATED SPECIES
All the more common *Croci*

GROWTH HABITS
Perennial bulb
Origin: Western Mediterranean region
Range: Cultivated commercially in France, Iran, Italy, Kashmir, Sicily, and Spain

CULINARY USES
Saffron gives Spanish paella its golden color and glorious scent. It is especially good with shellfish, as it has a slightly iodine-like, oceanic scent that implies freshness. It is easy to think of saffron as a southern ingredient, for all the Mediterranean cuisines use it—think of the bouillabaisse of Marseilles or *risotto alla milanese* from Lombardy—but it is also very popular in Scandinavian countries. Up north, saffron is used to flavor and color baked goods such as breads, cookies, and cakes. Saffron is used with poultry and lamb, especially in Moroccan tagines, and in sauces, soup, and stews.

Saffron is said to be one of the secret ingredients in Benedictine and in green Chartreuse. Fernet Branca contains a small amount of saffron.

Saffron gets its perfume from safranal, its golden yellow color from the pigment crocin, and its bitter taste from picrocrocin.

COMMENTS
Saffron blooms in the autumn. About half of the *Crocus* species bloom in the fall. Most people, more familiar with the spring bloomers, are surprised by these bulbs that bloom with chrysanthemums.

Don't expect to grow your own saffron and save money on this costliest of spices. The effort involved in plucking and drying thousands of pistils from the blossoms (which are about three inches from the ground) is certainly beyond *my* endurance. Do not be fooled by low-cost "false saffron," either. Also known as American saffron, bastard saffron, false saffron, Mexican saffron, and safflower, *Carthamus tinctoris* is a member of the Asteraceae family. Yes, its carotenoid pigments will dye your food yellow, but not as gloriously as saffron; nor will they provide the wonderful scent and charming faint bitterness of the real thing. Safflower does yield a good cooking oil and its shoots and flowers are edible.

Consumed in large quantities, saffron can become a narcotic. Considering its expense, it is not likely to provide much competition to more traditional drugs.

43. Lamiaceae (formerly Labiatae): The Mint Family

Alpine Basil Thyme: *Acinos thymoides*

OTHER COMMON, ETHNIC, OR SCIENTIFIC NAMES

Acinos vulgaris, basil balm, basil thyme, common calamint, hoary mountain mint, mother of thyme, mountain mint, thyme basil, thymos acinos, wild basil. Basil thyme has been known scientifically as *Calamintha acinos* (sometimes with species name capitalized), *Calamintha ascendens, Calamintha menthifolia, Calamintha sylvatica, Calamintha offinalis,* and *Satureja Acinos.*
Italy: Niebita

RELATED SPECIES

Pycnanthemum incanum: Hoary mountain mint
Pycnanthemum montanum: Mountain mint

GROWTH HABITS

Annual (or short-lived perennial)
Origin: Europe
Range: Temperate regions

CULINARY USES

This herb is said to be thyme-like or camphoraceous in flavor (which one would expect from the variety of names the plant has acquired), but milder. The leaves and flowering tops have been used in marinades for game, especially hare.

Showy savory, *Calamintha grandiflora,* has tangerine-scented foliage that is used, dried, in herbal teas, or fresh in fruit salads.

Pycnanthemum incanum contains pulegone (up to 10,000 ppm), menthone (up to 10,000 ppm), limonene (up to 1,200 ppm), isomenthone (up to 900 ppm), and menthol (up to 800 ppm).

Pycnanthemum montanum contains isomenthone (up to 4,900 ppm), camphor (up to 3,900 ppm), camphene (up to 1000 ppm), pulegone (up to 800 ppm), 1,8-cineole (up to 700 ppm), and just enough menthone to provide a minty taste.

Anise Hyssop: *Agastache foeniculum*

OTHER COMMON, ETHNIC, OR SCIENTIFIC NAMES

Blue giant hyssop, fennel giant hyssop, fragrant giant hyssop. Sometimes listed as *Lophanthus anisatus.*

Agastache mexicana (sometimes listed as *Agastache anethiodora*): Toronjil
(Mexico), Mexican giant hyssop
Agastache nepetoides: Catnip giant hyssop
Agastache rugosa: Korean mint, wrinkled great hyssop
Agastache urticifolia: Giant hyssop, sawtooth mountain mint

GROWTH HABITS
Biennial or perennial
Origin: North America
Range: Wild or cultivated, common in Plains, but sporadic in the eastern
United States

CULINARY USES
Teas are brewed with flowers and leaves. Dried or fresh, the downy heart-
shaped leaves are used to season fruit compotes. The herb has a definite licorice
flavor, even though it is not related to anise or fennel. It shares the sweetness
of licorice. Fresh leaves and purple flowers can be used in salads. A lemon-
scented tea is brewed from *Agastache mexicana,* in Mexico, as a digestive.

COMMENTS
Anise hyssop should not be confused with true hyssop, *Hyssopus officinalis,*
or any of the other herbs that include "hyssop" in their names.

Balm: *Melissa officinalis*

OTHER COMMON, ETHNIC, OR SCIENTIFIC NAMES
Balm gentle, balm lemon, bawlme, balm-mint, common balm, bee balm,
lemon balm, sweet balm, garden balm, honey plant
Estonia: Sidrunmeliss
Finland: Sitruunamelissa
France: Baume, citronelle, citronne, herbe du citron, mélisse, piment des
abeilles, piment des ruches, ponchirade, thé de France
Germany: Citronenkraut, Bienenkraut, Honigblume, Melisse,
Zitronenkraut, Zitronenmelisse
Iceland: Hjartafró, sítrónumelissa
Iran: Badrangbuye, farandj moschk
Italy: Melissa
Mexico: Melisa, toronjil
Netherlands: Bijenkruid, citroenmelisse, melis
Norway: Sitronmelisse
Poland: Melisa lekarska
Portugal: Cidreira, erva-cidreira
Russia: Limonnik, melissa limonnaya

Spain: Balsamita maior, toronjil, toronjiña
Sweden: Citronmeliss, hjärtansfröjd
Turkey: Melisa, ogul otu
Vietnam: Rau kinh gioi, tiatô

CULTIVAR
'Variegata'

GROWTH HABITS
Perennial
Origin: Southern Europe
Range: Europe and eastern United States

CULINARY USES
Its mild lemon-and-mint-scented leaves are used in teas and in cooking.
They have an almost candy-like quality to their flavor because there is no
trace of acidity. This means that you can add balm to vinaigrettes without increasing their astringency. Leaves can be minced and added to mayonnaise, or
to flavor whipped cream for desserts. Lemon balm enlivens oils and vinegars.

Try rubbing crushed balm leaves on lamb before roasting. They can also be
combined with sage in stuffings for poultry. Add fresh young leaves to salads,
especially fruit salads, or compotes using tart fruits like black currants.

The herb is alleged to be one of the "secret" ingredients in anisette, Benedictine, yellow and green Chartreuse, Pernod, and vermouth. Formerly, it
was used in absinthe. Claret cup is a complex mixture of red Bordeaux wine,
balm, borage, orange, cucumber, cognac, and seltzer.

Balm contains citronellal (up to 3,000 ppm), geraniol (up to 1,100 ppm),
and germacrene-D (up to 1,000 ppm), and neral (up to 900 ppm), along with
dozens of other aromatic compounds.

COMMENTS
Some cultivars of balm have a slight soapy taste that makes their use in
salads less than desirable. Tasting is the only way to know when, and how
much of, an herb should be used.

Many times the term "balm" is meant to refer to balsam (the firs, *Abies*
spp. [q.v.]), as in "balm of Gilead." Likewise, the French *baume* and Italian
balsamo do not refer to *Melissa officinalis*. To add another level of confusion,
the term "balsam" is also used for a number of plants of the genus *Impatiens*.

Basil: *Ocimum basilicum*

OTHER COMMON, ETHNIC, OR SCIENTIFIC NAMES
Anise basil, anise-scented basil, Asian basil, basilie, basill, common basil,
sweet basil, sweet genovese, tea bush, Thai basil. An old botanical name for
basil is *Ocimum bullatum*. Some British herbals list the genus as *Ocymum*.

Algeria: Hbaq
Arabic: Raihan
Burma/Myanmar: Pinzainpinzin
China: Hun que, lo le, yu-heung, yu xiang cai
Costa Rica: Albahaca
Denmark: Basilikum
East Timor: Manjeriku, ruku
Estonia: Vürtsbasiilik
Ethiopia: Besobila
Finland: Basilika
France: Basilic, basilic commun, basilie, herbe royale
Germany: Basilienkraut, Basilikum, Königskraut
Greece: Vasilikos
Hungary: Bazsalikom
Iceland: Basilíka
India: Barbar, dhalatulasi, gulal tulsi, janglitulshi, pachcha, ramkasturi,
    rudrajada, sabje, suwndutala, tirunitru, tulsi
Indonesia: Daun kemangi, daun selasih, indring, kermangi, ruku,
    manjeriku selasih
Iran: Shaahesprahm
Israel: Reihan
Italy: Basilico, genovese profumitissima, misiricoli, piccolo verde
Japan: Meboki, me boki
Malaysia: Daun kemangi, daun selaseh
Mexico: Albáhaca
Morocco: Hboq
Netherlands: Basilicum, baziel, bazielkruid, koningskruid
Norway: Basilikum
Panama: Albahaca fina, toronjil
Philippines: Balanoi, balinoi, bidai, sulasi
Poland: Bazylia pospolita
Portugal: Manjericão
Romania: Busuioc
Russia: Bazilik, dushistiye vasil'ki, dushki
South Africa: Basilikum
Spain: Alabega, albacar, albahaca, alfábega
Sri Lanka: Maduru-tala, suwendi-tala
Swahili: Mrihani
Sweden: Basilika, basilkaört
Thailand: Bai horapa, bai manglak, bai kaprao, horapa, kaprow, mangluk
Turkey: Feslegen, reyhan
Vietnam: Cay ich gioi, chi sa, e tia, hathuong, hung que, pak bua le phe,
    rau e, rau que, tchow ze tang, thaokai, ytou

'Anise': Bai manglak (Thailand); horapa (Thailand); indring
(Indonesia); rau hung que, rau que (Vietnam); tulsi (India); anise
basil, hairy basil, licorice basil. A purple-stemmed plant with a
pronounced anise scent.

'Aussie Sweetie': Slow to bolt

'Cinnamon': Round three-inch, bright green leaves with sweet cinnamon
taste and a hint of clove. Northern India. Good in chutneys.

'Citriodorum': Lemon-scented basil

'Crispum': Curly basil, lettuce leaf basil—large (4"–5") puckered leaves
with strong basil flavor. This Japanese import makes an interesting
wrapper for foods. A small caveat: *Ocimum crispum* has been used as a
name for perilla (q.v.).

'Genovese': Sweet genovese. This has green and purple leaves and a basil
flavor with hints of anise and clove.

'Licorice': Long narrow leaves, with a flavor reminiscent of anise or
French tarragon. Originally from India and Pakistan. The stems
and veins are distinctly purple. If used to make an herbal vinegar, it
provides a lovely rosy color.

'Mammoth': Mammoth basil, monstruoso

'Minimum': Bush basil, dwarf basil, Greek basil; tiny, bright green leaves
with sweet, mild clove flavor. Origin is Indian but has been a standard
in Europe since the sixteenth century. 'Nano Compatto Vero' is a
variety of *Ocimum basilicum* 'Minimum'. Its anise and clove flavors are
more pronounced. French fine leaf basil is another, hardier, variety.
Its tiny leaves have a floral sweetness, with a hint of mint in the finish.
Ocimum minimum is another name for the cultivar.

'Morpha': Purple-stemmed plant used in the cooking of India and
Malaysia. It has narrower leaves than *Ocimum basilicum* 'Anise'.

'Mrs. Burns': Mrs. Burns basil

'Piccolo': Piccolo verde fino basil. It has longish glossy bright green
leaves, with a sweet floral anise scent. European.

'Purpurascens': Horapa (Thailand); black opal basil, dark opal basil,
opal basil, purple ruffles. Typical basil scent and flavor, but spicy,
with perhaps a hint more clove. Its deep purple, ruffled leaves make a
beautiful garnish for appropriately flavored dishes. This cultivar was
created in the 1950s at the University of Connecticut.

'Siam Queen': Siam queen basil, Thai basil

'Thrysiflora': Thrysiflora basil—long, narrow green leaves on an odd
pyramid-shaped plant. This is the sweetest basil, indigenous to India
and Pakistan, but used in Thai cooking, as well.

'True Thai': Siam queen basil; spicy, licorice-like scent

Ocimum americanum: Lemon basil (*Ocimum canum* × *Ocimum basilicum purpurescens*)—long, dull grayish leaves, pronounced lemon scent. A natural hybrid.

Ocimum americanum: Wild basil (Australia); elega lenga

Ocimum canum: Manglak (Thailand); meng luk, partminger (Kenya and South Africa); khasa-khasa (Sri Lanka); luk manglak (Thailand); curry leaf, holy basil seeds: tookmuria, tucmeria (India)

Ocimum citriodorum: Manglak (Thailand); Thai basil

Ocimum gratissimum: Akeni, amana, efinrin, furugena, iniri, mfang, nchaawu (Nigeria); krapow (Thailand); clove basil, East Indian basil, green basil, hoary basil, tea bush, tulsi. Musky scent is unpleasant (see Comments, below) in quantity, so use sparingly. The cultivar called 'Viride' has a lemon-thyme scent.

Ocimum kilimandscharicum: Camphor basil; shrub with grayish hairy leaves and pronounced camphor scent. This East African plant is useful as a source of camphor for medicines, but it has no real place in the kitchen. Hybrid: *Ocimum kilimandscharicum* × *purpurescens:* African blue basil

Ocimum micranthrum: Peruvian basil

Ocimum sanctum (also known as *Ocimum tenuifloru* and *Ocimum tenniflorum*): Babui tulsi, kalotulsi, krishnamula, oddhi, madurutala, sivatulasi, thulasi, tulasa, tulasigidda, tulasii (India); besobila (Ethiopia); bidai, sulasi (Philippines); kha phrao, kha phrao daeng, kha phrao khaao, kraprao, kaprow (Thailand); bai kaprao, che tak me, e do, erung, e tia, hung thai (Vietnam); laun (Burma); Krishna's leaves, holy basil, sacred basil—leaves are purple, with green undersides, and have strong clove flavor. Purple tulsi or Krishna tulsi is a cultivar of this species, called 'Purple'. It is one of the few basils that does not have mucilaginous seeds.

GROWTH HABITS

Annual

Origin: Tropical Old World

Range: Temperate regions to tropics

CULINARY USES

Is there be a better-known use for basil than the *pesto alla genovese* of Liguria? It has become famous enough to spawn a number of alternate pesto-like sauces. Parsley pesto. Cilantro pesto. Mint pesto. Famous enough to encourage the marketing of several ready-made pesto-in-a-jar imitations. Some people know pesto only from these pathetic preparations. Not surprisingly they wonder, what's the big deal? Only pesto made from freshly picked basil can answer that question.

Many herb books and cookbooks will tell you that you can freeze pesto (without the cheese) for use in the winter. Sure, or you can just buy a jar of the surrogate stuff. If you want the real thing, eat it in the summer. If you must have pesto in the winter, grow some basil in a pot placed in a sunny window. It won't have the sun-drenched perfume of basil from the garden, but it will be closer than the other options.

Pistou is a pesto-enhanced vegetable soup from the south of France.

In high summer, fresh home-grown tomatoes and basil are an unbeatable combination. Try sprinkling some basil vinegar on them. This vinegar is also interesting when used to deglaze a nonstick pan used to sear large sea scallops.

Try basil-flavored olive oil instead of butter on corn on the cob, or as a seasoned dip for bread at the table. This Italian approach is not only tastier but makes good nutritional sense. Like other herbal oils, basil oil is made by steeping the chopped herbs in warm, not hot, olive oil until all the flavor is extracted. If needed, the oil can be strained and the process can be repeated until the desired strength is achieved. A microwave can be used to speed the process; just be careful not to *cook* the herbs.

Basil makes a good flavoring for sausages, its sharp clove-like quality punctuating the rich fat of meats like pork and duck. Try rubbing crushed fresh basil leaves on goose or venison before roasting.

Basil is good with fat fish, such as salmon or eel, and also with eggs, egg-plant, and spinach. Add it to bean soups. A little basil enlivens the cooking liquid for peas, beans, lobster, mussels, potatoes, and shrimp.

Together with coconut, hot chiles, and lemongrass, basil helps to create the complex layers of flavor in many Thai dishes. Basil is used in Ethiopian cooking, in *berberé,* the ever-present hot pepper paste, and in the flavored, clarified butter called *niter kebbeh.* This fat is the primary cooking medium in Ethiopia. *Ocimum gratissimum* is used in the cooking of Ghana, as a season-ing for meats, in teas, and in salads. Dried purple basil is used in the cooking of Turks and Armenians.

"Italian Seasoning" is a name for several different mixtures of herbs and spices that are sold commercially. They often contain basil.

The tiny pale-violet-to-white flowers are borne on terminal clusters. They are also edible and make elegant garnishes. Basil leaves make excellent gar-nishes, fresh or fried. Purple varieties look better than green leaves when fried. When fried, much of their flavor is lost to the cooking fat, but for some dishes the strong basil presence may be overpowering anyway.

Basil is used in the formulation of some aromatic liqueurs, such as Char-treuse (although Merory does not include it in any of his versions of these herbal liqueurs).

Basil seeds of several species contain a mucilaginous substance that has been used in a number of places (such as Indonesia, Mexico, and Thailand) to thicken various cooling beverages: *cherbet tokhum* is based on water, but others may contain coconut milk.

Basil's wonderfully aromatic and complex flavors and scents derive from an assortment of varying amounts of estragol (up to 9,000 ppm), methyl chavicol (up to 8,800 ppm), linalool (up to 8,700 ppm), eugenol (up to 8,600 ppm), plus *trans*-cinnamic-acid and *trans*-cinnamic-acid-methyl-ester (up to 7,000 ppm each). *Ocimum sanctum* also contains camphor, terpenes, and thymol.

OTHER USES

Albáhaca is a Mexican name for a particular type of basil that is used as a kind of trap for evil spirits. It is unlikely that superstitious people would cook with it; they would be more concerned with finding a safe way to dispose of the herbal equivalent of spiritual toxic waste.

COMMENTS

Keep the basil pinched back to encourage bushy growth and to help prevent the setting of séed. Many basils become musky in scent and flavor if allowed to flower. A vigilant pair of scissors can keep a patch of basil productive and tasty throughout the summer. Once picked, basil is very short-lived. In the refrigerator, it will quickly develop extremely unattractive black spots.

Save purple basil for uses that showcase its color and texture; if you plan to season a cooked dish with basil, use the green variety or even dried basil.

Herb royale is another name for southernwood (which see, under MUGWORT). Rau que, the Vietnamese name for basil, is also used for mint.

Ocimum citriodorum is not listed in *Hortus Third*.

How many times must I see the word "unpleasant" in herb books? Yes, I sometimes use the word, as I do above to describe the musky scent of *Ocimum gratissimum,* and sometimes that is exactly what I mean. The truth, however, is that all tastes are acquired through experience and repetition. If another culture joyfully uses something our own finds disgusting, it is almost certain that we have not taken the time to learn to love it. Admittedly, some substances, such as asafoetida (q.v.), take more time than others.

Bee Balm: *Monarda didyma*

OTHER COMMON, ETHNIC, OR SCIENTIFIC NAMES

Basil balm, bergamot, fragrant balm, horse mint, horseradish, Indian's plume, Indian's red balm, lemon mint, low balm, monard, Oswego tea, pagoda plant, red balm, rignum, rose balm, scarlet balm, sweet horsemint, Sweet Mary, wild bergamot
England: Gold melissa, Indian nettle
Estonia: Aedmonardaa
Finland: Teeminttu, väriminttu

France: Bergamote, monarde ponctuée, thé d'Oswego
Germany: Blumenmelisse, Goldmelisse, Monarde, Zitronenmonarde
Italy: Bergamotta, monarda
Netherlands: Bergamotteplant, monarda, Oswego thee
Norway: Etasjeblomst, hagehestemynte
Portugal: Monarda
Spain: Bergamota, monarda
Sweden: Blodröd temynta, temynta

Bee balm has many cultivars; they are mostly distinguished by floral color. The most common domesticated *Monarda* has crimson-colored flowers and grows twice as tall as its wild cousin. 'Lavender' is a cultivar that has a lemon-mint scent that makes it more desirable as an herbal tea (see Culinary Uses, below).

RELATED SPECIES

Monarda austromontana: Mexican bergamot, Mt. Pima oregano
Monarda citriodora (sometimes listed as *Monarda pectinata*): Betoníca (Mexico); lemon bee balm, lemon bergamot, lemon mint, wood betony—a citrus-scented plant indigenous to the southern Appalachians
Monarda clinopodiodia: Basil balm, horsemint, white basil balm
Monarda fistulosa: Wild bergamot; has a lovely pinkish lavender flower and is about 18 to 24 inches tall. The cultivar 'Oregano de la Sierra' (*Monarda fistulosa menthaefolia*) is used as a seasoning for soft, fresh cheeses and for strong-flavored meats such as game or young goat (*cabrito*). It is sometimes listed as *Monarda menthaefolia*.
Monarda odoratisima: Coyote mint, mountain pennyroyal, pennyroyal
Monarda puntcata: Dotted mint, horsebalm, horsemint

GROWTH HABITS

Perennial
Origin: New England to Georgia
Range: Temperate regions

CULINARY USES

Dried leaves are brewed as herbal teas, although some books suggest using *Monarda* flowers. Perhaps tastes in teas have changed since that recommendation first appeared in print. If any of the authors of those texts had bothered to taste these flowers, they would have discovered a strong, warm, oregano-like flavor, with an accompanying numbness of the tongue, something like that caused by Szechuan peppercorns (q.v.).

These flowers are better used for seasoning and garnishes. You *could* eat an entire flower, but it would probably overpower anything else in the meal.

Better to treat these aromatic explosions as you would the bay leaves on a pâté or the dried chiles in a Chinese stir-fry: look, enjoy their savor, but leave them on the plate.

An obvious way to sidestep the flowers' domineering tendency is to limit the quantity of *Monarda* that actually reaches the plate. The bouquet garni, especially one using leaves rather than flowers, was invented for this purpose, and if you wish to flavor a hearty soup with *Monarda,* that would be the solution.

Using *Monarda* as a garnish, try sprinkling a few petals (actually, tubular flowers—the familiar pompon is not a single flower but a radiating mass of individual flowers) on a savory beef consommé or on top of a grilled tomato. They could also be used in salads (in limited quantities, of course) or to garnish roasted meats sauced with rich reductions of stock and wine.

Fresh leaves might make an interesting garnish for tall drinks—a Bloody Mary made with habanero-infused vodka comes to mind. Certainly, no one would complain about the assertiveness of the wild bergamot.

Monarda citriodora is used by Hopis to flavor game, especially harc.

The warmth of *Monarda didyma* comes from linalool (up to 9,600 ppm), 1,8-cineole (up to 2,700 ppm), *p*-cymene (up to 1,800 ppm), limonene (up to 1,300 ppm) and γ-terpinene (up to 1,200 ppm), as well as dozens of other aromatic compounds.

Monarda fistulosa contains many of the same compounds, but the balance is different and it is more strongly flavored; it contains geraniol (up to 29,500 ppm), thymol (up to 20,800 ppm), carvacrol (up to 19,900 ppm), *p*-cymene (up to 15,800 ppm), and γ-terpinene (up to 11,300 ppm).

Monarda punctata is more like *Monarda fistulosa* than *Monarda didyma,* containing thymol (up to 27,600 ppm), carvacrol (up to 12,500 ppm), 1,8-cineole (up to 6,800 ppm), α-terpineol (up to 4,500 ppm), and dihydrocarvyl acetate (up to 4,500 ppm).

OTHER USES

Bee balm is a commercial source of oil of thyme; it is also used in potpourri.

COMMENTS

I have read that the flowers can be crystallized, but I can't think of a dish that would benefit from a sugar-coated blast of carvacrol and thymol.

No relation to true bergamot, a citrus species (q.v.).

Betony: *Stachys officinalis*

OTHER COMMON, ETHNIC, OR SCIENTIFIC NAMES

Bishopswort, hedge nettle, wood betony, woundwort. It has been listed botanically as *Stachys Betonica* and *Betonica officinalis.*

France: Betoine officinale, epiare officinale
Germany: Betonie, Feuerkraut, Heilbatunge, Heil-zeist, Zehrkraut

RELATED SPECIES
Stachys affinis: Chinese artichoke, chorogi, crosnes du Japon, Japanese
artichoke, knotroot

GROWTH HABITS
Perennial
Origin: Eurasia
Range: Temperate regions

CULINARY USES
The only gastronomic uses I have encountered for this essentially decorative herb have been in teas and in an herbal beer. Betony is quite astringent,
containing achillein, rosmarinic acid, and tannins.
The related species, *Stachys affinis,* has edible tuberous roots.

Bugle: *Ajuga reptans*

OTHER COMMON, ETHNIC, OR SCIENTIFIC NAMES
Ajuga, bugleweed, carpet bugle. Sometimes listed as *Ajuga repens, Ajuga
Tottenhamii,* or *Ajuga variegata.*

GROWTH HABITS
Annual or perennial
Origin: Europe
Range: Naturalized, even weedy, in North America

CULINARY USES
Young shoots can be used in salads.

COMMENTS
The leaves are said to contain compounds that are similar to the digitalis
found in foxglove, *Digitalis purpurea,* which is to say they may be toxic.
Ajugas spread by runners, as do strawberries and myrtle. While this makes
them good candidates for use as groundcovers, they can be invasive.

Calamint: *Calamintha nepeta*

OTHER COMMON, ETHNIC, OR SCIENTIFIC NAMES
Basil thyme, lesser calamint, mill mountain, mountain balm, mountain
mint. Also known botanically as *Clinopodium nepeta, Satureja calamintha,* and
Satureja nepeta.

Germany: Bergminze
Italy: Calaminta, nepitella

'Glandulosa': Also known as *Calamintha officinalis*
'Nepeta': Also known as *Calamintha nepetoides*

RELATED SPECIES
Calamintha acinos (sometimes listed as *Acinos arvensis*): Acinos, basil thyme
Calamintha grandiflora: Large-flowered calamint, mint savory, mountain balm, showy savory, showy calamint. Cultivar: 'Variegata'
Calamintha clinopdium subs. *Morie:* Za'ater dial wad (Morocco)
Calamintha sylvatica: Calamint

GROWTH HABITS
Shrubby perennial
Origin: Mediterranean region
Range: Temperate regions

CULINARY USES
Aromatic leaves are used in a bouillabaisse-like soup from Corsica.

COMMENTS
The name "calamint" is associated with a number of other species and genera, including *Acinos thymoides, Acinos alpinus, Clinopodium vulgare,* and *Satureja georgiana.*

Catnip: *Nepeta cataria*

OTHER COMMON, ETHNIC, OR SCIENTIFIC NAMES
Catmint, cat's wort, nep
Mexico: Hierba del gato, hierba gatera, nepeta

CULTIVAR
'Citriodora': Lemon-scented catnip

RELATED SPECIES
Nepeta Mussinii: Catmint

GROWTH HABITS
Perennial
Origin: Eurasia
Range: Naturalized in North America

CULINARY USES

Catnip is related to the mints, oregano, and marjoram (q.v.) and can be used in herbal teas. It has a curious savory scent and a bitter taste. Although we tend not to think of it as a kitchen herb, it has been used in soups and stews since the fifteenth century. It was popular in sauces and as a condiment in eighteenth-century England. Alone, it might be a bit musky, but combined with parsley and garlic it would be an interesting garnish on a ragu of assorted mushrooms. The lemon-scented cultivar is said to be more attractive to people than to cats.

Catnip contains, among it numerous compounds, nepetalactone (up to 9,900 ppm), caryophyllene (up to 3,200 ppm), caryophyllene oxide (up to 2,400 ppm), and β-farnesene (up to 260 ppm).

OTHER USES

There do seem to be some differences of opinion among connoisseurs. I'm referring, of course, to the fur-bearing consumers of catnip products. It is obvious that cats like the stuff. Some cats indulge in the drug freely, some in an extremely stingy manner, some furtively. While most cats prefer the dried herb, as in all other matters feline, individuality is the rule. Some cats will lie in the garden and graze until nothing but slimy stumps of nepeta are left.

Catnip
Nepeta cataria

From Blackwell,
Herbarium Blackwellianum, vol. 3

Cuban Oregano: *Plectranthus amboinicus*

OTHER COMMON, ETHNIC, OR SCIENTIFIC NAMES
Country borage, Greek oregano, false oregano, Spanish thyme, stygian thyme
Australia: Five-in-one
East Timor: Soldar
Indonesia: Daun kucing, daun kambing
Malaysia: Daun bangun-bangun
Philippines: Oregano, suganda
Portugal: Oregano
Vietnam: Can day la, rau cang, rau thom lun
West Indies: French Tobago thyme, Spanish thyme

CULTIVAR
'Variegated'

RELATED SPECIES
Coleus amboinicus (sometimes listed in old botanical texts as *Coleus aromaticus;* see Comments, below): Oreganon (Mexico); country borage, Indian borage, Spanish thyme
Plectranthus madagascariensis: No common name found. Edible tubers are used in Madagascar.
Plectranthus purpuratus: Vick's plant

GROWTH HABITS
Perennial (in the tropics)
Origin: East Indies, possibly Africa
Range: Wild in Malaysia. Cultivated from India to Southeast Asia, the Caribbean islands, and tropical Americas

CULINARY USES
The fresh leaves are used to season fish and *cabrito* (young goat) in the Caribbean. They are sometimes chopped in chile pastes (something like jerk seasoning, but without the strong onion and ginger presence). The leaves are the primary seasoning in the Cuban black bean soup *frijoles negros.* A kind of salsa, made by mincing the leaves together with various unripe fruits, is served as an accompaniment to rice.

In Java and Malaysia, the leaves are used in curries, especially with goat or strong-smelling fish.

The leaves are sometimes used to flavor beers and wines in India. They have been brewed as herbal tea and cooked as potherbs. Roots and young plants of *Coleus amboinicus* are eaten in South America. The fragrant leaves are eaten as potherbs in India. The roots of *Coleus barbatus* are pickled in India.

This powerful-smelling herb seems to contain large amounts of thymol, which would account for some of its misleading common names.

COMMENTS

This species is not listed in *Hortus Third*. A possible reason is that "country borage" is also a name for *Coleus amboinicus*, which—depending on the source—is either the same species or a closely related species. *Coleus aromaticus* is an outdated name for *Plectranthus amboinicus*, according to *The Oxford Companion to Food*.

Cumberland Rosemary: *Conradina verticillata*

OTHER COMMON, ETHNIC, OR SCIENTIFIC NAMES
Mountain rosemary

CULTIVAR
'Compact Gray Conradina'

RELATED SPECIES
Hortus Third says the genus contains four species, and it lists only one domesticated plant, *Conradina canescens*. However, some nurseries carry as many as five species, plus cultivars.
  Conradina brevifolia: Shortleaf rosemary
  Conradina glabra: Panhandle conradina
  Conradina grandiflora: Large-flowered rosemary
  Conradina sp: Low gray conradina
  Conradina sp: Santa Rosa conradina

GROWTH HABITS
Shrubby perennial
Origin: Southeastern United States
Range: Appalachians

CULINARY USES
Used like true rosemary (q.v.).

COMMENTS
Cumberland rosemary is an endangered species in the wild. In fact, all the *Conradina* species are rare. It is only reasonable and responsible to use domestically raised plants.

Dittany: *Cunila origanoides*

OTHER COMMON, ETHNIC, OR SCIENTIFIC NAMES
American dittany, common dittany, dittander, fever plant, frostweed, headache tea, high pennyroyal, Maryland dittany, Spanish hops, stone mint, sweet horsemint, wild basil

France: Origan dictame
Germany: Diptam, Dosten Diptam
Italy: Dittamo cretico
Spain: Dictamo

GROWTH HABITS

Perennial
Origin: Eastern North America to Uruguay
Range: Eastern North America

CULINARY USES

Leaves and flowers are used in bitters, Pernod, and vermouth. The leaves taste a bit like oregano and have been used, with chives, garlic, salt, and black pepper, to make seasoned olive oil for dipping bread at the table. Both dried and fresh, the leaves are also used in teas.

COMMENTS

Do not confuse this with another plant named dittany. That one is also known as false dittany (q.v.), fraxinella, gas plant, burning bush, and white dittany, *Dictamnus albus*. It is a member of the *Rutaceae*.

Dittany
Cunila origanoides

From Woodville, *A supplement to Medical botany,* vol. 4

Dittany of Crete: *Origanum dictamus*

OTHER COMMON, ETHNIC, OR SCIENTIFIC NAMES
Crete dittany, hop marjoram. Dittany of Crete is sometimes listed botanically as *Amaracus dictamnus* and *Origanum cyriacum.*

GROWTH HABITS
Shrubby perennial
Origin: Crete and Greece
Range: Temperate regions

CULINARY USES
The leaves, dried or fresh, have an aromatic quality that works well with meats and fish. The herb combines well with other Mediterranean seasonings, such as garlic, parsley, and thyme. The dried flowering tops are sometimes brewed into an herbal tea.
Dittany of Crete contains carvacrol and pulegone.

COMMENTS
Do not confuse this species with dittany, *Cunila origanoides* (q.v.)

Germander: *Teucrium chamaedrys*

OTHER COMMON, ETHNIC, OR SCIENTIFIC NAMES
Chamaedrys, green germander, wall germander
France: Germandree officinale
Germany: Echter Gamader
Italy: Camedrio
Mexico: Camedrio
Spain: Xamedrios

RELATED SPECIES
Teucrium canadense: Snakeweed
Teucrium massiliense: Cha tô dât (Vietnam)
Teucrium polium: Polei-gamander (Germany); tüylü kisa mahmut
   (Turkey); felty germander, golden germander
Teucrium pseudo-hyssopus: Bastard hyssop
Teucrium scorodonia: Escordia (Mexico); ambroise, garlic sage, hind heal,
   large-leaved germander, sage-leaved germander, wood sage

GROWTH HABITS
Perennial
Origin: Europe
Range: Temperate regions

Flowering tops are used in bitters, herbal liqueurs, and vermouth. In eighteenth-century Jersey, they were used, like hops, to flavor and clarify beer.

Sage-leaved germander, *Teucrium scorodonia,* has also been used to help clear beer and add the desired bitter flavor. The leaves are not used directly but are made into a strong tea, called ambroise, that is added to the fermenting wort. It is difficult to imagine how such beer would taste; the plant has a distinct garlic aroma. *Scorodon* is Greek for "garlic."

Extracts of *Teucrium polium,* like germander, are used in vermouth.

COMMENTS

The FDA restricts the use of all *Teucrium* spp. to alcoholic beverages.

Bastard hyssop is not to be confused with true hyssop, *Hyssopus officinalis* (q.v.).

Ground Ivy: *Glechoma hederacea*

OTHER COMMON, ETHNIC, OR SCIENTIFIC NAMES

Alehoof, field balm, gill-over-the-ground, ground ivy, nepeta, runaway robin. Formerly known scientifically as *Nepeta glechoma.*
Germany: Gundermann
Mexico: Hiedra terestre

GROWTH HABITS
Perennial
Origin: Europe
Range: Naturalized in North America

CULINARY USES

Leaves are used in herbal teas. Alehoof was supposedly used by the Saxons as a bittering agent in beer making. The young leaves of ground ivy can be eaten in salads. Their flavor and scent season Italian risottos.

COMMENTS

Ground ivy can easily become a pest, overrunning gardens and lawns.

Horehound: *Marrubium vulgare*

OTHER COMMON, ETHNIC, OR SCIENTIFIC NAMES

Candyweed, coughweed, common horehound, hoarhound, marvel, water horehound, white horehound
France: Marrube blanc
Germany: Gemeiner Andorn

Italy: Manrubio, marrubio, masto
Mexico: Marrubio
Spain: Marrubio blanco, marroyo

RELATED SPECIES
Ballota nigra: Black horehound

GROWTH HABITS
Perennial
Origin: England and Mediterranean region
Range: Naturalized in North America, Europe, Asia, North Africa

CULINARY USES
Horehound is best known as old-fashioned hard candy or cough drops. It has a bitter, balsamic, and peculiarly musky, root-beer-like flavor. Craig Claiborne has described it as "rather unpleasant, perverse tasting." With increasing age, I have noticed that one person's "perverse" is another person's "curious," or yet another person's "fascinating."

Horehound is both pungent and bitter, but it *does* have its culinary uses. Tiny amounts (for instance, one leaf) can be used to flavor the braising liquid for a pot roast. Use it as you would use bay leaves, discarding the leaf when straining the sauce. It has been used in herbal beers, liqueurs, and syrups. Supposedly, leaves have been candied.

It is rumored that horehound can be used in cakes, cookies, and herbal teas, but I have yet to find any convincing recipes to try.

Horehound contains only traces of the usual flavoring compounds but lots of tannins (up to 70,000 ppm) and marrubiin (up to 10,000 ppm).

Hyssop: *Hyssopus officinalis*

OTHER COMMON, ETHNIC, OR SCIENTIFIC NAMES
Former scientific names for this species were *Hyssopus aristata* and *Hyssopus vulgaris.*
Denmark: Ysop
Estonia: Harilik iisop
Finland: Iisoppi
France: Herbe sacré, hysope
Gaelic: Isop
Germany: Eisop, Joseph, Kirchenseppl, Ysop
Iceland: Ísópur
Italy: Issopo, issopo celestino, ossopo
Netherlands: Hyssop, ipse, paddekruid
Norway: Isop
Poland: Hyzop lekarski

Russia: Yssop
Spain: Hisopo
Sweden: Isop
Turkey: Çördük otu

'Alba': White hyssop
'Grandiflora': Large flowered hyssop
'Rosea': Pink hyssop
'Rubra': Red hyssop

RELATED SPECIES
Agastache rugosa: Korean mint, wrinkled great hyssop
Agastache foeniculum: Anise hyssop, blue giant hyssop, fennel giant
   hyssop, fragrant giant hyssop, horsemint, giant hyssop

GROWTH HABITS
Shrubby perennial
Origin: Mediterranean region
Range: Dry temperate regions

CULINARY USES
Leaves are used in sweetened herbal teas, flavorings for cordials and wines, fruit salads, game, lamb pâtés, sausages, soups, and stews. Hyssop leaves make suitable garnishes for fat fish and for game, such as duck, goose, and pheasant. Dried leaves can be added to fruit pies, especially apricot or peach. Leaves and flowering tops can be added to salads, sauces, and condiments.

Honey derived from hyssop blossoms is highly prized. Hyssop leaves are supposedly among the secret ingredients in Benedictine, as well as in Chartreuse (both yellow and green) and Pernod. *Agastache foeniculum* is used as a seasoning and a tea.

Hyssop gets its minty, resinous, ginger-like flavor and aroma from β-pinene, l-pinocamphene, and traces of dozens of other terpinoids. The piney flavor is especially pronounced in dried hyssop.

OTHER USES
Extracts used in cosmetics, perfumes, and potpourri.

COMMENTS
The flavoring power of fresh hyssop is quite forceful; use it sparingly until you develop a feel for it.

The "hyssop" mentioned in the Bible is not this species but probably one of the many herbs known today as za'atar (q.v.). According to Fleisher and Fleisher, the species most likely to have been the biblical hyssop is *Majorana syriaca.*

This "horsemint" is not the same as *Mentha longifolia* (q.v.).

Hyssop
Hyssopus officinalis

From Woodville,
Medical botany, vol. 1

Many other herbs have "hyssop" in their names, several of which can be found in this book.

Konivari: *Hyptis suaveolens*

OTHER COMMON, ETHNIC, OR SCIENTIFIC NAMES
Bush tea plant, desert lavender, salvia, sangura
Colombia: Hierba de la muela
Mexico: Chan
Panama: Purga-purga

RELATED SPECIES
Hyptis emoryi: Desert lavender
Hyptis pectinata: Comb hyptis
Hyptis verticillata: John Charles (Jamaica); paleca (Panama)

GROWTH HABITS
Tropical shrub
Origin: Tropical America
Range: Common weed in pastures, Mexico to Argentina

Leaves are used as a mint-like herbal tea. Leaves are also toasted and ground and then mixed with honey and water to make a pungent beverage called *bate* in Mexico. Mucilaginous seeds have been used, like basil seeds, as a thickener for some soups. *Hyptis pectinata* is used in Nigeria as a seasoning. It is also used to flavor rum in Madagascar.

Konivari contains 1,8-cineole (4,500 ppm), α-caryophyllene(480 ppm), limonene (390 ppm), thujane (325 ppm), α-phellandrene (285 ppm), and some twenty other flavor components.

Lavender: *Lavandula angustifolia*

OTHER COMMON, ETHNIC, OR SCIENTIFIC NAMES

English lavender. Also known botanically as *Lavandula vera* or *Lavandula offinalis*.

Denmark: Lavendel
Estonia: Tähklavendel
Finland: Tupsupäälaventeli
France: Lavende
Gaelic: Lus-na-tùise
Germany: Lavendel
Hungary: Levendula
Iceland: Lofnarblóm
Iran: Ostukhudus
Italy: Lavanda
Mexico: Alhucema, espliego, lavanda
Morocco: Khzama (*Lavandula vera*)
Netherlands: Lavendel, spijklavendel
Norway: Lavendel
Poland: Lawenda waskolistna
Russia: Lavanda
Sweden: Lavendel
Tunisia: Khezama
Turkey: Lavanta

CULTIVARS

There are many cultivars, culinarily equal. Popular cultivars include 'Hidcote', 'Munstead', 'Sharon Roberts', 'Twickie Purple', the primary difference being the color of the flowers, which range from white to deep purple.

RELATED SPECIES

Lavandula dentata: French lavender
Lavandula spica (also known as *Lavandula latifolia*): Spick, spik, spike lavender

Lavandula stoechas: False nard, French lavender, Italian lavender, Spanish lavender
Lavandula viridis: Green lavender, yellow lavender (pale, nearly white, yellow flowers)

Lavandula × intermedia: Lavender grosso, lavandin (France, Germany, Spain); lavandino (Italy). This is a hybrid of *Lavandula angustifolia* and *Lavandula spica,* sometimes listed as *Lavandula fragrans* or, simply, *Lavandula hybrida.*

GROWTH HABITS

Perennial
Origin: Mediterranean region
Range: Temperate regions

CULINARY USES

Edible flowers are often crystallized in sugar. Lavender is used in jams, syrups, and vinegars.

Use flower spikes to garnish iced drinks such as herbal teas or lemonade. A trace of lavender oil lends a slightly bitter, floral note to Benedictine and Chartreuse. A small number of flowers can be minced together with other fresh herbs for flavoring vinaigrettes for salads. In Australia, the blossoms of lavender are used to flavor a cheese called Hillcrest Farm Curd Truckle.

Almost all of the production of *Lavandula × intermedia* is in France. Lavandin is grown in immense purple fields in Haute-Provence for the perfume industry. The local bees, caring nothing for human commerce, manufacture an exquisite lavender-scented honey. Not surprisingly, the dried blossoms are sometimes included in the mixtures sold as "Herbes de Provence."

Lavender's slightly alkaline floral scent and bitter taste are primarily provided by linalyl acetate (approximately 40 percent) and linalool (approximately 30 percent), though its perfume is enhanced by several other compounds.

Spike lavender tastes and smells more aromatic and rosemary-like. It contains borneol, cineol, linalool, and pinene. The hybrid, lavandin, is much stronger (and less sweet) smelling than the species, with a distinct scent of camphor.

OTHER USES

Source of oil of lavender, perfume ingredient. Sachets, potpourri. The dried herb perfumes bedlinens.

COMMENTS

Lavandula spica is hardier than other lavenders.
Khezama is also used as a name for marjoram in Tunisia.

Marjoram: *Origanum majorana*

Annual marjoram, knotted marjoram, marjoram, pot marjoram, sweet marjoram. Formerly known by the scientific name *Majorana hortensis*. Since the Latin alphabet did not originally contain a "J," the various names for this species are often spelled with an "I" in the place of the "J."

Arabic: Marzanjush
China: Ma-yueh-lan-hua
Estonia: Aedmajoraan, majoraan
Finland: Meirami
France: Marjolaine, origan
Germany: Majoran, Wurstkraut
Greece: Mandzurána
Hungary: Majoránna
Iceland: Kryddmaera, marjoram
India: Mirzam josh
Iran: Avishan, marzangoosh
Israel: Majoran asovit
Italy: Maggiorana, persa, persia
Japan: Mayorana
Mexico: Mejorana
Morocco: Mrdeddouch
Netherlands: Marjolein
Norway: Merian
Poland: Majeranek
Portugal: Manjerona
Russia: Majoran
Spain: Almáraco, marduix, mejorana
Sweden: Mejram
Tunisia: Khezama
Turkey: Kekik mercanköshk, mercankosk (use of these names is rare)

CULTIVARS

'Aurea', 'Creeping Gold Marjoram' or 'Golden Marjoram', and 'Variegated Marjoram'

RELATED SPECIES

Majorana syriaca: Za'atar (Israel)

GROWTH HABITS

Perennial, cultivated as an annual
Origin: Northern Africa, southwestern Asia
Range: Temperate regions

CULINARY USES

Used with green vegetables (great with lima beans), goose, turkey, pork, lamb, eggs, herbed compound butters, and salad dressings. Marjoram adds flavor to the cooking liquid used in preparing carrots, peas, spinach, and zucchini.

Rub it on game and poultry before roasting. Ground marjoram is a component of poultry seasoning, along with thyme, sage, rosemary, oregano, ginger, and black pepper. As you might guess from the German name *Wurstkraut,* the herb makes an important contribution to the flavor of sausages, although more often in lands closer to the Mediterranean. It is always an ingredient in "Herbes de Provence." Marjoram is also a component of the spice blend *épice parisienne.*

Young leaves are good in tomato-based seafood chowders and in tomato or brown sauces. The *pizzaiola* of Naples is a classic sauce based on garlic, marjoram, and tomatoes. In Italy, marjoram is used to season fish, soups, and stews. Chopped fresh leaves give character to bland cheese dishes like ricotta-filled ravioli.

Although it seems unlikely, marjoram is indicated in some recipes for altvater, Campari, Fernet Branca, and vermouth. It has been used in place of hops in herbal beers.

The seeds are used as an aromatic seasoning in candies and condiments, with meats, and in soft drinks.

Marjoram has a warm Mediterranean sort of scent with hints of aromatics like resin or camphor (similar to sage and rosemary) and a slight flowery component. Marjoram contains linalool, methyl chavicol, 1,8-cineol, eugenol, and terpineol. Marjoram can be distinguished from the similar oregano by the absence of carvacrol and thymol (see ZA'ATAR).

OTHER USES

Potpourri

COMMENTS

Khezama is also used as a name for lavender in Tunisia.

Mint: *Mentha* spp.

OTHER COMMON, ETHNIC, OR SCIENTIFIC NAMES

Algeria: Fliyou, nah'nah
Arabic: Naa-naa, na nal
Brazil: Hortelã
Cambodia: Pak hom ho
East Timor: Ortalan
Ethiopia: Iban, naana

France: Mentha, menthe
Germany: Minze
Greece: Diósmos, méntha, thiósmos
India: Podina, pudina
Iraq: Naanaa, na a na
Italy: Menta
Laos: Pak hom ho
Libya: Fliyou
Malaysia: Daun pudina
Mexico: Menta, yerba buena
Morocco: Fliyou, nana
Philippines: Hierba buena
Poland: Mieta
Portugal: Hortelã
Russia: Mentol, myata pyeryechnaya, myata zyelyonaya
Spain: Menta, yerba buena
Sri Lanka: Meenchhi
Thailand: Bas sa ra nai, by kaprow
Tunisia: Bnadaq, fliyou, nana
Vietnam: Bacha, ha to, hung, hung bac ha, hung cay, hung lui, que,
   rauthoon, rau hung que, rau que, rau thom, rau tuom, tia to

CULTIVARS

Mentha Pulegium 'Erecta': Upright pennyroyal
Mentha spicata 'Crispata': Crispata
Mentha spicata 'Crispii': Crispii
Mentha suaveolens 'Variegata': Pineapple mint

RELATED SPECIES

Hedeoma drummondii: New Mexican pennyroyal, poleo, toronji. Used like
   peppermint, in herbal teas.
Hedeoma Pulegiodes: Menta (Costa Rica); poleo (Mexico); American
   pennyroyal, hedeoma, mock pennyroyal, pudding grass, squaw mint,
   stinking balm, thickweed, wild peppermint
Mentha aquatica: Butenaj, butnege, butunage (Iraq); hung dui lang, lung
   que, rau hung, rau thom (Vietnam); Wasserminze (Germany); garden
   mint, watermint, wild water mint
Mentha arvensis: Hierba buena (Philippines); hung bac ha, hung lui
   (Vietnam); menta selvatica (Italy); ortalan (East Timor); corn mint,
   field mint, Japanese mint, wild pennyroyal. This is the mint used in
   most Asian cuisines.
Mentha australis: River mint (Australia)
Mentha citrata: Grapefruit mint, orange bergamot mint. This may be a
   cultivar of *Mentha aquatica* 'Citrata'.

Mentha diemenica: Kosciuko, slender mint (Australia)

Mentha longifolia: Egyptian mint, English horse mint, horse mint, round-leaved mint. Used in Afghanistan to flavor fresh cheese curds, and in India for chutneys. *Longifolia* is sometimes confused with *Mentha spicata* or *sylvestris* or *tomentosa.* In dried form, *longifolia* is the species of mint used in Turkish cooking.

Mentha Pulegium: Fliyou (Algeria, Libya, Morocco, and Tunisia); menta (Turkey); mentha puleggio (Spain); menthe pouliot (France); Polei (Germany); poleo, puleggio (Italy); European pennyroyal, lurk-in-the-ditch, pennyroyal, piliolerial, pudding grass, run-by-the-ground

Mentha Requienii: Corsican mint, menthella, creme-de-menthe plant

Mentha rotundifolia: Mastranto (Mexico); apple mint

Mentha sativa: L'herba sana (Spain); hairy mint, marsh mint, water mint, whorled mint

Mentha spicata (sometimes listed as *Mentha niliaca* or *Mentha viridis* or *Mentha cardiaca*): Frauen Munze (Germany); herba Santa Maria, hierba buena (Mexico); hortelã (Brazil); menthe de Notre Dame (France); myata zyelyonaya (Russia); naa-naa (Arabic); fliyou, nana (Morocco); fish mint, garden mint, green mint, lamb mint, mackeral mint, our lady's mint, sage of Bethlehem, spearmint, spire mint

Mentha suaveolens (formerly listed as *Mentha rotundifolia* or *Mentha* × *rotundifolia* or *Mentha rotundifolia* × *Mentha suaveolens*): Apple mint. Cultivar: 'Variegata'

HYBRIDS

Mentha × *piperita* (formerly known as *Mentha aquatica* × *Mentha spicata* and *Mentha piperita*): Ananoukh, nane (Turkey); bac ha, hung que, rau thom, tia to (Vietnam); bai saranae, bai sa ra nai, saranae (Thailand); bohe, bok hoh, heung-fa-chio, pak hom ho, xiang hua cai (China); chetnimaragu, jech-chak-kirai, meenchi, phudino, podina, pothina, pudina, putiyina (India); daun pudina, janggat (Indonesia); daun pudina, pohok (Malaysia); diósmos, idíosmos, ménda (Greece); Edelminze, Englische Minze, Minze, Pfefferminze (Germany); éqama, nanah (Arabic); hakuka (Japan); fodormenta (Hungary); hierbabuena, menta, piperita (Spain); iban, naana (Ethiopia); meenchi (Sri Lanka); menta pepe, menta peperina, menta piperita (Italy); menta (Mexico); menta (Hungary, Portugal); mentã (Romania); menthe anglaise, menthe poivrée, sentebon (France); mieta, mieta pieprzowa (Poland); minta, mynta, piparminta (Iceland); mionnt (Gaelic); mjata pjerechnaya, myata pyeryechnaya (Russia); na'na' (Israel); nanah, nane (Iran); nauna (Afganistan); pebermynte (Denmark); pepermunt (Netherlands); pepparmynta (Sweden); peppermynte (Norway); pereminde (Swahili); piparminttu (Finland); piparmünt (Estonia); pohok (Malaysia); rau huong lui (Vietnam); yang po ho or paoh-ho

(China); yerba buena (Philippines); brandy mint, candy mint, curled mint, curly green, lamb mint, lammint, peppermint

Mentha × Aquatica 'Citrata': Lemon mint

Mentha × Aquatica: Basil mint

Mentha × Gentilis: Red mint, Scotch mint. Sometimes given, mistakenly, as *Mentha cardiaca.*

Mentha × Gracilis: Scotch spearmint

Mentha × Gracilis 'Madalene Hill': Double mint

Mentha × Gracilis 'Variegata': Ginger mint

Mentha × piperita 'Citrata': Peperina (Italy); bergamot mint, brandy mint, eau de cologne mint, lemon mint, orange mint. Said to be used in Earl Grey tea. Formerly given as *Mentha citrata.*

Mentha × piperita 'Crispa': Black peppermint, curly

Mentha × piperita 'Crispata': Fuzzy spearmmint, large leaf spearmint, spearmint 'Kentucky Colonel'

GROWTH HABITS

Perennial

Origin: Old World

Range: Temperate regions to the tropics

CULINARY USES

Don't write off mint as just a knee-jerk garnish for a glass of iced tea or lemonade. This familiar sweet herb can be minced and added to cream cheese, ice cream, sorbets, fruit salads (especially those containing pineapple), baked fish, and roast lamb. That may seem an oddly disparate group of foods, but there are more to come: combine it with yogurt and cucumbers for an Indian raita, or use it as a garnish for hummus or pea soup (in fact, most bean dishes are enhanced by a bit of mint). In the Middle East, a similar yogurt-cucumber dish is made, usually with garlic and dill as well. This dish is known as *cacik* in Turkey, or *tzatzikia* in Greece. *Keftedes* or *kofta,* Middle Eastern meatballs, often contain mint and cinnamon. Interestingly, *albondigas* (a Mexican soup containing meatballs) also incorporates mint. The rice and lamb filling for stuffed grape leaves is usually flavored with lemon and mint. *Hortopitta,* another Greek dish, is a kind of pie filled with rice and spinach, seasoned with mint, along with cinnamon, dill, and parsley. Similarly, *flauones kyprioukes,* in Cyprus, is a quiche-like pie of cheese perfumed with mint.

Haloumi (sometimes spelled Halloumi) is a brine-cured cheese from Greece and Cyprus containing chopped mint. When made, this mostly sheep or goat cheese is dipped in hot water and kneaded, like mozzarella, so it has an elastic consistency.

Mint is popular in most Arabic cultures. Anywhere Islamic people have spent time, their culinary influence survives. Mint is used in Sicily because of the Saracens (a European name for the Muslims and Berbers who occupied the island in the Middle Ages). Similarly, cumin and saffron are used in

Spain because the Moors (a European name for the Muslims from Morocco) controlled it for most of the eighth through the fifteenth centuries. It is still used to flavor rice in Estremadura, the Portuguese Riviera.

The Iraqi mint, butnege (*Mentha aquatica*), is always used in dried form. It is used in the casserole called *tishreeb bajilla* or *tashreeb baqilla,* made with fava beans. Other tashreebs can be made with okra, yogurt, or chickpeas in place of fava beans. According to Nina Jamil-Garbutt, the word *tashreeb* refers to stock thickened with pieces of bread, although Paula Wolfert has found sources in which it means lamb's or sheep's trotters. Butnege is often associated with vegetable dishes in Iraqi cuisine, such as salads of lettuce or beets, or chard stuffed with a pilaf-like mixture of onions and rice. Jamil-Garbutt's 1985 book *The Baghdad Kitchen* recommends substituting any dried mint if butnege is unavailable.

The same species is used, in Vietnam, in combination with daun kesom (q.v.) as a garnish for dumplings or in the filling of imperial rolls. It is also the chosen mint for *laab,* the raw beef dish from Laos. Mint's fresh taste is a perfect foil for the fatty flavor of some meats, as it is used for lamb in the Middle East. In Thailand, it serves the same function in *yam nang mu,* a kind of salad containing pork skin.

Try adding mint to the cooking liquid for vegetables, such as carrots, peas, or potatoes. Use it in salad dressings (tabouleh is a classic example). Add mint and lemon zest to whipped cream as an accompaniment to ripe figs.

Mint is, of course, used in jelly, but it is also useful in vinegars and flavored oils. The leaves can be used as a garnish for desserts, either fresh or crystallized.

Various mints are used in cordials, such as Creme de Menthe. Benedictine, Fernet Branca, Grand Marnier, and vermouth, for example, contain peppermint. Menthol is part of yellow Chartreuse's formulation. Pippermint is another French liqueur that is flavored with mint. A less-sweet version is the Italian brandy called Grappa alla Menta. The Italian Mentucca, or Centerbe, includes mint among the hundred-odd herbal ingredients collected in Abruzzi.

Pennyroyal, seldom considered a culinary herb today, used to be used as a seasoning for pork. A small amount, along with some curry powder, can be added to eggs. It was generally used in combination with sweeteners, such as honey. It was used in teas also. Extracted essential oils are still used in some commercial flavorings.

Typically mints contain menthol. Peppermint contains (in addition to its menthol) l-menthyl acetate, cadinene, menthone and l-limonene. *Mentha arvensis* contains l-menthol (up to 29,500 ppm), (+)-octan-3-one (up to 27,000 ppm), pulegone (up to 24,900 ppm), menthol (up to 24,300 ppm) and menthone (up to 24,000 ppm). Pennyroyal has (in addition to the expected 3,700 ppm of menthol) pulegones (up to 19,400 ppm), isomenthone (up to 8,400 ppm), and menthone (up to 6,100 ppm), plus traces of several other aromatics and a substantial amount of tannin (up to 40,000 ppm). Spearmint replaces much of the menthol with carvone (up to 20,000 ppm), (+)-dihydrocarvone (up to 13,700 ppm), 1,8-cineol (up to 9,300 ppm), linalool (up to 9,000 ppm), and limonene (up to 9,000 ppm), and, as is typical of mints, perhaps a hundred other terpinoids and esters.

OTHER USES
Essential oils

COMMENTS
Mint will take over any garden space available. Be prepared to put in a barrier to the spreading stolons, or spend the rest of your life pulling out the unwanted intruders.

A short look at the list of mints above suggests that the names of mints (and related genera) can be quite confusing. Vietnamese mint (*Polygonum pulchrum,* q.v.) is not actually a mint. *Rau que,* a Vietnamese word for mint, is also the name for basil. "Horse mint" is used as a name for some of the *Monardas* (see WILD BERGAMOT). Lemon mint, *Monarda citriodora,* is another bergamot that carries the mint name. These examples only hint at the bewilderment possible in English; a look at mint names in other languages offers only more muddle.

Poleo is used for several different mints, but also refers to a Mexican savory, *Satureja oaxacana* (q.v.).

The Iraqi name *butnege,* in all of its forms, is also applied to a savory-like plant called *Micromeria fruticosa* 'Druce'. I have not been able to find this species, but the genus *Micromeria* is an old name for what is now known as *Satureja* (see SUMMER SAVORY, THRYBA, and YERBA BUENA).

The naming of mints sold in nurseries and garden shops can be extremely variable. The cavalier manner in which common names and scientific names are used in such places is little more than an invitation to argument.

Moldavian Balm: *Dracocephalum Moldavica*

OTHER COMMON, ETHNIC, OR SCIENTIFIC NAMES
Dragonhead, Moldavian dragon's head

GROWTH HABITS
Annual
Origin: Europe and Asia
Range: Naturalized in Europe and North America

CULINARY USES
Leaves are used in herbal teas when a lemony quality is desired. Young shoots are eaten in salads.

Motherwort: *Leonurus cardiaca*

OTHER COMMON, ETHNIC, OR SCIENTIFIC NAMES
Mexico: Agripalma, cardiaca, chiquiza

RELATED SPECIES
Leonurus sibiricus: Chivirico, Siberian motherwort

GROWTH HABITS
Perennial
Origin: Mediterranean region
Range: Cosmopolitan weed

CULINARY USES
Flowers are used in teas. They can also be used as a seasoning for soups made with legumes. Breweries have used the flowering tops in place of hops in ales, beers, and stout.

Roots of *Leonurus sibiricus* are served with pork in China, where young growth is prepared as a potherb.

In addition to as much as 3,500 ppm of assorted alkaloids, motherwort contains caryophyllene (up to 200 ppm), α-humulene (up to 175 ppm), α-pinene (up to 28 ppm), linalool (up to 4 ppm), limonene (up to 2 ppm), and traces of dozens of other compounds.

Native Mint: *Prostanthera* spp.

OTHER COMMON, ETHNIC, OR SCIENTIFIC NAMES
Mintbush, native peppermint

RELATED SPECIES
Prostanthera lasianthos: Victorian Christmas bush
Prostanthera nivea: Snowy mintbush
Prostanthera rotundifolia: Round-leaf mintbush

GROWTH HABITS
Shrub or shrubby perennial
Origin: Southeast Australia and Tasmania
Range: Australia

CULINARY USES
Native mint's peppermint-like flavor and scent can be used anywhere mint would be used: compound butters, herbed breads, sauces (including pestos), and flavored vinegar. The flavor is enhanced by a slight eucalyptus or woody scent. Native mint can be used in sauces for desserts, especially

those involving cream. It might also make an interesting addition to a balsamic vinaigrette.

Available in the form of an essential oil.

COMMENTS

In Australia, the name "native mint" also refers to many peppermint-scented species of eucalyptus.

Oregano: *Origanum vulgare*

OTHER COMMON, ETHNIC, OR SCIENTIFIC NAMES

Italian oregano, French marjoram, marjoram, Mexican sage, pot marjoram, oregan, organy, origanum, wild marjoram

Arabic: Anrar
Estonia: Harilik pune
Finland: Mäkimeirami
France: Doste, marazolette, marjolaine bâtarde, marjolaine sauvage, origan, pelevoué, penevoué, thé rouge, thym de berger
Germany: Dost, Dosten, Kostets, Oregano, Oreganum, Topf-majoroni, Wilder Majoran
Greece: Oríganon, rígani, rigany, righani
Iceland: Bergminta, oreganó
Iran: Avishan kuhi
Italy: Erba acciuga, origano, origano rigamo, regamo; riganu (in Sicily)
Mexico: Oregano
Netherlands: Wilde marjolein
Norway: Bergmynte, kung
Philippines: Suganda
Poland: Dziki majeranek, lebiodka pospolita
Portugal: Onrégão
Russia: Dushitsa
Spain: Orégano, orenga
Sweden: Kungsmynta, vild mejram
Turkey: Izmir kekigi, farekulagi, mercan kösk, kekik, yabani mercankosk

CULTIVARS

'Aureum', 'Dark Oregano', 'Dwarf Oregano' or 'Compactum Nanum', 'Compact Pink Flowered', 'Crinkle Leaf', 'Golden Marjoram', 'Golden Oregano' or 'Golden Creeping Oregano', 'Gold Variegated Marjoram', 'Jim Perry's Oregano', 'Seedless Oregano', 'Silver Oregano', 'Variegated Oregano', 'Viride' or 'White Oregano', 'White Anniversary Oregano'

Origanum vulgare subs. *hirtum* (also known as *Origanum hirtum* or *Origanum heracleoticum*): Karakekik (Turkey), Greek oregano, marjoram, pot marjoram, winter sweet marjoram, za'atar. Cultivars include 'Greek Oregano', 'Italian Oregano', and 'Sicilian Oregano'.

RELATED SPECIES

Origanum compactum 'Benth': Za'tar, za'tar-al-hamir, Za'tar tadlawi (Morocco)

Origanum elongatum: Za'tar riffi (Morocco)

Origanum micranthum: Kekik (Turkey)

Origanum syriacum: Dag kekegi, yaban kekegi (Turkey)

Origanum tytthanum (sometimes listed as *Origanum vulgare* subs. *gracile*): Kirghiz oregano, Russian oregano

HYBRID

An oregano-marjoram hybrid called "cooking oregano," "culinary oregano," "hardy marjoram," or "Italian oregano" is almost as hardy as the species, but it tastes and smells more like marjoram.

GROWTH HABITS

Perennial

Origin: Europe, the Mediterranean region to central Asia

Range: Temperate regions

CULINARY USES

Dried oregano is familiar to anyone who has eaten pizza or indeed anything from the Mediterranean region. The fresh herb is quite different. It is hotter and has an intense aromatic quality that requires restraint on the part of the cook.

Many cookbooks make the blanket suggestion that you should use a smaller amount of dried herbs than fresh (usually stating that a half teaspoon of dried herb is equivalent to one tablespoon of fresh herb). This may be true of some herbs, but it is definitely not the case with members of the oregano/marjoram group. Accepting such advice at face value can result in some unpalatable, if not inedible, fare. Always taste and smell your ingredients before adding them to a dish. It is the only way to be certain of their quality and intensity.

A simple dish like linguine with white clam sauce can be overpowered by fresh oregano, but it benefits from the milder dried oregano and fresh parsley. Add dried oregano to the drawn butter served with boiled shellfish: clams, lobster, and shrimp. Combine black pepper, oregano, parsley, scallions, and thyme to make a rub for baked firm fish, such as grouper, mahimahi, or marlin.

Obviously, any pairing with tomatoes is likely to be a success, but the same is true with beans, onions, potatoes, and spinach. Oregano is useful in marinades for game, lamb, beef, pork, and poultry, especially chicken, guinea hen, and pheasant. Good with eggs and in pickling, salads, and soups.

Use fresh oregano in vinegars, flavored oils, and compound butters. Toss a few stems of oregano on top of the coals while barbecuing to impart a savory flavor.

Oregano can be brewed as an herbal tea. *Thé rouge* is made from the deep pink flower heads. Hymettus honey, a glory of the Greek countryside, is derived mainly from the blossoms of mountain herbs like the oreganos, savories, and thymes.

Origanum vulgare hirtum, especially the cultivar 'Greek Oregano', is usually sold as oregano. In most cases, any "oregano" you buy in the grocery store is probably not oregano at all, but winter marjoram. Consequently, all the uses you normally think of for oregano apply equally well to winter marjoram.

A popular beverage in Morocco is hot milk flavored with oregano. According to Paula Wolfert, za'tar-al-hamir (*Origanum compactum* Benth) is, for Moroccans, the true za'tar. She writes that it is used in "everything including *Babbouche* (the snail soup); cucumber salad; fish tagines; pasta-type balls (called *Berkkukes*) and in my recipe for *smen* in my book." The mountain herb za'tar riffi (*Origanum elongatum*) is used in Morocco to flavor local honeys.

The Turkish word *farekulagi* means "mouse ears," an excellent description of the plant's leaves. In Turkey, *kekik* and similar words are used as generic names for a group of herbs that include various oreganos, marjorams, savories, and thymes (see THYME). For example, in the Antalya region, *Origanum onites* is known as *tas kekik,* while *canakkale kekigi, kara ot, kekigi,* and *keklik otu* all refer to *Origanum vulgare,* in and around Istanbul. The *kekik* from the Tarsus Mountains is *Origanum micranthum,* but *dag kekegi* and *yaban kekegi* is *Origanum syriacum* from Antakya. In Mersin, *Origanum majorana* is called *guy otu* (in Turkish, *kara* means "dark or black," and *yaban* or *yabani* means "wild").

In England, the goat's milk cheese called Innes sometimes contains oregano.

Oregano's characteristic flavor and scent result from its carvacrol and thymol, along with traces of 4-terpineol, β-bisabolene, and caryophyllene. The flavor of za'atar (*Origanum vulgare* hirtum) is characterized by carvacrol and γ-terpinene, although it does contain some fourteen other flavoring compounds.

OTHER USES
Scented soaps

"Oregano" is used as a name in Mexico for a number of species of the *Lippia* genus, and it is never applied to *Origanum* spp. The name "oregano" is, however, used in Mexico for *Lantana involucrata,* an unrelated plant (actually a shrub verbena, known as "Alampana" in Colombia) that is used in the same ways as oregano. To add to the confusion, other *Lantanas* have common names like "yellow sage" and "polecat geranium," also unrelated to plants with similar names.

"Za'tar" or "za'atar" are generic names for a whole group of Middle Eastern herbs from the genera *Origanum, Calamintha, Thymus,* and *Satureja.* There is a lot of overlap between the za'atar and kekik groups.

Patchouly: *Pogostemon cablin*

OTHER COMMON, ETHNIC, OR SCIENTIFIC NAMES
Dhalum wangi, pachupat, patchouli, patcha pat, pucha-put, tilam wangi. Also known botanically as *Pogostemon patchouli.*
Germany: Patchouli
Indonesia: Nilam
Italy: Patchouli
Spain: Pachuli

RELATED SPECIES
Pogostemon heyeanus: Java patchouli, Malayan patchouli, smooth patchouli

GROWTH HABITS
Perennial
Origin: Malaysia
Range: Cultivated in Brazil, Indonesia, Malaysia, Madagascar, Paraguay, the Seychelles

CULINARY USES
Fresh leaves have been used as a seasoning. When dried and cured (like tea), the leaves develop essential oils used in chewing gums and some commercial baked goods.

Pogostemon heyeanus is used to flavor a liquor in Java.

Patchouly contains benzaldehyde, eugenol, cinnaminaldehyde, and patchouly alcohol. The extracted oil has a peculiar musty odor, reminiscent of Brazil nuts (*Bertholletia excelsa*).

OTHER USES
Most patchouly is used in the manufacture of perfumes.

The genus is mentioned, but not listed, in *Hortus Third*.

Perilla: *Perilla frutescens*

OTHER COMMON, ETHNIC, OR SCIENTIFIC NAMES
Beefsteak leaf, beefsteak plant, Chinese basil, wild sesame. Previous scientific names for perilla include: *Perilla crispa, Perilla nankinensis, Ocimum frutescens,* and *Ocimum crispum.*
China: Bai su zi, chi ssu, hung sha yao, tyu ssu, yeh ssu, zi su
Germany: Chinesische Melisse, Perilla, Schwarznessel, Wilder Sesam
India: Ban tulsi, bhanjira
Japan: Aka-shiso (red); ao-shiso (green); egoma, oba, shiso
Korea: Kkaennip, tulkkae
Thailand: Ngaa khee mon
Vietnam: Tia to

CULTIVARS
'Aromatic Flatleaf Perilla', 'Curled Perilla' or 'Curly Perilla', 'Green Cumin', 'Lemon Perilla'
'Altropurpurea': Red perilla, purple perilla, crispy perilla, aka shiso or shiso noha (Japan). Dark purple foliage
'Crispa': Green perilla or ao shiso (Japan). Green or bronze foliage with bright purple, wrinkly edges
'Lanciniata': Red perilla with deeply serrated leaves

GROWTH HABITS
Annual
Origin: China, Southeast Asia, west to the Himalayas
Range: Naturalized in eastern United States; weedy

CULINARY USES
The herb's flavor is cilantro-like, with hints of cinnamon, lemon, and mint. Green and bronze varieties are gingery, with a sweet finish. Reddish purple forms are not as intensely flavored as the green varieties. Bronze perilla is the variety most often used in food. Use fresh leaves in salads (especially those that include cucumbers), fruit salads, and stir-fries.

Flowers and buds (*hojiso* or *mejiso*) garnish soups or fish.

The tiny seed pods are sometimes added to *shoyu* to make a condiment to accompany tempura. The seeds, when pressed, yield a cooking oil that is very high in polyunsaturated fat.

Red perilla provides the color of *umeboshi,* the Japanese salted "plums" (which are actually a kind of apricot), and the glowing pink of preserved

Perilla
Perilla frutescens

From Weinmann,
Phytanthoza iconographia, vol. 3

ginger. After perilla is pickled with umeboshi, the leaves are dried and pulverized to make the condiment *shiso momiji,* a kind of seasoned salt. It is traditionally served with tofu and some tempuras. It is also an ingredient in several varieties of canned Japanese pickled vegetables.

Red perilla is known as *rau tio to* in Vietnam, where its hairy leaves are prized for their slightly bitter citrus and cinnamon-like flavor. *Rau kinh gioi,* or green perilla, has a hot, lemony, faintly basil-like flavor that the Vietnamese like in salads, or they use the leaves as they would lettuce, as a wrapper of hot foods.

Perilla contains perilla aldehyde, perilla ketone, perillene, α-pinene, and pinene.

OTHER USES

Perilla is also raised in Japan for oilseeds.

COMMENTS

I had heard that oba is used as a garnish for sushi, but confirmation proved to be very elusive. While oba's description sounded a bit like that of *Perilla frutescens* 'Crispa', there had been no mention of purple edges on the leaves, so I had my doubts. I searched in dozens of books for oba, never finding the slightest mention of the herb. Recently, I had some sushi made with burdock roots (*gobo*). I noticed a thin, ruffled line of green surrounding the burnt-orange pickled roots in the center of the nori-wrapped roll. I questioned the sushi chef about it, and he answered "Japanese mint." I asked if he meant shiso. When he nodded (seemingly surprised that this extremely un-Japanese eater knew anything at all about the food), I saw my chance. Did he know of a leaf called oba? Lo and behold: oba is green perilla. Not all answers are to be found in books.

Some people develop allergic skin rections to perilla aldehyde in the leaves.

Tia to is also the Vietnamese name for the leaves of the caraway plant (q.v.).

Rau kinh gioi has been used as a name for lemon balm, *Melissa officinalis* (q.v.).

Rosemary: *Rosmarinus officinalis*

OTHER COMMON, ETHNIC, OR SCIENTIFIC NAMES

Compass plant, compass weed, old man, polar weed. An old scientific name for the plant is *Rosmarinus coronarium*.

Arabic: Ikil al-jabal
China: Mi-tieh-hsian
Denmark: Rosmarin
Estonia: Harilik rosmariin
Finland: Rosmariini
France: Ecensier, incensier, romarin, rosmarin
Gaelic: Ròs mhuire
Germany: Rosmarin
Greece: Arismári, dendrolívano, diosmaríni
Iceland: Rósmarín, saedögg
Iran: Eklil kuhi
Italy: Ramerino, rosmarino
Japan: Mannenro
Mexico: Romero
Netherlands: Rozemarijn
Norway: Rosmarin
Poland: Rozmaryn lekarski
Portugal: Alecrim
Russia: Rozmarin
Spain: Romaní, rosmario, romero
Sweden: Rosmarín
Turkey: Biberiye

CULTIVARS

The plant has many cultivars, mostly identical gastronomically. They are distinguished primarily by differences in growth habit (such as the low-growing prostrate or trailing rosemary, *Rosmarinus officinalis* 'Prostratus') and color of the flowers. Of culinary interest are 'Blue Spire' or 'Blue Spears', 'Escondito', 'Golden Rain' or 'Joyce de Baggio'. The leaves of 'Gorizia' are said to be mild, with a ginger-like scent. Of interest for their distinctive flowers are 'Albiflorus', 'Majorica Pink', 'Miss Jessopp's Upright', 'Mrs. Howard's Creeping', 'Nancy Howard', 'Severn Sea', and 'Tuscan Blue'.

GROWTH HABITS

Evergreen shrub

Origin: Mediterranean region. The Greek name, *dendrolívano,* suggests
   Lebanon as the original source of the plant.

Range: Frost-free temperate regions

CULINARY USES

Lavender-lipped flowers are milder in taste than the leaves, so they can be used in salads and garnishes. The floral cultivars listed above would all make beautiful edible garnishes. The flowers, with some help from Italian bees, yield an aromatic honey. French Narbonne honey is derived from rosemary blossom nectar. Leaves and flowers are used in herbal teas, often with tansy. The blossoms are sometimes crystallized.

Rosemary-flavored vinegars are delicious when used for deglazing the pan after roasting fresh pork or sautéing pork chops. Rosemary-scented wine or jelly can also be used in the preparation of rich meats.

Fresh and dried leaves as seasoning and garnish for fish and meats, especially lamb and poultry. Roast pork, or suckling pig, especially the aristas of Florence, benefit from the warm flavors of rosemary, garlic, and cloves. In Rome, rosemary is used to season lamb, not pork. The herb is occasionally used with fish, as in Provençal's red mullet with rosemary.

Rosemary can be used—very sparingly—in salad dressings. A little goes a long way. Save stems after removing leaves for storage; they make excellent flavored skewers for shish-kabobs. Alternatively, the twigs can be placed under meats while they are grilled.

Rosemary is good with beans and polenta and also makes interesting compound butters. It might appear to be too strong and resinous for use in cheeses, but it has been utilized in some. In England, the goat's milk cheese called Innes sometimes contains rosemary, and the soft cheese known as Perrouche is often sold with a crust of chopped rosemary.

Place a sprig of fresh rosemary in the red wine used for poaching oranges. Campari's orange flavor is enhanced by the savory aromatic quality of rosemary. Mince a small amount of fresh rosemary with pitted Calamata olives, add olive oil and fresh-ground black pepper, and use the mixture to coat penne pasta or small new potatoes.

Rosemary leaves get their typical aromatic presence from rosmarinic acid (up to 25,000 ppm), 1,8-cineol (up to 8,100 ppm), bornyl acetate (up to 5,000 ppm), borneol (up to 4,200 ppm) and camphor (up to 5,800 ppm). The flowers don't contain camphene or camphor so they don't taste as piney or resinous. Unlike the leaves, the flowers contain a little tannin.

OTHER USES

Flowering tops yield an aromatic oil used in perfumes and soaps.

COMMENTS

I read that a couple of decades ago, an archeologist in Rome had noticed some rosemary growing in an oddly regular fashion. Digging ten to twelve feet below the surface, he discovered the ruins of a small house. An ancient Roman had planted the rosemary conveniently close to the kitchen door. Long after the occupants had passed on to their culinary rewards, and their house crumbled, the rosemary lived on. Century after century, the soil built up over the spot, rising slowly enough for the rosemary to keep its head above the horizon. Now *that's* a perennial.

Protect (or bring indoors) in colder climates. "Compass plant," "compass weed," and "polar weed" are all used as names for rosin weed, *Silphium paciniatum*.

Rosemary Mint: *Poliomintha incana*

OTHER COMMON, ETHNIC, OR SCIENTIFIC NAMES

Desert rosemary, eagle feather medicine, hoary rosemary mint, oregano, purple sage

RELATED SPECIES

Poliomintha longiflora: Mexican oregano, orégano

GROWTH HABITS

Perennial
Origin: Southwestern United States
Range: Wild desert plant

CULINARY USES

The dried aromatic leaves are used as a seasoning. Fresh leaves are cooked with beans or added to omelets and frittatas. *Poliomintha incana* is a popular herb among the Hopi of northeastern Arizona, while *Poliomintha longiflora* is favored by the Kickapoos of Texas and Mexico.

Poliomintha incana contains pulegone (up to 777,000 ppm), α-terpineol (up to 20,000 ppm), 8-hydroxy para menth-4-en-3-one (up to 14,000 ppm), *trans*-iso-pulegone (up to 13,000 ppm), *cis*-iso-pulegone (up to 1,000 ppm).

COMMENTS

Poliomintha is not listed in *Hortus Third*.

"Mexican oregano" is also the name for *Lippia graveolens* (q.v.). *Poliomintha longiflora* has a similar flavor and uses.

Sage: *Salvia officinalis*

OTHER COMMON, ETHNIC, OR SCIENTIFIC NAMES

Common sage, garden sage, ramona, sawge
Arabic: Maryamiya
China: Ching-chieh
Estonia: Salvei
Finland: Rohtosalvia, salvia
France: Sauge, thé de la Grèce
Gaelic: Athair liath, slan lus
Germany: Salbei
Greece: Alisfakiá, faskomiliá
Hungary: Zsálya
Iceland: Salvía
India: Bhui-tulsi, sathi, kammarkas
Iran: Mariam goli
Iraq: Semsem barri
Italy: Salvia
Netherlands: Franse thee, salie, selft, selve, tuinsalie
Norway: Salvie
Poland: Szalwia lekarska
Portugal: Salva
Russia: Shalfey
Spain: Sàlvia
Sweden: Kryddsalvia, salvia
Turkey: Adacayi

CULTIVARS AND SUBSPECIES

'Berggarten Sage', 'Dwarf Sage' or 'Nana', 'Golden Sage' or 'Aurea', 'Gold Variegated Sage', 'Holt's Mammoth Sage' or 'Giant Sage', 'Icterina', 'Purple Sage' or 'Purpurea' (or even 'Purpurescens'), 'Town of Bath', 'Tricolor Sage' or 'Variegated Sage'
Salvia officinalis subs. *minor:* Dalmatian sage
Salvia officinalis subs. *prostrata:* Prostrate sage (pronounced balsamic flavor)

RELATED SPECIES

Salvia aethiopis: African sage
Salvia argentea: Silver clary sage
Salvia arizonica: Arizona creeping sage

Salvia azurea: Wild blue sage

Salvia blepharophylla: Mexican sage

Salvia cacaliaefolia: Central American sage

Salvia candelabrum: Candelabrum sage

Salvia carduacea: Thistle sage

Salvia Clevelandii: Blue sage

Salvia coccinea: Chia, scarlet sage, tropical sage

Salvia columbariae: Chia, golden chia

Salvia discolor: Peruvian sage

Salvia divinorum: Ska maría pastora (Mexico, Oaxaca only); Yerba de la pastora (Mexico); diviner's sage, Mexican hallucinogenic sage

Salvia Dorisiana: Fruit sage. Cultivated as an annual. Originated in Honduras. Its scent is reminiscent of grapefruit and pineapple.

Salvia elegans (sometimes listed as *Salvia rutilans*): Pineapple sage. Steep in apple juice before making jelly. The leaves and red flowers make a good garnish for cold drinks or fruit salads. Tiny fritters of pineapple sage leaves are made; their aromatic fruity quality serve as counterpoint to the richness of cream.

Salvia forskahlei: Eastern European sage

Salvia fruticosa (sometimes listed as *Salvia trilobata* or *Salvia triloba*): Greek sage. Strong sage quality, with a rosemary-like scent.

Salvia fulgens: Cardinal sage, Mexican red sage

Salvia glutinosa: Hardy sage, Jupiter's distaff, yellow sage

Salvia grandiflora: Balsamic sage

Salvia greggii: Autumn sage

Salvia guaranitica: Blue sage, nutmeg sage

Salvia hispanica: Chia (Mexico); chia sage, Mexican chia

Salvia involucrata: Roseleaf sage; has ink flowers

Salvia lavendulaefolia (sometimes listed as *Salvia lavendulifolia*): Narrowleaf sage, Spanish sage; this is a wild sage, smelling of eucalyptus.

Salvia leucantha: Mexican bush sage

Salvia lyrata: Lyreleaf sage

Salvia madrensis: Forsythia sage

Salvia mellifera: Black sage

Salvia microphylla: Red sage; has red flowers

Salvia patens: Gentian sage

Salvia pomifera: Apple-bearing sage

Salvia pratensis: Meadow clary sage, meadow sage

Salvia repens repens: Creeping sage

Salvia roemeriana: Cedar sage

Salvia Sclarea: Muscateller Salbei (Germany); salvia muscatel (Spain); sauge scarée (France); clary sage, clear eye, see-bright

Salvia sonomensis: Sonoma creeping sage
Salvia spathacea: Pitcher sage
Salvia tiliaefolia: Tarahumara chia sage
Salvia transylvanica: Transylvanica sage
Salvia triloba: Greek sage
Salvia uglinosa: Winter blooming sage
Salvia Verbenaca: Christ's eye, clary sage, oculus christi, vervain sage,
   wild clary, wild English clary, wild English sage
Salvia verticillata: Whorled clary sage
Salvia viridis: Ada çayi (Turkey); Salbei (Germany); annual clary sage,
   painted sage, red-topped sage, tricolor sage. Use its blue-violet, pink,
   or white flowers in salads or as a garnish.

GROWTH HABITS
   Perennial
   Origin: Northern coast of the Mediterranean
   Range: Temperate regions

CULINARY USES
   Flowers are used in salads and as garnishes. Leaves are used in poultry
stuffings, especially with onions, and are a key ingredient in sausages made
with pork, duck, or goose. The leaves can be used with soft cheeses, butters,
jellies, and vinegars. They are also good with tomatoes, eggs, and onion soup
and are sometimes used in herbal teas.
   Sage is included in the recipes for a number of herbal liqueurs known as
digestifs. Campari and vermouth are typical of these bitter concoctions.
Chartreuse is another; it uses the extracted oil of clary sage.
   "Italian Seasoning" is a name for several different commercial mixtures of
herbs and spices. These preparations often contain sage.
   Fruit sage, *Salvia Dorisiana,* is good with baked fish or roast beef.
   Golden chia, *Salvia columbariae,* is a source of the grain called chia, which
is used with other grains as a starch, or for its thickening properties in fruit
juices. Its leaves are used as a seasoning, and its sprouts are eaten in salads.
Mexican chia, *Salvia hispanica,* is the primary source of the grain. The seeds'
mucilaginous property when wet allows them to adhere to unglazed ceramic,
which making it possible to "grow" Chia Pets.
   Hardy sage, *Salvia glutinosa,* is used in Holland to flavor a local wine. *Salvia indica,* for which there does not seem to a common name in English, is
used in India as a flavoring for beer. Meadow sage, *Salvia pratensis,* is more
bitter than most sages and has been used to flavor beers and wines.
   Tricolor, or variegated, sage, *Salvia officinalis,* has the usual sage flavor but
makes a beautiful garnish for cold meats (the leaves lose their color if exposed to heat).

A savory garnish, or the basis for a quick sauce for stuffed pasta, is sautéed fresh sage leaves. The sage leaves become crispy and aromatic, but milder than you might expect.

Sage has had some use in cheese making. It is used in some marbled English hard cheeses. Cumberland Farmhouse tastes of sage. The juice of sage is used to flavor Sage Derby, while the leaves themselves have a much stronger presence in Sage Lancashire. Outside of the British Isles, the only notable sage-infused cheeses I have found were some Vermont Cheddars.

Almost all sages contain borneol, camphor, cineol, pinene, and thujone (see Comments, under MUGWORT), although different cultivars, species, and varietals vary in proportions of these compounds, and occasionally in the addition or subtraction of key components. *Salvia lavendulaefolia,* for example, contains more camphor and cineol than *Salvia officinalis,* but its flavor is flat and rather uninteresting because it doesn't contain thujone, which provides the slight bitter edge normally found in sage.

OTHER USES
Potpourri

COMMENTS
Clary sage forms large puckered, velvety, silvery leaves; to me, its aroma, like that of boxwood, is reminiscent of rutting tomcat. I know that tastes change with time, but I am going to need some serious cultural evolution before I will be able to think of it as a culinary herb.

"Indian sage" is a name used for boneset, *Eupatorium perfoliatum,* which is obviously not a sage at all. Similarly, "wood sage" is actually sage-leaved germander, *Teucrium scorodonia.*

Skullcap: *Scutellaria galericulata*

OTHER COMMON, ETHNIC, OR SCIENTIFIC NAMES
Marsh skullcap
Mexico: Esculetaria

GROWTH HABITS
Perennial
Origin: Northern Hemisphere
Range: Temperate regions

CULINARY USES
The leaves are bitter but not aromatic. They are used in herbal teas.

Skullcap contains substantial amounts of tannin (up to 35,000 ppm), plus caryophylline (up to 180 ppm), *trans*-b-farnesene (up to 100 ppm), menthone (up to 60 ppm), and α-humulene (up to 20 ppm).

Summer Savory: *Satureja hortensis*

OTHER COMMON, ETHNIC, OR SCIENTIFIC NAMES
Calamint, satureja leaf, savory. *Satureja* appears in various botanical texts
as *Acinos, Calamintha, Clinopodium,* and *Micromeria.*

Arabic: Nadgh
China: Hsiang-po-ho
Estonia: Piparrohi
Ethiopia: Tosinyi
Finland: Kesäkynteli
France: Herbe de Saint-Julien, sariette
Gaelic: Garbhag ghàraidh
Germany: Bohnenkraut, Kölle, Pfefferkraut, Saturei, Winterbergminze
Greece: Thrombi
Hungary: Csombor
Iceland: Sar
Italy: Erba cerea, santoreggia, timo
Mexico: Ajedrilla
Netherlands: Bonenkruid, koele, kunne, peperkruid, scharekruid,
tuinbonenkruid
Norway: Bønneurt, sar
Poland: Czaber ogrodowy
Portugal: Segurelha
Romania: Cimbru
Russia: Chabjor
Spain: Ajedrea, saborija, sabroso, sajolida
Sweden: Kyndel
Turkey: Sater otu

RELATED SPECIES
Clinopodium vulgare (sometimes called *Satureja vulgaris* or *Calamintha
Clinopodium*): Basil, basilweed, dog mint, field basil, hedge basil, hedge
calamint, wild basil
Satureja oaxacana: Hierba de borracho, poleo (Mexico)
Satureja spicigera: Creeping winter savory
Satureja viminea: Costa Rican mint bush, Jamaican mint bush

GROWTH HABITS
Annual
Origin: Mediterranean region
Range: Dry temperate regions

CULINARY USES
Savory is used in baked goods, with eggs, and with fish and meats. Both
delicate meats, like veal, and strong-tasting meats, like mutton or goat,

benefit from its warm, aromatic strength. It is especially good in stuffings for chicken and turkey, and in vinaigrettes and sauces. It adds a warm aroma when cooked with beans, lentils, and—especially—limas. Finely minced with parsley and perhaps a little chervil, it makes a tasty garnish for soft cheeses.

In France, sprigs of savory are used with sheep's or goat's milk cheeses. Banon au Pèbri d'Aï, La Sariette, and Poivre d'Ane are savory-laced cheeses sold wrapped in chestnut leaves.

Hymettus honey, the Greek pastoral treasure, is derived mainly from nectar collected from mountain herbs like the savories and other aromatic Mediterranean plants.

The savories have a flavor between that of lemon thyme and oregano, but without the minty finish of thyme. They have been used in some bitter liqueurs and vermouth. Savory is fairly strong and should be used sparingly until you have a good understanding of its effects.

Satureja hortensis contains carvacrol (up to 57 percent of the essential oil) and a small amount of thymol, α-pinene, borneol, and dipentene.

COMMENTS

Timo, the Italian word for summer savory, also refers to thyme and winter savory.

Thryba: *Satureja thymbra*

OTHER COMMON, ETHNIC, OR SCIENTIFIC NAMES

Barrel sweetener, Persian za'atar, pink savory, satureia, za'atar franji (European hyssop), za'atar rumi (Roman hyssop)
Germany: Thrymba-bergminze
Turkey: Kaya kekigi

RELATED SPECIES

Satureja cuneifolia: Dag kekigi (a local name in Antalya, Turkey)
Satureja spicigera: Kekigi (a local name in Trabzon, Turkey)

GROWTH HABITS

Perennial
Origin: Eastern Mediterranean region
Range: Wild plant in Eastern Mediterranean countries

CULINARY USES

In Crete, thryba is the preferred herbal tea. Elsewhere, it is used to flavor stews, grilled meats (especially lamb), and vegetables.

OTHER USES

A strong tea made from thryba is used to clean and purify wine barrels each year, just before the new wine is to be transferred from the fermenting vats.

"Za'tar" or "za'atar" are generic names for a whole group of Middle Eastern herbs from the genera *Origanum, Calamintha, Thymus,* and *Satureja.*

European hyssop and Roman hyssop should not be confused with true hyssop, *Hyssopus officinalis.*

Thyme: *Thymus* spp.

OTHER COMMON, ETHNIC, OR SCIENTIFIC NAMES

Common thyme, garden thyme

Algeria: Za'after, zi'tra (*Thymus vulgaris*)

Arabic: Za'atar (*Thymus vulgaris*)

China: Ai-Hao (*Thymus vulgaris*)

Denmark: Timian (*Thymus vulgaris*)

Estonia: Aed-liivatee, liivatee (*Thymus vulgaris*); numm-liivatee (*Thymus serpyllum*)

Finland: Tarha-ajuruoho, timjami (*Thymus vulgaris*); kangas-ajuruoho (*Thymus serpyllum*)

France: Thym ordinaire (*Thymus vulgaris*); serpolet (*Thymus serpyllum*)

Gaelic: Lus an righ (*Thymus vulgaris*)

Germany: Römischer Quendel, Thymian (*Thymus vulgaris*); Wilder Thymian, Quendel (*Thymus serpyllum*)

Greece: Thmári (*Thymus vulgaris*); thiósmo (*Thymus serpyllum*)

Iceland: Timjan (*Thymus vulgaris*)

Iran: Awishan shirazi (*Thymus vulgaris*)

Iraq: Zaatar (*Thymus vulgaris*)

Italy: Timo (*Thymus vulgaris*); serpillo (*Thymus serpyllum*)

Mexico: Tomillo (*Thymus vulgaris*), yerba fina (only in Oaxaca)

Netherlands: Keukentijm, tijm, wintertijm (*Thymus vulgaris*); kruipende tijm, kwendel, wilde tijm (*Thymus serpyllum*)

Norway: Hagetimian, timian (*Thymus vulgaris*); kryptimian (*Thymus serpyllum*)

Poland: Tymianek wlasciwy (*Thymus vulgaris*)

Portugal: Timo, tomilho (*Thymus vulgaris*)

Russia: Bogoroditskaya trava, chebrets, timian (*Thymus vulgaris*)

Spain: Farigola, tomillo (*Thymus vulgaris*); serpol, serpoleto (*Thymus serpyllum*)

Sweden: Trädgårdstimjan, timjan (*Thymus vulgaris*); backtimjan (*Thymus serpyllum*)

Turkey: Adi kekik, esas kekik, pirzolasi, kekik (*Thymus vulgaris*), yabani kekik (*Thymus serpyllum*)

There are two primary and several lesser species of thyme, from a culinary point of view. The first primary species is *Thymus vulgaris,* known as common thyme, garden thyme, or narrowleaf French thyme. Its cultivars and their common names include 'Argenteus', silver lemon thyme, silver thyme; 'Aureus', golden lemon thyme; 'Doretta Klaber', Doretta Klaber thyme; 'Fragrantissimus', fragrantissimus thyme; 'Roseus', roseus thyme; and 'Silver Posy', silver posy thyme.

The second primary species is *Thymus serpyllum,* known as continental wild thyme, creeping thyme, lemon thyme, mother of thyme, or wild thyme. It has been listed erroneously as *Thymus serpyllum* augustifolius. Its cultivars and their common names include 'Aureus', golden creeping thyme; 'Citriodorus', lemon thyme (lemon scented); 'Lemon Curd', pink chintz (lemon scented); 'Snowdrift', snowdrift thyme; 'Vulgaris', common thyme, lemon thyme, or *Thymus serpyllum citriodorum.*

RELATED SPECIES

Thymus bleicherianus: Za'atar (Morocco)

Thymus broussonetii: Pine-scented thyme. Cultivars include 'Bois', which has the common names za'tar es swiri, z'itra (Morocco).

Thymus caespititus (also listed as *Thymus azoricus* or *Thymus micans*): Azores thyme, Cretan thyme. Pine and tangerine scented.

Thymus eucotrichus: Moonlight thyme

Thymus Herba-barona: Caraway thyme. Cultivar: 'Nutmeg', known by the common name nutmeg thyme. Smells strongly of caraway, with a hint of sage in the finish.

Thymus lanuginsosus (also listed as *Thymus praecox* 'Lanuginsosus'): Wooly thyme

Thymus mastichina: Mastic thyme, pine-scented thyme, Spanish marjoram

Thymus nummularius: Marjoram-leaved thyme

Thymus Pallasianus (also known as *Thymus odoratissimus*): No common name found. Cultivars include 'Doone Valley', which is lemon or citrus scented.

Thymus pallidus: Za'atar (Morocco)

Thymus praecox 'Arcticus' (sometimes erroneously listed as *Thymus serpyllum* 'Britannicus'): Mother of thyme. Cultivars include 'Albus', 'Coccineus', 'Skorpilii', and 'Splendens'.

Thymus pulegiodes (also listed as *Thymus montanus* or *Thymus chamaedrys* or *Thymus serpyllum glaber*): Broadleaf thyme. Cultivars include 'Alba', 'Coccineus', and 'Kermesinus', which are commonly known as wild thyme or creeping thyme.

Thymus Richardii (sometimes seen as *Thymus Richardii* 'Nitidus'): No common name found.

Thymus × citriodorus (sometimes listed as *Thymus fragratissimus* or *Thymus pulegiodes × Thymus vulgaris*): Silver lemon thyme. Cultivars include 'Argenteus', 'Aureus', 'Fragrantissimus', and 'Silver Queen'.

GROWTH HABITS

Perennial

Origin: Europe and Asia

Range: Temperate regions

CULINARY USES

Thyme is one of France's fines herbes. Fresh thyme leaves are much more flavorful than dried thyme. The leaves, along with bay leaves and parsley, are used in a bouquet garni, an essential for stocks, sauces, and marinades. Use fresh thyme in salad dressings, soups, and stews.

Dried thyme is a component of poultry seasoning, along with ground marjoram, sage, rosemary, oregano, ginger, and black pepper (q.v.). It is useful in sausages and pâtés made with pork, lamb, poultry, and game.

"Italian Seasoning" is a name for several different mixtures of herbs and spices that are sold commercially. They often contain thyme.

Try using lemon-scented varieties with chicken or fish, in marinades, as the aromatic component of a beurre blanc, or even to flavor unsweetened whipped cream to accompany cold dishes. They are especially good with shellfish, such as mussels. Pine-scented varieties work with lamb; caraway-scented varieties, with beef or pork. Combine black pepper, oregano, parsley, scallions, and thyme to make a rub for baked firm fish, such as grouper or mahimahi, or marlin.

Thyme is a natural with goat cheese, garlic, black olives, tomatoes, and zucchini. In England, the goat's milk cheese called Innes sometimes contains thyme. In Lebanon, Shankleish is a sun-dried cheese that is covered with dried thyme.

Mastic thyme, *Thymus mastichina,* is used for seasoning meats. As its name might indicate, *Thymus Herba-Barona* is the classic seasoning for a roast baron of beef. Azores thyme, *Thymus caespititus,* has been used to perfume custards.

The coarse wild thyme of Greece provides much of the nectar for the famous honey of Hymettus. A milder variety of this thyme is used to season game and pork.

In Turkey, *kekik* and similar-sounding words are used as generic names for a group of herbs that includes various oreganos, marjorams, savories, and thymes (see OREGANO). It can mean *Thymus longicaulis,* while *kekikor* is *Thymus praecox.* In the city of Boursa, for example, the name *kekik* refers to *Thymus bornmuelleri. Kekik yagi* is Turkish oil of thyme used as a seasoning ingredient.

Thyme is a component of several herbal liqueurs, lending its aromatic essence to Benedictine and Campari. The flavor and scent of the various thymes are the result of varying blends of carvacrol, anisyl alcohol, linalool, borneol, and geraniol, as well as many other aromatics.

Potpourri

COMMENTS
Bob Bragner, a correspondent in Turkey, tells me that "mixed with vodka, [*kekik yagi*] makes great Bloody Marys."

Many cultivars may actually be species other than *Thymus serpyllum,* but that is the way they are found in the market. To quote the authors of *Hortus Third,* "Most thymes grown in American gardens appear to be of confused identity and are often erroneously named." Having spent many hours trying to disentangle the strands of this subject, I have to say that the folks at *Hortus Third* have cultivated a charming and elegant variety of understatement.

One thyme, not mentioned above, is *Thymus serpyllum* 'Cimicinus'; the cultivar name translates from the Latin as "smelling of bugs," hardly a recommendation for inclusion in a kitchen handbook.

"Za'tar" or "za'atar" are generic names for a whole group of Middle Eastern herbs from the genera *Origanum, Calamintha, Thymus,* and *Satureja.*

Timo is also the Italian word for winter and summer savory.

White Dead Nettle: *Lamium album*

OTHER COMMON, ETHNIC, OR SCIENTIFIC NAMES
Archangel, dead nettle, dumb nettle, snowflake
Germany: Taubnessel

GROWTH HABITS
Perennial
Origin: Europe and Asia
Range: Naturalized in North America

CULINARY USES
The best-known dish using *Lamium* is the French *anguille au vert à la Flamande,* where it is used in combination with sorrel and eels. Leaves are used cooked, in omelets or as a potherb, or fresh, in salads. Flowers are sometimes candied.

COMMENTS
This species is not related to nettle, *Urtica dioca* (q.v.).

"Archangel" and "dead nettle" are other names for angelica (q.v.).

While the plant is sometimes used as a ground cover, it tends to become a pest, invading more desirable areas of gardens.

Winter Savory: *Satureja montana*

OTHER COMMON, ETHNIC, OR SCIENTIFIC NAMES
Bean herb
Ethiopia: Tosinyi
France: Sariette, savourée
Germany: Bohnenkraut, Winterbohnenkraut
Greece: Thrombi
Italy: Santoreggia d'inverno, timo
Spain: Saborija, sajolida
Turkey: Dag sater

GROWTH HABITS
Perennial
Origin: Mediterranean region
Range: Temperate regions

CULINARY USES
Winter savory is used much as is summer savory (q.v.). It is found in baked goods and combines well with eggs, fish, and meats. It is especially good in stuffings for poultry. Finely minced with parsley and chervil, it makes an attractive garnish for soft cheeses. It should be used in vinaigrettes (sparingly) and in sauces.

Beans of almost any kind are improved by the aromatic leaves of both savories, hence the German name *Bohnenkraut* ("bean herb").

The savories have a flavor something like lemon thyme, but without the minty finish of thyme. The taste of winter savory is similar to that of summer savory, but it is a little warmer and stronger. Winter savory contains carvacrol and thymol.

COMMENTS
Timo is also the Italian word for thyme and summer savory.

Yerba Buena: *Satureja Douglasii*

OTHER COMMON, ETHNIC, OR SCIENTIFIC NAMES
California yerba buena, Oregon tea, spearmint. Formerly known botanically as *Micromeria Chamissonis* or *Micromeria Douglasii*.

GROWTH HABITS
Perennial
Origin: Western United States
Range: Temperate regions

Micromeria myrtifolia: Tas nanesi (Turkey); micromeria

CULINARY USES
Yerba buena is used in Mexican cooking. It has been used as an herbal tea.
Yerba buena contains pulegone (up to 6,700 ppm), camphor (up to 5,900 ppm), isomenthone (up to 4,300 ppm), limonene (up to 1,500 ppm), and carvone (up to 2,300 ppm).

COMMENTS
Should not to be confused with *Mentha spicata,* more commonly known as spearmint.

Za'atar: *Origanum cyriacum*

OTHER COMMON, ETHNIC, OR SCIENTIFIC NAMES
Bible hyssop, Syrian oregano. Also known scientifically as *Majorana syriaca, Origanum maru,* and *Origanum syriacum.*
Greece: Rigany
Israel: Ezov, za'atar
Turkey: Kekik

CULTIVAR
'Aegypticum'

GROWTH HABITS
Perennial
Origin: Middle East (name suggests Syria)
Range: Dry temperate regions

CULINARY USES
Za'atar tastes like a cross between thyme, marjoram, and oregano (q.v.). It is used in the cooking of Morocco.
In several Middle Eastern countries, the spice mixture za'atar (see Comments, below) is combined with salt and olive oil and used as a topping (or dip) for bread. This usage is common among the Bedouins of North Africa as well.
The flavor of za'atar is characterized by carvacrol (70 percent) and *p*-cymene (10 percent), although it does contain some sixteen other flavoring compounds.

COMMENTS
Various mixtures are sometimes marketed as za'atar (or zathar; see SUMAC). Thyme and sumac combine in a common version. Another is comprised of thyme, salt, sumac, and toasted sesame. Yet another is made of thyme, sumac,

and summer savory. I have also seen a melange of marjoram, sesame, sumac, salt, and olive oil.

"Za'tar" or "za'atar" are generic names for a whole group of Middle Eastern herbs from the genera *Origanum, Calamintha, Thymus,* and *Satureja.* In Turkey, *kekik* is a generic name for a group of herbs that includes various oreganos, marjorams, savories and thymes (see OREGANO and THYME).

Bible hyssop should not be confused with true hyssop, *Hyssopus officinalis,* or any of the other herbs that include "hyssop" in their names.

Za'atar Farsi: *Thymus capitatus*

OTHER COMMON, ETHNIC, OR SCIENTIFIC NAMES
Conehead thyme, headed savory, maritime thyme, Persian hyssop, Spanish origanum, zathter. Za'atar farsi is also known botanically as *Coridothymus capitatus* and *Satureia capitata.*
Italy: Santoreggia

GROWTH HABITS
Shrubby perennial
Origin: Eastern Mediterranean Region
Range: Dry temperate regions

CULINARY USES
Its uses are similar to those of za'atar and thryba (q.v.). The essential oil is used in commercial flavorings for baked goods, candies, condiments, ice creams, soft drinks, and meats.

OTHER USES
Source of commercial Spanish origanum oil

COMMENTS
"Za'tar" or "za'atar" are generic names for a whole group of Middle Eastern herbs from the genera *Origanum, Calamintha, Thymus,* and *Satureja.*
Persian hyssop should not be confused with true hyssop, *Hyssopus officinalis,* or any of the other herbs that include "hyssop" in their names.

Za'atar Hommar: *Thymbra spicata*

OTHER COMMON, ETHNIC, OR SCIENTIFIC NAMES
Donkey hyssop, za'atar sahrawi (desert hyssop)

GROWTH HABITS
Shrubby perennial

Origin: Eastern Mediterranean region
Range: Temperate regions

CULINARY USES

Its uses are similar to those of za'atar and thryba (q.v.).

COMMENTS

"Za'tar" or "za'atar" are generic names for a whole group of Middle Eastern herbs from the genera *Origanum, Calamintha, Thymus,* and *Satureja.*

Desert hyssop or donkey hyssop should not be confused with true hyssop, *Hyssopus officinalis,* or any of the other herbs that include "hyssop" in their names.

44. Lauraceae (sometimes listed as Myrtaceae): The Laurel Family

Allspice: *Pimenta dioica*

OTHER COMMON, ETHNIC, OR SCIENTIFIC NAMES

Jamaica pepper, myrtle pepper, tail pepper, West-Indian bay leaves. Its old botanical names were *Eugenia pimenta, Pimenta officinalis,* and *Myrtus pimenta.*

Arabic: Bahar, bhar hub wa na'im
Denmark: Allehånde
Estonia: Harilik pimendipuu, Vürts
Finland: Maustepippuri
France: Piment, piment jamaique, poivre aromatique, poivre de la jamaique, toute-épice
Germany: Allgewürz, Englisches Gewürz, Jamaikapfeffer, Nelkenpfeffer, Neugewürz, Piment, Westindische Lorbeerblätter
Iceland: Allrahanda
Italy: Piment, pimento
Jamaica: Pimento
Mexico: Pepe di giamaica, pimienta jamaica, pimenta dulce, pimenta gorda
Morocco: Noioura
Netherlands: Jamaica peper, piment
Norway: Allehånde
Poland: Ziele angielskie
Portugal: Pimenta da jamaica
Russia: Yamaiskiy pjerets

Spain: Pimienta gorda, pimento, pimiento de jamaica
Sweden: Kryddpeppar
Turkey: Yeni bahar, yenibahar

RELATED SPECIES
Pimenta racemosa: Bay malagueta (Spain); bay, bay rum tree. Source of clove-like myrcia oil.

GROWTH HABITS
Tropical tree
Origin: Caribbean, Central America, Mexico
Range: Southern Florida

CULINARY USES
Dried berries are the familiar spice that smells and tastes like a mixture of cinnamon, cloves, nutmeg, and black pepper. Allspice is used in baked goods, condiments, and pickles; with fish, poultry, and meats; and in sauces, soups, and stews. These berries are ingredients in Benedictine and some gins.

Jamaican allspice berries are smaller, but they are said to be better flavored than the allspice from Central America and Mexico. *Monte Aguila* is a Jamaican liqueur—a bitter digestif—made with allspice.

The berries are used in *berberé,* the Ethiopian red pepper paste. They are also one of the components of the Iraqi spice mixture *boharat.*

Ground berries are used, in combination with other spices and salt, in the French seasoning *sel épice.* It is used with meats, especially in the cured meats and sausages that constitute French charcuterie. Ground allspice also appears in other charcuterie, such as bologna, head cheese, hot dogs, and pickled pig's feet. The leaves are similar in taste, but milder. They are used in herbal teas.

The main component of allspice's essential oil is eugenol (up to 85 percent), but there are also small amounts of 1,8-cineol, caryophellene, cineol, and methyl ether.

OTHER USES
Leaves are used in perfumes and as a commercial source of eugenol. Pimento oil, extracted from the leaves and fruit, has a carnation-like scent. It is used in cosmetics.

Leaves and twigs of *Pimenta racemosa* are distilled to produce oil of bay, which is used in the manufacture of bay rum and perfumes.

COMMENTS
In the Caribbean region, "pimento" is a catch-all term for almost any spice.

Avocado: *Persea americana* subs. *drymifolia*

OTHER COMMON, ETHNIC, OR SCIENTIFIC NAMES
Ahuacate, alligator pear, avocate, fuerte avocado, palta, salad fruit, vegetable marrow
Brazil: Abacate
East Timor: Avocat
Indonesia: Avocad, buah apokat
Mexico: Aguacate

RELATED SPECIES
Persea borbonia: Florida mahogany, laurel tree, red bay, swamp red bay, sweet bay, tisswood

GROWTH HABITS
Perennial tree
Origin: Central America
Range: Southern California and Florida

CULINARY USES
Of course, the fruit of *Persea americana* is the familiar avocado. It is delicious when combined with acids (to keep its unctuousness in check); try flavored vinegars (raspberry, basil, or balsamic), citrus juices, or tamarind juice (a tamarind/chipotle salsa made with avocados should be great). Slices of ripe avocado and Brie are ambrosial in an omelet, provided that you are on an all-fat diet. Avocados can be as much as 25 percent oil. Granted, it is unsaturated fat, but all fats, no matter how "healthy," supply nine calories per gram.

Guacamole, an old standard in the United States, is very different in places like Guatemala, Honduras, and El Salvador. In Central America, it usually contains cheese, mashed, hard-boiled eggs, and sometimes heavy cream.

The rich fruit has been made into "ice creams," notably the *sorvete de abacate* of Brazil. The fat green flesh, tasty at room temperature, is too bland when frozen, so it is sweetened and flavored with vanilla and dark rum.

The reason for including avocados here among the herbs has nothing to do with the fruit. The subspecies *drymifolia* represents the Mexican variety of avocado. Its leaves (known as *hojas de aguacates*), when cut or crushed, exude a lovely mint-licorice flavor that enhances bean dishes, salsas, and salads. They are used to wrap tamales. They might, if cut *chiffonade,* make an interesting bed for grilled fish, such as mahimahi or grouper. The leaves have been used as an herbal tea.

COMMENTS
If this subspecies is grown in the United States, it is probably in California (the small Mexican "race" of avocado is sometimes listed as a separate

species, *Persea drymifolia*), whereas the West Indian type can be grown only in southern Florida, where nearly tropical conditions exist. If I was going to try to grow an avocado (in the house) for its leaves, I think I would start with a Haas, rather than one of the large green varieties.

"Sweet bay" is also used as a name for *Magnolia virginiana*.

Bay Leaf: *Laurus nobilis*

OTHER COMMON, ETHNIC, OR SCIENTIFIC NAMES

Daphne, Grecian bay, laurier sauce, laurel, noble bay, noble laurel, olympic herb, roman laurel, sweet bay, sweet bay leaf, sweet laurel, true laurel

Algeria: Rand
Arabic: Ghar
China: Yueh-kuei
Denmark: Laurbaer
Estonia: Harilik loorberipuu
Finland: Laakerinlehti, laakeripuu
France: Laurier, laurier commun, laurier d'Apollon, laurier noble
Gaelic: Labhras
Germany: Lorbeer, Lorbeerbaum (tree), Lorbeerblatt (leaf)
Greece: Dáfni, dhafni
Hungary: Babér
India: Tejpat
Iran: Barg bu
Iraq: Warak el ghar
Israel: Aley daphna
Italy: Alloro, lauro
Japan: Gekkeiju
Mexico: Laurel de hoja larga
Netherlands: Laurier
Norway: Laurbaerblad
Philippines: Bitaog, laurel
Poland: Listek laurowy
Portugal: Lauro, loureiro, louro
Romania: Dafin
Russia: Lavr
Spain: Laurel, llorer
Sweden: Lager, lagerbärsblad
Turkey: Dafne yapregi, defne

CULTIVARS

'Angustifolia' (also known as 'Salicifolia'): Willow-leaf bay. Has narrow leaves.

'Aurea' (also known as 'Golden Bay'): Has yellowish leaves
'Undulata': Wavy-edged leaves

Cryptocarya moschata: Brazilian nutmeg. Bark and fruits are described as smelling like cinnamon, laurel, and mangos.

GROWTH HABITS
Broad-leafed evergreen shrubs or small trees
Origin: Mediterranean region
Range: Frost-free temperate regions

CULINARY USES
Bay leaves are a savory addition to sauces (especially those based on tomatoes), vegetable soups, and stocks, usually as part of a bouquet garni. They are sometimes used to flavor vermouth. They are good with poultry, in stuffings, or powdered in a rub before roasting beef, lamb, and veal. A pâté is often baked with a couple of bay leaves at the bottom of the pan (so they will show on top when the pâté is unmolded).

Bay leaves are used to flavor fish fumet, game marinades, soups, and stews. In Cadiz, bay leaves are used with shellfish. *Vatkuli* is a Finnish beef stew seasoned with bay leaves. A couple of leaves should be added to the liquid used for cooking artichokes, beets, carrots, and potatoes. They are used in baked goods and in pickling.

"Italian Seasoning" is a name for several different mixtures of herbs and spices that are sold commercially. They often contain bay leaves.

Not usually included among Chinese ingredients, bay leaves have been used to season breaded strips of pork in Shanghai's Lu Bo Lang restaurant.

The characteristic sweet warmth of bay leaves is a result of their cineol (up to 70 percent of the essential oil), pinenes, phellandrene, linalool, geraniol, and noticeable levels of eugenol. The berries contain most of the same compounds, plus cinnamic acid and methyl cinnamate, and have also been used as a seasoning. Berries are stronger flavored than the leaves, sometimes containing as much as three times the amount of essential oils.

OTHER USES
Bay leaves yield an essential oil used for perfumes, and they also appear in potpourri. The leaves are used decoratively as wreaths, a possible echo of their use in antiquity to crown victorious heroes and other great public figures (even then, major sports figures earned their laurels). The ancient Greeks added bay leaves to wine. They also burned them at Delphi to help the oracle to enter the requisite trance-like state for forecasting the future.

Their cineol content makes bay leaves useful for repelling insects from stored foods. A leaf kept in a container of dried beans, flour, or other staple will keep weevils and other small vermin away.

The only nonpoisonous "laurels" found in North America are *Laurus nobilis* and *Umbellularia californica* (q.v.). "Mountain laurel" is one of the toxic "laurels." In fact, it is not really a laurel; it is *Kalmia latifolia*.

The West African plant "French laurel," also known as "spicy cedar," is apparently not related to bay leaves.

Bois de Rose: *Aniba rosaeodora*

OTHER COMMON, ETHNIC, OR SCIENTIFIC NAMES
Brazilian rosewood, rosewood
France: Bois de rose
Germany: Rosenholz
Italy: Legno di rosa

RELATED SPECIES
Aniba rosaeodora var. *amazonica:* Brazilian bois de rose, Peruvian bois de rose

GROWTH HABITS
Evergreen tropical tree
Origin: Brazil and Peru
Range: South American rainforests

CULINARY USES
Extracts are used as commercial flavorings for baked goods, confections, and soft drinks.

Brazilian bois de rose oil and Peruvian bois de rose oil are distilled from the variety 'amazonica' and contain less linalool than cayenne bois de rose oil, which is made from the species. Linalool can make up as much as 87 percent of cayenne oil. Other contributing notes come from terpenes, dipentene, methyl heptanol, eugenol, and nerol.

OTHER USES
Essential oil is used in the cosmetics industry.

California Laurel: *Umbellularia californica*

OTHER COMMON, ETHNIC, OR SCIENTIFIC NAMES
Balm of heaven, California bay, California olive, headache tree, Oregon myrtle, myrtle, peppernut tree, pepperwood, sassafras laurel, spicebush, spicetree. Also seen listed as *Laurus regalis, Laurus regia, Oreodaphne californica,* and *Tetranthera californica.*

Litsea glaucescens: Mexican bay laurel
Litsea pringlei: Laurel de hoja redonda (Mexico); laurel

GROWTH HABITS
Evergreen shrub
Origin: Southwestern United States
Range: Temperate regions

CULINARY USES
Pungent dried leaves have been used as one would use bay leaves (see Comments, below). Their scent is quite different from that of true bay leaves, however. They are sweet, like bay leaves, but the clove-like quality is absent and they have a resinous quality that some people find offensive. They add a distinctive presence to baked fish as well as to roasted poultry and game. They have been used in stews, such as chili, and in soups. Native Americans in California are said to have used the seeds as a seasoning.

The leaves of California laurel contain umbellulone (up to 15,600 ppm), 1,8-cineole, 3,4-dimethoxyallylbenzene, thymol, and terpinen-4-ol.

Mexican bay laurel is used in the flavorings industry. It contains sabinene and terpinen-4-ol.

COMMENTS
Umbellone is a toxic substance that can affect the central nervous system if eaten in quantity. Some people experience skin irritation if exposed to the foliage. It can also affect the respiratory tract if the dust of dried leaves is inhaled.

Cassia: *Cinnamomum aromaticum*

OTHER COMMON, ETHNIC, OR SCIENTIFIC NAMES
Bastard cinnamon, Canton cassia, cassia-bark tree, cassia, cassia aromaticum, cassia lignea, China hunk cassia, Chinese cassia, Chinese cinnamon, Hunan cassia, Kwangsi cassia, Kwantung cassia, Yunnan cassia. *Cinnamomum cassia* is its old scientific name.
Arabic: Darseen, kerfee
China: Kuei, kwei, rou gui pi
Colombia: Algarrobo
Costa Rica: Abejon
East Timor: Ai-kameli
Estonia: Hiina kaneelipuu
Ethiopia: K'erefa
Finland: Kassia, talouskaneli
France: Canéfice, canelle de chine, casse

Germany: China-Zimt, Chinesischer Zimt, Zimtcassie
Iceland: Kassía
India: Dalchini, tej pattar (leaves)
Indonesia: Kayu manis
Italy: Cannella della Cina, cassia, legno di cassia
Japan: Bokei, kashia keihi
Korea: Gae-pi
Malaysia: Kayu manis
Morocco: Karfa
Netherlands: Bastaardkaneel, kassie, valse kaneel
Nicaragua: Ahumada
Norway: Kassia
Russia: Korichnoje derevo
Spain: Canela de la China, casia
Sweden: Kassia
Thailand: Bai kravan (leaves), ob choey, ob cheuy

RELATED SPECIES

Cinnamomum burmannii: Canelle de padang (France); Indonesische
    kaneel (Netherlands); Indonesischer Zimt, Padang-Zimt (Germany);
    kayu manis padang (Indonesia); jaavankaneli (Finland); kayu manis
    padang (Malaysia); Batavia cassia, Batavia cinnamon, cassia vera,
    fagot cassia, Indonesian cassia, Indonesian cinnamon, Korintji cassia,
    Korintji cinnamon, Java cassia, Macassar cassia, Padang cassia, Timor
    cassia
Cinnamomum Camphora (also listed as *Camphora officinalis*): Alcanfor
    (Spain); camphre (France); canfora (Italy); hon-sho (Japan); Kampfer
    (Germany); kapuru-gaha, ohba-Kusu (Taiwan); yusho (China);
    camphor tree
Cinnamomum fistulosa: Arbol de la vela or cañafístula (Mexico); candle
    tree, purging cassia (or Indian laburnum, *Cassia fistula*)
Cinnamomum Louririi: Canelle de cochinchine (France); que (Vietnam);
    Saigon-Zimt, Vietnamesischer Zimt (Germany); saigonkaneli
    (Finland); annam cassia, cassia-flower tree, Danang cassia, karfa,
    Saigon cinnamon, Tonkin cassia, Vietnam cassia, Vietnamese
    cinnamon
Cinnamomum tamala (sometimes listed as *Cinnamomum tejpata*): Indisches
    Lorbeerblatt (Germany); kanelilaakeri (Finland); laurier des Indes
    (France); lauro indiano (Italy); mahpat, patta akulu, patraka, talisha,
    talishappattiri, tamaal patra, tejapatra, tej pat, tejpata, tejpatra,
    (India); tejpat (Turkey); thitchabo (Burma/Myanmar); Indian bay leaf

GROWTH HABITS
Evergreen tropical tree

Origin: China
Range: Burma/Myanmar, Malaysia, southern China, and Vietnam

CULINARY USES

Dried bark is cassia, a cinnamon-like spice that is stronger and less delicate than true cinnamon. The dried unopened buds are also used as a spice.
Much commercial "cinnamon" (especially in the United States) is actually
cassia.

Cassia is used in baked goods; condiments such as ketchup and chili sauce;
and some curries, chutneys, and preserves. The ground bark is used, in combination with other spices and salt, in the French seasoning called *sel épice.* It
is used with meats, especially in French charcuterie.

Camphor, *Cinnamomum Camphora,* hard as it may be to believe, is used as
a seasoning in Borneo. Indigenous to China, Japan, and Taiwan, it can be
grown in the southern parts of the United States. Its leaves, or chips of its
wood, are used by the Chinese to produce the smoke for the dish known as
camphor and tea-smoked duck.

Cinnamomum Louririi is found only in Southeast Asia. Its dried bark is sold
much as is cassia, which is less expensive than true cinnamon. In China,
a vermouth-like wine called *kweilin gui hua jiu* is made from the blossoms.
Cassia leaves and buds, known as *ob choey* (Thailand), are sometimes substituted for curry leaves (q.v.).

Traces of cassia are found in anisette, Benedictine, and some gins.

Cinnamomum burmannii, from Indonesia, and *Cinnamomum Louririi* are
used interchangeably in commercial flavorings applications, although they
possess slight differences in flavor and aroma. Cassia's essential oil contains
most of the same flavoring elements as true cinnamon (up to 90 percent cinnaminic aldehyde) with some coumarin, but eugenol is missing. The fruit
pulp also contains sugars, hydroxymethyl anthraquinone, and tannin.

OTHER USES

Source of camphor (distilled from the wood)

COMMENTS

Do not confuse this plant with cassie (see ACACIA) or with senna, *Cassia
alata* (see ROOIBOS).

Dalchini is also the Indian word for cinnamon. *Indonesisches Lorbeerblatt*
and "Indian bay leaf" are also names for the unrelated *Eugenia polyantha.*

Cinnamon: *Cinnamomum zeylanicum*

OTHER COMMON, ETHNIC, OR SCIENTIFIC NAMES

Canella, Ceylon cinnamon, dar el cini, Seychelles cinnamon, Sri Lanka cinnamon, true cinnamon. Cinnamon has appeared in some botanical texts as

Cinnamomum verum. The old herbalist's and apothecary's terms for cinnamon were *Cortex Canellae Albae* (the bark of *Cinnamomum zeylanicum*), *Cortex Cinnamomi Ceylanici* (the bark of *Cinnamomum zeylanicum,* specifically that from Sri Lanka), and *Flores Cinnamomi* (the flower of *Cinnamomum zeylanicum*).

Afghanistan: Dolchini
Algeria: Quarfa
Arabic: Qurfa
Burma/Myanmar: Hminthin, thit-ja-bo-gauk
China: Jou kuei
Colombia: Alcanfor
Czech Republic: Skorice
Denmark: Kanel
Estonia: Tseiloni kaneelipuu
Finland: Ceyloninkaneli, kaneli
France: Cannelle
Gaelic: Caineal
Germany: Ceylonesischer Zimt, Echter Zimt, Sri-Lanka-Zimt, Zimtblüte
Greece: Kanéla
Hungary: Fahéj
Iceland: Kanell
India: Dalchini, erikkoloam, illavangam, karuvappadai, kurundu, lavangamu, lavangapatta, nagkesar
Indonesia: Kaju manis, manis djangan
Iran: Dar chini
Iraq: Darjeen, darseen
Italy: Cannella
Japan: Seiron-nikkei
Malaysia: Kayu manis
Morocco: Dar el cini
Netherlands: Kaneel
Norway: Kanel
Panama: Alcanfor
Philippines: Canela
Poland: Cynamon
Portugal: Canela
Romania: Scortisoara
Russia: Koritsa
Spain: Canela
Sri Lanka: Kurundu
Swahili: Mdalasini
Sweden: Kanel
Thailand: Op cheuy
Tunisia: Kerfa

Turkey: Tarçin
Vietnam: Que

GROWTH HABITS
Evergreen tropical tree
Origin: Sri Lanka
Range: Tropics

CULINARY USES

The dried bark is true cinnamon. The plant is also known as canella. Finer than all substitutes, it has a lingering, ethereal sweetness that is missing in the somewhat coarse hotness of cassia (q.v.). Cinnamon is used in baking (apples, peaches, and pumpkin, of course, but also in cherry pies) and pickling. It works well in desserts (great on vanilla ice cream), sauces (especially Greek meat sauces), and stuffings.

The ground bark is used, in combination with other spices and salt, in the French seasoning *sel épice,* used in French charcuterie. Egyptian and Tunisian versions of the French *quatre épices* contain cinnamon, although the original French recipe does not. Cinnamon adds just the right autumnal warmth to charm a dinner of game.

Cinnamon is used in Thai curries based on Indian recipes (such as *gaeng mussaman*). Cinnamon is an ingredient in the Persian spice mixture *advieh* and in the Iraqi spice blend *boharat*. Cinnamon is essential to Greek tomato sauces, always combined with olive oil, often with honey. The syrup used on Greek pastries is almost always perfumed with cinnamon.

Cinnamon was one of the main commercial products on the old spice routes that connected the tropical East and spice-hungry Europe. As a result, it appears in every cuisine touched by the Arab traders. Ethiopia is no exception. Two foundation ingredients determine the flavor of Ethiopian dishes: *berberé* pepper paste and *niter kibbeh,* a spicy butter used in almost every dish. Cinnamon is essential to both.

Cinnamon is reported to be among the secret ingredients in Benedictine, as well as in Campari, yellow Chartreuse (in the form of cinnamon oil), and Grand Marnier. Cinnamon is probably an ingredient in Angostura Bitters, too. It was an ingredient in the now-forbidden absinthe. Cinnamon sticks are the ideal stirrers for hot winter libations, such as grog, mulled wine or cider, hot toddies, or even coffee. Cinnamon is used in some herbal and black tea blends, but the cheaper, hotter cassia is more common.

True cinnamon contains eugenol (the essential oil that flavors cloves and allspice) and cinnaminic aldehyde, which is the primary flavoring agent. It also contains caryophyllene, cineol, cinnamic acid esters, safrole, and terpenes. Ceylon cinnamon also contains benzaldehyde, furfural, linalool, α-phellandrene, and pinene.

Cinnamon makes an appearance in amaretto, anisette, gin, Kümmel, Morello Ratafia, and vermouth. Its leaves are used commercially to produce clove oil. They yield large amounts of eugenol, but none of the cinnaminic aldehydes found in the bark.

COMMENTS

Not all sources agree about cinnamon's place in Benedictine. They do agree about cassia's presence, but I'll have to take their word for it; my palate cannot make that distinction within the context of nearly two dozen herbs and spices.

Most commercial users do not distinguish between cassia and cinnamon, in spite of the differences mentioned above. Since cassia is cheaper, expect to see a lot more of the hotter material sold as cinnamon.

Dalchini is also the Indian word for cassia.

Filé: *Sassafras albidum*

OTHER COMMON, ETHNIC, OR SCIENTIFIC NAMES

Ague-tree, cinnamon wood, fennel wood, gumbo-filé, gumbo-zab, hack-matack, laurus sassafras, mitten tree, saloop, saxifrax, tea tree. *Sassafras varifolium* is an old scientific name for this plant. I have also seen the name *Sassafras trifolium* used, referring to the tree's peculiar trait of bearing three different kinds of leaves on the same plant.

Estonia: Valkjas sassafras
France: Laurier sassafras
Germany: Fenchelholzbaum, Fleberbaum
Italy: Sassafrasso
Mexico: Sasafrás
Poland: Sassafras roznolistny
Spain: Sasafrás

GROWTH HABITS

Shrub or tree
Origin: Eastern United States
Range: Temperate regions

CULINARY USES

Powdered inner bark and/or leaves of sassafras are dried and ground to make filé, which is added to gumbos as a thickener (see BITTER LEAF).

Sassafras is a key flavoring in root beer and sarsaparilla (q.v.). Teas are made from roots and bark. During World War II, a sassafras tea called grub hyson was used as a coffee substitute.

Filé's essential oil is almost 90 percent safrole (see Comments, below) plus traces of several terpinoids.

OTHER USES

Filé is used in some perfumes.

COMMENTS

Filé should be added to gumbos *after* cooking; if allowed to boil, filé can become unpleasantly stringy.

Filé may be carcinogenic. Oil of sassafras consists of up to 80 percent safrole. Safrole has caused liver damage and cancer in some laboratory animals. While this does not necessarily mean that it is dangerous to humans, why risk it? The FDA requires all extracts of leaves and bark to be free of safrole if used in foods. According to Bremness, ethyl alcohol is fourteen times more carcinogenic than safrole. (If this sounds familiar, see Comments about thujone, under MUGWORT.)

The flavor supplied by filé is subtle, especially compared to that of the highly seasoned foods to which it is added. There are lots of other ways to thicken a sauce. Louisiana's cooks have used okra and roux for this purpose for ages.

Filé
Sassafras albidum

From Köhler, *Köhler's Medizinal-Pflanzen,* vol. 2

"Hackmatack" has been used as a name for tamarack, juniper, lodgepole pine, white cedar, spirea, and balsam poplar.

Spice Bush: *Lindera benzoin*

OTHER COMMON, ETHNIC, OR SCIENTIFIC NAMES
Benjamin bush. This may be the same species as *Styrax benzoin,* in which case it is known as gum benjamin or, in Mexico, as *benjuí* or *estoraque.*

GROWTH HABITS
Deciduous shrub
Origin: Eastern United States
Range: Wild in moist woods

CULINARY USES
Bark, leaves, and twigs are used in spicy herbal teas. The twigs were used as food and medicine by the Cherokees. Dried berries are used like allspice (q.v.).

OTHER USES
Benzoin is used in the manufacture of perfumes and medicines.

COMMENTS
Sometimes confused with sweet shrub, *Calycanthus floridus* (q.v.).

45. Leguminosae (sometimes listed as Fabaceae): The Pea or Pulse Family

---

Abrus: *Abrus pulchellus*

RELATED SPECIES
Abrus is part of the Faboideae, a subfamily of the Leguminosae.
Abrus precatorius: Goonteh, gunga (India); coral bead plant, crab's eye, Indian licorice, jequirity bean, love pea, prayer beads, precatory bean, red bead vine, rosary pea, weather plant, weather vine, wild Indian licorice

GROWTH HABITS
Tropical vine
Origin: Tropical Africa to Southeast Asia
Range: China

Roots supply an anise-like essence. The roots contain glycorrhysin.

OTHER USES
The seeds have often been made into necklaces, which can be a dangerous practice; see Comments, below.

COMMENTS
The seeds of all *Abrus* species are extremely poisonous. Eating a single seed can be fatal.

Acacia: *Acacia dealbata*

OTHER COMMON, ETHNIC, OR SCIENTIFIC NAMES
Black wattle, mimosa flowers, silver wattle. Some older botanical texts list this species as *Acacia decurrens* var. *dealbata*.
France: Mimosa
Germany: Akazie, Mimose
Italy: Gaggia (cassie), mimosa
Spain: Acacia (cassie), mimosa

RELATED SPECIES
Acacia is part of the Mimosoideae, a subfamily of the Leguminosae.
Acacia Catechu: Acacia au cachou (France); catec (Spain); catecu terracahu (Italy); black catechu, cashoo, catechu, cutch, gambier, gambir, khair, wadalee-gum. Astringent taste due to tannin content. Formerly used as a preservative in beers, as hops are today.
Acacia Cavenia: Cassie romaine (France); espino cavan
Acacia concinna: Soap pod
Acacia decurrens: Black wattle, mimosa, wattleseed
Acacia Farnesiana: Aromo (Panama); aromo, guisache, huisache (Mexico); pela, una de cabra (Colombia); cassie, cassie ancienne, opopanax, popinac, sponge tree, sweet acacia, West Indian blackthorn
Acacia floribunda: Wattleseed (Australia)
Acacia longifolia: Wattleseed (Australia)
Acacia Senegal: Gombier blanc, mska (Morocco); gum arabic, Sudan gum arabic
Acacia smallii: Huisache (Mexico); sweet acacia
Acacia spectabilis: Mudgee wattle
Pistachia lentiscus: Al mastaki (Iraq); sakiz (Turkey); chios Mt. Atlas, lentisk tree, mastic

GROWTH HABITS
Shrub

Origin: Tasmania and Australia

Range: Mostly grown in California and Hawaii

Leaves are used in India as a seasoning for sweet-sour chutneys. The tart leaves of *Acacia concinna* are used just like tamarind, to impart a complex sour taste to the dishes of Southeast Asia. They are used in a marinade for fish in Laos.

Acacia flowers' nectar is the source of a delicious French honey. The Basque liqueur Izarra (similar to Chartreuse in that it is available in both green and yellow forms) is made from Armagnac, eau-de-vie, a number of herbs, and acacia honey. Catechu has been used as a source of bitterness in beer making.

The dark brown wattleseeds are usually ground. They have a roasted flavor, something like a combination of chocolate and coffee, with a hint of hazelnut. They add a browned note to sauces for meats, but they also supply an interesting flavor to sweet dishes made with batters or to ice cream. The ground seeds lend their toasted flavor to fresh pasta. The flavor is often extracted by infusion in hot water-based liquids. The results are strained, the solids discarded, and the remaining liquid used, as is, or reduced.

Mastic, *Pistachia lentiscus,* has a sweet anise-and-vanilla-like scent that makes it useful in desserts. Its resinous gum is popular in Sardinia and is used as a seasoning in Egypt. Mastiche is a liqueur, flavored with mastic, in Turkey and Greece. Cypriots and Greeks, especially those who live on the isle of Chios, also make *mastic,* or *masticha,* a pungently sweet mixture of mastic gum and anise seed.

The flowers of mudgee wattle, *Acacia spectabilis,* are first marinated in brandy, then deep-fried, and served as a dessert (see ELDERBERRY).

Acacia flowers have a violet scent. They contain anisic acid, cassie aldehyde, octadecylen, and palmitic acid. Fruits can contain as much as 300,000 ppm of tannins.

Flowers are used in manufacture of perfumes. Gum arabic is derived from the related *Acacia nilotica.*

"Catechu" is another name for betel nuts (also known as areca nuts or pinang), which are actually the seeds of *Areca catechu,* a species of palm. They are a popular drug all over India and Southeast Asia. *Acacia Catechu* should not be confused with *Areca Catechu* or *Uncaria gambir* (a member of the *Rubiaceae* family that is also known as gambier catechu and pale catechu).

Astragalus: *Astragalus membranaceus*

OTHER COMMON, ETHNIC, OR SCIENTIFIC NAMES
Milk vetch
China: Huang-chi

RELATED SPECIES
Astragalus is part of the Faboideae, a subfamily of the Leguminosae.
Astragalus boeticus: Swedish coffee
Astragalus gummifer: Kthira (Iraq); tragacanth
Astragalus Wootonii: Locoweed

GROWTH HABITS
Perennial
Origin: China
Range: Temperate zones

CULINARY USES
Several species within this genus yield gum tragacanth, which is used as a thickener and binder in commercial condiments, ice creams, pie fillings, salad dressings, and sauces. The seeds of *Astragalus boeticus* have been roasted and ground for use as a coffee substitute in Germany and Hungary.

OTHER USES
The fruits of *Astragalus hamosus* resemble worms. They are sometimes added to salads as a kind of edible practical joke.

COMMENTS
Toxic glycosides occur in several species in this genus. *Astragalus Wootonii* is one of many plants called "locoweed," because it has poisoned—literally intoxicated—livestock that have fed upon it.

Broom: *Spartium junceum*

OTHER COMMON, ETHNIC, OR SCIENTIFIC NAMES
Basam, bisom, bizzom, breeam, browne, broom tops, cola de caballo, green broom, Spanish broom, weaver's broom
France: Genêt
Germany: Ginster, Pfriemenginster
Italy: Ginestra
Spain: Ginestra
Turkey: Borcak

Cytisus Scoparius (sometimes listed as *Spartium Scoparium* or *Sarothamnus Scoparius*): Genêt à balais (France); Besenginster (Germany); Scotch broom

GROWTH HABITS
Shrub
Origin: Mediterranean region
Range: Naturalized in southern California

CULINARY USES
Broom flowers have a sweet, honey-like balsamic scent. They yield a scented extract that is used commercially for flavoring ice cream, chewing gum, pastries, and soft drinks.

The plant's green tops are bitter and have been used in beer making (before the advent of hops). Unopened flower buds can be pickled in brine, like capers.

The flowers of Spanish broom contain 1,18-octadecanediol, caprylic acid, juncein, and luteolin glucosides and myristic acid; the bitter leaves contain quercetin.

Broom
Spartium junceum

From Desfontaines,
Atlantica, sive Historia plantarum, vol. 2

OTHER USES

Used as a yellow dyestuff and a source of fibers. Essential oil from the flowers is used in perfumes, especially in combination with oils from ylang-ylang (q.v.).

COMMENTS

Broom contains cytisine, a poisonous alkaloid commonly found in laburnum, *Cytisus laburnum.*

Spartium junceum is not related to butcher's broom, *Ruscus aculeatus* (q.v.).

Chepil: *Crotalaria longirostrata*

OTHER COMMON, ETHNIC, OR SCIENTIFIC NAMES
Rattlebox
Guatemala: Chilpilín
Mexico: Chepil, chipil, chipiles

RELATED SPECIES
Crotalaria plumila: Romerillo (Mexico); crotalaria

GROWTH HABITS
Shrubby perennial
Origin: Mexico
Range: A wild plant, growing in waste places and on the sides of the road, rarely cultivated.

CULINARY USES
The leaves, tasting a bit like sorrel, are used in Chiapas and Oaxaca to season rice dishes and *tamales.* The leaves are exported, frozen, from Guatemala.

COMMENTS
The name *chipiles* is used for a number of *Crotalaria* species.

Clover: *Trifolium pratense*

OTHER COMMON, ETHNIC, OR SCIENTIFIC NAMES
Cleaver grass, cow grass, golden flower vegetable, peavine clover, purple clover, trefoil
Jamaica: Ceracee, cerasse
Mexico: Trebol morado
Russia: Clever

CULTIVARS
'Perenne': Mammoth clover
'Sativum': Sativum

RELATED SPECIES
   Trifolium is part of the Faboideae, a subfamily of the Leguminosae.
   Trifolium repens: Trebol flor bianco (Mexico); white clover

GROWTH HABITS
   Perennial
   Origin: Europe
   Range: Naturalized in North America

CULINARY USES
   Aside from providing the nectar for most of the honey sold—at least in the United States—this plant is used primarily as an ingredient in herbal teas. The sprouts and young leaves are used in salads and on sandwiches.
   In China, the young leaves are stir-fried. The dried leaves are powdered and used as a condiment for rice. In Shanghai, *Trifolium pratense* is known as "burr clover." It is stir-fried in lard and oil and then sauced with sorghum-based yiang he wine, soy sauce, salt, and sugar.
   White clover is sometimes used to flavor syrups. Otherwise, the uses are the same as those of red clover.

OTHER USES
   Clover is often planted as a cover crop on fallow fields. Not only does clover yield usable silage, but the nitrogen-fixing nodules on its roots provide natural fertilizer.

COMMENTS
   Several clovers are also known as Irish shamrocks. Although clover's three-lobed leaves are similar, they should not be confused with true Irish shamrocks, which are members of the Oxalidae (see WOOD SORREL). "Trefoil" is a descriptive name shared by both groups of plants.

False Acacia: *Robinia pseudacacia*

OTHER COMMON, ETHNIC, OR SCIENTIFIC NAMES
   Black locust, pseudo-acacia, yellow locust
   Germany: Falsche Akazie
   Greece: Akakía
   Italy: Acacia
   Spain: Acácia
   Turkey: Yalanci akasya

CULTIVARS
   Hortus Third lists over a dozen varieties and cultivars of this species.

RELATED SPECIES
   Robinia is part of the Faboideae, a subfamily of the Leguminosae.

    Deciduous tree
    Origin: Eastern and central United States
    Range: Temperate regions everywhere

CULINARY USES

The flowers of false acacia have a delicious vanilla-like scent. The only direct culinary use found for them is in a dessert fritter (see ELDERBERRY). Most of the Italian honey crop each year is derived from the nectar of false acacia. The seeds can be pressed to yield a cooking oil.

COMMENTS

How do we know which flowers are used by bees to make the honeys we consume? After all, we can't very well follow them as they make their rounds. Determining the floral sources used to be a rather inexact process, but science has found a way to obtain more accurate results. Honey is not 100 percent pure, although you won't hear that from the folks who market it. You can always find a tiny amount of sediment at the bottom of the golden liquid. That sediment contains pollen from the plants that have been visited by the bees. Every species of flowering plant produces pollen grains that are unique to that species. The pollen grains' "fingerprints" identify the anonymous product. Knowledge derived from such study has improved both the yield and the quality of honey by identifying desirable and undesirable plants in the bees' collecting area.

Fenugreek: *Trigonella foenum-graecum*

OTHER COMMON, ETHNIC, OR SCIENTIFIC NAMES
    Bird's foot, Greek hay, Greek hayseed
    Arabic: Hilbeh, hulba
    Burma/Myanmar: Penantazi
    China: Hu lu ba
    Egypt: Helba
    Estonia: Kreeka lambalääts, põld-lambalääts
    Ethiopia: Abish
    Finland: Sarviapila
    France: Fénugrec, trigonelle, sénégrain, sénegré
    Germany: Bockschorn, Griechisch Heu
    India: Methi, vendiya keerai (leaves); menthae soppu, methi ka beej,
        methi sag, menthulu, menthulu kooraku, ventayam (seeds); kasoor
        methi, mente, mentula, mentikura, methika, methini, methri, methro,
        mithiguti, sag methi, uluhaal, vendayam, venthiam (unspecified,
        probably seeds)

Iran: Shabaliidag, shambelileh
Iraq: Helbah
Italy: Fieno greco, trigonella
Malaysia: Halba
Mexico: Alhova, fenogreko
Morocco: Helbah
Netherlands: Fenegriek
Norway: Bukkehornkløver
Poland: Kozieradka pospolita
Portugal: Feno-grego
Russia: Pazhitnik grecheskiy, shambala
South Africa: Meti (name used mainly by Malaysian émigrés)
Spain: Alholva, fenigreco
Sri Lanka: Uluhaal
Swahili: Uwatu
Sweden: Bockhornsklöver
Turkey: Chaiman, poy

RELATED SPECIES
Trigonella arabica: Nafal
Trigonella corniculata 'Kasuri': Kasuri methi (India)

GROWTH HABITS
Annual
Origin: Southern Europe, Asia
Range: Cultivated in India and North Africa

CULINARY USES
Fenugreek is available as ground or whole seeds and as an extract. Ground seeds are occasionally used with vanilla and butterscotch, but they more commonly flavor pickles and cheeses. The dried leaves and seeds of fenugreek are used in Ethiopian *berberé* paste.

Fenugreek and turmeric are the main ingredients in most commercial "curry powders." Leaves are used in India as an ingredient in some curries and in the masala used in tandoori cooking. They are especially prized in combination with potatoes or spinach. The leaves flavor Indian breads, as well. In the United States, if the leaves can be obtained at all, they are in sun-dried form. The seeds are part of the Indian spice mixture called *panch phoron*. Vegetables, and any of a number of the puréed legumes, called dals, are seasoned with panch phoron.

Hilbeh is a kind of Middle East salsa made of chopped tomatoes, seasoned with zhug (see glossary) and fenugreek. Nafal, *Trigonella arabica,* is used by the Bedouins of North Africa to flavor their ghee-like *samin.*

Seeds can be sprouted for use in salads or on sandwiches.

Fenugreek
Trigonella foenum-graecum

From Köhler, *Köhler's
Medizinal-Pflanzen,* vol. 2

Fenugreek's curious maple-like aroma is primarily the result of β-carotene, coumarin, and kaempherol, along with several alkanoles, lactones, and sesquiterpenes. Glycosides and quercetin provide the bitterness.

OTHER USES
Extracts are used in the formulation of imitation rum and imitation maple flavorings. Leaves are useful in potpourri.

Goat's Rue: *Galega officinalis*

OTHER COMMON, ETHNIC, OR SCIENTIFIC NAMES
Everlasting clover, French lilac, pestilence plant, pock plant, Spanish holy hay, spot plant, wild holy hay
France: Sanfoin d'espagne
Germany: Ewigen Klee, Geissklee
Turkey: Keçi salaki

CULTIVAR
'Alba'

  Perennial
  Origin: Central Europe to eastern Mediterranean region
  Range: Cosmopolitan weed

CULINARY USES
  Juice expressed from the plant is used in place of rennet for curdling milk in cheese making.

COMMENTS
  This French lilac, *Galega officinalis,* is not related in any way to lilac, *Syringa vulgaris* (q.v.). The former has been listed by the USDA as a "noxious weed."

Licorice: *Glycyrrhiza glabra*

OTHER COMMON, ETHNIC, OR SCIENTIFIC NAMES
  Black sugar, Italian licorice, lycorys, Spanish juice, Spanish licorice, sweetwood. It has also been known as *Liquirtia officinalis.* The ancient Romans called it *radix dulcis,* or "sweet root."
  Arabic: Arpsous, arq-sous
  Burma/Myanmar: Noekiyu
  China: Gan cao, kan ts'oi
  Denmark: Lakridsplante
  Estonia: Lagritsa-magusjuur, magusjuur
  Finland: Lakritsi
  France: Réglisse
  Germany: Lakritze, Süßholz
  Greece: Glikóriza, jiámpoli
  Iceland: Lakkrís
  India: Atimaduram, jashtimodhu, jethi madh, madhuka, mithi lakdi,
     muleti, yasthimadhu
  Iran: Shirin bajan
  Italy: Liquirizia, regolizia
  Mexico: Orozuz, palo dulce, regalís
  Mongolia: Nakhalsa (leaves)
  Morocco: Arksous
  Netherlands: Zoethout
  Norway: Lakrisrot
  Poland: Lukrecja gladka
  Russia: Lakrichnik, solodka gladkaya
  Spain: Orozuz, ragaliz
  Swahili: Susu

Sweden: Lakrits
Wales: Lacris

RELATED SPECIES
Glycyrrhiza asymmetrica: Meyan (Turkey)
Glycyrrhiza echinata: Dikenli meyan (Turkey), spiny-fruited liquorice, wild licorice
Glycyrrhiza lepidota: American licorice
Glycyrrhiza uralensis (sometimes listed as *Glycyrrhiza uralinsis*): Chinese licorice, gum-juo
Ononis spinosa (sometimes listed as *Ononis arvensis* or *Ononis repens*): Wild licorice, rest harrow

GROWTH HABITS
Perennial
Origin: Mediterranean region
Range: Cultivated commercially in southern Europe and western Asia

CULINARY USES
Licorice is used as a flavoring for root beer, candy, and tobacco products. Its flavor combines well with mint.

In Morocco, licorice is used with snails in *boubbouche.* It is also used to flavor squid. In Mongolia, an herbal tea is made from the leaves. The roots are also used for herbal teas and appear in some gin recipes.

Wild licorice, *Ononis spinosa,* is used like true licorice, but the young shoots are also eaten as a potherb.

Glycyrrhizin is the source of licorice's sweetness. The "licorice" flavor is, of course, anethole; it is a flavor that appears among totally unrelated families of plants.

COMMENTS
Most licorice-flavored spirits are actually flavored with anise, fennel, or star anise. The only one I have encountered that actually gets its primary flavoring from *Glycyrrhiza glabra* is the Italian *grappa alla liquiriza.*

OTHER USES
Potpourri

Melilot: *Melilotus officinalis*

OTHER COMMON, ETHNIC, OR SCIENTIFIC NAMES
Yellow sweet clover, yellow melilot, melist

RELATED SPECIES
Melilotus elegans: Kokula yonca (Turkey); Steinklee (Germany)
Trigonella caerula: Blue melilot, curd herb, sweet trefoil

GROWTH HABITS
  Annual
  Origin: Eurasia
  Range: Naturalized in the United States

CULINARY USES
  Some Polish vodkas are flavored with melilot seeds and foliage. In Switzerland, the dried leaves of blue melilot, *Trigonella caerula,* are used as a flavoring for other cheeses, such as Sapsago (also known as Grüner Käse, Glarner Kräuterkäse, and Schabzieger) and Gruyère. They are used in herbal teas, or blended with black tea in China. The Tyrolean bread *brotwürze* is flavored with dried leaves and flowers of blue melilot.

COMMENTS
  If these plants are not dried properly, fungi will cause the development of dicoumarol, a coumarin-like toxic substance that is a dangerous anticoagulant.

Mesquite: *Prosopis glandulosa*

OTHER COMMON, ETHNIC, OR SCIENTIFIC NAMES
  Argentina: Algarrobo
  Chile: Algarrobo
  Nicaragua: Acacia de catharino
  Panama: Algarrobo

CULTIVARS
  'Glandulosa': Honey mesquite, honey pod
  'Torreyana': Western honey mesquite

RELATED SPECIES
  Prosopis chilensis: Algaroba, Hawaiian mesquite, kiawe, mesquite
  Prosopis juliflora: Aroma, manca-caballo (Panama); manca-caballo, trupilla (Colombia); mesquite
  Prosopis pubescens: Screw bean, tornillo

GROWTH HABITS
  Small tree
  Origin: Kansas to Mexico
  Range: Native to the U.S. Southwest

CULINARY USES
  Mesquite is best known as the classic fuel for smoky-flavored barbecues in the American Southwest, although it has other culinary uses also. Based on archaeological evidence, mesquite was second only to agave in the diet of Mexican Indians in the period 6000 BCE to 1580 CE. Today, the blossoms are

used in teas and in salads. The mature pods contain a sweet pulp, something like tamarind, that has can be made into beer and sweet wines. They are also eaten raw or roasted. The seeds have been cooked like baked beans, with salt pork and molasses.

Similarly, the wood of kiawe, *Prosopis chilensis,* is used in Hawaii as fuel for barbecues; the pods and edible seeds are used to make a beverage called *atole* and appear as an ingredient in beer. The nectar from the blossoms is said to yield an excellent honey.

Screw bean, *Prosopis pubescens,* has similar uses, but the pods are also boiled to release their sugar content; then the resulting liquid is reduced to a molasses-like syrup.

COMMENTS

It's always been common knowledge (at least among Texans) that mesquite provides the longest-lasting, best-smelling firewood for the tastiest Texas-sized barbecues. Nowadays, mesquite charcoal can be purchased in places far, far from Texas.

Parkia: *Parkia* spp.

OTHER COMMON, ETHNIC, OR SCIENTIFIC NAMES
Indonesia: Peteh
Japan: Nejire-fusamame
Malaysia: Petai
Thailand: Sataw, sator

RELATED SPECIES
Parkia is part of the Mimosoideae, a subfamily of the Leguminosae.
Parkia biglobosa (also known as *Parkia africana*): Monkey cutlass, nutta
Parkia filicoidea: West African locust bean
Parkia javanica (also known as *Parkia roxburghii*): African locust,
    kedawung, kedaung
Parkia speciosa: Nitta tree, peté, peteh

GROWTH HABITS
Tropical tree
Origin: Southeast Asia,
Range: Tropical areas, worldwide

CULINARY USES
The seeds of *Parkia biglandulosa* are dried and roasted for use as a coffee substitute. The pulpy fruits are fermented into a ripened, cheese-like paste that is used, like miso or fermented bean curd, as an enriching seasoning. A

similar ingredient, called *kinda* or *netetou,* is made from the pulp of monkey cutlass, *Parkia biglobosa.* That plant's seeds are also used like coffee, in *café du Sudan.* Yet another fermented parkia paste, made from West African locust bean, *Parkia filicoidea,* is called *dawadawa.*

The seeds of nitta tree, *Parkia speciosa,* are eaten boiled, fried, raw, or toasted. The pods are said to taste like garlic and are used the same way. Flowers and leaves are eaten as salads.

Rooibos: *Aspalathus linearis*

OTHER COMMON, ETHNIC, OR SCIENTIFIC NAMES
Red bush, red tea, rooibosch, rooibos tea

RELATED SPECIES
Cassia alata: Alexandre (Russia); bajagua, dorance, hierba de playa, lenguevaca, lucutema, lucutena, majaguilla, majaguillo, mocuteno (Colombia); hojasenn, senn, te de sen (Mexico); laureno (Panama); senne (France); Sennesblätter (Germany); wild senna (Jamaica); candlestick cassia, cure-all candle-plant, Christmas candle, empress, ringworm cassia, senna

GROWTH HABITS
Evergreen shrub
Origin: South Africa
Range: Temperate regions

CULINARY USES
Leaves are used in herbal teas, traditionally by bushmen and Khoikhoin (once called "Hottentots" by colonials). The Khoikhoin have extensive trading networks and have spread useful herbs (culinary, medical, ceremonial, and what we might call "recreational" herbs) all over southern Africa. Cinnamon and/or other seasonings are often added to rooibos tea.

Rooibos is sometimes sold in the United States as kafree tea.

Rooibos adds color and flavor to marinades, sauces, soups, and stews. Senna (*Cassia alata*) has some slight utilty as a bitter industrial flavoring, generally for tobacco (see Comments).

COMMENTS
Culinary use of senna should be limited as it has strong laxative properties. Senna is included in this book in an attempt to prevent confusion resulting from its scientific name. In spite of its genus, senna is not related in any way to the cinnamon-like cassia, *Cinnamomum Cassia* (also *Camphora officinalis*); see CINNAMON.

Tamarind: *Tamarindus indica*

OTHER COMMON, ETHNIC, OR SCIENTIFIC NAMES

Imlee, Indian date. An outdated scientific name for tamarind is *Tamarindus officinalis*.

Arabic: Sbar, tamar hindi
Burma/Myanmar: Ma-gyi-thi
Cambodia: Ampil khui (unripe); ampil tum (ripe)
China: Asam koh
East Timor: Sukaer
Estonia: Tamarindipuu
Finland: Tamarindi
France: Tamarin
Germany: Indische Dattel, Sauerdattel, Tamarinde
India: Amli, chinch, huli, kainya, siyambula, tentuli, puli
Indonesia: Asam
Iran: Tamr-e hendi
Iraq: Tamir hind
Italy: Tamarindo
Laos: 'Kham
Malaysia: Asam
Netherlands: Assem, indische dadel
Okinawa: Tama-rindo
Philippines: Salomagi, sampalok
Russia: Indiyskiy finik
Spain: Tamaríndo
Sri Lanka: Siyambala
Swahili: Ukwaju
Thailand: Kham
Vietnam: Cay me, khoua me, mak kham, me

RELATED SPECIES

Dialium cochinchinense (also known as *Dialium ovoideum*): Gal siyambala (Sri Lanka); kallu pullium (India); kanji, keranji (Malaysia); kaa yee, khleng, naang dam, yee (Thailand); velvet tamarind
Dialium guineense: Velvet tamarind, Sierra Leone tamarind
Dialium indum: Tamarind plum

GROWTH HABITS

Evergreen tree
Origin: India, possibly Africa
Range: Southernmost Florida

Tamarind might seem to be excludable from this book, but it is used more as a flavoring than a fruit. The pulp, once its large seeds are removed, adds a velvet texture, a rich brown color, and a sweetly tart flavor (somewhere between that of lemon and prune) to sauces. It deepens the flavor—and color—of curries, chutneys, salsas, and satés. It is an ingredient in Worcestershire sauce.

The cuisine of the Philippines has a sophisticated approach to sour flavors. Many different plants supply the desired tart flavor (and only a truly uninspired cook would stoop to the use of mere vinegar or lemon juice). Underripe tamarind fruit and tamarind leaves are key elements in the Filipino spectrum of sharp seasonings.

Tamarind is used in cold drinks in India, and a small amount of tamarind syrup in a tall glass of soda water is an Italian refresher that leaves iced tea panting in the shade. *Tamarindo* is an almost identical Mexican soft drink. Tamarind tea is popular in the Middle East.

Tamarind's tart flavor is a delightful foil to rich meats, such as duck or goose. Mark Miller's *The Great Chile Book* contains a recipe for tamarind chipotle sauce that fits the bill perfectly (sautéed soft-shelled crabs, always delicious, were even better with this smoky, tangy, velvet-textured sauce).

Dulces de tamarindo are Guatemalan sweets made from tamarind pulp and sugar. In Mexico, tamarind pods, dusted with powdered chile, are sold as confections. You have to chew or suck the sweet/sour/hot pulp off the rather large stones. If you're looking for a less tiresome way to enjoy this particular flavor combination, you're in luck. A commercially made Thai candy utilizes similar ingredients; thankfully, the toffee-like confection is produced without tamarind seeds.

The fruit has been used to make wine.

The *Dialium* species are used as tamarind, but their lower acidity requires greater amounts of fruit to achieve the same results.

Tamarind's sour quality is a result of fruit acids, but its flavor and scent are influenced by alkylthiazoles, cinnamic acid, ethyl cinnamate, geraniol, limonene, methyl salicylate, pyrazine, and safrole.

Tolu: *Myroxylon balsamum*

OTHER COMMON, ETHNIC, OR SCIENTIFIC NAMES

Balsam of tolu, quinoquino, tolu balsam. Tolu is sometimes listed scientifically as *Myroxylon peruiferum*.

France: Baume du tol
Germany: Tolubalsam

Italy: Balsamo del tol
Spain: Balsamo tolu

CULTIVAR
'Pereirae' (sometimes listed as *Myroxylon pereirae*): Balsamo, balsamo
  peru (Spain); balsamo del peru (Italy); baum du pérou France); tache
  (Colombia); balsam of Peru, black balsam, Indian balsam, Peruvian
  balsam

GROWTH HABITS
Tropical tree
Origin: Venezuela and Peru
Range: Grown in India, Sri Lanka, Sumatra, and the West Indies

CULINARY USES
Tolu has an acrid taste but a pleasantly aromatic scent, reminiscent of cinnamon, hyacinths, and vanilla. It is the source of tolu balsam, used in the
flavorings industry for candies, ice cream, and soft drinks. Balsam of Peru is
sometimes added to *aguardiente,* a high-powered alcoholic beverage made in
Guatemala.

All parts of the tolu tree contain benzyl benzoate, benzyl cinnamate, and
vanillin.

OTHER USES
It is used in perfumes and soaps.

Tonka Bean: *Dipteryx odorata*

OTHER COMMON, ETHNIC, OR SCIENTIFIC NAMES
Tonco bean, tonquin bean. Its old scientific name was *Coumarouna odo-
rata*. Pharmaceutically, it appears as *Semen Tonco.*
  Brazil: Rumara
  Finland: Tonkapapu
  France: Fèves de tonka
  Germany: Tonkabohne
  Italy: Favatonka
  Netherlands: Tonkaboon
  Spain: Habatonca

RELATED SPECIES
Dipteryx is part of the Faboideae, a subfamily of the Leguminosae.
Dipteryx oppositifolia: Tonka bean (formerly *Coumarouna oppositifolia*)

GROWTH HABITS
Tree
Origin: Tropical South America

Range: Commercially cultivated in Africa, British Guiana, Brazil, Ceylon, and Venezuela

CULINARY USES
The plant has a floral, new-mown-hay scent. Tonka beans have been used to flavor cordials like Grand Marnier and Cointreau. Their flavor is also part of Angostura Bitters. Tonka beans contain coumarin, which develops when the beans are soaked in alcohol and allowed to ferment (see Comments, below).

OTHER USES
Potpourri, perfumes

COMMENTS
While used commercially—outside the United States—as a flavoring, coumarin is a dangerous substance that can cause serious liver damage. It has been used as an adulterant of vanilla extracts, a practice that is illegal in the United States but common in Mexico.

46. Liliaceae: The Lily Family

Aloe: *Aloe Perryi*

OTHER COMMON, ETHNIC, OR SCIENTIFIC NAMES
Socotrine aloe, Zanzibar aloe
France: Aloès

RELATED SPECIES
Aloe barbadensis (sometimes mistakenly listed as *aloe vera*): Zábila (Mexico); Barbados aloe, Curaçao aloe, medicinal aloe, unguentine cactus
Aloe socotrina: Bombay aloe, Moka aloe, Turkey aloe, Zanzibar aloe

GROWTH HABITS
Perennial
Origin: Socotra (an island in the Indian Ocean, since 1967 a part of Yemen)
Range: Temperate to tropical regions

CULINARY USES
In Nigeria, the peoples of the Bani River region chop the leaves of aloe, then pickle them in lime juice.

Aloe is supposed to be one of the bitter ingredients in Fernet Branca and Benedictine. It is flavored by aloin and barbaloin.

OTHER USES

The wood is sometimes used as incense.

COMMENTS

"American aloe" is actually *Agave americana,* a close relative to the plant that gives us tequila and mescal (see AGAVE).

Butcher's Broom: *Ruscus aculeatus*

OTHER COMMON, ETHNIC, OR SCIENTIFIC NAMES

Box holly, Jew's myrtle

GROWTH HABITS

Evergreen shrub
Origin: Mediterranean region (Azores to Iran)
Range: Southern United States

CULINARY USES

Added to egg or rice dishes, the young leaves and shoots have an astringent quality that diminishes upon cooking.

Butcher's Broom
Ruscus aculeatus

From Woodville, *A supplement to Medical botany,* vol. 4

This species is not related to broom, *Spartium* spp. (q.v.).

Checkered Lily: *Fritillaria Roylei* subs. *Hook*

RELATED SPECIES
Fritillaria meleagris: Fritillaire (France); Kiebizei, Schachblume
(Germany); fritillary, snake's head

GROWTH HABITS
Perennial
Origin: Himalayas
Range: Cool temperate regions

CULINARY USES
Used in Chinese soup containing pears and pork.

COMMENTS
Fritillaria meleagris is poisonous.

Golden Needles: *Hemerocallis* spp.

OTHER COMMON, ETHNIC, OR SCIENTIFIC NAMES
Day lily, lily buds
China: Chin cheng tsai, gum-chum, jin-pi, kim-choi
Japan: Kanzō, wasuregusa
Korea: Pet kup julgi
Okinawa: Kanso
Thailand: Dok mai jin
Vietnam: Kim cham

GROWTH HABITS
Perennial
Origin: East Asia
Range: Temperate areas

CULINARY USES
Dried buds are known as golden needles, perhaps most familiar in the
United States in the classic Mandarin dishes moo shu pork and hot and sour
soup. The buds are eaten fresh in salads and cooked as a vegetable. Young
leaves are eaten as a vegetable in Japan.

Fermentation occurs during the drying process, yielding a haunting tart
flavor that is absent in the fresh buds.

Sarsaparilla: *Smilax ornata*

OTHER COMMON, ETHNIC, OR SCIENTIFIC NAMES

Catbrier, greenbrier, Jamaica sarsaparilla, red-bearded sarsaparilla. Sarsaparilla is sometimes found in older botanical texts as *Smilax Medica* and *Smilax officinalis.*
France: Salsepareille
Germany: Sarzaparilla, Sassaparilla, Sarsaparillawurzel
Italy: Salsapariglia
Spain: Salsaparilla

RELATED SPECIES

Smilax aristolochiaefolia: European sarsaparilla
Smilax China: China root
Smilax cordifolia: Colcomeca, culculmeca, raiz China, zarzaparilla
  (Mexico); China root, Mexican sarsaparilla
Smilax reglii: European sarsaparilla

GROWTH HABITS

Woody vine
Origin: Central America, Jamaica, Mexico
Range: Central America, Jamaica, Mexico

CULINARY USES

Sarsaparilla has a sweet, slightly bitter, anise-like flavor that is reminiscent of root beer. It is used in candies, herbal teas, and soft drinks.

Roots of *Smilax China* are eaten as starchy vegetables in China. Its spicy root beer–like flavor is used in industrial flavorings.

Sarsaparilla roots and bark contain cinchonin, rutin, tannin, and compounds specific to the genus: parillin, sarasaponin, sarsaparilloside, sarsaponin, sarsasapogenin, smilagenin, smilasaponin, and three smilax-saponins.

COMMENTS

The wild sarsaparillas of North America (*Araliaceae,* see ARALIA) are sometimes substituted for the true South American sarsaparillas, which are members of the Lilaceae family. Sarsaparillas provide creamy heads on some beers and soft drinks.

Tassel Hyacinth: *Muscari comosum*

OTHER COMMON, ETHNIC, OR SCIENTIFIC NAMES

Cipollino, feather hyacinth, purse tassel. Sometimes seen listed as *Hyacinthus comosum* and *Leopoldia comosa.*
France: Muscari à toupet

Germany: Schopfige Bisamhyazinthe
Greece: Kremmydola
Italy: Cipollotto col fiocco, lampascione, pampasciune, vamppagiolo

Muscari racemosum: Grape hyacinth
Muscari weissii: Arap sümbülü (Turkey); Traubenhyazinthe (Germany)

GROWTH HABITS
Perennial bulb
Origin: Western Europe and North Africa
Range: Temperate regions

CULINARY USES
The bulbs, parboiled and then tossed in a simple vinaigrette, are eaten as antipasti. The bulbs of grape hyacinth are used in the same manner, in Crete, Italy, and a number of other locations in the eastern Mediterranean region.

COMMENTS
The bulbs, sometimes sold as *cipollino,* should not be confused with the small flat onions called *cipollini.*

Yucca: *Yucca brevifolia*

OTHER COMMON, ETHNIC, OR SCIENTIFIC NAMES
Beargrass, Joshua tree, soapweed

RELATED SPECIES
Yucca aloifolia: Dagger plant, Spanish bayonet
Yucca baccata: Spanish bayonet, yucca
Yucca filamentosa: Adam's needle, needle palm, Spanish bayonet
Yucca glauca: Beargrass, soapweed, soapwell, Spanish bayonet
Yucca schidigera: Mojave yucca

GROWTH HABITS
Perennial
Origin: North America
Range: Southern United States

CULINARY USES
Petals are candied, used in salads, or fried in fritters (see ELDERBERRY). The young seeds have been used as a cooked vegetable. Yucca root extracts are used as a flavoring for root beer and as an aid in the formation of a creamy head on the drink.
Yucca baccata contains traces of β-carotene.

COMMENTS

The common names for yuccas, such as "Adam's needle," "soapweed," "Spanish bayonet," and "Spanish dagger," are used indiscriminately for many different species of yucca. Local names are often interesting but rarely trustworthy.

47. Magnoliaceae: The Magnolia Family

Champaca: *Michelia Champaca*

OTHER COMMON, ETHNIC, OR SCIENTIFIC NAMES

Chêmpaka, fragrant champaca. Sometimes listed in old botanical texts as *Micheaua champaca*.

RELATED SPECIES
Michelia alba: Ginkô boku, yü lan
Michelia figo: Banana shrub

GROWTH HABITS
Evergreen shrub
Origin: Northern India
Range: India to Malaysia, southern Florida

CULINARY USES

Champaca has been used as a commercial flavoring. Flowers smell like ylang-ylang and taste like violets. Champaca has edible fruit. The bark is bitter and aromatic.

The blossoms of *Michelia alba* are used to flavor black teas.

OTHER USES

Used in manufacture of perfumes. It has been used as an adulterant in cinnamon.

Native Pepper: *Drimys lanceolata*

OTHER COMMON, ETHNIC, OR SCIENTIFIC NAMES

Mountain pepper, pepper tree, Tasmanian pepper. Also known botanically as *Tasmannia aromatica, Tasmannia lanceolata, Drimys aromatica,* or *Winteriana lanceolata*.

Germany: Australischer Pfeffer, Bergpfeffer, Tasmanischer Pfeffer

Tasmannia insipida: Pepper tree
Tasmannia stipitata: Dorrigo pepper

GROWTH HABITS
Dioecious evergreen small tree or shrub
Origin: Australia
Range: New South Wales, Tasmania, Victoria; grows at altitudes of
2,400 to 4,500 feet in moist places

CULINARY USES
Both leaves and berries are peppery. The deep purple berries are about
the size of whole allspice. Dried and ground, they are used like black pepper,
though they are somewhat hotter. The berries can be used fresh, but they
are more frequently available frozen or as a ground spice. They are a natural
combination with game but can also be used in breads, compound butters,
pasta, and sauces. Native pepper is an excellent component of forcemeats
for sausage or pâté, and it adds a pungent note to marinades and glazes for
barbecue.

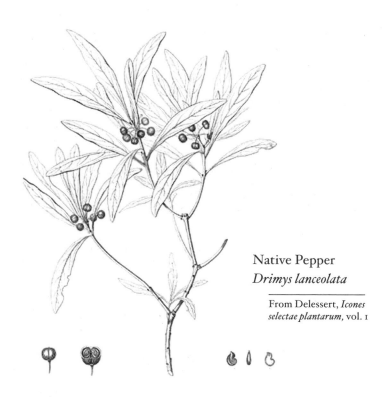

Native Pepper
Drimys lanceolata

From Delessert, *Icones
selectae plantarum,* vol. 1

It lacks the resinous bouquet of *Piper nigrum,* but its heat—found largely in the seeds—comes on very gradually, building in intensity in a very satisfying manner. The berries impart a pale mauve tint to light-colored sauces. If this is not desirable, a similar flavor can be obtained by using the leaves (fresh or dried) in place of the berries.

COMMENTS

The characteristic pungency of native pepper will not stand up to prolonged cooking; the herb is usually added at the last minute.

Sweet Bay: *Magnolia virginiana*

RELATED SPECIES
Magnolia grandiflora: Magnolia

GROWTH HABITS
Shrubby tree (evergreen in the southern United States)
Origin: Eastern United States
Range: Cool temperate regions

CULINARY USES
Magnolia grandiflora is sometimes pickled in Devonshire, England.

COMMENTS
"Sweet bay" is also used as a name for *Persea Borbonia.*

Winter's Bark: *Drimys winteri*

OTHER COMMON, ETHNIC, OR SCIENTIFIC NAMES
Chachaca, New Granada winterbark, palo de mambo, true winter's bark, winter's cinnamon, wintera, wintera aromatica

GROWTH HABITS
Evergreen tree
Origin: Chile and Argentina
Range: Tropical upland forests

CULINARY USES

Winter's bark has been used as a substitute for cinnamon. In Brazil and Mexico, it is powdered and used as a table condiment. Extracts of winter's bark are used in the commercial flavorings industry. They contain drimin and driminic acid.

"Winter's bark" is used as a name for Malambo bark, or Matias bark, *Croton Malambo.* The flavor of *Croton Malambo* is said to be more like that of calamus than cinnamon. The plant has been used as a substitute for Peruvian bark as well. False winter's bark, *Cinnamodendron corticosum,* is from Jamaica and is also known as red canella and mountain cinnamon. Its flavor and scent are similar to those of true winter's bark.

This genus does not appear in *Hortus Third.*

48. Malvaceae: The Mallow Family

Alaches: *Anoda cristata*

OTHER COMMON, ETHNIC, OR SCIENTIFIC NAMES
Halachas. Also known scientifically as *Anoda acerifolia, Anoda Dilleniana, Anoda hastata, Anoda lavateroides,* and *Anoda triangularis.*

GROWTH HABITS
Annual, sometimes perennial
Origin: Southern United States, Mexico, West Indies, South America
Range: Naturalized in frost-free regions

CULINARY USES
Halachas is a wild herb found in eastern Mexico. It has downy arrowhead-shaped leaves and purple blossoms. It is used to season local squashes, along with chiles, garlic, and onions. Shoots, flowers, and leaves are eaten.

Hollyhock: *Alcea rosea*

CULTIVAR
'Nigra': Black Hollyhock

RELATED SPECIES
Althea pallida: Blasse Stockrose (Germany); hatmi (Turkey)

GROWTH HABITS
Biennial
Origin: Asia Minor
Range: Temperate regions

In Egypt, the leaves are used in cooking. Both flowers and buds are eaten in salads. The petals have been used in herbal teas. The petals of the cultivar 'Black Hollyhock' are used as a vegetable coloring for herbal teas and wines.

Marsh Mallow: *Althaea officinalis*

OTHER COMMON, ETHNIC, OR SCIENTIFIC NAMES

Althaea root, cheeses, hock herb, mallards, mauls, mortification root, schloss tea

France: Guimauve, guimaure officinal, mauve
Germany: Echter Eibiscu, Stockmalve
Greece: Molólcha
Italy: Altea officinale, bismalva, malva
Spain: Altea comn, malví

RELATED SPECIES

Malva neglecta: Common mallow. Used in stewed chicken dishes in Greece.
Malva sylvestris: Ebegümeci (Turkey); Wild Malva (Germany); cheeses, common mallow, high mallow, khobbeiza, mallow
Malva verticillata: Mallow (or *Malva crispum*). Used in salads.

GROWTH HABITS

Perennial
Origin: China
Range: Temperate regions

CULINARY USES

The fresh seeds are eaten alone or in salads. The flowers can be added to salads or used as garnishes. Leaves are useful in salads or as a flavoring for oils or vinegars. They can also be eaten as a potherb. Leaves and young shoots of *Malva sylvestris,* sweated in olive oil, become an ingredient in salads served from North Africa to Turkey. Cooked rice, flavored with dill, onion, and parsley, is the filling for stuffed mallow leaves in Turkey. Shoots can be boiled, steamed, or stir-fried. They are used in soups and stews. Extracts from the roots are used for flavoring soft drinks and desserts.

Musk Mallow: *Malva moschata*

OTHER COMMON, ETHNIC, OR SCIENTIFIC NAMES
Cutleaf mallow

CULTIVARS
'Alba', 'Rosea'

RELATED SPECIES
Abelmoschus eculentus: Algalia, candia, gombo, guicombo, lagarto
(Colombia); gumbo (Jamaica); naju (Panama); okra, gumbo, gombo,
lady's finger, quimbombo

GROWTH HABITS
Perennial
Origin: Mediterranean region
Range: Cool temperate regions

CULINARY USES
Flowers can eaten in salads or used as a garnish.

COMMENTS
Do not confuse musk mallow, *Malva moschata,* with musk seed, *Abelmoschus*
moschatus (q.v.) or musk mallow, *Hibiscus Moscheutos* (q.v.), even though the latter two scientific names are occasionally interchanged.

Musk Seed: *Abelmoschus moschatus*

OTHER COMMON, ETHNIC, OR SCIENTIFIC NAMES
Ab-el-mosch, ambrette, ambrette seed, bamia moschata, capu kanassa,
Egyptian alcée, galu gasturi, ketmie odorante, musk mallow, musk okra, target-
leaved hibiscus. It was formerly known scientifically as *Hibiscus Abelmoschus.*
Colombia: Algalia, almizclillo, lagarto
Germany: Ambrakörner, Bisornkörner, Moschuskörner
Italy: Ambretta
Jamaica: Wild okra
Spain: Abelmosco

RELATED SPECIES
Hibiscus acetosella: Asatsuki, asam susur, false roselle, som kop
Hibiscus bifurcatus: Flor de paisto, vinaigre
Hibiscus cannabinus: Hemp-leaved hibiscus, kenaf

GROWTH HABITS
Evergreen shrub in the tropics
Origin: Tropical Asia
Range: Grown as an annual in temperate zones

CULINARY USES
Roots of musk seed are used in baked goods, candy, and ice cream. Arabs
sometimes use the seeds as a flavoring for coffee. Outside of Islamic countries,

the seeds are used to flavor liqueurs (see below). The seed capsules are used in soups and as a seasoning for pickles. Essential oils derived from the seeds are used in commercial flavorings for baked goods, candies, ice cream, and non-alcoholic beverages.

The seeds were originally intended to be used as a substitute for true musk, which is derived from the scent glands of male Himalayan or Siberian musk deer, *Moschus moschiferus.*

Asatsuki, *Hibiscus acetosella,* is used in Africa like sorrel, to add a tart bite to soups and stews. Also in Africa, hemp-leaved hibiscus, *Hibiscus cannabinus,* is used in combination with the cheese-like pulp of the fruit of parkia (q.v.) to make a kind of condiment called *kwa'do.*

Musk seed's floral, earthy, or musky flavor suggests brandy and is reportedly a component of liqueurs such as amaretto, Benedictine, bitters, and vermouth. The source of these flavors is farnesol and hexadecenolactone.

OTHER USES
Used in the manufacture of perfumes.

COMMENTS
Do not confuse musk mallow, *Abelmoschus moschatus,* with musk mallow, *Hibiscus Moscheutos* (q.v.), or musk mallow, *Malva moschata* (q.v.).

Rose Mallow: *Hibiscus Moscheutos*

OTHER COMMON, ETHNIC, OR SCIENTIFIC NAMES
Abelmusk, common rose mallow, musk mallow, swamp rose mallow, wild cotton. Formerly known as *Abelmoschus Moscheutos.*
Colombia: Almizclillo
Panama: Algodoncillo

GROWTH HABITS
Perennial, cultivated as an annual
Origin: Eastern United States
Range: Temperate regions

CULINARY USES
Teas, garnishes. Provides the red color in some popular commercial herbal tea blends (for example, Red Zinger).

OTHER USES
Seeds are used in the manufacture of perfumes.

COMMENTS
Do not confuse musk mallow, *Hibiscus Moscheutos,* with musk mallow, *Abelmoschus moschatus* (q.v.), or musk mallow, *Malva moschata* (q.v.).

Roselle: *Hibiscus sabdariffa*

OTHER COMMON, ETHNIC, OR SCIENTIFIC NAMES
Florida cranberry, hibiscus, Indian sorrel, Jamaica flower, Jamaican sorrel,
Java jute, rama, red sorrel, rosella
  Algeria: Bqoul
  Arabic: Karkade
  Burma/Myanmar: Chinbaung ywet
  France: Carcadé, karkade, oseille rouge, oseille de guinée
  Germany: Carcadé, Karkadeh, Rosella
  India: Pulincha kira
  Italy: Carcadé
  Japan: Rozeru
  Mexico: Flor de jamaica, jamaica
  Portugal: Azeda de guiné, vinagreira
  Senegal: Bisap
  Spain: Carcadé, quimbombó chino, sereni
  Sri Lanka: Rata bilincha
  Thailand: Krachiap, krachup daeng

CULTIVARS
  'Altissima': Raised for fibers (though it is sometimes used for food, the
    same as 'Sabdariffa')
  'Sabdariffa': Rosella (Colombia); vinuela (Spain); Jamaica sorrel, Roselle.
    Raised for edible portions of flowers.

RELATED SPECIES
  Hibiscus rosa-sinensis: Bunga raya (Malaysia); bussouge (Japan); fa jasum,
vadamal (India); Chinessischer Roseneibisch (Germany); çin gülü (Turkey);
fu shong hua (China); gumamela bulaklak (Philippines); palo de la reina,
papo, tapo (Panama); pejo (Colombia); saattu mal, watha wal (Sri Lanka);
woro wari (Indonesia); Chinese hibiscus, choblac, hibiscus
  Modiola caroliniana: Cheeses, mauve

GROWTH HABITS
  Perennial, raised as an annual
  Origin: India and Tropical Asia
  Range: Cultivated in Southern Florida, naturalized throughout tropics
    (Africa, Central America, China, Thailand and the West Indies)

CULINARY USES
  The sour-tasting calyx (the sheath around the flower bud) and bracts
are used in chutneys, jams, jellies, juice drinks, sauces, and wines, often in
combination with rose hips. The calyxes can be added to the recipes for
rather bland homemade wines, providing a lovely rosy color, fruity flavor,

and tartness that might otherwise be lacking. *Agua de flor de Jamaica* is a Mexican version of iced Red Zinger tea sold in the United States. The petals of *Hibiscus rosa-sinensis* are made into pickles in India and China.

Leaves and stems are eaten as vegetables, as a flavoring for curries, and, if young, as a salad herb. The leaves are made into a sweet beverage, flavored with ginger. A similar beverage is popular among the Cajuns of Louisiana made with the leaves of *Modiola caroliniana*.

The flowers are used to flavor rum in Jamaica. A number of sweet-sour mixed drinks are made using ginger, lime juice, roselle, and rum. Shandy, or Shandy Carib, is a bottled mixture of lager beer and "sorrel" (which, in the Caribbean, means roselle) that is available in stores in Trindadian communities.

In Australia, the fruits are made into jam. Their sour, rhubarb-like overtones make the berry preserves an interesting base for sauces to accompany meats.

Seeds are eaten in Africa.

The sour flavor is provided by citric acid.

Roselle
Hibiscus sabdariffa

From Bonpland,
Description des plantes

The FDA restricts the use of roselle to alcoholic beverages.

49. Meliaceae: The Mahogany Family

Juran: *Aglaia odorata*

OTHER COMMON, ETHNIC, OR SCIENTIFIC NAMES
Chinese perfume plant, mock lime
Spain: Falsa lima

GROWTH HABITS
Tropical tree
Origin: China and southeast Asia
Range: Indoors, or southern Florida and California

CULINARY USES
The spicy, vanilla-scented blossoms are used to perfume tea. The bitter blooms and leaves of *Melia Azedarach* are used to flavor a Laotian salad made with beef from water buffaloes.

Margosa: *Azadirachta indica*

OTHER COMMON, ETHNIC, OR SCIENTIFIC NAMES
Free tree of India, neem tree. Also listed botanically as *Azadarachta samimensis, Melia Azedarach,* and, probably in error, as *Azadirachira indica.*
East Timor: Nemba
India: Neem, vapu

GROWTH HABITS
Evergreen tropical tree
Origin: Burma/Myanmar and Pakistan
Range: South Asia, Caribbean, and Central America

CULINARY USES
Bengalis like bitter flavors, frequently using fenugreek or the bitter melon they call *karela* to impart the desired bitterness to their dishes. Neem leaves and flowers are about ten times as bitter as karela. Consequently, they are powdered and added sparingly to vegetable dishes, such as eggplant fried in mustard oil, or to appetizers like the lentil-based, *falafel*-like *urad dal.*

Margosa is sometimes available in the United States in the form of dried leaves.

50. Monimiaceae: The Monimia Family

Boldo: *Peumus boldus*

OTHER COMMON, ETHNIC, OR SCIENTIFIC NAMES
Baldina, boldea, boldoa fragrans, boldo leaves, boldus. Has been listed botanically as *Boldu boldus, Boldea fragrans,* and *Peumus boldos.*
France: Boldo
Germany: Boldoblätter
Mexico: Boldo

GROWTH HABITS
Evergreen shrub
Origin: Chile, Peru
Range: Southern California

CULINARY USES
Boldo is a spicy, aromatic, burning component of some recipes for bitters. Both leaves and bark are used. Boldo also has edible fruits, which are said to be sweet and aromatic.
Its peculiar odor has been compared to the aroma of epazote (q.v.). It contains 1,8-cineole, ascaridol, cymol and linalool. The leaves also contain a number of bitter, quinine-like alkaloids.

OTHER USES
Has been used as a flavoring, to mask the taste of some medicines.

Peruvian Nutmeg: *Laurelia serrata*

OTHER COMMON, ETHNIC, OR SCIENTIFIC NAMES
Chile laurel. Also known botanically as *Laurelia aromatica.*

RELATED SPECIES
Laurelia sempervirens: Chilean laurel

GROWTH HABITS
Subtropical tree or shrub
Origin: South America and New Zealand
Range: Grown in Chile

CULINARY USES
Fruit, leaves, and seeds are used as seasoning in Peru. The bark and leaves of *Laurelia sempervirens* are used the same way in Chile.

  See Comments, under Nutmeg.

Plume Nutmeg: *Atherosperma moschata*

OTHER COMMON, ETHNIC, OR SCIENTIFIC NAMES
New Holland nutmeg, Tasmanian sassafras tree

GROWTH HABITS
Tree
Origin: Australia
Range: Temperate regions

CULINARY USES
The bark of plume nutmeg is used in herbal teas.

51. Moringaceae: The Moringa Family

Moringa: *Moringa pterygosperma*

OTHER COMMON, ETHNIC, OR SCIENTIFIC NAMES
Calamungay, drumstick leaves, drumstick vegetable, horseradish, horserad-ish tree, Indian asparagus, kalamungay, oil of ben tree, saragaro, segava, sajjan ki phalli (pods), sargvani sing. Moringa is also known as *Moringa oleifera.*
East Timor: Ai-moringu
India: Muruggai, sahijan, seeng, sekta-ni-sing
Indonesia: Kelor, sai jar
Japan: Wasabi no-ki
Malaysia: Buah keloh, kelor
Nepal: Nihura
Philippines: Malunggay talbos, marungay
Samoa: Lopa
Sri Lanka: Murunga (bean), murunga kolle (leaf)
Thailand: Ma-rum (bean), phak-ma-rum (leaf)
Vietnam: Ba dau dai, chum ngay

RELATED SPECIES
Moringa oleifera: Angela (Colombia); jacinto (Panama); horseradish tree
Moringa ovalifolia: Phantom tree

GROWTH HABITS
Deciduous tree

Origin: India
Range: Cultivated and naturalized widely in frost-free areas

CULINARY USES

Fruits ("drumsticks") are eaten as vegetables, in curries (in Burma/ Myanmar), and in soups. They are pickled in India.

Flowers and young leaves are eaten raw, in salads, or cooked, as potherbs or in curries and soups. Fresh leaves are an important ingredient in many boiled dishes from the Philippines, especially those made with chicken, fish, or pork.

The leaves are relatively high in protein, and the seeds are a source of edible oil that is used on salads in the Caribbean islands. The plant is valuable enough in India for an improved hybrid to be developed for agricultural use.

Roots are said to be used like horseradish, grated as a condiment. All parts of the plant are said to taste like mustard. The flowers of this locust-like tree are honey scented.

OTHER USES

Oil of ben, pressed from the seeds, is odorless and nondrying. This makes it useful as a fixative for scents in the manufacture of perfumes. It is also used as a lubricant for delicate mechanisms such as watches.

COMMENTS

While the roots *are* hot and pungent, they are not related to true wasabi (q.v., under RADISH).

52. Myricaceae:
The Bayberry or Wax Myrtle Family

Sweet Gale: *Myrica gale*

OTHER COMMON, ETHNIC, OR SCIENTIFIC NAMES

Bog myrtle, candleberry, Dutch myrtle, English bog myrtle, gale, meadow fern. Its former scientific name was *Gale palustris*.

Estonia: Harilik porss
Finland: Suomyrtti
France: Galé odorant, myrique
Gaelic: Rideag
Germany: Gagel, Gagelstrauch, Sumpfmyrte
Italy: Mirica
Norway: Pors

Poland: Woskownica europejska
Spain: Mirto holandés
Sweden: Pors

Myrica cerifera: Malagueta (Mexico); American bayberry, American
vegetable wax, candleberry, southern bayberry, tallow shrub, wax
berry, wax myrtle
Myrica pennsylvanica (also seen as *Myrica cerifuga*): Northern bayberry
Comptonia peregrina: Sweet fern

GROWTH HABITS
Deciduous shrub
Origin: North America, Eurasia
Range: Cool temperate regions

CULINARY USES
Use berries and leaves as a seasoning, much as you would use bay leaves
(q.v.). The leaves and twigs are fragrant but bitter and astringent. At one time
the leaves were used in place of hops in the production of gale beer in York-
shire. Sweet gale is said to aid in the formation of a good head on beers.

The leaves of northern bayberry, *Myrica pennsylvanica,* have been used in
chowders, crab boils, soups, and stews. Like bay leaves, they are removed
before service. The dried berries have been used much as allspice berries are
used. Leaves of *Comptonia peregrina* are used as herbal tea.

Wax myrtle contains α-pinene, β-carotene, γ-terpinene, limonene, and
linalool, among other elements.

OTHER USES
The aromatic wax from both species of bayberries is used to make candles. The berries of sweet gale lack wax.

COMMENTS
Sweet gale is not related to bay leaves, myrtle, or nutmeg, in spite of similar-sounding scientific names and similar flavors.

53. Myristicaceae: The Nutmeg Family

Nutmeg: *Myristica fragrans*

OTHER COMMON, ETHNIC, OR SCIENTIFIC NAMES
Moscat nut, myristica, nux moschata, sadhika. Nutmeg was formerly
known scientifically as *Myristica officinalis* and *Myristica aromata.*

Nutmeg and mace are two different parts of the same plant. Nutmeg is the hard nut or seed. It is generally treated as a separate spice with its own set of names. (Note: when no distinction between nutmeg and mace has been specified in a text, the equivalent non-English name is listed here as "nutmeg.")

Arabic: Basbasa, josat al teeb
Burma/Myanmar: Zalipho thi
China: Rou dou kou, tou k'ou
Denmark: Muskatnød
Estonia: Lõhnav muskaadipuu
Ethiopia: Gewz
Finland: Muskottikukka
France: Muscade, noix de muscade
Germany: Muscatnuß
Greece: Moskhokário, moskokárido (both nutmeg and mace)
Iceland: Mskat
India: Jaiphul, jathikka, javitri, sadikka, taifal, wasa-vasi
Indonesia: Pala
Iran: Djus hendi
Iraq: Jose boa, lebb joz'l tayeb
Italy: Noce moscata, macis
Japan: Nikuzuku
Malaysia: Buah pala
Mexico: Nuez moscado
Morocco: Gouza
Netherlands: Nootmuskaat
Norway: Muskatnøtt
Portugal: Noz moscado
Russia: Muskatniy orekh, sushonaya shelukha muskatnogo orekha
Samoa: Atong-ula
Spain: Moscada, nuez moscada
Sri Lanka: Sadikka
Swahili: Basibasi, kungumanga
Sweden: Muskotnöt
Thailand: Luk chand
Turkey: Küçük hindistancevizi

Mace is the red covering, or aril, that surrounds the nutmeg. It is peeled off the hard "nut" before its long drying process begins. It is generally treated as a separate spice with its own set of names: *Arillus Myristicae, Myristica officinalis, Myristica moschata,* macis, muscadier.

France: Fleur de muscade, macis
Germany: Macis, Muskatblüte
Iceland: Masi
India: Javitri

Indonesia: Fuli, sekar pala
Iraq: Ghesher joz'l tayeb
Italy: Mace
Finland: Muskottipähkin
Greece: Moskhokário, moskokárido (both nutmeg and mace)
Malaysia: Kembang pala
Mexico: Macis
Morocco: Bsilbsa
Netherlands: Foelie
Norway: Muskatblomme
Spain: Maciás
Sri Lanka: Wasa-vasi
Sweden: Muskotblomma
Thailand: Dauk chan
Vietnam: Dau khau

RELATED SPECIES
Horsfieldia irya: Warun

GROWTH HABITS
Evergreen tree
Origin: Moluccas (Indonesia)
Range: Cultivated commercially in Brazil, Costa Rica, India, Indonesia,
  Sri Lanka, and the West Indies (Grenada)

CULINARY USES
Nutmeg is used in baking and puddings as well as with meats such as pâtés, poultry, sausages (for example, bologna, head cheese, hot dogs, and liverwurst), lamb dishes (especially Greek and Middle Eastern dishes), and stews. The ground spice is combined with other spices and salt to produce the French seasoning called *sel épice*. Nutmeg is one of the four ingredients in *quatre épices*. Both seasonings are used with meats, especially in French charcuterie.

Nutmeg is often added to dairy-based sauces; indeed, béchamel is only a milky paste without it. A tiny amount of freshly grated nutmeg, floating on a cup of hot cocoa, is a huge improvement over marshmallows, and certainly better for you than whipped cream. If you still crave sweetened butterfat, try making nutmeg-flavored ice cream.

Nutmeg is often paired with spinach, its warm sweetness balancing the slightly sour bitterness of the greens. Mace and nutmeg seem to be two of the secret ingredients in anisette, Benedictine, green Chartreuse (in the form of extracted mace oil), yellow Chartreuse, Pernod, and vermouth. Absinthe formulations often included nutmeg. According to Chaucer, nutmeg gave flavor to ale in the fourteenth century.

Mace, a sweet spice, might seem out of place in Worcestershire sauce, but it is there, along with the even more unlikely pickled walnuts, mushrooms, and sherry. Mace is useful in baking, with fish and poultry, in pickling, and in soups and stews. It also appears in some recipes for Benedictine and gin.

Nutmeg and mace are often ingredients in the Moroccan spice mixtures called *ras el hanout*. It is also featured in the Iraqi spice blend *boharat*.

In Indonesia, the fruit that surrounds the nutmeg and mace is eaten with a *sambal*, or pepper paste. It is also candied, or made into jam or preserves. The fruit is said to have the typical nutmeg taste and aroma. The flesh of the fruit is brewed into an alcoholic drink (see Comments, below).

Nutmeg's flavor and scent result from the combination of pinenes, camphene, *p*-cymene, dipentene, linalool, plus noticeable levels of eugenol and many other aromatics.

OTHER USES

Nutmeg yields essential oils that are used in the manufacture of perfumes and soaps. Nutmeg butter, a more substantial fat extracted from the nuts, is used in cosmetics and skin creams.

COMMENTS

A number of other plants are also called "nutmeg." Do not be misled by Brazilian nutmeg, *Cryptocarya moschata* (q.v.); calabash nutmeg, or African nutmeg, *Monodora myristica* (q.v.); California nutmeg or stinking nutmeg, *Torreya californica* (q.v.); clove nutmeg or Madagascar nutmeg, *Ravensara aromatica;* or Peruvian nutmeg, *Laurelia serrata* (q.v.).

The intoxicating scent of fresh nutmeg can be smelled a mile off the leeward side of Grenada. Apparently, nutmeg has been used as an intoxicant, less figuratively, but that is beyond the scope of this book.

54. Myrsinaceae: The Myrsine Family

Areuj Kathembang: *Embelia ribes*

OTHER COMMON, ETHNIC, OR SCIENTIFIC NAMES
Memory enhancer

GROWTH HABITS
Evergreen shrub or tree
Origin: Southeast Asia
Range: Tropics and subtropics

The tart leaves are eaten cooked on their own, or used like tamarind (q.v.), as a souring agent for curries and soups. The fruits add their sweet-sour flavor to tropical beverages.

OTHER USES
Black pepper has been adulterated with the dried fruits of *Embelia ribes.*

55. Myrtaceae: The Myrtle Family

Aniseed Myrtle: *Backhousia anisata*

GROWTH HABITS
Evergreen shrub or small tree
Origin: Eastern Australia
Range: Sometimes planted in Florida

CULINARY USES
Aniseed myrtle has a gentle licorice flavor with a sweet finish that is best suited for desserts that include cream or fruits, especially pears and apricots.

Available as dried herb or essential oil. The volatile flavor is easily lost through cooking, so the herb should be used in uncooked dishes or added near the end of cooking.

The plant's flavors are a result of citral, citronellal, geranial, linalool, myrcene, and neral.

Cajeput: *Melaleuca leucadendron*

OTHER COMMON, ETHNIC, OR SCIENTIFIC NAMES
Paperbark tree, river tea tree, swamp tea tree, weeping tea tree, white tea tree, white wood. Also known scientifically as *Melaleuca cajuputi.*

RELATED SPECIES
Melaleuca alternifolia: Tea tree
Melaleuca quinquenervia (also known as *Melaleuca viridifolia):* Contains
   niaouli oil

GROWTH HABITS
Shrubby tree
Origin: Australia, Moluccas, New Guinea

Range: Tropical, not cultivated in the United States, according to *Hortus Third*

Cajeput leaves have a camphor-like scent that is aromatic, simultaneously cooling and warming—a bit like camphor, cardamom, mint, and rosemary. The leaves have been used in herbal teas.

Cajeput contains α-terpineol, benzoic aldehyde, cineol, dipentene and l-limonene. *Melaleuca alternifolia* contains 1,8-cineole, terpinen-4-ol, terpinolene, α-terpinene, and γ-terpinene.

OTHER USES

Used to add scent to soaps

COMMENTS

The scientific name, *Melaleuca leucadendron,* refers to this species, but it is also applied to a whole group of trees that supply cajuput oil.

Cloves: *Syzygium aromaticum*

OTHER COMMON, ETHNIC, OR SCIENTIFIC NAMES

Previous scientific names for cloves include *Caryophyllus aromatica, Eugenia aromatica, Eugenia Caryophyllata,* and *Jabosa Caryophyllis.*

Afghanistan: Kala
Algeria: Oud onqronfel
Arabic: Habahan, qaranful
Brazil: Cravo da India
Burma/Myanmar: Ley nyin bwint
Chile: Yerba del clavo (dried roots)
China: Ding heung, ting hsiang
Estonia: Harilik nelgipuu
Ethiopia: K'rinfud
Finland: Neilikka
France: Girofle
Germany: Nelke
Greece: Kariofílli, moschokárfi
Hungary: Szegfü
Iceland: Negull
India: Grampu, labanga, laung, lavanga, shriisanjnan
Indonesia: Cengké
Iran: Mikhak, nebos
Iraq: Krunful
Israel: Tziporen
Italy: Garofano

Japan: Choji
Malaysia: Bunga cingkeh
Mexico: Clavo de olor
Morocco: Oud el nouar
Netherlands: Kruidnagel
Norway: Nellik
Philippines: Clavo de comer
Poland: Gozdziki
Portugal: Cravinho, cravo
Romania: Cuisoare
Russia: Gvozdika
Spain: Clavo, jerofle clavus
Sri Lanka: Karabu nati
Swahili: Karafuu
Sweden: Kryddnejlika, kryddnejlikor, nejlikor
Thailand: Khan plu
Turkey: Karinfil
Vietnam: Hanh con

RELATED SPECIES

Eugenia aggregata (sometimes listed as *Myrciaria edulis*): Cherry-of-the-Rio-Grande. Cultivated in California and Florida.

Eugenia aqueae: Watery rose apple

Eugenia dombeyana (sometimes listed as *Eugenia Dombeyi*): Brazil cherry, grumichama, grumixameira

Eugenia floribunda (sometimes listed as *Myrciaria eloribunda*): Murta, rumberry

Eugenia Luschnatiana: Pitomba

Eugenia malaccensis: Malay apple, mountain apple

Eugenia michtlii: Brazilian cherry

Eugenia myrtifolia: Bush cherry, red myrtle

Eugenia paniculata: Brush cherry

Eugenia polyantha (also known as *Syzygium polyanthum*): Daun salam (Indonesia and Malaysia); Indonesisches Lorbeerblatt (Germany); lauro d'Indonesia (Italy); laurierblad (Indonesia); Indonesian bay leaf

Eugenia polycephaloides: Maigang

Eugenia stipitata: Araca-boi

Eugenia tomentosa: Cabelluda

Eugenia uniflora: Barbados cherry, Brazil cherry, Cayenne cherry, pitanga, Surinam cherry

Eugenia Uvalha (sometimes listed as *Eugenia Uralha*): Uralha, uvalha

Psidium guajava: Guava

Syzgium cumini: Duhat, jambolan, Java plum

Syzygium jambos: Rose apple

Evergreen tree
Origin: Moluccas (Indonesia)
Range: Cultivated in tropical areas around the world

CULINARY USES

Cloves are the dried unopened flower buds of a tropical tree. The glossy, evergreen leaves contain the same essential oil that provides the aromatic heat of cloves, so they can be used in cooking, but they are not available outside the areas in which they are grown.

Cloves are an ingredient in the French spice mixture *quatre épices,* as well as in the related seasoning blend incorporating salt, *sel épice.* Both are used with meats, especially in the cured meats and sausages that constitute French charcuterie. Other meats flavored with cloves include hams, sausages made of blood or liver, head cheese, and more prosaic items like bologna.

Dauphin, or Thiérache, is an ancient cheese from Flanders, seasoned with cloves, black pepper, parsley, and tarragon. The Dutch cheese Nagelkaas (or Friese Nagelkaas) is often sold studded with cloves, *piqué,* like an onion or ham.

Cloves lend their warmth to candies, cakes, mulled wine, meats (such as ham, sauerbraten, sausage), salad dressings, and sauces. Inserted in whole onions, *piqué,* they are useful in stocks. They are found in some herbal liqueurs, such as Benedictine, Campari, and Grand Marnier, and in Angostura Bitters. They also appear in recipes for amaretto, anisette, Fernet Branca, gin, vermouth, and both colors of Chartreuse. Russians are warmed by okhotnichya, hunter's brandy, a concoction consisting of alcohol, cloves, and other flavorings. Gorny doubnyak is a bitter Russian liqueur flavored with cloves and other ingredients (see glossary for both Russian drinks).

Cloves make an appearance in several recipes for Worcestershire sauce. Cloves are also used in Thai curries based on Indian recipes. In Ethiopia, the chile-based paste *berberé* often contains cloves. In Persian cooking, ground cloves are an ingredient in the spice mixture called *advieh.* They are among the ingredients in *boharat,* an Iraqi spice blend.

Most of the clove species have aromatic leaves and tart edible fruits. *Hortus Third* lists five species as "good for making jams and jellies."

In the Philippines, the bark is used to flavor *basi,* a fermented drink made from sugarcane (q.v.).

Cherry-of-the-Rio-Grande, *Eugenia aggregata,* has edible fruit said to taste like—you guessed it—cherries.

Cloves are commonly available in the United States in powdered form or as whole cloves. The whole form is preferable; powdered spices fade quickly as their essential oils volatilize away from the vastly increased surface area created by grinding.

All parts of *Syzygium aromaticum* contain eugenol, the primary, and characteristic, ingredient. The leaves also contain napthalin. The flower buds contain eugenol acetate, β-caryophyllene, and vanillin in addition to the eugenol.

OTHER USES

Oil of clove is an industrial flavoring and a mild anesthetic. It is mixed with zinc oxide to make the temporary fillings used by dentists. It is an ingredient in some perfumes. It is not distilled from the cloves themselves, but from the leaves, stems, and twigs.

In Indonesia, a kind of cigarette, called *kretek,* is made with cloves.

Cloves are often stuck in oranges to make pomanders, a charmingly quaint form of air freshener.

COMMENTS

Eugenia is to the new world what *Syzygium* is to the old.

In some Latin American cultures, various parts of the clove tree are considered to have aphrodisiacal properties. I don't know if such assertions are true, but the stories about cloves are interesting because they shed some light on the way such beliefs can be started.

First, it is not much of a stretch to associate spiciness, especially hot and sweet spiciness, with amorous activity. A chef friend has told me that he considers all good cooking to be a kind of seduction. He meant it in a broader sense than sexual, but by no means did he intend to disparage the erotic aspects of food.

Second, physiologically, eugenol (the primary essential oil in all parts of the clove tree) causes a slight numbing of any tissues to which it is applied. Many of the products used to prolong sexual encounters make use of "destimulation" in this way, using other anesthetics (a small aside: "an-esthetic" is a curious word in itself, in this context).

Third, many plants are supposed to have aphrodisiacal characteristics because of physical resemblance between parts of the plant and parts of the body. Cloves, and parts of the clove root, are vaguely phallic in form. Because of the level of joyful expectation, or immoderate optimism (depending on one's vantage point), even a vague resemblance is resemblance enough.

Finally, and closely related to the previous paragraph, is what may be called the linguistic rationale. *Clavo,* in Spanish, means "nail." Nails are phallic, both in form and function. It is no coincidence that an American slang term for sexual conquest is the verb "to nail."

Many of the fruits, listed under "Related Species," above, have from time to time been included in the genus *Syzygium,* only to be switched back to *Eugenia,* or over to *Myrciaria.* Fortunately, there does not seem to be any credibility (or edibility) issues jeopardized by this confusion. Be prepared for a paper chase if you wish to positively identify any of these fruits.

"Indonesisches Lorbeerblatt" and "Indian bay leaf" are also names for the unrelated *Cinnamomum tamala.*

Eucalyptus: *Eucalyptus globulus*

OTHER COMMON, ETHNIC, OR SCIENTIFIC NAMES
Australian fevertree, blue gum, globulus, gum tree, Tasmanian blue gum
Australia: Gumleaf, peppermint (names refers to several *Eucalyptus* spp.)
Colombia: Eucalipto
Costa Rica: Eucalipto
East Timor: Ai-bubur metin, ai-bubur mutin
France: Eucalyptus globuleux, gommier bleu
Germany: Blauer Eucalyptusbaum, Eukalyptusblume
Italy: Eucalipto
Mexico: Eucalipto
Spain: Eucalipto

RELATED SPECIES
Eucalyptus amygdalina: Black peppermint
Eucalyptus cinerea: Argyle apple
Eucalyptus coccifera: Mt. Wellington peppermint
Eucalyptus dives: Broad-leaved peppermint
Eucalyptus elata: River peppermint
Eucalyptus Nicholii: Narrow-leaved black peppermint, Nichol's willow-
   leaved peppermint
Eucalyptus piperita: Sydney peppermint
Eucalyptus pulchella: White peppermint
Eucalyptus radiata: Gray peppermint
Eucalyptus Risdonii: Silver peppermint
Eucalyptus Robertsonii: Robertson's peppermint
Eucalyptus Smithii: Blackbutt peppermint
Eucalyptus stuartiana: Apple eucalyptus
Eucalyptus tenuiramis: Silver peppermint

GROWTH HABITS
Tree
Origin: Australia
Range: Naturalized in California and Hawaii, planted in Arizona

CULINARY USES
Eucalyptus has a tonic and astringent quality that is useful in cough drops and some baked goods. The resinous eucalyptus flavor, reminiscent of lemon and peppermint, combines well with caramel or honey for dessert sauces, or in garlic-and-coriander-scented honey as a glaze for grilled meats.

Eucalyptus is available as dried leaves or essential oil. The oil is quite strong and must be diluted for use in sauces.

Eucalyptus contains cineol, eucalyptol, pinene, and terpineol.

COMMENTS

The University of California at Davis warns about this species in its Wildland Invasive Species Program.

Lemon Myrtle: *Backhousia citriodora*

OTHER COMMON, ETHNIC, OR SCIENTIFIC NAMES

Lemon ironwood, lemon scented myrtle, sweet verbena tree
Germany: Zitronenmyrte

GROWTH HABITS

Evergreen shrub or small tree
Origin: Eastern Australia
Range: Sometimes planted in Florida

CULINARY USES

Lemon myrtle, like lemongrass or lemon verbena, offers a refreshing citrus scent without the overpowering acidity of the fruit from which it takes its name. Its slight lime-like scent is appealing in dessert sauces and in marinades for chicken and fish, as might be expected, but also with pork. Lemon myrtle can be added to the flour when making fresh pasta.

The sap is collected and reduced, like maple syrup. It has the characteristic caramel notes of maple syrup, but with a subtle citrus scent.

Lemon myrtle is available in the form of an essential oil. The volatile flavor is easily lost through cooking, so it should be used in uncooked dishes or added near the end of cooking.

COMMENTS

While the fresh leaves *are* lower in acid than lemons, there is enough to curdle milk if the leaves are cooked in it. A small amount of honey or sugar, added before the lemon myrtle, is said to minimize curdling.

Myrtle: *Myrtus communis*

OTHER COMMON, ETHNIC, OR SCIENTIFIC NAMES

Greek myrtle, Swedish myrtle, sweet myrtle
Arabic: As, hadass
Bulgaria: Mirt
Estonia: Harilik mürt
Finland: Myrtti

France: Myrte
Gaelic: Miortal
Germany: Brautmyrte
Greece: Mirtiá
India: Bilati-mehedi, habulas, kulinaval, vilayatimehndi
Iran: Mord
Israel: Hadas
Italy: Mirto, mortella
Japan: Ginbaika
Mexico: Arráyan, capulín, mirto
Netherlands: Mirte
Poland: Mirt
Romania: Mirt
Russia: Mirt
Spain: Arrayán, mirto, murtró
Turkey: Mersin agaçi

CULTIVARS

'Dwarf Myrtle', 'German Myrtle', 'Polish Myrtle', and 'Triloba' or 'Sacred Myrtle'

Myrtle
Myrtus communis

From Jaume Saint-Hilaire,
Traité des arbrisseaux

Evergreen shrub
Origin: Mediterranean region
Range: Temperate regions

CULINARY USES

Flower buds, once the bitter green parts have been removed, can be added to salads. The flowers themselves make good garnishes. Myrtle has been used as an additive in beers. A spice is made from the dried and ground berries and flowers.

The leaves are a good flavoring for roast pork but should be used with restraint, or added at the end of the cooking process. Young goat and lamb are seasoned with myrtle and roasted over wood fires in Sardinia.

The leaves, twigs, and berries have a spicy, resinous, juniper-like flavor that has occasionally been used to enhance the apparent strength of some wines (see MELEGUETA PEPPER) and also flavor the Italian spirit *grappa alla mirtillo.*

Myrtle in all forms is somewhat astringent. It contains pinene, camphene, cineol, dipentene, geraniol, and myrtenol.

OTHER USES

Dried flowers are used in potpourri. *Eau d'ange* is a toilet water made from myrtle flowers.

COMMENTS

Creeping myrtle and periwinkle are not related to this myrtle; they are actually *Vinca major* and *Vinca minor,* West and East Coasts, respectively. This is an important distinction to make, as both *Vincas* contain poisonous alkaloids (vinblastine and vincristine) that can damage the liver and kidneys of anyone consuming any portion of the plants. Some evidence of cytotoxic and neurological activity has been associated with these plants.

The FDA restricts the use of *Myrtus communis* to alcoholic beverages.

Niaouli Leaf: *Melaleuca viridiflora*

OTHER COMMON, ETHNIC, OR SCIENTIFIC NAMES

Bottle brush, honey myrtle. Also known scientifically as *Melaleuca Wilsonii.*

GROWTH HABITS

Shrubby tree
Origin: Australia
Range: Australia and Indonesia

Creeping Myrtle
Vinca major

From Jaume Saint-Hilaire,
Traité des arbrisseaux

CULINARY USES

Used in the flavorings industry, extracts of niaouli contain cineol, eucalyptol, pinene, and valerianates. Niaouli has a bitter almond and eucalyptus-
like scent.

56. Naiadaceae: The Naiad Family

Cape Pondweed: *Aponogeton distachyus*

OTHER COMMON, ETHNIC, OR SCIENTIFIC NAMES
Cape asparagus, water hawthorn
South Africa: Untie, waterblommetjie

CULTIVARS
'Giganteus', 'Grandiflora', 'Lagrangei'

GROWTH HABITS
Tropical perennial

Origin: South Africa
Range: Naturalized in some rivers in France

CULINARY USES
The flowering spikes are pickled or cooked as potherbs. The tuberous roots are roasted as a starchy vegetable on the southeast coast of Africa.

57. Nyctaginaceae: The Four O'Clock Family

Four O'Clocks: *Mirabilis jalapa*

OTHER COMMON, ETHNIC, OR SCIENTIFIC NAMES
Beauty of the night, marvel of Peru. Four O'clocks are sometimes listed botanically as *Mirabilis uniflora*.
Colombia: Don diego de noche, tabaquillo
Panama: Buenas tardes

GROWTH HABITS
Perennial
Origin: Tropical Americas
Range: Temperate, worldwide, but treated as an annual, except in frost-free areas

CULINARY USES
Mirabilis leaves are said to be eaten in Nepal (see Comments, below).

COMMENTS
According to *Hortus Third,* there is one species of *Mirabilis* that is native to the Himalayas, which would suggest that it is *that* species, rather than *Mirabilis jalapa,* that is eaten. Unfortunately, *Hortus Third* does not list the species.

58. Nympheaceae: The Water Lily Family

Lotus Lily: *Nelumbo nucifera*

OTHER COMMON, ETHNIC, OR SCIENTIFIC NAMES
East Indian lily, sacred lotus. Lotus lily is sometimes identified in old botanical texts as *Nelumbo nelumbo* or *Nymphaae speciosa.*
China: Leen ngau
India: Nadru
Japan: Renkon

'Alba Grandiflora', 'Alba Striata', 'Pekinensis Rubra', 'Pekinensis Rubra Plena', 'Rosea Plena'

RELATED SPECIES
Nelumbo lutea (sometimes listed as *Nelumbo flavescens*): American lotus, pond nuts, water chinquapin, wonkapin, yanquapin, yellow nelumbo
Nymphaae caerulea: Egyptian lotus, or *Nymphaae Lotus*

GROWTH HABITS
Aquatic perennial
Origin: Southeast Asia to Australia
Range: Cultivated throughout Asia, naturalized in parts of the United States

CULINARY USES
The lotus lily is a source of culinary and aesthetic pleasure throughout Asia. The plant provides a number of different foodstuffs. The leaves are used to wrap parcels of rice and chopped meats before baking or steaming. Shredded young leaves are cooked as potherbs. They are available, dried, in some Asian markets in the United States. The petals are used as garnishes or cooked as vegetables. The entire flower is used as an edible bowl for cooked foods.

The seeds, once the bitter germ is removed, are used in soups. They are toasted, salted, and eaten like peanuts. When they are cooked and sweetened, they are used to make the filling for moon cakes, a Chinese dessert. Chinese eight jewel or eight treasure are dishes that usually contain lotus seeds.

The roots look like white yams with holes drilled through the length. They have a slightly sweet taste and a texture something like water chestnut or raw potato. Boiled, they become the Japanese dish called *nimono*. The holes are often stuffed with varying ingredients: in Japan it might be mustard greens, in China it might be a purée of mung beans. Cooked slices of lotus root are a frequent ingredient on Chinese cold platters, often in combination with slices of pork kidney and shiitake mushrooms slow-cooked in soy sauce. In China, the whole roots are sometimes simmered with pork and dried squid.

All parts of the plant are eaten throughout Southeast Asia, especially in Thailand.

Starch from the roots is used as a thickener in several Asian cuisines.

COMMENTS
The elegant form of the lotus flower has found its way into the art of every country in which the plant grows.

59. Oleaceae: The Olive Family

Ash: *Fraxinus excelsior*

OTHER COMMON, ETHNIC, OR SCIENTIFIC NAMES
European ash, holarrhen
France: Frêne élevé
Germany: Eberesche, Esche
Morocco: Lissan ettir

RELATED SPECIES
Fraxinus ornus: Flowering ash, manna, manna ash
Fraxinus angustifolia (sometimes listed as *Fraxinus oxyphylla*): Narrow-leaf
    ash

GROWTH HABITS
Tree
Origin: Europe and Asia Minor
Range: Cool temperate regions

CULINARY USES
Ash leaves have been added to beers. The bark has been used, like quinine, in bitters.
The tart fruits of narrow-leaf ash, *Fraxinus angustifolia,* are said to be used
as a seasoning in Morocco.
Resin from the hardened sap of *Fraxinus ornus* is used in the commercial
flavorings industry. It contains mannitol.

OTHER USES
The plant's strong, straight-grained wood is frequently used for baseball
bats, tool handles, and cabinet work.

COMMENTS
The common names and uses of plants named "ash" are sometimes confusing (see also PRICKLY ASH, *Aralia spinosa;* MOUNTAIN ASH, *Sorbus aucuparia;* and SZECHUAN PEPPER, *Zanthoxylum piperitum*).
"Manna" is also the name for a lichen, *Leconora esculenta,* that is eaten in
the Middle East; this may be the manna of the Old Testament. It also refers
to resins derived from camel's thorns, two species of the genus *Alhagi.*

Common Lilac: *Syringa vulgaris*

OTHER COMMON, ETHNIC, OR SCIENTIFIC NAMES
France: Lilas
Germany: Lila, Lilafarbe
Italy: Lillia

CULTIVARS
Many cultivars, but not intended for the kitchen.

RELATED SPECIES
Syringa microphylla: Sung lo cha (China); little leaf lilac

GROWTH HABITS
Deciduous shrub
Origin: Southeast Europe
Range: Temperate regions

CULINARY USES
Flowers can be used in fritters, candied, or as a flavoring in compound butters. They can garnish dishes that have a presence strong enough to survive the intense perfume of the lilacs. Lilac prunings can be used to smoke fish or lamb, which adds a slightly floral aroma to the mild smoky flavor.

The blossoms of sung lo cha, *Syringa microphylla,* are used (as might be expected from its Chinese name) as an herbal tea.

Fragrant Olive: *Osmanthus fragrans*

OTHER COMMON, ETHNIC, OR SCIENTIFIC NAMES
Sweet olive, tea olive. Sometimes listed, botanically, as *Olea fragrans.*

RELATED SPECIES
Olea europaea (known pharmaceutically as *Oleum Olivarum*): Aceituna (Spain); azeitona (Portugal); eliá (Greece); euroopa Õlipuu (Estonia); jaitun, julipe, saidun (India); măsline (Romania); ólífa (Iceland); olajbogyó, olajfa (Hungary); Ölbaum, Oliif (Germany); olijf (Netherlands); oliva (Italy); oliva (Spain); zaytun (Arabic); zeituni (Swahili); zeytin (Turkey); common olive. Cultivars include 'Ascolano', 'Barouni', 'Manzanillo', 'Mission', and 'Sevillano'
Osmanthus americanus: American olive, devilwood, wild olive. This is the only indigenous American species and is said to bear edible fruit.

GROWTH HABITS
Evergreen shrub

Origin: Eastern Asia
Range: Frost-free areas

CULINARY USES

Flowers are used as garnishes in China. They are used crystallized (candied), fresh, or preserved in a sugary, alcohol-laced syrup or brine. The blossoms also flavor black teas, cordials, and wines. They perfume sweet Chinese dishes such as lotus seed soup and steamed pears, as well as some pastries.

The fruits are sometimes sold as cassia blossom jam, even though there is no connection with either cassia (q.v.) or the unrelated *Cassia* genus (see, under ROOIBOS).

Jasmine: *Jasminum Sambac*

OTHER COMMON, ETHNIC, OR SCIENTIFIC NAMES

Arabian jasmine, biblical jasmine, pikake, sambac mo le hwa
France: Jasmin
Germany: Jasmin
Italy: Gelsomino
Spain: Jazsmin
Thailand: Dok malee, mali
Turkey: Yasemin

CULTIVARS

'Grand Duke of Tuscany': Doubled flowers

RELATED SPECIES

Jasminum grandiflorum: Spanish jasmine
Jasminum officinale: Poet's jasmine
Jasminum paniculatum: Jasmine, sieu hing hwa
Jasminum polyanthum: Jasmine

GROWTH HABITS

Tropical evergreen shrub
Origin: Asia
Range: Frost-free areas

CULINARY USES

A mixture of this species and *Jasminum paniculatum* flavors black tea in China. The best jasmine teas are made by placing the just-opening flowers near the drying leaves of tea, so the leaves can absorb the perfume from the flowers. Cheaper grades simply add extracts of jasmine. Occasional jasmine flowers in the tea do not necessarily mean that the tea was actually flavored by the flowers; in fact, some of the cheapest grades are disguised in this way.

Extracts flavor baked goods, candies, and chewing gum.

Flowers (and flower essence) are used in Thailand to flavor syrups for desserts and rice dishes. Thais make a traditional coconut custard dessert, called *songaya,* that is sweetened with palm sugar and perfumed with jasmine water.

Essential oils from poet's jasmine, *Jasminum officinale,* are used to perfume a number of commercial confections, including maraschino cherries.

Jasmine gets its citrus-flower, bittersweet qualities from a group of alcohols: nerol, nerolidol, and terpineol; plus esters: benzyl acetate and linalyl acetate; plus *p*-cresol, eugenol, and other aromatics.

OTHER USES

Jasmine is used in the perfume industry.

COMMENTS

Some jasmines have been reported to be poisonous, for example, Carolina jasmine (also known as Carolina yellow jasmine, evening trumpet flower, gelsemium, sempervirens, wild woodbine, yellow jasmine, and yellow jessamine), *Gelsemium sempervirens.* It is not related to the true jasmines. It belongs to the Loganiaceae family, which includes plants such as strychnine, or nux vomica.

60. Orchidaceae: The Orchid Family

Vanilla: *Vanilla planifolia*

OTHER COMMON, ETHNIC, OR SCIENTIFIC NAMES

Bourbon vanilla, Mexican vanilla. Also known as *Epidendrum vanilla, Myrobroma fragrans,* and *Vanilla fragrans.*

Arabic: Wanila
China: Hsiang-tsao, hsiang-ts'ao
Colombia: Bejucillo
East Timor: Fanili
Estonia: Harilik vanill
Finland: Vanilja
France: Vanille
Germany: Vanille
Greece: Vanília
Hungary: Vanilia
Iran: Vanil
India: Vanikkodo
Indonesia: Paneli

Italy: Vaniglia
Japan: Banira, bauira
Netherlands: Vanille
Norway: Vanilje
Portugal: Baunilha
Romania: Vanilie
Russia: Vanil'
Spain: Vainilla
Swahili: Lavani
Sweden: Vanilj
Turkey: Vanilya

RELATED SPECIES

Vanilla pompona: Antilles vanilla, Guadelupe vanilla, pompona, vanillons, West Indian vanilla

Vanilla Tahitensis: Tahiti vanilla. Hybrid of *Vanilla planifolia* × *Vanilla pompona,* which may have originated in Guadeloupe.

GROWTH HABITS

Perennial vine

Origin: Tropical America

Range: Tropical America, cultivated in India, Mexico, Madagascar, Papua New Guinea, southeast Asia, Micronesia, Polynesia, and Uganda

CULINARY USES

The most highly prized vanilla is made from *Vanilla planifolia,* although both species and their hybrid are used to produce commercial vanilla.

Vanilla beans are said to be among the secret ingredients in Benedictine.

Vanillin, the primary flavoring in the beans and the extract, was one of the first flavorings to be synthesized (in Germany, during the 1880s). However, real vanilla contains minute traces of many other compounds, such as piperonal and heliotropine, that add a complex richness that cannot be matched by vanillin alone. One analysis indicated 163 additional compounds that influence the flavor of "natural" vanilla; others report as many as 250 compounds.

OTHER USES

Vanilla Tahitiensis is used in the manufacture of perfumes. It contains piperonal, an essential oil that smells of heliotropes.

COMMENTS

Some so-called vanilla extracts, especially cheaper grades found in Mexico (many of which do not actually contain extracts but synthetic vanillin), have been adulterated with coumarin. It is a sweet but toxic substance found in many plants, commercially produced primarily from tonka beans (q.v.). In the United States, the FDA restricts the use of coumarin to nonfood products only.

We often hear of wines having "some vanilla in the nose." This is not mere pretentiousness on the part of wine snobs. Some wines are aged in oaken barrels, and the wood of some species of oak actually contain vanillin. If the wine sits in contact with the wood long enough, it absorbs some of that vanillin. Since—as we have so often heard—time is money, wines that come by their vanilla scent honestly tend to be more expensive, although less fastidious winemakers sometimes throw oak chips into the wine vats for a quick blast of vanilla-like oakiness.

61. Oxalidaceae: The Oxalis or Wood Sorrel Family

Cucumber Tree: *Averrhoa bilimbi*

OTHER COMMON, ETHNIC, OR SCIENTIFIC NAMES
Belimbi, sour finger carambola, tree sorrel
Colombia: Grosella carambola
India: Bilimbikai
Indonesia: Belimbing wuluh
Malaysia: Belimbing asam
Philippines: Belimbing, camias, pias
Thailand: Madun, ta-ling-pling
Sri Lanka: Billing

RELATED SPECIES
Averrhoas carambola: Grosella caranbola (Colombia); tiriguro (Costa Rica); caramba, carambola, Chinese star fruit, country gooseberry, five-angled fruit, star fruit

GROWTH HABITS
Tropical evergreen tree
Origin: Malay Peninsula
Range: Cultivated in tropical regions

CULINARY USES
The tart, gherkin-like fruits are cooked and made into preserves. Their sour juice is used by Filipinos as other people would use vinegar or lemon juice, or, for that matter, as medieval cooks would have used verjuice, the squeezings of underripe green grapes. Marinades, salad dressings, and cleansing sorbets come to mind as possible uses.

Indonesians use the tart fruits in fish curries, pickles, and *sambals*. Thais mix slices of the perishable fruit with hot chiles to make a salsa-like condiment. Colombians make preserves from the flowers.

Wood Sorrel: *Oxalis acetosa*

OTHER COMMON, ETHNIC, OR SCIENTIFIC NAMES
Cuckowes meat, fairy bells, hallelujah, lady's sorrel, sour trefoil, stickwort, stubwort, surelle, three-leaved grass, wood sour
Costa Rica: Acedera
France: Alléluja, pain de coucou
Germany: Sauerklee
Greece: Xiníthra
Ireland: Seamsog
Italy: Acetosella, iuliole
Mexico: Acedra
Scotland: Gowke meat
Spain: Agrella

RELATED SPECIES
Oxalis acetosella: European wood sorrel, Irish shamrock
Oxalis corniculata: Vinagrillo (Spain); sourgrass, wood sorrel
Oxalis dichondrifolia: Raíz de la chata (Mexico); wood sorrel
Oxalis hedysaroides: Sanguinaria (Colombia)
Oxalis pescaprae: Eksi yonca (Turkey); Nickender Saurklee (Germany); suring (South Africa, among Cape Malays); yellow sorrel (also seen as *Oxalis pes-caprea*)

GROWTH HABITS
Annual
Origin: Europe
Range: Temperate regions

CULINARY USES
Uses are the same as those of sorrel (q.v.), except that wood sorrel's different leaf shape suggests more decorative uses as well. It looks something like a shamrock or clover, which could make it useful as a garnish. Lemonade-like drinks have been made with the sour leaves, sometimes with the addition of orange peel or violet syrup.

COMMENTS
I have grown a deep purple variety, called 'Triangularis', that I used in salads. I have not been able to discover its species, although it may be a cultivar of *Oxalis violacea*.

European Wood Sorrel
Oxalis acetosella

From Woodville, *Medical botany,* vol. 1

Wood sorrel, like sorrel and rhubarb, gets its kick from oxylates, which can be poisonous in quantity.
Oxalis acetosa is not listed in *Hortus Third.*

62. Paeonaceae: The Peony Family

Peony: *Paeonia officinalis*

OTHER COMMON, ETHNIC, OR SCIENTIFIC NAMES
Common peony, double peony, king of flowers

RELATED SPECIES
Paeonia lactiflora: Chih shao (China); peony

GROWTH HABITS
Perennial
Origin: Southern Europe
Range: Temperate regions

The seeds have a hot spicy flavor and were at one time used as a spice. Like melegueta pepper (q.v.), peony seeds suggest greater alcoholic strength for some ales. They were popular in England during the fourteenth century.

The flowers are used in herbal teas and in salads. They are eaten as vegetables in Japan, where they are known as "the food of dragons."

The roots of *Paeonia lactiflora* contain traces of a few of the chemicals that interest us, but only benzoic acid and galloyl-tannins appear in significant amounts.

Paeonia officinalis's roots also contain benzoic acid, but less than *Paeonia lactiflora*.

63. Palmae: The Palm Family

Coconut: *Cocos nucifera*

OTHER COMMON, ETHNIC, OR SCIENTIFIC NAMES
Coconut palm
Burma/Myanmar: Ungbin
East Timor: Nuu
Estonia: Kookospalm
Finland: Kookospähkinä
France: Noix de coco
Germany: Kokosnuß
Iceland: Kókoshneta
India: Kobari, mar, nadiya, nalikeram, naral, narikela, polgaha, tenkaya, thengu
Indonesia: Kelapa
Iran: Anaargeel
Italy: Cocco
Netherlands: Kokosnoot
Spain: Coco fruto
Swahili: Dafu, nazi
Thailand: Maprow
Vietnam: Cot dua

GROWTH HABITS
Palm tree
Origin: Probably Melanesia
Range: Tropical and subtropical regions

While neither herb nor spice, coconut is frequently used as a flavoring ingredient. Coconut milk is the foundation of much Thai and Indonesian cuisine. The nuts also provide a great deal of the world's supply of cooking fats. The saturated fat, often snubbed in the United States for health reasons, is still preferred in many places because of its superiority in producing very crisp fried foods.

Date Palm: *Phoenix dactylifera*

RELATED SPECIES
Borassus flabellifer: Doub palm, Palmyra palm, tala palm, toddy palm, wine palm

GROWTH HABITS
Tree

Origin: West Asia and North Africa

Range: Grown commercially in Arizona, California, Iraq, and North Africa

CULINARY USES
The fruit of the date palm is well known. The trees are also tapped for their sap, which can be drunk fresh or allowed to ferment. The palm wine that results from fermentation is called *lagmi, laqmi,* or *legmi* in southern Tunisia and is sometimes flavored with rue (q.v.). The yeast-rich fermented juice is also used to leaven flatbreads. A similar palm wine is made in Central America of the sap of another palm (*Acrocomia Panamensis*), known in Panama as *pacorza* and in Costa Rica as *palma de vino*.

The characteristically sticky surface of date fruits are a natural trap for air-borne yeasts. This tendency, combined with the fruits' high sugar content, makes them an ideal starter for fermented drinks. In fact, the oldest beer recipe known, from the nineteenth century BCE, used dates this way (Fritz Maytag's Anchor Brewery more recently revived this ancient beer as Ninkasi, named for the Sumerian goddess of brewing). Turks make *bouza,* a kind of beer, from dates and bulghur wheat. *Buza* is a similar brew, made in Israel, that substitutes pearled millet flour for the bulghur. Some Israeli buza is, in turn, distilled to yield the more potent *boukha* or *buhja*.

Jaggery is Indonesian date sugar made from the sap of the Palmyra palm, *Borassus flabellifer*. Muslim Touaregs boil the unfermented sap to obtain either a thick syrup or a jaggery-like date sugar called a *robb*. Similar date sugars are used as an emergency energy source by some Pacific Islanders, who transport small loaves of the stuff in little cylindrical cases that look like the poison dart quivers carried by some natives of the South American rainforest. The loaves are said to keep for years.

64. Pandanceae: The Screw-pine Family

Pandang: *Pandanus odoratissimus*

OTHER COMMON, ETHNIC, OR SCIENTIFIC NAMES
Breadfruit, hala, kewd, nicobar bread-fruit, pandanus leaf, screwpine, textile screwpine, umbrella tree
Colombia: Palma de tornillo
Denmark: Skruepalme
Estonia: Lōhnav pandan
Finland: Kairapalmu
France: Pandanus
Germany: Schraubenbaum, Schraubenpalme
India: Kaitha, kewra, kia, mogil, rampe, tale hoovu, thazhai
Indonesia: Daun pandan
Italy: Pandano
Malaysia: Daun pandan
Micronesia: Kaina
Netherlands: Pandan, schroefpalm
Norway: Skrupalme
Philippines: Pandang mabango
Polynesia: Ara, fa, hala
Portugal: Pandano
Spain: Pandano
Sri Lanka: Rampe
Sweden: Skruvpalm
Thailand: Bai toey
Vietnam: Lu dua

RELATED SPECIES
Pandanus amaryllifolius (also known as *Pandanus latifolius*): Bai toey, paanae wo-nging, toey hom, pandan, pandan-mabango (Thailand); dua thom (Vietnam); pandan rampai, pandan wangi (Malaysia); rampe (Sri Lanka); curry leaf, daun pandan, dwarf pandan, dwarf screw pine, pandanus leaf
Pandanus brosimus: Padang (New Guinea)
Pandanus conioides: Padang (New Guinea)
Pandanus dubius: Padang (Solomon Islands)
Pandanus fascicularis: Mudu kekiya (Sri Lanka); padang, tali (India); kewda
Pandanus latifolius: Rampe (Sri Lanka)
Pandanus leram: Nicobar breadfruit, Nicobar Island breadfruit
Pandanus tectorius: nearly identical to *Pandanus odoratissimus*

GROWTH HABITS

Small tropical tree

Origin: Southeast Asia

Range: Grows in subtropical United States (southern Florida). Young trees can be grown in greenhouses, further north.

CULINARY USES

Pandang, Nicobar Island breadfruit, and *Pandanus utilis* produce edible fruits and seeds. They are used in Hawaiian cooking. Polynesians use the fruit much as others use chewing gum. Before the advent of chicle-based gums, spruce gum was used the same way in the United States.

The various species of *Pandanus* are used throughout the southern subcontinent of Asia. In Sri Lanka, they enhance yellow rice dishes. In Indonesia, risotto-like dishes called *nasi kunyit* are flavored with daun pandan. Likewise, some of the biryanis of India are perfumed with *kewra water* (see below), made from padang.

In the South Pacific, four plants provide nearly all the vegetable and starch needs of the islanders' diet: coconuts, breadfruit, yams, and pandang.

In the Marshall Islands, there are at least eight different names for pandang. One of the more unusual preparations is *mokan,* or pandanus paste. It is

Pandang
Pandanus odoratissimus

From Jacquin, *Fragmenta botanica*

314

a kind of reduced preserve, only slightly softer than fruit-leather. The bracts of Nicobar breadfruit (*Pandanus leram*) are used to perfume coconut oil.

Pandang is available in Southeast Asia as fresh, frozen, or dried leaves. An extract, called *toey* in Thailand, is made from the blossoms of screwpine. It is used to flavor desserts and other dishes. A similar essence, called *tewra* (or *kewra water,* or *kewda water*), is made in India from *Pandanus fascicularis.*

In Indonesia, daun pandan is often added to soy milk before it is curdled into tofu. It is also used to make confections, called *chendol* and *nyonya kuey,* enjoyed in Indonesia and Malaysia.

Curry leaf, *Pandanus latifolius,* is used to flavor—obviously—curries in Sri Lanka. An essence extracted from the plant flavors desserts, jellies, and soft drinks.

Pandanus spp. have a honey-like scent that is reminiscent of hazelnuts and vanilla. Phenyl ethyl alcohol makes up 60 to 80 percent of the essential oil. Pandanus contains several piperidine-like alkaloids and a number of floral-scented constituents.

OTHER USES

Leaves are used for the manufacture of baskets, hats, ropes, twine, and woven mats, and in the tropics for thatched roofs. The flowers yield an essential oil that is used in perfumes.

COMMENTS

While pandang is sometimes called breadfruit, it is not at all similar to the breadfruit of HMS *Bounty* fame. The breadfruit that Captain Bligh introduced successfully (eventually, but not on the voyage interrupted by Fletcher Christian) into the West Indies was actually *Artocarpus altilis.*

According to *Hortus Third,* over 650 species are included in the *Pandanus* genus, although it lists only a small selection. There is much confusion of names within this genus, which is to be expected, considering the vast area in which the plants are found and the cultural isolation of the inhabitants of that area. It is very likely that the few species listed above do not truly represent the range of species and breadth of uses for *Pandanus.*

"Curry leaf" has been used as a name for *Ocimum canum* in Africa (see BASIL), and for *Murraya Koenigii* (q.v.).

65. Papaveraceae: The Poppy Family

Poppy: *Papaver somniferum*

OTHER COMMON, ETHNIC, OR SCIENTIFIC NAMES
Ahiphenalm, breadseed poppy, garden poppy, opium poppy

Burma/Myanmar: Bhainzi
China: Ying-shu
Colombia: Ababol
Denmark: Opiatvalmue
Estonia: Magun, unimagun
Finland: Oopiumiunikko, uniko
France: Coquelicot, pavot
Gaelic: Codalion
Germany: Mohn
Greece: Paparona (*Papaver Rhoeas*)
Hungary: Mák
Iceland: Birki, valmafrae
India: Abhini, aphu, kus kus, postaka
Italy: Paparina, paparinula (*Papaver Rhoeas*), papavero, papavero
    sonnifero
Malaysia: Kas kas
Netherlands: Heulbol, maankop, slaapbol, slaappapaver
Norway: Valmue
Poland: Mak, mak lekarski
Portugal: Papoila dormideira, papoula
Romania: Mac
Spain: Ababa, adormidera, amapola, rosella
Sweden: Vallmo

CULTIVARS
'Hungarian Blue-seeded Poppy', 'Hutterite Poppy', 'White Persian Poppy'

RELATED SPECIES
Papaver nudicaule: Iceland poppy
Papaver orientale: Oriental poppy
Papaver Rhoeas: Klatsch-mohn (Germany); mümmülü (Turkey);
    quiquiriquic (Spain); common poppy, corn poppy, field poppy,
    Flanders poppy, Shirley poppy
Papaver stylatum: Gelencik (Turkey); Mohn (Germany); poppy

GROWTH HABITS
Perennial
Origin: Southeast Europe and western Asia
Range: Temperate regions

CULINARY USES
Poppy seeds, when toasted, acquire a nutty flavor with a hint of dustiness
in the finish, a warm, nostalgic taste that comforts the palate. These seeds,
also known as *Mohn,* are commonly used in baking. Hard rolls and bagels are
often garnished with the seeds, as are the *rundstykke* and *tebirkes* of Denmark.

Mohn are often used as a sweetened filling for crêpes, Danish pastries, hamantaschen, streudels, and other baked goods. The seeds are often combined with lemon as a flavoring for muffins.

All of the cultivars listed above are used for the edible seeds. 'Hungarian Blue-seeded Poppies' provide the bulk of the world's supply, but Indians, Japanese, and some Scandinavians prefer the white seeds produced by 'White Persian Poppies'. Poppy seeds make a pleasant addition to salad dressings. The seeds are also good cooked in hot butter and then tossed with fresh noodles. White poppy seeds are among the ingredients in *shichimi* (seven spice mixture), along with black hemp seeds, black sesame seeds, chile, mandarin orange peel, nori (seaweed), and Szechuan pepper.

White poppy seeds are ground and added to curries in India, primarily for their thickening properties, but they do add a nutlike flavor as well. The oil from white poppy seeds is used as a salad oil and for cooking. In France, it is known as *olivette*.

A bright red syrup is made from the petals of the Flanders poppy, *Papaver Rhoeas*. Young greens of Flanders poppy can be eaten as a potherb, cooked with olives, as in Italy and the south of France. They are added to baked goods in Turkey.

COMMENTS

This plant is the infamous opium poppy. Planting it could attract unwanted attentions from the authorities. There aren't any other compelling (legal) reasons for growing the plant, so why bother? The Iceland poppy, *Papaver nudicaule,* also contains the alkaloids that make opium poppies *flora non grata*. Poppy seeds do not contain any opiates but can lead to false positive results on drug tests designed to detect use of opiates.

66. Passifloraceae: The Passionflower Family

Passion Fruit: *Passiflora edulis*

OTHER COMMON, ETHNIC, OR SCIENTIFIC NAMES
Passionflower, purple granadilla, purple passionfruit
Hawaii: Lilikoi
Panama: Ala de murcielago

CULTIVARS
'Alice', 'Black Knight', 'Crackerjack', 'Edgehill', 'Frederick', 'Kahuna', 'Lacey', 'Paul Ecke or Ecke Select', 'Purple Giant', 'Rainbow Sweet', 'Red Giant', 'Red Riviera', 'Red Rover', 'Sunnypash'

A subspecies, *Passiflora edulis* subs. *flavicarpa,* has two cultivars, 'Brazilian Golden' and 'Golden Giant' (or 'Yellow Giant').

Passiflora incarnata: Passionflower
Passiflora quadrangulis: Giant granadilla
Passiflora rubra: Pomme de liane zombie

GROWTH HABITS
Tropical vine
Origin: Brazil
Range: Naturalized in South America and Caribbean Islands. Cultivated in California, Hawaii, Mexico, and Australia

CULINARY USES
The fresh fruit is eaten, but it is the juice of the passion fruit that has made the most impact on the culinary world. It is used to flavor all kinds of baked goods, candies, fruit soups, soft drinks, and sherbets. Aside from canned drinks intended for children—such as Juicy Juice—there is a soft drink called Passaia. Taken one step further, the fermented juice is the wine *parchita seco.* The juice of two species, *Passiflora mixta* and *Passiflora manicata,* is combined with milk for use as a beverage in South America.

The unripe fruits of giant granadilla, *Passiflora quadrangulis,* are used as a cooked vegetable. They are either steamed or boiled, or sliced, breaded, and fried in butter, then seasoned with nutmeg and black pepper.

The corn-based beverage *chicha* is sometimes flavored with *Passiflora rubra.* Passion fruit contains kaempferol, quercetin, and rutin.

OTHER USES
Hortus Third mentions that the genus of *Passiflora* contains four hundred species. Most of the species in cultivation are grown for their decorative, not culinary, value.

COMMENTS
Pomme de liane zombie, *Passiflora rubra,* is rumored to possess narcotic properties, hence its common name and inclusion in chicha, which often has ceremonial uses. Chicha is combined with dangerous—or at the very least questionable—ingredients in different places. It has always been associated with magic and shamanism.

67. Pedaliaceae: The Pedalium Family

Sesame: *Sesamum indicum*

OTHER COMMON, ETHNIC, OR SCIENTIFIC NAMES
Benne, bhene, teel. Sesame used to be listed scientifically as *Sesame orientale* and pharmaceutically as *Semen Sesami.*

Algeria: Djeldjane
Arabic: Sasim, soum soum
Brazil: Gergelim
Burma/Myanmar: Hnan si
China: Zhi ma
Estonia: Harilik seesam
Finland: Seesami
France: Sésame, till
Germany: Sesam, Vanglo
Greece: Sousámi
Iceland: Sesamfrae
India: Ashadital, bariktil, chitelu, ellu, gingelly, mittho-tel, nuvvulu,
   rashi, til, tisi, yallu (seeds); nallenai, nuvalu nuna, thil ka thel (oil)
Indonesia: Wijen
Iraq: Semsem
Italy: Sesamo
Japan: Kuro goma (black); muki goma, shiro goma (white)
Malaysia: Bijan
Mexico: Ajonjolí, sesamo
Morocco: Jinjelan
Netherlands: Sesamzaad
Philippines: Linga
Portugal: Gergelim
Spain: Ajonjolí, sésamo
Sri Lanka: Thala
Swahili: Ufuta
Sweden: Sesam
Thailand: Nga dee la
Turkey: Sousma, susam
Vietnam: Me, vung

CULTIVARS
'Black Seeded Sesame', 'Black Thai Sesame', 'Brown Turkey Sesame', 'Tan
Anatolia Sesame', 'White Seeded Sesame'

RELATED SPECIES
Ceratotheca sesamoides: False sesame
Pedalium murex: Burra gookeroo
Sesamum alatum: Gazelle's sesame, tacoutta
Sesamum radiatum: Black beniseed, ekuku

GROWTH HABITS
Annual
Origin: Tropics
Range: Texas to Florida

White seeds are used in breads, candies, *tahini* (a paste of ground raw seeds), and Chinese sesame paste (ground roasted seeds); as a cooking oil (pressed from raw seeds, the light-colored and mild-flavored kind of sesame oil found in health food stores); and as Chinese sesame oil (pressed from roasted seeds, and used for flavoring oriental foods). The latter, darker oil is known in China as *ma yau* or *tee ma yau.* In India it is called *ka tel,* while the Japanese use the name *goma abura.* White seeds garnish meat dishes of such diverse ethnicity as satés, mole poblano, and teriyaki.

Toasted black seeds are used to garnish Japanese dishes, such as sweetened omelets. The black varieties are milder and less bitter than the light-colored seeds. Black sesame seeds are among the ingredients in *shichimi* (seven spice mixture), along with black hemp seeds, chile (q.v.), Mandarin orange peel, nori (seaweed), poppy seeds (q.v.), and Szechuan pepper (q.v.).

Sprouted seeds are used in salads. Sesame oil is sometimes known as gingelly oil.

Leaves are sometimes used as a potherb. They are steamed and then braised with a little soy sauce for use as a garnish for rice in Korea. The leaves are used in some tea blends in Mexico. The stems of *Pedalium murex* and *Sesamum radiatum* have been used for their mucilaginous thickening properties, although *Sesamum radiatum* is said to have an unpleasant smell.

Sesame seeds contain olein, palmitin, sesamin, and stearin.

68. Pinaceae: The Pine Family

Balsam Fir: *Abies balsamea*

OTHER COMMON, ETHNIC, OR SCIENTIFIC NAMES
Balm, balm of Gilead
Mexico: Abeto

GROWTH HABITS
Evergreen shrub
Origin: Canada to West Virginia and Iowa
Range: Cool temperate regions

CULINARY USES

In Modena, Italy, balsamic vinegar spends part of its time maturing in a cask made of Italian fir. In the Franche-Compté of France, hard candies flavored with fir resin, called *Vosges pastilles,* are popular.

The extracted oil is used to flavor some baked goods. It combines well with citrus-scented herbs.

Balsam fir contains bornyl acetate, phellandrene, and pinene.

Balsam fir resin is used in adhesives for medical and scientific purposes. The incredibly pure, clear resin is used to cement the cover glass on microscope slides.

COMMENTS
"Balm of Gilead" is a name for canary balm, *Cedronella canariensis,* alternately known as *thé de canaries.* It is also known scientifically as *Cedronella triphylla. Commiphora opobalsamum,* a shrub of Old World deserts, provided the "balm of Gilead" mentioned in the Bible.

Pine: *Pinus* spp.

OTHER COMMON, ETHNIC, OR SCIENTIFIC NAMES
Piñon
Germany: Edeltanne
Italy: Pignoli (nuts)
Korea: Jaht (nuts)
Mexico: Pino
Turkey: Fistik (nuts)

RELATED SPECIES
Pinus cembroides: Mexican pinyon pine
Pinus Gerardiana: Chilghoza pine, Gerald's pine, Nepal nut pine
Pinus koraiensis: Korean pine
Pinus Lambertiana: Giant pine, sugar pine
Pinus monophylla: Nut pine, single-leaf pinyon pine, stone pine
Pinus pinea: Fiustik çami (Turkey); Pinie (Germany); Italian stone pine, stone pine, umbrella pine
Pinus quadrifolia: Parry pinyon pine
Pinus Sabiniana: Digger pines
Pinus Torreyana: Soledad pine, Torrey pine

GROWTH HABITS
Evergreen Tree
Origin: Northern Hemisphere
Range: Temperate to subarctic regions

CULINARY USES
It sounds unlikely, but pine trees *do* have some culinary uses. Some of the varieties with stiff needles, such as Austrian pine, *Pinus nigra,* make charming skewers for small dishes like mezes or tapas. They are used this way in Japan. The needles are also used to flavor and garnish clear soups.

Sandarac, a resin derived from the sap of Scotch pine, *Pinus sylvestris,* is used to flavor the famous retsina wines of Greece. It has also been used to flavor some beers. Pine barrels are used for one of the maturing stages of balsamic vinegar in Emilia-Romagna, Italy.

A lovely Italian variation on the New England clambake makes use of pine needles, as well. Dried needles are spread on a large, flat stone, forming a bed maybe two or three inches thick and a couple of feet in diameter. Scrubbed and debearded mussels are arranged on top of the needles. Just before the mollusks are served, the needles are set afire. They burn quickly, giving off just enough heat to open the mussels and endowing them with a piney perfume.

Chopped dried pinecones are said to be among Brother Bernardo Vincelli's original recipe for Benedictine.

The seeds of American *Pinus monophylla,* the nut pine, are useful. Pignoli, piniones, pignons, pinyons, or pine nuts are also borne in the cones of *Pinus quadrifolia, Pinus Torreyana, Pinus cembroides,* and *Pinus Sabiniana.* In Europe, the seeds are obtained also from *Pinus pinea,* and in Asia, they are gathered from *Pinus Gerardiana, Pinus koraiensis,* and *Pinus Lambertiana.* Pine nuts are delicious when toasted to release their resinous fragrance. The Italian pine nut–studded macaroons known as pignoli are the perfect accompaniment to espresso, offering just a little sweetness to balance the bitter coffee. The simple, elegant pignoli often outshine the showier cannoli and babas au rhum.

Pine nuts make a great garnish for salads and, of course, they are the only proper thickener for *pesto alla genovese.* Koreans use pine nuts as garnishes for meat, in desserts, and even as an addition to kimchee. Hua Yuan, a long-gone restaurant in New York City's Chinatown, used to serve a simple dish that consisted of nothing but pine nuts, chicken, carrots, celery, and garlic. Everything was chopped to the same size as the nuts, stir-fried, then sauced with concentrated chicken stock and sesame oil to coat the tiny pieces of vegetable. The dish was simple but delicious.

Pine nuts are used in many Middle Eastern rice dishes. In Arabic, they are known as *snober.* In Turkey, they are called *fistik. Dolma fistik* means "pine nuts for stuffed grape leaves." Armenians use them in the same way (although they would, no doubt, prefer that their cooking not be mentioned in the same breath as that of the Turks).

The Portuguese make a pine nut brittle called *pinhoada* (*pinhão* is Portuguese for "pine nut"). A similar pine nut candy, *saeng pyeon,* comes from Korea and is flavored with fresh ginger and toasted cinnamon.

The needles of *Pinus montana* contain bornyl acetate, cadinene, phellandrene, and pumilone terpenes.

OTHER USES

Pinecones make good fire starters, and they are sometimes included in potpourri.

COMMENTS

The "pine needles" (as well as the cones and seeds) listed in some flavoring treatises may also refer to white spruce, *Picea glauca,* which contains bornyl acetate, cadinene, lauric aldehyde, limonene, and pinene, or to Douglas fir, *Pseudotsuga Menziesii.*

Silver Fir: *Abies alba*

OTHER COMMON, ETHNIC, OR SCIENTIFIC NAMES
White spruce

GROWTH HABITS
Evergreen tree
Origin: Central and southern Europe
Range: Cool temperate regions

CULINARY USES
Spruce gum was once a popular confection in the United States. Today it is only a curiosity.

Spruce bark is used in the manufacturing of some French cheeses. In Savoie, the soft cheese Vacherin des Beauges, or Vacherin des Aillons, is wrapped in a ribbon of the inner bark of spruce trees. Vacherin du Haut-Doubs is similar but has a stronger, more resinous flavor.

Spruce contains bornyl acetate, cadinene, lauric aldehyde, limonene, and pinene.

69. Piperaceae (sometimes listed as Peperomiaceae): The Pepper Family

---

Culantro de Montana: *Peperomia acuminata*

OTHER COMMON, ETHNIC, OR SCIENTIFIC NAMES
Radiator plant

RELATED SPECIES
Peperomia maculosa: Cilantro peperomia
Peperomia pellucida: Cang cua (Vietnam); ketumpangan ayer (Malaysia); olasiman ihalas, sahica-puti, ulasiman-bato (Philippines); pak krasang (Thailand); rangu-ranga (Indonesia); rau cangcua (Vietnam); suna kôsho (Japan); greenhouse tea plant, peperomia

GROWTH HABITS
Succulent perennial
Origin: Northern South America
Range: Naturalized in Hawaii

The leaves of *Peperomia acuminata,* fresh or dried, are used as a seasoning in tropical portions of the Americas. *Peperomia maculosa* tastes like, and is used as, cilantro (q.v.). *Peperomia pellucida* is employed as an herbal tea, in salads, and as a potherb.

Cang cua has an odd odor, smelling as if were stored with uncooked fish.

COMMENTS

Culantro de monte is a name used in the Caribbean, usually referring to *Eryngium foetidum,* a plant that is more closely related to sea holly (q.v.). "Cilantro," of course, usually means the foliage of coriander.

Some of the *Peperomia acuminata* sold in the United States is actually *Peperomia elongata* var. *guianensis.*

Pepper: *Piper nigrum*

OTHER COMMON, ETHNIC, OR SCIENTIFIC NAMES

Black pepper, white pepper, pepper plant, vine pepper
Arabic: Bhar, filfil
Brazil: Pimienta do reino
Burma/Myanmar: Nga-youk-kuan
China: Hu jiao li, woo jiu
Denmark: Peber
East Timor: Pimenta
Estonia: Must pipar
Ethiopia: K'undo berbere
Finland: Pippuri
France: Poivre
Germany: Pfeffer
Greece: Pipéri
Hungary: Borsó
Iceland: Pipar
India: Gulki, mirich, krishnadi, kuru-mulagu, marichan, menasu, milagoo, miris, miriyalu, vella
Indonesia: Lada, merica
Iran: Abeeyad, philphili
Iraq: Felfel
Israel: Pilpel
Italy: Pepe
Japan: Kosho
Laos: Phik noi
Malaysia: Lada
Mexico: Pimienta

Morocco: Elbezar
Netherlands: Peper
Nigeria: Ada, ivere, oziza
Norway: Pepper
Philippines: Paminta
Poland: Pieprz
Portugal: Pimenta
Romania: Piper
Russia: Pjerets
Spain: Pimienta
Sri Lanka: Gammiris
Swahili: Pilipili
Sweden: Peppar
Thailand: Cha plu, prik thai
Turkey: Biber
Vietnam: Hat-trieu

RELATED SPECIES

Piper aduncum: Gusanillo (Spain); higuillo, wild pepper

Piper angustifolium (also known as *Artanthe elongata*): Herba matico, mateco, matica, matico, yerba matico (Spain)

Piper auritum (also known botanically as *Piper sanctum*): Acuyo, candela de ixote, hoja de anis y momo, hoja santa, santilla de comer, tlamapaquelite, tlanepa, yerba santa (Mexico); anisillo, hoja de ajan, hoja de anis, hoja de la estrella, hierba santa, santamaria, santilla de comer (Costa Rica); bulath (Sri Lanka); matarro (Honduras); cordoncillo (Spain); Méxicanischer Blattpfeffer (Germany); Santa Maria (El Salvador); Mexican pepper leaves, sacred pepper, root beer plant

Piper betle: Betel leaves, betel pepper, paan (India); phluu (Thailand)

Piper cubeba: Cabé java (Indonesia); cubeba, kababat (Iraq); cubèbes, poivre aqueue, poivre du java (France); cubebepeper (Netherlands); cubera (Mexico); dikiy pjerets, kubeba (Russia); Javanischer Pfeffer, Kubebenpfeffer, Schwanzpfeffer, Stielpfeffer (Germany); kabab-chini, kankol, tadamiri, thippli, tokamiriyalu (India); kamukus (Indonesia); kebbaba (Algeria); kabebba (Morocco); kubebapeppar (Sweden); kubeebapipar (Estonia); cubeb pepper, Java peppercorn, Javanese pepper, tailed pepper

Piper darienense: Duermeboca (Panama)

Piper excelsum: Kawakawa, New Zealand peppertree

Piper guinense (also known as *Piper Clusii* and *Piper guineense*): Aschantipfeffer, Clusiuspfeffer, Falscher Kubebenpfeffer, Guineapfeffer (Germany); poivre du kissi (France); Ashanti pepper, Benin pepper, Clusius pepper, false cubeb pepper, Guinea cubebs

Piper interitum: Tetsi

Piper longum (may be the same species as mountain long pepper, *Piper sylvaticum*): Balinesischer Pfeffer, Bengalischer Pfeffer, Jaborandi-Pfeffer, Langer Pfeffer, Stangenpfeffer (Germany); bi ba (China); cabé bali (Indonesia); chanchala, darfilfil, hippali, magha, pipali, thippali (India); dar felfel (Morocco); felfel daraz (Iraq); långpeppar (Sweden); langwerpige peper (Netherlands); pikk pipar (Estonia); poivre long (France); timiz (Ethiopia); Balinese pepper, Bengal pepper, Indian long pepper, jaborandi, long pepper

Piper lolot: Lo lot (Vietnam); lolot

Piper marginatum: Aniseto (Dominican Republic); licorice scented

Piper ornatum: Celebes pepper

Piper palmeri: Matico (Mexico); matico pepper

Piper retrofractum (sometimes listed as *Piper officinarum*): Cabe merah (Indonesia); Javanese long pepper. Indigenous in Malaysia

Piper sarmentosum: Bo la lot (Vietnam); cha plu (Thailand); daun kadok (Malaysia); phak i leut (Laos); betel leaf, wild betel leaf

Piper tuberculatum: Cordoncillo, cordoncillo blanco (El Salvador); pimienta longa (Mexico)

GROWTH HABITS

Tropical vine
Origin: Southern India and Ceylon
Range: Old World tropics

CULINARY USES

This is the only true pepper. Black pepper is made from the dried unripe fruits. The green berries are allowed to ferment, encouraging the growth of a fungus, *Glomerella cingulata,* which provides the black color and develops latent flavors in the berries. The berries are then dried, producing the characteristically shriveled, wrinkled appearance. If the berry is allowed to ripen but the skin (pericarp) is rubbed off before drying, the resulting product is white pepper. The primary reason for choosing white pepper for a dish is its color (or rather, its lack of color). It has some of the heat (from the active ingredient, piperine) of black pepper, but the aromatic properties that distinguish black pepper from other sources of culinary heat seem to reside in the pericarp. Pepper is used with fish, meats (roasts, sausages, and, of course, steak au poivre), and salad dressings. It is delicious on fresh strawberries.

Lampong pepper, from Indonesia, is the most common variety of black pepper in use in the United States, with some competition from Penang pepper and Singapore pepper. Alleppi pepper, Mangalore pepper, and Tellicherry pepper are higher grades of pepper from India; their higher cost is justified by their more complex and aromatic scent. Other varieties of note include pepper from Madagascar, Siam (Thailand), and Saigon (Ho Chi Minh City,

Vietnam); note that outdated place-names are still used to identify these products.

Most white pepper is made from Muntock pepper, a variety grown on Banka, an island near Sumatra. Sarawak pepper is used to a lesser extent. It is grown in northern Borneo.

Green peppercorns are also harvested in unripe condition, but they are pickled, either in brine or vinegar; freeze-dried; or dehydrated. This prevents the darkening fermentation that strips black pepper of the faintly resinous quality that the green peppercorns retain. This slightly piney taste is especially appealing with game, such as venison or duck, or with rich meats like lamb. For this reason green peppercorns often appear in pâtés and other products of the charcuterie.

Black pepper and possibly Ashanti pepper are among the vast and shifting list of ingredients in Ethiopia's *berberé*. In Morocco, it is included in the spice mixture called *la kama,* commonly used in soups and stews, and *ras el hanout.* In Persian cooking, black pepper is occasionally included in the spice mixture called *advieh.* It is one of the ingredients in the Iraqi spice mixture known as *boharat.*

Ashanti pepper, *Piper guineense,* is said to be milder than black pepper, *Piper nigrum.* It is used in western Africa just as black pepper is used, and its

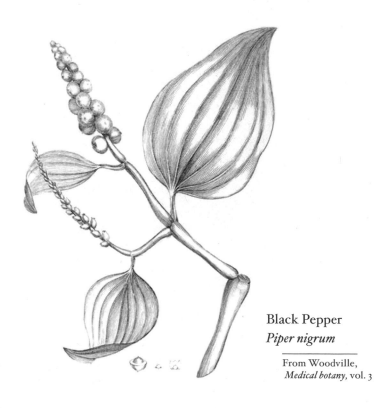

Black Pepper
Piper nigrum

From Woodville,
Medical botany, vol. 3

leaves are used to season soups; ashes from the burning of the plant are used as a salt substitute.

Pertsovka is a Russian vodka (a form of nastoika) flavored with hot chiles and cubeb pepper. Cubebs are also used in Morocco as an ingredient in *ras el hanout*. It has a slightly numbing heat and a long-lasting bitter finish.

Ground white pepper is used, in combination with other spices and salt, in the French seasoning called *sel épice*. A simpler mixture, without the salt but still containing white pepper, is *quatre épices*. Both seasoning mixtures are essential to French charcuterie.

"Italian Seasoning" is a name for several different mixtures of herbs and spices sold commercially. They often contain pepper.

Molho brasiliero, "Brazilian sauce," is a kind of green salsa made with black pepper, lime juice, and other spices and herbs.

Piper longum is generally used in pickling or in the North African *ras el hanout,* although it was preferred over black pepper by the Romans. It has a more resinous flavor, and a heat that affects the back of the throat.

Many cheeses have more than a passing acquaintance with black pepper. The Belgian Vacheloo is flavored with pepper, while the soft, triple-cream Princ' Jean Met Peper is rolled in it. England also has a soft cheese log rolled in pepper; it has the very French-sounding name Roubiliac. The English

Long Pepper
Piper longum

From Blackwell,
A curious herbal, vol. 2

Cubeb Pepper
Piper cubeba

From Köhler, *Köhler's Medizinal-Pflanzen*, vol. 2

also have Week-ender, flavored with lemon pepper, chives, garlic, and parsley. Other British cheeses containing pepper are the Stilton-like Vulscombe, which also contains garlic and herbs, and the Gouda-like Walda, which is flavored with green peppercorns. Sussex Slipcote is a soft, Boursin-like cheese, sold in boxes, that is available flavored either with garlic, crushed black pepper, or a mixture of herbs.

Other pepper-laced cheeses from the British Isles include Kilshanny, from County Clare, in Ireland; Ballindalloch, a Scottish goat cheese containing black pepper and caraway seeds; and St. Finan's, a hard cheese made from sheep's milk in Scotland that sometimes contains cracked peppercorns. The Welsh have their Cadern, a Cheddar-like cheese flavored with Port and black pepper, and Pant-Ys-Gawn, a Boursin-like fresh cheese, redolent of black pepper, chives, and garlic.

The French, who probably produce and consume more varieties of cheese than any other culture, have not neglected black pepper. Boulette de Cambai is a fresh cheese containing parsley, pepper, tarragon, and chives. Boursin, of course, is famous as a mass-produced triple-cream cheese, available in either a mantle of cracked peppercorns or flavored with garlic and an assortment of herbs. Other pepper-covered French cheeses include Pélardon and, occasionally, Brie. Bougnat, sometimes called Poivre d'Auvergne,

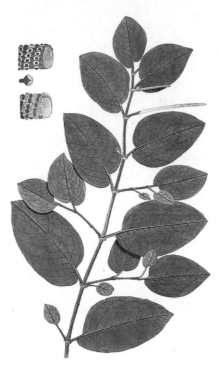

Cordoncillo
Piper tuberculatum

From Jacquin, *Icones
plantarum rariorum*, vol. 2

is seasoned only with pepper. Dauphin, or Thiérache, is an ancient cheese from Flanders that is seasoned with black pepper, cloves, parsley, and tarragon. Gapron, Gaperon, and Le P'Ail are relatively low-fat cheeses made with black pepper and garlic. The Netherlands uses black pepper in some of its Edams and Goudas (Pompadour is one of these Gouda-like cheeses). In Italy, whole peppercorns are sprinkled throughout the body of the cheese called Majocchino.

The leaves of *Piper angustifolium* are used in commercial flavorings. *Piper auritum*'s leaves are said to smell like sarsaparilla and are used to season tamales in Costa Rica. The berries of *Piper auritum,* smelling like cinnamon and anise, are used as a condiment.

The leaves of *Piper betle* get their name from their use; they are chewed with betel nuts, *Areca Catechu* (see Comments, under ACACIA).

The large, spicy, licorice/nutmeg/black pepper–flavored leaves of *Piper sanctum* are used in herbal teas. They are also used as a seasoning for egg dishes, fish, salsas (such as *mole verde*), and tamales.

Piper tuberculatum's spicy leaves are used as food wrappers in Thailand, just as grape leaves are in the Middle East.

White pepper contains pinenes, β-caryophyllene, d-limonene, piperidine, piperine, and l-a-phellandrene. Black pepper contains the same, only substituting camphor for l-a-phellandrene and adding chavicine.

Cubeb pepper contains β-cubebene, copaene, cubebol, d-cadinene, and α-cubebene.

Long pepper contains more piperine than black pepper, plus several related piperine compounds.

Piper methysticum contain benzoic acid, bornyl cinnamate, and cinnamic acid.

OTHER USES

A drink made from the roots of *Piper methylisticum* is used in political and religious rituals in Micronesia. The bitter, nonalcoholic, but apparently euphoria-inducing drink is prepared by the women, who chew the roots before spitting them into coconut milk. The finished alkaloid-laced brew is used only by the men during tightly controlled ceremonies.

At one time, it seemed unlikely that the kava-kava ritual would catch on among trendy, politically correct thrill-seekers in the United States. However, there is an easier way to indulge in kava-kava. It is now on the market, in pill form, wherever alternative medications are sold.

Masho-hara and yauardi-hena are names for snuffs made from varying *Piper* species. *Piper interitum* is used to make a snuff that is, not surprisingly, called *Tetsi*.

Essential oils and oleoresins from pepper are used in the perfume industry.

COMMENTS

The ancient Romans have a reputation for many kinds of excess, and their culinary attitudes were not exceptional in this regard. The dinner with Trimalchio, from *The Satyricon* of Petronius, was of course a joke, but without an element of truth, no satire is possible. Some historians have speculated that Romans suffered from exposure to high levels of lead from their plumbing and that the intensely flavored dishes they preferred were necessary palliatives for their poisoned palates.

It seems unlikely that large numbers of Romans could have had such high levels of lead in their systems that it affected their sense of taste, and it seems even more improbable that their individual affliction altered the collective taste of the empire. Perhaps the wealthy Romans who *could* afford indoor plumbing were the very people who set the standards for gastronomic excellence, exerting disproportionate influence on their culture. Their illness affected their taste, but their prestige affected their culture.

Chile pepper (q.v.) is not related to this pepper in any way. It is a *Capsicum*, related to bell peppers, potatoes, tomatoes, and eggplant. It is called "pepper" because of wishful thinking on the part of one Christopher Columbus. Due to a small error in calculation, he thought he was on the other side of the globe, where true pepper was—and is—grown.

Pink peppercorns are not related to pepper, either. They are *Schinus terbinthifolius* (q.v.).

Mignonette is a chef's term for freshly cracked black pepper. It should not be confused with Mignonette, *Reseda odorata* (q.v.). *Bhar* is Arabic for "all-spice" as well as "pepper."

Of all the complaints voiced by people who do not care for spicy (that is, *hot*) food, the most common is that it will destroy the stomach, or stomach-lining, of habitual eaters. No medical or scientific evidence has been found to confirm this wild fear, at least as far as the much hotter *Capsicums* are concerned. Black pepper, however, *has* been implicated in some ulceration of stomach-linings.

70. Plantaginaceae: The Plantain Family

Common Plantain: *Plantago major*

OTHER COMMON, ETHNIC, OR SCIENTIFIC NAMES
Cart-track plant, ribwort, white man's foot
Costa Rica: Llanten
Mexico: Llanten

RELATED SPECIES
Plantago coronopsis: Buck's horn
Plantago juncoides: Seaside plantain
Plantago lanceolata: Spitzwegerich (Germany)

GROWTH HABITS
Perennial
Origin: Northern Europe and Asia
Range: Cosmopolitan weed

CULINARY USES
All species of plantain are edible. Young leaves can be used as a salad green, while older leaves become bitter and are better cooked. The seeds become gelatinous when soaked (like chia and basil; q.v.) and can be used as a thickener for soups. The seeds have been dried and ground as flour.

Plantago juncoides, a species found in the eastern United States, is reputed to be the best of the *Plantagos,* as a culinary herb, while *Plantago coronopsis* is the plantain of preference in France.

Plantain leaves contain benzoic acid, cinnamic acid, *p*-coumaric acid, *p*-hydroxybenzoic-acid, and vanillic acid, but tannins predominate.

COMMENTS
This plantain is unrelated to the green banana plantain, or plantano, of the *Musa* genus.

71. Poaceae (formerly Gramineae): The Grass Family

Buffalo Grass: *Hierchloeodorata*

OTHER COMMON, ETHNIC, OR SCIENTIFIC NAMES
Russian buffalo grass, sweet grass, vanilla grass
Poland: Subrowka
Russia: Zubrovka

GROWTH HABITS
Perennial
Origin: Northern Hemisphere
Range: New Mexico (high altitudes) to Alaska, Europe, and Asia

CULINARY USES
The vanilla-flavored leaves are used in Russia to flavor vodka (*vodka-zubrovka*). The grass gives the vodka a greenish cast. The essential oil derived from buffalo grass is used commercially in France to perfume candies, soft drinks, and tobaccos.

Dog Grass: *Agropyron repens*

OTHER COMMON, ETHNIC, OR SCIENTIFIC NAMES
Couch grass, durfa grass, twitch grass, quack grass, quick grass, quitch grass, scutch, tritveum, witch grass. Dog grass also appears in older scientific texts as *Triticum repens*.
France: Chiendent commun, chiendent rampant, petit chiendent
Germany: Gemeine Quecke, Hundsquecke, Kriechende Quecke
Italy: Gramigna
Russia: Pirey polzutchy
Spain: Grama officinal

GROWTH HABITS
Perennial
Origin: Eurasia
Range: Naturalized all over the United States

CULINARY USES
The rhizomes of dog grass, with their medicinal, slightly maple-like taste, are found in commercial baked goods, candies, ice creams, and soft drinks. They contain malic acid, mannite, and triticin. Their sweetness is supplied by inosite and glucose.

This harmful weed spreads rapidly by means of creeping rhizomes (see Comments, under MINT).

Lemongrass: *Cymbopogon citratus*

OTHER COMMON, ETHNIC, OR SCIENTIFIC NAMES

Camel's hay, citronella, oil grass, geranium grass, melissa grass, oil plant, West Indian lemongrass, fever grass. Sometimes seen listed botanically as *Andropogon nardus* var. *ceriferus, Cymbopogon flexuosus,* and *Andropogon schoenathus.* Old pharmaceutical names for lemongrass include *Herba Andropogonis* and *Herba Citronellae.*

Brazil: Caipim limão
Burma/Myanmar: Zabalin
Cambodia: Bai mak nao
China: Cang-mao, ching tong, heung mao tsu, xiang mao cao
Costa Rica: Yerba de limón, zacate de limón
Denmark: Citroengraes
East Timor: Du'ut moring
Estonia: Harilik sidrunhein
Finland: Sitruunaruoho
France: Verveine
Germany: Zitronengras
Iceland: Sítrónugras
India: Ghandia, sera, servi-pillu, vasanai-puthu
Indonesia: Sereh
Italy: Cimbopogone
Japan: Remon gurasu, remon-sou
Malaysia: Serai
Mexico: Hierba luisa, te limón, zacate de limón
Netherlands: Citroengras
Nigeria: Achara ehi, akwkuo, ikonti, koko oba, myoyaka
Philippines: Citronella, harani, salay, tanglad
Portugal: Capim-santo, erva-cidreira
Singapore: Laska
Spain: Te de limón, zacate de limón
Sri Lanka: Sera
Thailand: Ta krai
Vietnam: Tao doo (Hmong); sa, xa

CULTIVAR

'Nardus' (sometimes listed as *Cymbopogon nardua* or *Cymbopogon nardus*):
Hierba de limon (Spain); limoncilla (Colombia); citronella grass, nard

Cymbopogon flexuosus (sometimes listed as *Andropogon nardus* var. *flexuosus*): East Indian lemongrass

Cymbopogon martinii (sometimes listed as *Cymbopogon martini* or *Cymbopogon sofia*): East Indian geranium, gingergrass, palmarosa, rosha grass

GROWTH HABITS

Perennial (cultivated as an annual)

Origin: Southern India, Ceylon

Range: Frost-free areas and in greenhouses

CULINARY USES

Lemongrass appears in both Thai and Vietnamese cooking. The combination of lemongrass with coconut milk, *nam pla,* and chile is the signature of Thai cuisine. The addition of basil or cilantro or chives as aromatics provides the typically complex flavor of Southeast Asian cuisine.

In Nigeria, lemongrass appears in teas and pepper soups.

Lemongrass is used in sweet herbal teas. *Te limón,* as its name suggests, is used as tea in Mexico, especially at breakfast. In Greece, lemongrass is used to provide the tartness of yogurt during fasts, when dairy products are not used.

The herb is used in baked desserts, candies, chewing gum, gelatin desserts, liqueurs, and soft drinks.

Lemongrass's main flavoring is citral (as *cis*-citral and *trans*-citral), augmented by geranyl acetate, methyl heptenone, myrcene, and linalool. East Indian citronella grass contains citral (up to 85 percent of the essential oil), citronellal, geraniol, nerol, and farnesol. West Indian citronella grass contains citral, aldehydes, furfural, myrcene, dipentene and citronellal.

The gingery, cumin-like flavor, and rose-like scent of *Cymbopogon martinii* are due to citral, citronellal, dipentene, farnesol, and geraniol.

OTHER USES

Lemongrass is cultivated in Florida as a source of lemongrass oil. It is used in the manufacture of perfumes and scented soaps. In southern California and Florida, nard is grown for its citronella oil.

Indian lemongrass, *Cymbopogon flexuosus,* is a source for a variety of lemongrass oil known as *verveines des Indies. Cymbopogon martini* yields an essential oil known as *palmarossa.*

COMMENTS

"Indian lemongrass" and *Cymbopogon flexuosus* are used as synonyms for *Cymbopogon citratus,* although the flavorings industry considers them to be separate species.

Sugarcane: *Saccharum officinarum*

Ka-thee
Mexico: Caña de azucar

RELATED SPECIES
Saccharum sinense: Chinese sweet cane

GROWTH HABITS
Perennial
Origin: Southeast Asia
Range: Cultivated in warm areas everywhere. Louisiana and Texas are
large producers in the United States.

CULINARY USES
Sugarcane has culinary uses that extend beyond mere sweetening. Molasses, in varying strengths and coloration, is a byproduct of the refining process. Likewise, rum comes in a range of flavors and colors. Other alcoholic beverages are made from sugarcane besides rum: *Betsa betsa* is a kind of wine made in Madagascar, and *guarapo* is a primitive fermented drink made in South America. *Boj* is a crude brew made by the Kekchi Indians of Guatemala. *Basi* is a wine-like beverage made from sugarcane in the Philippines. In Brazil, *cachaça* and several rum-like brandies are made from sugarcane. One is called *mata-bicho* or "animal killer." The 151 proof rum of the Caribbean seems a close relative.

In Beijing, young shoots of sugarcane are cut in thin slivers, then cooked in a broth of chicken stock and rice wine. This soupy dish is known as stewed cane shoots in wine sauce. In Taiwan, a refreshing summer soup is made by cooking sweet potatoes and pineapple in a slightly salted sugar syrup; it is served ice cold.

In Thailand, sugarcane is included in soupy fish "stews." A forcemeat of seasoned shrimp is packed around a piece of sugarcane, then roasted to make an amusing Vietnamese version of a *gyro*. Slivers of the resulting "meat" are sliced off, wrapped in lettuce leaves with tomatoes and other garnishes, and eaten like tiny burritos. At the end of the meal, the "skewer" of sugarcane is chewed as a kind of integral dessert.

The unopened flowers of sugarcane are added to soups, stews and stuffings in several Asian cuisines. They are also eaten raw, dipped in sauces, as snacks. They are known as *dok-oi* in Thailand, *kon-tse-hua* in China, *satoukibi-no-hana* in Japan, *tebao-endog* in Indonesia, *tebu-telur* in Malaysia, and *tubo bulaklak* in the Philippines.

Sugar, like salt, has the remarkable property of bringing out and highlighting the flavors of other foods. Small amounts, barely noticeable in themselves, can add a great deal of flavor to dishes through their ameliorative (in the broadest sense) powers. In this context, sugar is still a spice.

Sugar and salt share another property: they are hygroscopic, that is, they attract water. This makes them good preservatives for foods. The reason has to do with osmosis and the structure of the organisms that cause food spoilage. Osmosis is the tendency of water to migrate from areas of greater concentration to areas of lesser concentration across a semipermeable membrane. A living cell is basically a thin membranous sac containing a watery mixture of biological goodies. If one of these "germs" tries to colonize a food that is high in sugar or salt, there will be a strong difference between the water concentration inside and outside the cells of the "germ." The resulting osmotic pressure literally bursts the cells open, killing them.

Heating sugar (sucrose)—caramelizing it—causes the formation of hundreds of different flavored and scented compounds. This is the reason that a "caramel" or "toffee" candy is much more satisfying than a simple lump of sugar, at least to an adult palate. This is part of the chemical transformation of mirepoix from mere chopped vegetables to a rich brown foundation for other flavors in stocks and sauces. The trick is that many of these reactions do not take place until the temperature reaches 310° F, which means that much of the water must be boiled off first. If you want this richness of flavor in a water-based product, the water must be replaced *after* the caramelization takes place.

Under certain conditions, the fermentation of glucose produces small amounts of diacetyl, the main flavoring compound in butter. Perhaps this was the original inspiration for butterscotch (and brittles and pralines).

OTHER USES

Sugar syrups have been used as the basis of many medicines, herbal and otherwise, for ages (see BORAGE).

COMMENTS

Twenty years ago, sugar occupied the pariah's chair currently held by fat. We tend to swing, like some frantic pendulum, between excesses of self-indulgence and self-deprivation based on overreaction to the media's exaggeration of the scientific insights of the moment. As a prototypical omnivore, I suspect that varied and balanced diets permit the occasional sampling of just about anything without harm. Unexamined excess is the real culprit in our dietary malaise.

Sugar is derived from many sources, of course, but sugarcane has a special place in history. At one time, sugar was so rare in Europe that it was treated as a spice and was part of the pharmacopoeia. With the discovery of the New World and its favorable climate, sugar became a major commodity. Unfortunately, it was an extremely labor-intensive crop. Slavery, on an unprecedented scale, was the horrible answer to Europe's craving for sugar. Sidney Mintz's book *Tasting Food, Tasting Freedom* follows the societal changes wrought by the sugar industry. Aside from the obvious negative aspects of the massive forced exodus from Africa to the Americas, some very interesting cultural and culinary practices evolved. Raymond Sokolov's delightful little book *Why We Eat What We Eat* chronicles some of the creative collisions that resulted, on both sides of the Atlantic, from the discovery of the New World.

Vetiver: *Vetiveria zizanioides*

OTHER COMMON, ETHNIC, OR SCIENTIFIC NAMES
Khas-khas, khus-khus. *Andropogon muricatus* is its old scientific name.
France: Vétiver
India: Khus

GROWTH HABITS
Tropical grass
Origin: India and tropical South Asia
Range: Wild in many tropical areas. Cultivated in Haiti, India, Java, and on Reunion Island.

CULINARY USES
Vetiver has been said to have a scent that resembles that of asparagus. It has been used to flavor sorbets and other desserts in India and Nepal. Khus essence is derived from the rhizomes. Khus is used to flavor soft drinks and syrups in Bengal.

The bitter aromatic roots contain benzoic acid, vetiverol (sesquiterpenes), and vetiverone (sesquiterpene ketones).

OTHER USES
Perfumes, potpourri, incense

72. Polygalaceae: The Milkwort Family

Rhatany Root: *Krameria triandra*

OTHER COMMON, ETHNIC, OR SCIENTIFIC NAMES
Mapato, Peruvian rhatany, pumacuchu, red ratanya. Some old herbals and apothecaries used the Latin name *Radix Ratahiae*.
France: Ratania
Germany: Ratanhia, Ratanhiawurzel

Italy: Ratania
Spain: Raiz para los dientes

RELATED SPECIES
'Krameria argetea: Brazilian rhatany, para rhatany

GROWTH HABITS
Shrub
Origin: South America
Range: Peru (Andes)

CULINARY USES
Used in commercial flavorings, especially for candies, ice cream, soft drinks, and alcoholic beverages. Extracts from the dried roots have been used to flavor some Ports.

The roots and bark of rhatany contain tannins. The roots of senega contain methyl salicylate, *p*-coumaric acid, *p*-methoxycinnamic acid, and valerianic acid.

OTHER USES
Used in toothpastes.

73. Polygonaceae: The Buckwheat Family

Bistort: *Polygonum bistorta*

OTHER COMMON, ETHNIC, OR SCIENTIFIC NAMES
Adderwort, Easter ledges, Easter mangiant, oderwort, osterick, pink plumes, snakeweed, twice writhen, wild chard. *Polygonum* is sometimes listed as *Persicaria.*
Inuit: Ipich, ma-shu, nizekmeektak
France: Renouée bistorte
Germany: Natterwurtz, Wiesenknöterich
Mexico: Bistorta
Russia: Vodianoy Peretz

CULTIVAR
'Superbum'

RELATED SPECIES
Polygonum cognatum: Turkish madimak. Dried leaves are used in pilafs.
Polygonum hydropiperoides (sometimes listed as *Persicaria hydropiper,*
    Polygonum hydropiper, Polygonum odoratum, or *Polygonum punctatum*):

Akantatar, katkeratatar (Finland); benitade (Japan); bitterblad, bitterpilört (Sweden); chilillo, pimienta de agua (Mexico); daun kesum (Malaysia); duizendknoop, waterpeper (Netherlands); goretc perichnyi, vodyanoii peretc (Russia); laksa-yip (China); lua ler, luam lows, rau ram (Vietnam); lus an fhògair (Gaelic); mõru kirburohi (Estonia); pa pao, pak pai (Thailand); pakarmul (India); pimienta acuática (Spain); poivre d'eau, renouée (France); rdest ostrogorzki (Poland); tade (Japan); vaspeppar (Norway); vodianoy peretz (Russia); Vietnamesischer Koriander, Wasserpfeffer (Germany); American water smart weed, arsesmart, common smartweed, hot arsesmart, laksa plant, mild water pepper, pepperwort, smartweed, Vietnamese coriander, Vietnamese mint, water pepper

Polygonum sachalinense: Japanese knotweed, giant knotweed; native wild plant

GROWTH HABITS

Perennial
Origin: Northern Europe and Asia
Range: Temperate regions

CULINARY USES

Bistort is used in England for Easter ledges pudding (also known as Easter herb pudding), usually in combination with lady's mantle (*Alchemilla xantho-chlora*) and lady's thumb (*Polygonum persicaria*).

Bistort
Polygonum bistorta

From Woodville, *Medical botany,* vol. 1

Some species are more acidic and peppery than others. As the leaves of rau ram, *Polygonum pulchrum,* become older, they become redder in color and hotter in flavor. Only the young leaves are used in raw Vietnamese dishes, especially the kim chee–like *du'a cân.* Young leaves are added as a garnish to creamy soups and cooked dishes containing noodles. Their arugala-like flavor is slightly bitter, with a soapiness that is reminiscent of cilantro, and it has a citrus finish. Young leaves and roots can be used raw in salads.

The leaves of *Polygonum hydropiperoides* are used fresh, all over southeast Asia, but especially in Vietnam. Their lemony, cilantro-like aroma is prized as a last-minute addition to soups, such as the famous *pho.* Their characteristic scent is derived from decanal, decanol, and dodecanal. Tadonal provides a short-lived biting heat, and rutin adds a bitter finish to the flavor.

Older roots are better as cooked vegetable. Older leaves are used as a potherb.

Bistort's roots contain gallic acid and tannins. These provide astringency but no other taste and little or no scent.

Polygonum hydropiperoides contains traces of many aromatic compounds, but its primary constituents are tannins and rutin.

OTHER USES
Bistort's high level of tannins made it useful to the tanning industry, at least before hemlock bark replaced it in the nineteenth century, only to be replaced in turn by chromium salts. Some polygonums have been used as dyestuffs.

COMMENTS
Excessive use can cause light-sensitive reactions in susceptible individuals.

Daun Kesom: *Polygonum odoratum*

OTHER COMMON, ETHNIC, OR SCIENTIFIC NAMES
Asian cilantro, Cambodian mint, fragrant knotweed, hot mint, lady's thumb, laksa leaf, lemon coriander, perennial coriander, persicary, smartweed, Vietnamese coriander, Vietnamese mint, water pepper. Daun kesom is sometimes listed as *Persicaria odorata, Polygonum pulchrum,* or *Polygonum hydropiper.*
Indonesia: Daun kesom, daun laksa
Laos: Phak pheo
Malaysia: Daun kesom, daun laksa, kasum
Singapore: Daun kesom, daun laksa
Thailand: Pak pao, phak phai
Vietnam: Nghe, rau ram

Polygonum multiflorum: Fo ti (Japan); hu shou wu (China)

Polygonum persicaria: Haru-tade, heartweed, lady's thumb, red leg; native wild plant

Polygonum sachalinense: Japanese knotweed, giant knotweed; native wild plant

Polygonum tartaricum: Buckwheat, tartary buckwheat

Rheum officinale: Ruibarbo (Colombia); ruibarbo (Mexico); rhubarb root

Rheum Rhabarbarum: Garden rhubarb, pie plant, rhubarb, wine plant

GROWTH HABITS

Perennial (in frost-free regions)

Origin: Vietnam

Range: Grown as an annual in cold climates

CULINARY USES

These leaves have a scent reminiscent of eucalyptus, lemon, and cilantro and are used in Southeast Asian curries. One source describes their flavor as "intense, akin to a concentrated mixture of basil and mint." They have a somewhat astringent quality as well.

Daun Kesom

Polygonum odoratum

From Jaume Saint-Hilaire,
La flore et la pomone françaises, vol. 5

Some species are more acidic and peppery than others. Usually, only the young leaves are used in Vietnamese dishes. They are often paired with poultry, duck eggs, and the pickled cabbage dish *du'a cân.*

Lady's thumb, *Polygonum persicaria,* is used in England for Easter ledges pudding, usually in combination with lady's mantle, *Alchemilla xanthochlora,* and bistort, *Polygonum bistorta* (q.v.).

Buckwheat, *Polygonum tartaricum,* yields edible seeds of the same name. An extract of rhubarb root, *Rheum officinale,* is used as an commercial flavoring. Fo ti (*Polygonum multiflorum*) roots contain anthraquinones and β-carotene.

COMMENTS

Do not confuse the fo ti above with fo ti tieng, *Hydrocotyle asiatica* subs. *minor* (q.v.).

Polygonum persicaria was formerly known scientifically as *Persicaria vulgaris.* "Vietnamese mint" is another name for rau hung cay, which actually is a mint.

Sorrel: *Rumex scutatus*

OTHER COMMON, ETHNIC, OR SCIENTIFIC NAMES

Buckler-shaped sorrel, French sorrel, garden sorrel, little vinegar plant, meadow sorrel, red top sorrel, sourgrass

France: Oseille
Germany: Sauerampfer
Greece: Xinolápathon
Italy: Acetosella
Mexico: Lenguas de vaca
Poland: Szczaw
Portugal: Azeda
Russia: Shcavyei'
Spain: Agrella

CULTIVAR

'Oseille de Belleville'

RELATED SPECIES

Rumex abyssinicus: Spinach rhubarb
Rumex acetosa: Cuckoo's meat, cuckoo sorrow, garden sorrel, gowke meat, green sauce, sour dock, sour grabs, sour sabs, sour sauce, sour suds
Rumex acetosella: Sangre de toro (Colombia); shavel (Russia); vinagrillo (Spain); common sorrel, field sorrel, sheep sorrel, red sorrel
Rumex buceplophorus: Çoban degnegi (Turkey); Stierkopf-ampfer (Germany)

Rumex crispus: Vinagrillo (Spain); curly dock

Rumex hymenosepalus: Caniagre, tanner's dock, wild rhubarb

Rumex Patientia (sometimes listed as *Rumex crispus*): Curled dock, garden patience, herb patience, monk's rhubarb, patience dock, patience herb, rumex, sour dock, spinach dock, yellow dock

Rumex sagittatus: Soorèngan, surengan

GROWTH HABITS

Perennial

Origin: Europe and Asia

Range: Temperate regions

CULINARY USES

Sorrel is used in salads, sauces, and stews. It is good as a cooked potherb, especially with lamb or veal. Its acidity is appreciated when it accompanies the unctuousness of goose, roast pork, or sweetbreads. A classic sorrel soup is made of rich chicken stock enriched with sorrel and sautéed onions, thickened with heavy cream and egg yolks.

Sorrel is used to stuff bony fishes, such as shad or pike. The oxalic acid is supposed to soften the small "floating" or forked bones that are difficult to remove before cooking. *Rumex acetosa* is similarly used with fish in Italy. There is little evidence that oxalic acid could actually soften those bones, at least at nontoxic concentrations.

The acidic juice of sorrel leaves is used, like rennet, for curdling milk in cheese making.

Surengan, *Rumex sagittatus,* is used in Java as a souring agent in curries (see TAMARIND). *Rumex abyssinicus* and *Rumex hymenosepalus* are frequently eaten, the leaves much as spinach is used, the stalks like rhubarb. The young leaves of *Rumex acetosella* are cooked before being added to salads in Italy, but they are included raw in Turkish salads. Their sour note lends excitement to beans, such as favas or lentils. *Rumex acetosa* provides a similar edge to bulghur wheat pilafs in Turkey.

Sorrel and the unrelated wood sorrel (q.v.) have a pleasant sour tang, but they lack the citrus quality of lemon juice. Both plants get their zip from oxalic acid, as does rhubarb. Sorrel also contains citric acid and malic acid. Sheep sorrel (*Rumex acetosella*) contains anthraquinones and coumarins, and its characteristic astringent sour flavor comes from ascorbic acid, oxalic acid and other oxylates, rutin, tannins, and tartaric acid.

COMMENTS

The name *lenguas de vaca* is applied generically to a number of *Rumex* species.

The sour bite of sorrel is barely noticeable early in the year. Later, the older leaves can become quite unpalatable as oxalic salts accumulate. The brief time between these extremes is the connoisseur's holy grail.

Oxalic acid is poisonous in quantity, but it is unlikely that someone would willingly eat enough to do any damage. The acid does react badly with metals, however. As a general rule, you should always use nonreactive cookware with any acidic ingredients.

74. Polypodiaceae: The Polypody Family

Bracken: *Pteridium aquilinum*

OTHER COMMON, ETHNIC, OR SCIENTIFIC NAMES
Brake, eagle fern. Has been listed botanically as *Ptiridium aquilinum*.
Colombia: Helecho de aguilo
Costa Rica: Alambrón, helecho alambre, helechón
Germany: Farnkraut
Japan: Warabe
Spain: Helecho

GROWTH HABITS
Perennial fern
Origin: North America
Range: Native or naturalized in temperate Northern Hemisphere to the tropics

CULINARY USES
Fresh fiddleheads and roots are eaten as vegetables, especially in Asia. Some Korean markets carry dried fiddleheads.

It is said that the dried roots have been added to flour for bread baking by peoples as diverse as the Maoris of New Zealand, Native Americans, and Canary Islanders. In Japan, starch derived from the rhizomes is used in dumplings. The bitter roots have been used like hops in beer brewing.

OTHER USES
Bracken is sometimes used where a gardener requires a thick patch of fern foliage. It is not, however, recommended for such use (see Comments, below).

COMMENTS
Bracken has been proven to contain carcinogens that affect humans. Cultures that habitually use bracken as food show a higher than normal incidence of gastric cancers. Bracken is also toxic to livestock. This is unfortunate because the ferns spread rapidly, underground, by way of a network of hairy rhizomes. They can quickly displace more desirable forage plants.

Maidenhair Fern: *Adiantum pedatum*

OTHER COMMON, ETHNIC, OR SCIENTIFIC NAMES

Hair fern, sweet fern. Maidenhair fern is sometimes listed as *Adiatum capillus-veneris,* but that name may refer to a European species.

Colombia: Caballera de Venus, cilantrillo
France: Capillaire, cheveux de Vénus
Germany: Frauenhaar
Italy: Capilera
Mexico: Culantrillo del pozo, helecho culantrillo
Panama: Culantrillo de piedra
Spain: Capelvenere

RELATED SPECIES

Diplazium esculentum: Daun pakis, sayur paku (Indonesia); daun paku
(Malaysia); ferntop, vegetable fern
Dryopteris filix-mas: Male fern

GROWTH HABITS

Perennial fern
Origin: North America and East Asia
Range: Temperate woods

CULINARY USES

Maidenhair fern has a tart, bittersweet flavor and an aromatic scent. It has been used as a tea in the Arran Islands. Maidenhair fern is said to be one of the secret ingredients in Benedictine.

Capillaire is a syrup flavored with maidenhair and orange water; it is sometimes combined with fruit juices.

Diplazium esculentum is native to Southeast Asia but naturalized in southern Florida. It is used as a vegetable, while leaves are new, in Indonesia. Male fern, *Dryopteris filix-mas,* is used as a flavoring for breads and beers in Norway.

Maidenhair fern contains gallic acid and tannins. The roots of sweet fern contain benzoic acid, butyric acid, glycyrrhizin, isovalerianic acid, and methyl salicylate.

OTHER USES

It is used in scents for hair tonics.

COMMENTS

The FDA restricts the use of maidenhair fern to alcoholic beverages.

The plant should not be confused with maidenhair tree, another name for the gingko tree, *Gingko bilobia,* also known as *Ichô* or, in China, *ya chiaou tzu.* The nuts of this tree are popular in several Asian cuisines; in China they are called *bark gor* or *pai kua,* and in Japan they are *ginnan.* They are also eaten in Korea. Gingko trees drop an incredible number of putrid-smelling fruits anywhere that trees of both sexes are planted. Properly segregated, however, they are a useful landscaping tree. Their snaky, unbranched boughs are covered along their entire length with lovely notched fan-shaped leaves. A mature gingko, in autumn, is delightfully yellow, from top to bottom.

The French name for this, *cheveux de Vénus,* is also applied to *Nigella sativa,* nigella (q.v.).

There is also an unrelated maidenhair berry, *Gautheria hispidula* (sometimes listed as *Chiogenes hispidula* or *Chiogenes serpyllifolia*), that grows in Canada and Maine. It is also known as creeping snowberry or moxie plum. It is not a fern but a heath, a member of the *Ericaceae,* and closly related to wintergreen (q.v.).

75. Pontederiaceae: The Pickerel Weed Family

Water Hyacinth: *Eichornia crassipes*

OTHER COMMON, ETHNIC, OR SCIENTIFIC NAMES
Water orchid

GROWTH HABITS
Aquatic perennial
Origin: Tropical South America
Range: Naturalized in southeast United States

CULINARY USES
The leaf stems of water hyacinth are used in Thai cooking, especially in sour soups (see Comments, below).

OTHER USES
Water hyacinth has the useful property of extracting large quantities of heavy metals from waters and soils in river beds. If the plants are periodically removed from the waterways, the heavy metals that have been absorbed into the plants can be removed from the ecosystem (see Comments, below).

COMMENTS
Avoid eating water hyacinths that grow in waters polluted by heavy metals.
Water hyacinths have few natural enemies and have completely clogged waterways in Florida. Manatees consume huge quantities of water hyacinth, but the needs of the manatees and of the boaters who use these waterways are not entirely compatible.

76. Portulacaceae: The Purslane Family

Anacampseros: *Anacampseros albissima*

RELATED SPECIES
Anacampseros papyracea: No common name found

GROWTH HABITS
Succulent perennial
Origin: Southern and Southwestern Africa
Range: Desert succulents

CULINARY USES
Both species of *Anacampseros* are used to make beer-like beverages in Africa.

Purslane: *Portulaca oloraceae*

OTHER COMMON, ETHNIC, OR SCIENTIFIC NAMES
Continental parsley, French pusley, hog parsley, miner's lettuce, pigweed
Arabic: Baklee
Australia: Munyeroo (Aborigine)
China: Kwa-tsz-tsai
France: Pourpier
Germany: Portulak
Greece: Andrákli, glistrítha
India: Kulfa
Indonesia: Krokot
Iraq: Barbeen
Italy: Mbrucacchia, porcellana, portulaca
Japan: Suberi-hiyu
Malaysia: Gelang pasir
Mexico: Verdolagas
Netherlands: Postelein
Philippines: Olasiman
Spain: Verdolaga
Sri Lanka: Genda-kola
Thailand: Phak bia-yai

CULTIVARS
'Giganthea', 'Goldgelber Purslane' (also known as 'Pourpier Doré' or 'Golden Purslane'), 'Multibranch Purslane'

Calandrinia micrantha: Chivitos (Mexico); bird's tongue
Claytonia lanceolata: Groundnut
Montia perfoliata: Cuban spinach, miner's lettuce, winter purslane
Portulaca grandiflora: French pusley, garden portulaca
Portulaca sativa: Golden purslane, kitchen garden portulaca

GROWTH HABITS
Annual
Origin: India
Range: Common wild plant, weedy in waste places

CULINARY USES
Purslane's young leaves, with their mild acidic flavor, are eaten in salads, especially with tomatoes. This use is popular in Greece and the Middle East, especially in Syria. The French make *salade de pourpier* with the leaves of purslane. The leaves' cool, crunchy presence is a fine foil for pungent foliage like mustard greens in salads. They are also used as a potherb. When cooked, purslane has a thickening property, much like the okra used in gumbos. Purslane is used in soups, often in combination with garbanzos or sorrel. In Greece, purslane leaves are added to omelets. They are good chopped in soft cheeses.

Large stems can be pickled. Sprouted seeds are sometimes eaten in salads. The seeds are milled into flour by the Aborigines of Australia.

Groundnut, *Claytonia lanceolata,* has edible tubers.

OTHER USES
Portulacas are used primarily as garden annuals.

77. Primulaceae: The Primrose Family

Primrose: *Primula vulgaris*

OTHER COMMON, ETHNIC, OR SCIENTIFIC NAMES
Spring primula

CULTIVARS
'Alba', 'Atropurpurea', 'Azurea', 'Caerulea', 'Grandiflora', 'Lilacina', 'Lutea', 'Rosea', 'Rubra'

RELATED SPECIES
Primula veris: Cowslip, paigle

GROWTH HABITS
Perennial

Origin: Eurasia
Range: Temperate regions

CULINARY USES

The blossoms of both *Primula vulgaris* and *Primula veris* are used to make herbal teas and wines. Primroses are made into preserves and pickles. They can also be crystallized for use as garnishes on desserts. A few fresh blossoms look good in salads, too. The leaves can be used in stuffings for poultry or cooked as a potherb.

COMMENTS

"Cowslip" is either a name, or part of a name, for lungwort, *Pulmonaria officinalis* (q.v.); marsh marigold, *Caltha palustris* (see Comments, under CALENDULA); and bluebells, *Mertensia virginica*.

78. Punicaceae: The Pomegranate Family

Pomegranate: *Punica granatum*

OTHER COMMON, ETHNIC, OR SCIENTIFIC NAMES
Apple of Carthage, grenadine
Afghanistan: Anar
Arabic: Roman, rumman
Brazil: Roma, romeira
Burma/Myanmar: Tha-le
China: Shi liu
Denmark: Granataeble
Estonia: Harilik granaadipuu
Finland: Granaattiomena
France: Grenade
Gaelic: Gràn ubhal
Germany: Granatapfel
Greece: Ródi
Iceland: Granatepli
India: Anar, anardana, dadam, dalimba, dhanimmapandu, madhubiija, madulam, matalam
Indonesia: Delima
Iran: Anaar
Israel: Rimon
Italy: Melagrana
Japan: Zakuro
Malaysia: Delima
Nepal: Daarim

Netherlands: Granaatappel
Norway: Granat
Philippines: Granada
Portugal: Romã
Romania: Rodie
Russia: Granatnik
Spain: Granada
Swahili: Komamanga, kudhumani
Sweden: Granatäpple
Turkey: Nar

GROWTH HABITS

Deciduous tree
Origin: Southern Europe and southern Asia
Range: In greenhouses or outdoors in frost-free regions

CULINARY USES

Aside from its use as a fruit, pomegranate provides a tart flavor and brilliant color that are delectable in marinades, for example, a roast chicken in Tuscany. In North Africa, chickens are often cooked in pomegranate juice. The tiny, gleaming, ruby-like fruitlets make a good garnish for rich meats.

In India, dried fruit and seeds of pomegranates are ground to make the spice *anardana* (or *annar-dana*), which is prized for its tart flavor.

The juice is the basis of pomegranate molasses. This reduced juice is known as *dibs riman* in Arabic, or *nar eksisi* in Turkish. In English, it is also known as pomegranate syrup or grenadine molasses. It has a sweet-sour, tamarind-like flavor, but a more appetizing color.

COMMENTS

The largest-selling grenadine syrup does not contain any pomegranate juice. It is a synthetic product whose only similarity to pomegranate is its intense red coloration, and whose only "natural" ingredients are water and sugar. Its flavor most strongly resembles a cross between artificial cherry and artificial strawberry.

79. Ranunculaceae:
The Crowfoot or Buttercup Family

American Cowslip: *Caltha palustris*

OTHER COMMON, ETHNIC, OR SCIENTIFIC NAMES

Kingcup, marsh marigold, may-blob, meadow-bright. A former scientific name for this species was *Caltha parnassifolia*.

American Cowslip
Caltha palustris

From Vallet, *Le jardin du Roy*

CULTIVARS
'Barthei', 'Monstruosa' (or 'Monstrosa Plena')

GROWTH HABITS
Perennial
Origin: Eurasia and North America
Range: Wild from Arctic Circle south to Tennessee

CULINARY USES
Cowslip leaves have been used as a potherb. The flowers have been made into wines. The buds are pickled, like capers. The cultivar 'Barthei' is known as *ezo ryûkin ka* in Japan. There, dumplings are made from the dried roots. The flowers are used in *tsukudani,* a sweet tasting, *miso*-like sauce.

COMMENTS
Cowslip, *Calendula officinalis* (q.v.), is not related to this plant; but is a member of the *Asteraceae.*

Nigella: *Nigella damascena*

OTHER COMMON, ETHNIC, OR SCIENTIFIC NAMES
Black cumin, devil-in-a-bush, fennel flower, love-in-a-mist, ragged lady, wild fennel

Arabic: Shamar
Egypt: Habbah sawda
Ethiopia: Tikur azmud
France: Nigelle
Germany: Schwarz Kümmel
Greece: Mavro
Iraq: Habbat soda

RELATED SPECIES

Nigella arvensis: Acker-schwarz Kümmel (Germany); çorek otu (Turkey); habet el soudane (Morocco); black bread weed, wild fennel

Nigella sativa: Aed-mustköömen, mustköömen (Estonia); charnushka (Russia); cheveux de Vénus, faux cumin, nigelle, poivrette, quatre épice, toute épice (France); çörekotu siyah, çörek otuy, shoushma (Turkey); czarnuszka siewna (Poland); habbet el beraka, habbah sauda, kamun aswad, sinouj (Arabic); jintan manis (Indonesia and Malaysia); kala jira, kalonji, kaluduru, karun jiragam, munga reala, nellajilakaira, shah jira, vengaya vidai, neeruli beeja, ullithnam (India); neidonkuka (Finland); nigèlla (Italy); Nigella, Schwarz Kümmel, Zwiebelsame (Germany); nigelle (Netherlands); niguilla, pasionara (Spain); svartkarve (Norway); svartkummin (Sweden); tikur azmud (Ethiopia); black cumin, devil-in-the-bush, fennel flower, onion seed, Roman coriander, siyah daneh, nigella, nutmeg flower, sweet cumin

GROWTH HABITS

Annual
Origin: Mediterranean region
Range: Temperate to tropical regions

CULINARY USES

Nigella is sometimes sold as "black onion seed," or simply "black seed," and is one of the many ingredients in garam masala. Despite its onion name, its flavor doesn't resemble onion at all; it has a bitter, resinous quality, a little like that of caraway without the warmth. Its German name translates literally as "black caraway." The seeds *are* black, but "caraway" reflects their flavor more than their appearance.

In the United States, Armenians often add nigella seeds to their braided cheeses (sometimes with mahleb, ground kernels of black cherry seeds). The Armenian cheeses Tel-banir and Haloumi are flavored with it.

The seeds garnish several Indian breads. They are also part of the Indian spice mixture called *panch phoron*. Vegetables, and any number of the puréed legumes called dals, are seasoned with panch phoron.

Nigella sativa is used all over the Eurasian region. It is used much as *Nigella damascena* but has additional uses as well. With the range of common names it has borne, it should come as no surprise that the seeds are used for

Nigella
Nigella damascena

From Köhler, *Köhler's Medizinal-Pflanzen,* vol. 3

seasoning. Preserved lemons in Morocco are flavored with it, among many other spices and herbs.

Nigella seed contains damascenin (and several other nigelline alkaloids), as well as a number of esters of terpene alcohols.

OTHER USES

The dried seedpods are often used in dried flower arrangements.

In India, black cumin is thought to prevent flatulence. Societies that are largely vegetarian—or at least those that consume a great deal of leguminous plants—seem to be plagued by thoughts about bodily gases (see EPAZOTE).

COMMENTS

Devil-in-a-bush is another name for *Saponaria officinalis,* better known as bouncing bet or soapwort. Cheveux de Vénus is a synonym for maidenhair fern (q.v.).

Wild Clematis: *Clematis vitalba*

OTHER COMMON, ETHNIC, OR SCIENTIFIC NAMES

Leather flower, traveler's joy, vase flower, virgin's bower

CULTIVARS
'Taurica'

GROWTH HABITS
Vine-forming perennial
Origin: Mediterranean region
Range: Temperate regions

CULINARY USES
Young leaves and sprouts are used in soups and as a garnish for egg and rice dishes.

80. Resedaceae: The Mignonette Family

Mignonette: *Reseda odorata*

OTHER COMMON, ETHNIC, OR SCIENTIFIC NAMES
Common mignonette
Germany: Reseda, Resede

CULTIVAR
'Grandiflora'

RELATED SPECIES
Reseda lutea: Wild mignonette
Reseda luteola: Dyer's rocket, weld

GROWTH HABITS
Annual
Origin: North Africa
Range: Commonly planted as an annual

CULINARY USES
Mignonette is used in the commercial flavorings industry. Extracts contain caprylic acid, eugenol, and phenols. The leaves of *Reseda phyteuma* are used as a potherb in Greece.

OTHER USES
Dyer's rocket, as its name might suggest, was at one time used as a source of a deep yellow dyestuff. Many *Resedas* have been used in the manufacture of perfumes.

COMMENTS
Mignonette is also a chef's term for freshly cracked black pepper, but it has nothing whatever to do with the herb *Reseda odorata*.

81. Rhamnaceae: The Buckthorn Family

Cascara Sagrada: *Rhamnus Purshiana*

OTHER COMMON, ETHNIC, OR SCIENTIFIC NAMES

Bearberry, bearwood, bitterbark, buckthorn, chittem, coffeeberry, Persian bark, sacred bark, wahoo, wild coffee. *Cascara Sagrada* was formerly known scientifically as *Cascara purshianus.*

Germany: Amerikanischer Faulbaum

Mexico: Aladierno, cascara sagrada

Russia: Joster, krushina

RELATED SPECIES

Rhamnus prinoides: Geisho, mofifi buckthorn

Zizyphus abyssinica: Catchthorn

Zizyphus Jujuba: Tsao (China); Chinese date, Chinese jujube, common jujube

Zizyphus mauritiana: Indian jujube

GROWTH HABITS

Deciduous shrub or small tree

Origin: Washington to California

Range: Cultivated in North America and Kenya

CULINARY USES

In Sonora, California, the nectar of cascara sagrada's flowers yields a dark, nongranulating, honey.

Bitter and acrid extracts are used in commercial flavorings. When the bitter elements are removed, the extracts are used in baked goods, ice cream, and soft drinks.

Chinese dates, or tsao, *Zizyphus Jujuba,* are ground in Korea to make *kochu jang,* a *miso*-like paste of chile, sweet rice, and soybeans. Chinese dates are available dried in Asian markets, usually packed in cellophane bags. Their most common form is smooth and red, but you may also find wrinkled black jujubes. The black ones have been smoked during the drying process. Their sweet-tart smokiness might be an excellent foil for the richness of pork or goose. Use them to replace some of the chipotles when you desire a sweet sauce with the smoke, but not all of the fire, of the jalapeños.

Indian jujube, *Zizyphus mauritiana,* provides the taste of the Venezuelan liqueur Crema de Poisigne. In Ethiopia, mofifi buckthorn, *Rhamnus prinoides,* flavors the sparkling mead called *tej,* as well as a smoky-tasting beer called *talla.* Catchthorn, *Zizyphus abyssinica,* is used in Malawi (once Nyasaland) to make the strong alcoholic brew *kachaso.*

OTHER USES

Cortex Rhamni Catharticae—the dried bark of buckthorn—yields a red-brown dyestuff; *Fructus Rhamni Catharticae*—the dried berries—yields a green dyestuff.

COMMENTS

Cascaras are strong purgatives, especially the fruits.

Maubi: *Colubrina elliptica*

OTHER COMMON, ETHNIC, OR SCIENTIFIC NAMES

Caribbean carob tree. Maubi is sometimes listed as *Colubrina arborescens* or *Colubrina reclinata,* the wild coffee listed below.

Trinidad: Mauby

RELATED SPECIES

Colubrina arborescens (sometimes listed as *Colubrina ferruginosa*): Wild coffee

GROWTH HABITS

Tree

Origin: Tropical Americas

Range: Caribbean, Hawaii

CULINARY USES

The bark is used to flavor a sweet drink also called *maubi* (or *mauby*) in the Caribbean. Other ingredients are anise, cinnamon, fresh ginger root, orange peel, and sugar.

COMMENTS

All the *Colubrinas* listed above may in fact be the same species.

New Jersey Tea: *Ceanothus americanus*

OTHER COMMON, ETHNIC, OR SCIENTIFIC NAMES

Mountain sweet, red-root, wild snowball

RELATED SPECIES

Ceanothus velutinus: Mountain balm

GROWTH HABITS
Shrub
Origin: Eastern United States
Range: Temperate regions

CULINARY USES
The leaves of New Jersey tea were used during the American Revolution as a substitute for tea imported from England.

82. Rosaceae: The Rose Family

Agrimony: *Agrimonia eupatoria*

OTHER COMMON, ETHNIC, OR SCIENTIFIC NAMES
Burr marigold, church steeples, cockleburr, harvest-lice, liverwort, philanthropos, sticklewort
France: Aigremoine eupatoire
Germany: Odermenning

Agrimony
Agrimonia eupatoria

From Woodville, *A supplement to Medical botany*, vol. 4

CULTIVAR
'Sweet Scented Agrimony'

GROWTH HABITS
Perennial
Origin: Mediterranean region
Range: Temperate regions

CULINARY USES
The apricot-scented cultivar listed above is said to be used in some herbal teas. Agrimony has a bitter and aromatic taste. According to Mrs. Grieve, the renowned British authority on herbs, it has been used in conjunction with other herbs (such as dandelion, betony, meadowsweet, and raspberry leaves), in place of hops, in herbal beers.
Agrimony contains tannin and an essential oil.

OTHER USES
Dyestuffs

COMMENTS
Agrimony is reputed to be an ingredient in some herbal liqueurs, but I've found no confirmation, so far.
Do not confuse with hemp agrimony, *Eupatorium cannabinum,* a member of the Asteraceae family.

Berries: *Rubus* spp.

OTHER COMMON, ETHNIC, OR SCIENTIFIC NAMES
Brambles (see also specific names below), cane berries. The old herbal and apothecary Latin name was *Eubatus Rubus.*

RELATED SPECIES
Rubus flagellaris: American dewberry
Rubus fructicosus: Blackberry
Rubus idaeus: Framboise, red raspberry
Rubus sanctus: Brommbeerstrauch (Germany), bögürtlen (Turkey), blackberry
Rubus villosus: Blackberry

GROWTH HABITS
Shrub
Origin: Northern Hemisphere
Range: Temperate regions

Other than the obvious uses for the berries themselves, the dried leaves are used in herbal tea blends. Their astringent taste, a result of tannins, does not resemble the flavor of the fruits, and the leaves are never used alone.

Burnet: *Poterium sanguisorba*

OTHER COMMON, ETHNIC, OR SCIENTIFIC NAMES

Burnet saxifrage, pimpinella sanguisorba. Burnet used to be known scientifically as *Sanguisorba minor.*
France: Sanguisorbe
Germany: Bibernette, Pimpinelle
Italy: Pimpinella
Mexico: Pimpinella blanca

RELATED SPECIES

Sanguisorba officinalis: Great burnet, burnet bloodwort

GROWTH HABITS

Perennial
Origin: Mediterranean region
Range: Temperate regions

CULINARY USES

Burnet's subtle cucumber-like flavor is not immediately apparent, but it gradually increases, seducing, rather than overpowering, the palate. It has a slight but pleasant alkaline bitterness. Its leaves can be used in salads, cordials, flavored vinegars, soft cheeses, and compound butters. Salad burnet should be the starting point for many civilized sandwiches. It is good in casseroles and creamed soups, such as asparagus or mushroom. The dried leaves can be added to French dressings (vinaigrettes). Fresh leaves are a pleasant addition to mayonnaise, combining well with rosemary and tarragon.

Both salad burnet and great burnet have been used in beers and in herb-flavored wine cups. The dried leaves are sometimes made into an herbal tea.

Burnet's delicate leaves, shaped like those of straberries, make a lovely garnish.

COMMENTS

Once a popular culinary and horticultural plant, burnet is due to make a comeback. What it lacks in drama is more than compensated by its charm.

Burnet's main drawback in the garden is that it is a prolific self-seeder. It should not be planted in a part of the garden where it can take over. If only one or two plants are desired, an attentive gardener can pick off the flower heads before they drop their seeds. Burnet grows radially, almost perfectly

Burnet
Poterium sanguisorba

From Weinmann, *Phytanthoza
iconographia,* vol. 4

flat, until just before it is about to flower. It then leaps up to its full height of one to two feet. It does grow well in pots outdoors, and a plant that I brought in for the winter doubled its summer growth in just one month on my kitchen counter. If planted in rich soil in the garden, it becomes quite lush.

European Mountain Ash: *Sorbus aucuparia*

OTHER COMMON, ETHNIC, OR SCIENTIFIC NAMES
   Quickbeam, rowan tree, sorb
   Bulgaria: Ofika
   Czech Republic: Jérabka
   Denmark: Røn
   Finland: Pihlajanmarja
   France: Sorbe
   Germany: Vogelbeere
   Greece: Sourbo
   Hungary: Veres berkenye
   Israel: Huzrar
   Italy: Sorbo

Japan: Nanakamado
Norway: Rogn
Poland: Jarzebina
Romania: Scorusua
Russia: Ryabina
Slovakia: Jerebina
Spain: Fresno alpestre
Sweden: Rönn

CULTIVARS

'Asplenifolia', 'Edulis' or 'Rowanberry', 'Fastigiata', 'Luteo-variegata', 'Moravica' or 'Mährische Eberesche', 'Rossica' or 'Russian Mountain Ash', 'Xanthocarpa'

RELATED SPECIES
Sorbus domestica: Service tree, sorb apple

GROWTH HABITS
Deciduous tree
Origin: Europe and Asia Minor
Range: North America

CULINARY USES

Fruits of several *Sorbus* species are used in jams, jellies, marmalades, and preserves. Some fruits are eaten fresh or dried. They have flavored ales, brandies, liqueurs (especially in Celtic, Gaelic, and Scandinavian countries), meads, vinegars, and wines. The juice is so tart that it can substitute for angostura in any cocktail recipe calling for bitters. *Sorbus aucuparia* and *Sorbus domestica* are used as a flavoring for French pear cider (Perry). The leaves and blossoms have been used as teas or as adulterants for black tea.

Rowan's astringent flavor is due to its high tannin and glycoside content.

COMMENTS

The common names and uses of plants named "Ash" have led to some confusion (see also PRICKLY ASH, *Aralia spinosa;* ASH, *Fraxinus excelsior:* and SZECHUAN PEPPER, *Zanthoxylum piperitum*).

The seeds of *Sorbus aucuparia* contain poisonous hydrocyanic acid and should always be removed before the berries are used or prepared for consumption.

Herb Bennet: *Geum urbanum*

OTHER COMMON, ETHNIC, OR SCIENTIFIC NAMES

Avens, blessed herb, cloveroot, colewort, goldy star, herba benedicta, way bennet, wild rye. *Carophyllatae* is an old name for the plant that no longer has any scientific relevance. Some apothecaries listed the plant as *Cardus Benedictus.*

France: Benoîte
Germany: Benedictenkraut, Nelkenwurz
Italy: Cano filiata, erba benedetta

RELATED SPECIES
Geum rivale: Chocolate root, purple avens, water avens

GROWTH HABITS
Perennial
Origin: Mediterranean region
Range: Temperate regions

CULINARY USES
Extracts of herb bennet roots are included in the formulations of altvater and amaretto. At one time, sachets of the herb flavored Augsburg ale. The leaves and pale yellow flowers may be added to salads and soups.
Geum rivale has likewise flavored ales, liqueurs, and wines.
The roots have an aroma that is reminiscent of cinnamon and cloves. They, or extracts of them, are used to season foods that blend well with those spices: apple pies, broths, hot ciders, and mulled wines (often with orange peel).
The herb's bitter flavor results from gein, and its spiciness comes from eugenol, the same essential oil that characterizes cloves and allspice.

OTHER USES
Ornamental

COMMENTS
Ancient herbals may not mean *Geum urbanum* when they use the term *Herba Benedicta.* This name is also associated with a number of other plants, among them hemlock and wild valerian. The common name "herb bennet" is also applied to poisonous water hemlock, *Cicuta maculata* (see Comments, under SKIRRET).

Lady's Mantle: *Alchemilla vulgaris*

OTHER COMMON, ETHNIC, OR SCIENTIFIC NAMES
Bear's foot, dewcup, leontopodium, lion's foot, nine hooks, stellaria
France: Pied de lion
Germany: Frauenmantel, Marienmantel

GROWTH HABITS
Perennial

Origin: Europe
Range: Temperate regions

CULINARY USES

The young leaves have a slightly bitter taste that makes them a good addition to salads. They are used in herbal tea blends, especially in Switzerland.

COMMENTS

Stellaria is the name for the genus that includes chickweed, or starwort. This totally unrelated plant is sometimes used in salads, as is lady's mantle.

Meadowsweet: *Filipendula ulmaria*

OTHER COMMON, ETHNIC, OR SCIENTIFIC NAMES

Bridewort, dolloff, lady of the meadow, meadsweet, queen-of-the-meadow. Formerly classed with *Spirea,* the old scientific name was *Spiraea Ulmaria*.
France: Reine des près
Germany: Mädesüss
Italy: Filipendula

CULTIVARS

'Aureo-Variegata': Leaves splotched with yellow
'Plena': Doubled flowers

GROWTH HABITS

Perennial
Origin: Europe and Asia
Range: Naturalized in North America

CULINARY USES

The flowers add almond flavor to beers, cooked fruits, jams, mead, wines, and teas. Fresh meadowsweet leaves flavor soups. The leaves contain coumarin, which is toxic but gives them a pleasant scent of fresh-mown hay.

OTHER USES

Add flowers and foliage to potpourri. The flowers and roots were once used in vegetable dying of wool.

Rose: *Rosa gallica* subs. *officinalis*

OTHER COMMON, ETHNIC, OR SCIENTIFIC NAMES

Apothecary's rose, French roses
Bulgaria: Shipka (hips)
China: Mei gui guo (hips)
Finland: Ruusukiulukka (hips)

France: Gratte-cul (hips), Rose
Germany: Hagebutten (hips), Rosa
India: Goolab
Iran: Gulab
Iraq: Warid joari (dried petals)
Italy: Rosa
Mexico: Rosa de castilla (dried rose buds)
Morocco: Rous el word
Netherlands: Rozebottel (hips)
Norway: Nype (hips)
Poland: Dzika róza (hips)
Spain: Rosa
Sweden: Nypon (hips)
Tunisia: Chouch el ward (dried and crushed)
Turkey: Itburnu (hips), gül (fresh), reçellik gül (dried)

CULTIVARS
Most modern cultivated roses are descended from this species.

RELATED SPECIES
Rosa canina: Hagebutte, Wildrose (Germany); dog rose
Rosa rugosa: Rugose rose, wrinkled rose; has huge orange hips.
Rosa eglanteria (also known as *Rosa Rubinosa*): Sweetbrier, eglantine
Rosa damascena: Bosora golabo, golabo, golap, gulab, gulabi, gulapha,
    gulisurkh, irosa, panniru, penimirpushpam, roja, shatadalaa, sudburg,
    tarana, vrittapuspa, (India); damascenerros, ros (Sweden); gul (Arabic);
    gul (Turkey); hninsi, nhin su bin, (Burma); kibuvits (Estonia); roos
    (Netherlands); rós (Iceland); rosa (Spain); roza, (Poland); ruusu
    (Finland); triandáfillo (Greece); ward (Arabic); waridi (Swahili);
    bussora rose, damask rose, English rose, rose

GROWTH HABITS
Perennial shrub or vine
Origin: Europe and Eurasia
Range: Naturalized in temperate regions everywhere

CULINARY USES
Rose petals from many species are used in candies, preserves, rose water,
salads, sorbets, syrup, and wine. Candied petals are used to garnish desserts.

Rose water (Arabic: *my warid; ma ward* in Morocco; *gül suyu* in Turkey),
or its more concentrated version, rose essence, is used in Indian and Middle
Eastern desserts such as fresh cheeseballs and *Lokum* (Turkish Delight). Rose
essence is known as *goolab* in India, *ayer mawar* in Malaysia, and *dok gulab* in
Thailand. The use of rose essence, like that of cloves and cinnamon, indicates
the influence of Indian cuisine on the cooking of Thailand. Dried rosebuds
are sometimes included in the Middle Eastern spice blend called *ras el hanout*.

They also appear in the Moroccan version of the classic French seasoning *quatre épices,* although they are not included in the original French mixture. Dried rose petals are among the ingredients in the Iraqi spice blend *boharat.*

At least three liqueurs are made from roses: Garnier's Crème de Roses, which also contains citrus elements and vanilla; *gul,* a Turkish elixir, similar to Crème de Roses; and a Greek version that also contains lemon. For a more potent, unsweetened spirit, look to the Italian grappa alla rosa. Oil of rose is an ingredient in Morello Ratafia. It, or rose water, is also used in some anisettes. French liqueurs have been made with roses: L'Huile de Roses and Parfait Amour. Shimpovka is a sparkling rose (not *rosé*) wine enjoyed in Siberia.

The petals can add their heady scent to honey. In Greece, honey is made by bees foraging among wild roses. A more intensely perfumed product (*gulangabin*) can be made by pouring heated honey over rose petals, steeping for two minutes, then straining the mixture. Alternatively, you could add rose water to honey and then reduce the mixture back to the original viscosity of the honey. Roses are sometimes added to mead.

Black tea is perfumed with rose blossoms in Japan. In China, a rose variety, called *tsing moi gui hwa,* is used the same way. In Shanghai, fried fish and preserved tofu is served with a rose-scented sauce. In Suzhou, a candy is made using rose petals. It has a soft, cotton-candy interior and a pink, rose-perfumed exterior.

In Germany, the leaves of *Rosa villosa* are infused to make *Deutscher Tee.*

Sweet herb vinegars flavored with roses can turn a simple fruit salad into an exotic treat. Rose syrup would be a pleasant accompaniment to custards and delicate puddings, a coeur à la créme, perhaps?

Rose hips (called "heps" or "haws" in some old books) are tart, acidic fruits that are useful for teas, jellies, and preserves. They are very high in vitamin C. Dog rose, *Rosa canina,* is an especially good source of hips for such culinary uses.

In Sweden, a cold soup called *nyponsoppa* is made with rose hips, water, sugar, and sometimes a little Madeira. It is thickened with potato starch and garnished with whipped cream and slivers of blanched almonds.

The flower's culinary features are provided by citronellol, damascenone, eugenol, geraniol, nerol, and phenyl ethyl alcohol.

OTHER USES

Potpourris, sachets, perfumes (attar of roses). Candles, soaps and, of course, incense are perfumed with roses.

COMMENTS

When preparing roses for use in any dish, wash carefully; in all likelihood the plants have been heavily sprayed with chemicals since insects love roses as much as we do. Blot on paper (or absorbent cotton) towels to remove excess moisture; you don't want to dilute the flavor and scent unnecessarily. Petals need to be trimmed before use as food. The heel (the greenish white

base of the petal) is unpleasantly bitter and must be clipped away with a pair
of sharp scissors.

Sloe: *Prunus spinosa*

OTHER COMMON, ETHNIC, OR SCIENTIFIC NAMES
Blackthorn
France: Prunellia
Germany: Schwarzdorn
Italy: Prugnolo
Mexico: Endrina
Spain: Bruniero

CULTIVARS
'Atropurpurea', 'Purpurea'

RELATED SPECIES
Prunus dulcis (also known as *Prunus amygdalus*): Almendra dulce (Spain);
amande douce (France); amandel (Netherlands); amandel (South
Africa); amêndoa (Portugal); amêndoa doce (Portugal); amígdalo
(Greece); badam, badama, badami, badamshirin, badamo, bedamu,
bilati badam, vadumai (India); badum (Iran); bian tao, ku xing ren,
tian wei bian tao (China); cno ghreugach (Gaelic); harilik mandlipuu
(Estonia); karvasmanteli, manteli (Finland); lawz (Arabic); lozi
(Swahili); mandel (Sweden); Mandel, Süßmandel (Germany); mandla
(Iceland); mandorla dulce (Italy); Mangel (Germany) migdal (Poland);
mindal (Russia); vaadaam (Iran); zoete amandel (Netherlands);
almond, sweet almond
Prunus dulcis subs. *amara* (also known as *Prunus amygdalus* subs. *amara*):
Almendra amara (Spain); amande amère (France); amêndoa amarga
(Portugal); bittere amandel (Netherlands); bittermandel (Denmark);
Bittermandel (Germany); bittermandel (Sweden); gorkiy mindal
(Russia); mandorla amara (Italy); bitter almond
Prunus mahaleb (also known as *Cerasus mahaleb*): Cerezo de Santa Lucia
(Spain); cerisier mahaleb, cerisier de Sainte-Lucie (France); ciliegio
canino, ciliegio di Santa Lucia, pruno odoroso (Italy); Felsenkirsche,
Mahaleb-Kirsche, Türkische Kirsche, Türkische Weichsel
(Germany); habbul malan (Iran); mahlab (Arabic); tunda la mahaleb
(Swahili); veikselinkirsikka (Finland); vejksel (Sweden); wichsel,
weichselkers (Netherlands); weichselbaer (Denmark); English cherry,
perfumed cherry, mahaleb cherry, rock cherry, St. Lucie cherry

GROWTH HABITS
Shrub

Origin: Eurasia
Range: Temperate regions

Bitter, sour extracts of bark, berries, and flowers are used in heavily sweetened liqueurs, such as sloe gin.

Tejocote: *Crataegus pubescens*

OTHER COMMON, ETHNIC, OR SCIENTIFIC NAMES
Hawthorn berry. The term *spinée,* used in medieval cookbooks, referred to the flowers of *Crataegus* spp.

RELATED SPECIES
Crataegus Azarolus: Azarole, Naples medlar
Crataegus pentagyna: Chinese thornapple
Crataegus laevigata (sometimes listed as *Crataegus oxycantha*): English
  hawthorn, hawthorn, may tree, quick-set thorn, whitethorn
Crataegus monogyna: English hawthorn

GROWTH HABITS
Thorny shrub
Origin: Mexico
Range: Frost-free regions

CULINARY USES
The one-inch fruits are used in Mexican cooking. Flower buds of *Crataegus laevigata,* called "bread and cheese," are added to salads in Wales. The fruits are eaten stewed, in preserves, or in candies in many places in Asia, Europe, and North America.

Wild Strawberry: *Fragaria virginiana*

OTHER COMMON, ETHNIC, OR SCIENTIFIC NAMES
Common strawberry, Virginia strawberry
Finland: Metsämansikka
France: Frais du bois
Italy: Fragola
Russia: Zemlianika

RELATED SPECIES
Fragaria moschata: Hautbois strawberry (European domestic strawberry)
Fragaria rosacea: Fraises des bois (France); Rügen (Germany); Alpine
  strawberry

Fragaria vesca: Erdbeere (Germany); fragola (Italy); fraise (France); fraulera (Spain); fresa (Mexico); wood strawberry, sow-teat strawberry, woodland strawberry

HYBRIDS
Fragaria × Ananassa: Garden strawberry, cultivated strawberry

GROWTH HABITS
Perennial
Origin: Eastern North America
Range: Temperate regions

CULINARY USES
All ripe strawberries are wonderful, of course, but the wild strawberry outdoes them all. It is small, rarely achieving thumbnail size, and too fragile for commercial use. However, its flavor, perfume, and glowing color are unmatched by anything you can buy.

Obviously, you can use the fruit just as you would use commercially raised strawberries: fresh, with cream, in jams and jellies, in syrups, in cordials (consult a may wine recipe).

The leaves can be used in teas and as a seasoning in meat broths. The leaves, like those of other berries, are somewhat astringent. They don't taste a bit like their fruits.

OTHER USES
Dried leaves are used in potpourri.

COMMENTS
Strawberries cause allergic reactions in some people; wild strawberries are no different.

To sit in a large patch of ripe wild strawberries, their scent rising in the sunlit air, is to understand why the ancients equated intoxication with divinity. You *may* succeed in picking enough to take some home; if so, you can make better strawberry preserves than you can possibly imagine. More likely, you will eat every berry that you find. It will not be time spent unprofitably.

83. Rubiaceae: The Madder Family

Cinchona: *Cinchona officinalis*

OTHER COMMON, ETHNIC, OR SCIENTIFIC NAMES
Calisaya, cardinal's bark, fever tree, Jesuit's bark, Jesuit's powder, Peruvian bark, quinine. Also known scientifically as *Cinchona calysaya*. The archaic apothecary name was *Cortex Chinae*.

France: Quinauina, quinquing
Germany: China Rinde, Chinarindenbaum
Italy: China
Mexico: Quina
Spain: Quina

RELATED SPECIES
Cinchona micrantha: Huanuco
Cinchona pubescens (formerly known as *Cinchona succirubra*): Quina roja
    (Mexico); cinchona bark, Jesuit's powder, Peruvian bark, red bark, red
    cinchona
Pausinystalia johimbe: Yohimbe

GROWTH HABITS
Evergreen tropical tree
Origin: Andes
Range: India, Java, and Sri Lanka

CULINARY USES
Used to flavor bitters and mixers such as tonic water, bitter lemon, and
Schweppes bitter orange (unfortunately, the latter is not available in the
United States). Extracts from the bark of *Cinchona pubescens* are used in fla-
vorings for commercial baked goods, condiments, ice cream, and mixers like
those mentioned above.

The extract also shows up in some recipes for Campari and Fernet Branca,
as well as some gins, vermouths, vodkas, and wines. Calisay is a sweet Spanish liqueur flavored with cinchona.

All cinchonas gets their bitter qualities from two sources: quinine (actually about thirty quinine-like alkaloids) and tannic acid. They are all used as
commercial sources of quinine. Yohimbe's bitter astringent taste is due to
quebrachine, tannins, and the alkaloid yohimbine.

Coffee: *Coffea arabica*

OTHER COMMON, ETHNIC, OR SCIENTIFIC NAMES
East Timor: Kafe arabica, kafe tropica
France: Café
Germany: Kaffe
Indonesia: Kopi
Italy: Caffe

CULTIVARS
'Bourbon Vermelho', 'Caturra', 'Columnaris', 'Erecta', 'Excelsis', 'Kona',
'Mundo Novo', 'Nana', 'Yellow'

Varieties: 'Antigua', 'Costa Rica', 'Java', 'Kenya, 'Mocha Mattari',
'Sumatra', 'Yergacheffe'

RELATED SPECIES
Coffea canephora (formerly known as *Coffea robusta*): Quillow coffee,
robusta coffee, wild robusta coffee
Coffea liberica: Liberian coffee
Coffea racemosa: Inhambane coffee
Coffea stenophylla: Highland coffee, Sierra Leone coffee
Coffea zanguebariae: Zanzibar coffee

GROWTH HABITS
Tropical Shrub
Origin: Tropical Africa
Range: Mountainous tropical areas around the world

CULINARY USES
Coffee beans are used as to make a beverage everywhere. The best coffees
are all made from *Coffea arabica* beans. Virtually all the coffee sold in cans
in the United States—and certainly all the instant coffee—is not made from
Coffea arabica but from *Coffea canephora.* This so-called robusta coffee is inferior in flavor and aroma, but it contains more caffeine. The other species
listed (with the possible exception of *Coffea stenophylla*) above are inferior
even to *Coffea canephora.*

In many places, especially those with Arabic-speaking populations, coffee is flavored with a variety of herbs and spices, as is noted elsewhere in this
book. In recent years, it has become common practice to produce "gourmet"
coffees with commercial (mostly artificial) flavorings. After the beans are
roasted, these essential oils are merely dumped in on top of the warm beans
and the mixture is stirred until the beans are uniformly coated. This "air-
freshener" approach seems to be intended for people who simply don't like
the taste of coffee. Needless to say, there is little point in using high-quality
arabica beans for such coffees.

Likewise, dark-roasted beans—espresso, French roast, Hispanic roasts
such as *cafe bustelo,* and Vienna roast—do not require the finest beans; the
ethereal aromas of kona or Jamaican blue mountain are simply volatilized
by the additional heat of dark roasting. By the way, some of the caffeine is
also lost during this extra roasting, but espresso still contains a high level of
caffeine, because the extraction of caffeine is more complete in an espresso
machine than in other coffee makers.

On the other hand, if a jolt to the nervous system is what you crave, you
might want to try making a tea from the leaves of *Coffea* species. The foliage
contains much more caffeine than the beans. In some areas where *Coffea
arabica* is grown, the bright red fruit (the part that surrounds the beans) is

chewed for a little acceleration. Of course, those same Andeans who use it this way regularly chew the leaves of *Erythroxilum coca*.

Coffee is also a flavoring in its own right. It is combined with chocolate to form the misnamed mocha. Coffee extracts are used in candies, baked goods, ice creams, soft drinks, and yogurts. Liqueurs, such as Kahlua, are flavored with coffee. Russians also enjoy okhotnichya—hunter's brandy—a warming concoction consisting of alcohol, coffee, and other flavorings (see glossary).

Strong coffee is sometimes added to tomato sauces to add complexity.

In Burgundy, a small smoky-tasting cheese called Laumes is rinsed with coffee as part of its curing process.

Coffee blossoms contain a fragrant nectar that yields an especially charming honey. It is often combined with orange-blossom honey—a nice conceit for breakfast.

When coffee beans are prepared, the seeds must be removed from the outer berry. This can be accomplished in two primary ways: wet or dry. The wet method generally removes the flesh of the berry before the curing process begins. In the dry method, the fleshy part of the berries is allowed to dry first, while the beans cure, before being scraped off by various means. In Yemen, these dried husks are removed but not discarded. They are boiled with spices and sugar to make a beverage called *quishr*.

There is one more, unconfirmed, method for removing the fleshy fruit from coffee beans. In Indonesia, the common palm civet, *Paradoxurus hermaphroditus,* is said to feed on only the ripest berries of the coffee trees. As the story goes, the beans pass through the animal's digestive tract intact, but fermentation and digestive enzymes are said to infuse beans with exceptionally rich flavor and aroma. Allegedly, the animal tends to leave its droppings in the same place, again and again, which makes it easy for the local natives to collect the processed beans. This coffee, *luwak* or *kopi luwak,* is quite rare (as few as five hundred pounds are produced annually) and understandably expensive, selling in the United States for as much as three hundred dollars per pound. There is, however, some disagreement among experts on whether or not *any* portion of this story—except, of course, for the high price of the beans—is true.

Gardenia: *Gardenia jasminoides*

OTHER COMMON, ETHNIC, OR SCIENTIFIC NAMES
Cape jasmine
Germany: Gardenie
China: Zhi-zi

CULTIVARS
'Fortuniana', 'Prostrata'

GROWTH HABITS
Evergreen shrub
Origin: China
Range: Frost-free areas

CULINARY USES
The flowers are used to flavor black teas. They have a scent like oranges and grapes, and a bittersweet, flowery flavor, like that of jasmine. The fruits provide a yellow food coloring in China.

Gardenia brasilensis and *Gardenia gummifera* are said to produce edible fruit. Gardenias contain benzyl acetate, linalool, and methyl anthranilate.

Kasembukan: *Paederia foetida*

OTHER COMMON, ETHNIC, OR SCIENTIFIC NAMES
Skunk vine
India: Nirgundi, pasaruni

GROWTH HABITS
Perennial vine
Origin: South Asia
Range: Invasive weed in Hawaii, Florida, and Texas

CULINARY USES
In combination with chiles and grated coconut, kasembukan is eaten as an accompaniment to white rice. The leaves are used as a potherb and as a seasoning for soups and vegetables.

COMMENTS
Foetida, as you might guess, comes from the Latin word for hideously ugly filth, the implication being that the stuff *smells.* The common name "skunk vine" should be another clue. Asafoetida (q.v.) shares this excremental reek. Fortunately, both plants lose their unpleasantness when they are cooked.

Woodruff: *Galium odoratum*

OTHER COMMON, ETHNIC, OR SCIENTIFIC NAMES
Bedstraw, cleavers, gosling grass, wuderove, wude-rova. Woodruff is sometimes seen listed in old botanical texts as *Asperula odorata,* as well as *Galium aparine.*

France: Aspérule odorante, muge de bois, muget de bois
Germany: Waldmeister
Italy: Asperula, stellina odorosa
Spain: Asperula

  Galium verum: Cheese rennet, cheese renning, lady's bedstraw, maid's
    hair, petty mugget, yellow bedstraw

GROWTH HABITS
  Perennial
  Origin: Mediterranean region
  Range: Temperate regions

CULINARY USES
  The dried leaves are used in herbal teas. The classic use for woodruff is as
the flavoring for may wine, but it also appears in a German digestif.
  Woodruff has a sweet aromatic scent that resembles a mix of violets and
tobacco, plus a strong whiff of new-mown hay that develops only after the
herb is dried. Woodruff contains citric acid, coumarin, and malic acid.
  Lady's bedstraw, *Galium verum,* is used as a dyestuff and formerly was used
to curdle and color milk in making cheeses (before rennet and annatto came
into use), especially Cheshire and Gloucester.

OTHER USES
  Dried leaves appear in potpourri and snuff. The dried herb is also used,
like lavender, to perfume bed linens. Dried roots used in vegetable dying,
yielding a characteristic red color.

COMMENTS
  Used dried leaves only; fresh leaves have no scent. Because of its coumarin
content, the FDA restricts the use of woodruff to alcoholic beverages.

84. Rutaceae: The Rue Family

Angostura: *Cusparia trifoliata*

OTHER COMMON, ETHNIC, OR SCIENTIFIC NAMES
  Its earlier botanical classification, now outdated, was *Galipea officinalis.*

RELATED SPECIES
  Cusparia febrifuga: Angostura
  Cusparia officinalis: Angostura

GROWTH HABITS
  Tropical tree
  Origin: Brazil
  Range: Tropical South America

CULINARY USES

Angostura is supposedly used to add a deep red color and bitter flavor to herbal liqueurs (digestifs); see Comments, below.

Angostura derives its aroma from cadinene, cusparine, galipene, galipol, and pinene and its bitter flavor from angosturin.

COMMENTS

The famous Angostura Bitters doesn't contain any angostura at all. It did at one time, but during the nineteenth century, rumors of contamination of angostura bark with the bark of strychnine, *Strychnos nux-vomica,* led to its reformulation. The story is similar to that of Pernod (see MUG-WORT). The bark of angostura is still used in some recipes for other bitters.

Bitter Orange: *Citrus Aurantium* subs. *Bergamia*

OTHER COMMON, ETHNIC, OR SCIENTIFIC NAMES

Bergamot, daidai, petitgrain. *Petigrain Bergamotte,* in old herbal texts, referred only to the leaves of the plant, while *Pericarpium Bergamottae* meant the peel of the fruit. Many members of the *Citrus* genus have been grouped and ungrouped botanically several times. It is not unusual to find this species listed as *Citrus bergamia.*

Arabic: Lemun adalya barnati, zahr
Burma/Myanmar: Shonsi, thanbaya
Denmark: Appelsin
Estonia: Apelsinipuu, bergamotipuu
Finland: Bergamotti
France: Bergamotte, bergamottier
Germany: Bergamotte, Sinessappel
Greece: Portokalí
Hawaii: Calamansi (calomondins)
Hungary: Narancs
Iceland: Appelsína, beiskjuappelsína, glóaldin
India: Dodan, kamala, kamala-tenga, kittile, narangam, narakam, naranga, narangi, naranji, sangtra, santra
Italy: Bergamotto
Netherlands: Bergamot, bergamot sinaasappel, bittere sinaasappel, oranje-appel
Norway: Appelsin
Romania: Portocală
Russia: Bergamot
Spain: Bergamota, cedro
Swahili: Chungwa

'Amar': Arancio amaro, arancio forte (Italy); burtuqual (Arabic); cheng, jin qiu, suan cheng (China); bigarad (Russia); Bitterorange, Pomeranze (Germany); bigarde, naranja agria, naranja amarga (Spain); bigaradier, bigarde, orange amère (France); daidai (Japan); daudang (Vietnam); hapanappelsiini, pomeranssi (Finland); pomeranets (Russia); pomerantsipuu (Estonia); som kliang (Thailand); bitter orange, sevilla orange, seville orange, sour orange

'Sinensis' (formerly known to apothecaries as *Pericarpium Aurantii* or *Cortex Aurantii fructus dulcis* and sometimes listed botanically as *Citrus sinensis*): Apelsin (Sweden); Apfelsine (Germany); apjelsin (Russia); appelsien, sinaasappel (Netherlands); appelsiini (Finland); arancia, arancia dulce (Italy); cam (Vietnam); guang gan, tian cheng (China); jeruk, jeruk manis (Indonesia); jeruk, jeruk manis (Malaysia); laranja (Portugal); nagaaruka (India); naranja, naranja china, naranja dulce (Spain); naranshi (Arabic); orange douce (France); orenji (Japan); sabraka (East Timor); som (Thailand); tapuz (Israel); blood orange or pigmented orange, China orange, sweet orange

RELATED SPECIES

Citrus reticulata: Mandarin orange, tangerine
Poncirus trifoliata: Bitter orange, hardy orange, trifoliate orange

HYBRIDS

Citrus × Citrofortunella 'Mitus': Kalamansi (Philippines); calamondin, calamansi

GROWTH HABITS

Evergreen shrub or tree
Origin: Vietnam
Range: Mediterranean region

CULINARY USES

Oil of bergamot is best known for creating the mysteriously spicy, flower-like scent of Earl Grey tea. The dried peel, along with cloves, is used to flavor other black tea blends, such as Constant Comment. It is also a good garnish for chicken and fish.

Tiny immature fruits of bergamots and calamondins are pickled in salt or vinegar. They are sometimes fried in coconut oil. Ripe fruits are served in Mexico with a paste of salt and minced chiles.

The peels of bitter orange are used in altvater, amaretto, gin, and Grand Marnier. Peels of sweet oranges are used in altvater, amaretto, anisette, yellow Chartreuse, gin, Grand Marnier, and Kümmel. Bitter orange, both fruit and peel, is used in Angostura Bitters and Campari. Both Valencia (sweet) and Spanish (bitter) orange peels are components of Benedictine.

Oils extracted from sweet and bitter oranges, as well as from lemons, are part of the complex flavor of Chartreuse. Russian okhotnichya—hunter's brandy—is a warming concoction consisting of alcohol, various citrus peels, and other flavorings (see glossary). Altvater adds unripe fruit to its complex mixture of herbs and citrus elements.

The juice of bitter orange is the foundation of *mojo criollo,* a Cuban marinade for pork containing bay leaves, cumin, garlic, and oregano. In Mexico, it is used to marinate grilled fish or, combined with cilantro and chile, poultry.

Bergamot, in the form of neroli oil, is used in akavit, anisette, Benedictine, Fernet Branca, and, at one time, absinthe.

Grand Marnier out-oranges all the other liqueurs. It contains all the oranges and lemons above, plus Curaçao orange peel and orange blossoms. Cointreau's formula is thought to be very similar. Curaçao orange peel also shows up in the formulas for altvater, amaretto, and Fernet Branca.

Flowers of this plant are used to make orange flower water, *zhaar,* in Morocco. They also appear in some recipes for anisette, Grand Marnier, and Kümmel.

Bergamot fruit gets its characteristic bitter citrus flavor and scent from bisabolene, limonene, linalool, linalyl acetate, pinene, and terpineol. Bergamot leaves contain, primarily, linalyl acetate. The flowers (neroli), like other orange blossoms, contain geraniol, linalool, linalyl acetate, methyl anthranilate, nerol, and phenyl ethyl alcohol. They have, in addition to the expected orange blossom scent, a bitter, clove-like quality.

The dried fruits of *Poncirus trifoliata* are used in China as a seasoning, while dried tangerine peel is known as *chin pei* or *gom pei* in that country. Orange-flavored preserves and wine are made from the fresh fruit of *Poncirus trifoliata* in China and Japan.

Petitgrain, the leaves and young shoots of bergamot, contain geraniol, linalool, linalyl acetate, and methyl anthranilate. Petitgrain is used by some distillers of gin. Petitgrain oil is also an ingredient in Chartreuse.

Aside from the well-known fruit, the peel of Mandarin orange, *Citrus reticulata,* is dried and used as a seasoning in China and Vietnam. It is known as *chen pi* in China.

The calamondin, *Citrus × Citrofortunella mitus,* is a very acid fruit, excellent for use in marmalades and "orange" soft drinks (ades); make sure to add plenty of sugar. The juice is used like lemon juice in Hawaii. In the Philippines, the juice is one of many sour ingredients that are part of the "signature" of the country's cuisine (much as lemon and oregano are in Greece).

The fragrant peels of sweet oranges contain citral and limonene, while their pith is bitter because of glycosides and rutin.

OTHER USES

Oil of bergamot is used in the manufacture of perfumes.

Bergamot is not related in any way to wild bergamot (q.v.).

The bergamot orange, *Citrus aurantifolium* subs. *aurantium,* seen in Florida and California is not this subspecies, but 'Bouquet', another cultivar of bitter orange. Bergamot orange is hardier than many species of sweet orange and frequently escapes wherever its preferred environment exists. Since it likes fresh-water shorelines and deep heavy soils, more wild bitter oranges are found in Florida than California.

Other common names for 'Bouquet' are bigarade (France), Seville orange and sour orange, Bitterorange (Germany), taronja amarga (Catalonian region of Spain), nerántzi (Greece), and arancio amaro (Italy). It is a source of neroli oil but is better known for its use in marmalades.

Boronia: *Boronia megastigma*

OTHER COMMON, ETHNIC, OR SCIENTIFIC NAMES
Brown boronia, scented boronia

CULTIVARS
'Harlequin', 'Heaven Scent', 'Jack McGuires Red', 'Lutea', 'Royale'

GROWTH HABITS
Evergreen shrub
Origin: Southwestern Australia
Range: Grown commercially in California

CULINARY USES
Boronia flowers are violet scented. The essential oil, *Boronia Absolute,* is said to smell of cinnamon, black currants, and tobacco. It is used in commercial flavorings for baked goods, candies, ice creams, and soft drinks.

Boronia contains β-Ionone, ethyl formate, geranyl acetate, linalool, and linalyl acetate.

OTHER USES
Used in the manufacture of perfumes.

Buchu Leaves: *Agathosma betulina*

OTHER COMMON, ETHNIC, OR SCIENTIFIC NAMES
Borosma. Buchu was formerly known scientifically as *Agathosma crenulata* and *Barosma Betulina.*
France: Bucco
Germany: Bukku

Italy: Bucco
Spain: Buch

RELATED SPECIES
Agathosma crenulata: Oval buchu

GROWTH HABITS
Perennial
Origin: South Africa
Range: Temperate regions

CULINARY USES
The leaves of both species of buchu flavor brandies in Tunisia and wines in South Africa. The leaves are the source of an essential oil used in the flavoring of commercial baked goods, beverages, candy, and condiments. The oil is said to have a scent reminiscent of camphor and peppermint (or, according to another source, a sweet scent and a bitter, rue-like taste).

Citron: *Citrus medica*

OTHER COMMON, ETHNIC, OR SCIENTIFIC NAMES
Cedar apple, median apple
Arabic: Utrujj
China: Ju yuan
Finland: Sukaattisitruuna
France: Cédrat
Germany: Zitronat-Zitrone, Zitrone
Greece: Kitron
Hungary: Citromsárga
Israel: Etrog
Indonesia: Jeruk bodong
Italy: Cedrata
Japan: Yuzu
Philippines: Cidra
Portugal: Cidra
Romania. Chitru, citra
Russia: Sladkiy limon, tsitron
Spain: Acitrón, cidra
Sri Lanka: Cidran
Thailand: Som mu, som saa
Turkey: Agaçkavunu

CULTIVARS
'Arcodactyla': Bushukan (Japan); Buddha's hand
'Ethrog': Etrog

Evergreen tropical shrub
Origin: India
Range: Cultivated in Mediterranean region, Southeast Asia, and the
West Indies. Sometimes planted in California and Florida.

CULINARY USES

True citron, *Citrus medica,* is an evergreen tree related to oranges and lemons. It comes in two basic varieties: sweet-fleshed cultivars, like 'Diamante', and sour-fleshed cultivars of the Corsican type. The thick rind is the only part used as preserved fruit. *Citrus medica* 'Bigarradia' is Italian bergamot (see BERGAMOT). *Citrus medica* subs. *limetta* is used as citron in a number of Asian cuisines. It is known as *jeruk bodong,* or *jeruk sekade,* in Indonesia; *yuzu,* in Japan; and *som saa,* in Thailand (see also CITRUS LEAVES).

Citron is familiar as the candied "fruit" in fruitcakes. Commercially, it is almost always dyed an unnatural red or a somewhat unsettling shade of green. It appears in many other baked goods as well as the occasional salad (see Comments, below).

An Italian lemonade-like beverage, called *acquacedrata,* is made from this fruit. *Citrus medica* is used in at least two liqueurs, Cédratine and Kitrinos.

COMMENTS

Most commercial "candied citron" is actually preserving melon, *Citrullis lanatus* 'Citroides', a cultivar of watermelon, grown for its thick, firm flesh. It is an annual member of the Cucurbitaceae that originated in tropical Africa and South Africa.

Citrus Leaves: *Citrus hystrix*

OTHER COMMON, ETHNIC, OR SCIENTIFIC NAMES

Double leaf lime, ghost's lime, ichang lime, Kaffir lime leaves, leech lime, wild lime. Also known as *Citrus papedia.*
Burma/Myanmar: Shauk-nu, shauk-waing
Cambodia: Krauch soeuch, kraunch soeuth
China: Fatt-fung-kam, suan gan yet
Denmark: Kaffir lime
France: Combava, limettier hérissé
Germany: Indische Zitronenblätter, Indonesische Zitronenblätter,
Kaffirlimette, Kaffernlimette, Kaffirzitrone
Indonesia: Daun jeruk perut, djeruk perut, jeruk perut, jeruk sambal
Malaysia: Daun limau purut, limau purut
Netherlands: Djeroek poeroet, Kaffir limoen
Philippines: Swangi
Singapore: Daun limau purut, limau purut

Sri Lanka: Kahpiri dehi, kudala-dehi, odu dehi
Thailand: Bai makrut, ma krut, makrut, som makrut
Vietnam: Chanh sac, truc

CULTIVARS AND RELATED SPECIES
Citrus amblycarpa: Leprous lime
Citrus microcarpa (also listed as *Citrus mitis*): Dayap (Philippines); limau
   kesturi (Malaysia and Singapore); kalamansi

GROWTH HABITS
Evergreen shrubs and small trees
Origin: Southeast Asia
Range: Frost-free areas all over the world

CULINARY USES
The leaves flavor curries and soups—particularly those containing fish—all over Southeast Asia, especially Thailand and Laos. In Indonesia, finely chopped lime leaves are served with roasted meats, often in combination with chile pastes. Lime leaves are an ingredient in *kecap.* The herb is available in the United States as dried leaves or a powder, although the leaves are the preferred choice. Where it grows, the plant is used both fresh and dried. The fruit rind is dried and candied or ground and added to curry pastes.

Dayap, *Citrus microcarpa,* a tiny fruit about three-eighths of an inch in diameter, is prized for its sour flavor. In the Philippines it is added to curries and pickles or used as a garnish, to be squeezed over fried noodles.

COMMENTS
Another ichang lemon is a cultivar of *Citrus ichagensis.* It is known as *hsiang yuan,* or *shangyuan,* in China.

Curry Leaves: *Murraya Koenigii*

OTHER COMMON, ETHNIC, OR SCIENTIFIC NAMES
Curry pak, Indian bay leaf, orange jessamine. Curry leaves are sometimes listed botanically as *Bergera Koenigii* or *Chalcas Koenigii.*
Burma/Myanmar: Pindosin, pyi-naw-thein, pyin daw thein
France: Caloupilé, feuilles de cari
Germany: Curryblätter, Indonesische Lorbeerblatt
Iceland: Karrílauf
India: Baisoppu, barsunga, basango, bowala, cariya patta, curry veppila,
   girinimba, kareapela, karepeku, karipat, karivepaku, katneem,
   karapincha, kariveppilai, karivepaku, kariyappila, kitha neem, meetha
   neem, suravi
Indonesia: Daun kari pla, daun salaam, karupillam
Italy: Fogli di cari

Laos: Dok kibe
Malaysia: Daun kari, karupilay
Netherlands: Kerriebladeren
Réunion: Caloupilé
Spain: Hoja
Sri Lanka: Karapincha
Swahili: Bizari, mchuzi
Thailand: Bai karee, hom kaek

RELATED SPECIES
Murraya exotica: Azahar de la india, azahar de la novia, jasmin de arabica, jazmin, mirto (Panama); Chinese box, satinwood
Murraya paniculata (formerly listed as *Citrus paniculata*): Orange jasmine, orange jessamine, satinwood, cosmetic-bark tree
Veppu maram: Neem

GROWTH HABITS
Tropical shrub
Origin: Southeast Asia; southern India, Sri Lanka
Range: Frost-free areas

CULINARY USES
These pungent aromatic leaves are found in Thai, Indian, and Indonesian "curries," as well as in chutneys and Indian pickles. The leaves are sometimes fried in the oil or ghee that is to be used in cooking, to flavor it, much as garlic or annatto is used. Curry leaves are sometimes ground together with chile, coriander seed, garlic, ginger, and lemongrass to make a curry paste. Cassia leaves can be used in their place.

Murraya exotica is said to produce edible fruits—with a peppery flavor—that are eaten in India.

Curry leaves get their curious tangerine-like aroma from essential oils containing β-caryophyllene (2.6 ppm), β-gurjunene (1.9 ppm), β-elemene (.6 ppm), β-phellandrene (.5 ppm), β-thujone (.4 ppm), and other aromatic compounds.

COMMENTS
The leaves lose their fragrance quickly when dried; if at all possible, use the leaves fresh.

"Curry leaf" is used as a name for members of several different genera, including *Helichrysum, Ocimum,* and *Pandanus.* "Indonesische Lorbeerblatt" and "Indian bay leaf" are also names for the unrelated *Cinnamomum tamala.*

False Dittany: *Dictamnus albus*

OTHER COMMON, ETHNIC, OR SCIENTIFIC NAMES
Burning bush, dittany, fraxinella, gas plant, white dittany

France: Dictame, fraxinelle
Germany: Aschwurz, Weisser Diptam
Italy: Dittamo
Spain: Dictam blanco

CULTIVARS
'Purpureus', 'Roseus', 'Ruber'

GROWTH HABITS
Perennial
Origin: Southern Europe to northern China
Range: Temperate regions

CULINARY USES
Dried leaves have been used as an aromatic, lemony herbal tea. Tea made from the cultivar 'Roseus' is said to taste more like almond and vanilla.

Roots and bark yield an extract that is used in the production of some aperitifs (see Comments, below).

OTHER USES
Lemon-scented extract from false dittany is used in the perfume industry.

COMMENTS
Do not confuse this with other plants named dittany, such as dittany, *Cunila origanoides* (q.v.) and dittany of Crete, *Origanum Dictamnus* (q.v.). The FDA restricts the use of *Cunila origanoides* to alcoholic beverages.

Jambol: *Acronychia laurifolia*

GROWTH HABITS
Tree
Origin: Tropical Asia
Range: Tropical Asia. One species, *Acronychia Baueri,* is grown in California.

CULINARY USES
In China, the young cumin-scented leaves of *Acronychia laurifolia* are eaten raw. This is unusual, as the Chinese do not have a tradition of eating salads. In Sri Lanka, the berries (also called "jambol") are eaten.

Lemon: *Citrus Limon*

OTHER COMMON, ETHNIC, OR SCIENTIFIC NAMES
Citronnier, leemoo, neemoo. Old apothecary's Latin names for lemon peel were *Cortex Citri Fructus, Limonis Cortex,* or *Pericarpium Citri.* The oil

was known as *Oleum Limonis.* The plant is also seen in some botanical texts as *Citrus medica* subs. *limonum.*

Arabic: Hamod, lemun, turung
Brazil: Limão
Burma/Myanmar: Shauktakera
China: Gou yuan, ning meng, xiang yuann, zhi qiao
Denmark: Citron
Estonia: Harilik sidrunipuu, näsaviljaline sidrunipuu
Finland: Limetti, sitruuna, sukaatti
France: Cédrat, citron, poncire commun
Germany: Limone, Sitroen, Zedrate, Zitronatszitrone, Zitrone
Greece: Lemóni, lemónia
Hungary: Zitrom
Iceland: Sítróna, skrápsítróna
India: Bijaura, cherunarakam, elimichcham, galgal, gilam, nebu, neebu, nimbu, nimmapandu, lembu, ruchaka, sedaran, sidalai, vijapura
Indonesia: Jeruk bodong, jeruk limon, jeruk nipis, jeruk sekade
Iran: Limun amadi, vaadrang
Israel: Etrog
Italy: Cedro, limone
Japan: Maru busshukan, remon, shitoron, yuzu
Malaysia: Jeruk asem, limao, limao nipis
Netherlands: Citroen, muskuscitroen
Poland: Cytryna
Portugal: Limão
Romania: Lámâie
Russia: Sladkiy limon, tsedrat, tsitron
Spain: Cidra, ethrog, limón
Swahili: Limau
Sweden: Citron
Thailand: Manao farang, ma nao leumg, som saa
Vietnam: Chanh tay, trai chanh

CULTIVARS
'Eureka', 'Lisbon', 'Meyer', 'Ponderosa', 'Rough', 'Villafranca'

RELATED SPECIES
Citrus aurantiifolia: Apog, dayap (Philippines); chanh ta (Vietnam); dehi (Sri Lanka); hapu laimipuu (Estonia); djeruk nipis, jeruk nipis (Indonesia); kagadi, kagji-nebu, nemu-tenga, nimboo (India); lai meng (China); lajm, lajm nastoyaschiy (Russia); lima acida, limão gelego (Portugal); lima, limetta (Italy); lima, limón agria (Spain); limau kesturi, limau nipis (Malaysia); limette, limette acide, limettier, limon (France); Limette, Limone (Germany); limetti (Finland);

limoen (Netherlands); límóna (Iceland); ma nao (Thailand); mexicano (Mexico); ndimu (Swahili); noomy basrah (Arabic); Basrah lemon, key lime, Mexican lime, Oman lemon, West Indian lime

Citrus latifolia: Bearss, Tahitian, or Persian limes

Citrus medica: Cultivar 'Bigarradia' is Italian bergamot (see CITRON).

Citrus microcarpa: Dayap (Philippines); limau kesturi (Malaysia)

Citrofortunella mitis: Kalamansi (Philippines); kalamondiinipuu (Estonia)

HYBRIDS

Citrus × spp.: Lavender Gem (alleged to be a cross between orange, grapefruit, and lemon)

Citrus × *amblycarpa:* Djeruk Limau (Indonesia)

Citrus × *junos:* Yuzu (Japan)

Citrus × *nobilis* (also known as *Citrus limettioides*): Limau manis (Malaysia), naran-kai (India), pani dodan (Sri Lanka), som khiew wan or som kleang (Thailand), sweet lime

GROWTH HABITS

Tropical evergreen tree

Origin: Southeast Asia

Range: Cultivated commercially in Italy and the United States (Florida and southern California)

CULINARY USES

As a fruit, the lemon is well known everywhere. As a flavoring, the colored part of the rind, or zest, is of interest in the context of this book. Lemon peel is used in a number of liqueurs: anisette, Benedictine, Fernet Branca, Grand Marnier, green Chartreuse, Liqueur d'Or, and some gins. Lemon peel was used in absinthe. In Russia, lemon-flavored vodka is known as Limonnaya. Ravello, Italy, produces Liquore di Limone, also known as Limoncello and as Profumi della Costiera (the perfume of the Amalfi coast). The liqueur has the clouded, slightly greenish look of lemon juice, but not the acidity; it has a sweetness from sugar, but its complexity suggests cinnamon or vanilla, although the only listed ingredients are alcohol, sugar, and lemon zest.

The cultivar 'Eureka' is the most commonly grown commercial lemon in California. 'Villafranca' makes up the primary lemon crop in Florida. Both of these lemons are thick skinned and quite sour. 'Meyer', however, is a golden, sweetly aromatic fruit, with a smooth skin and less bitter pith than the more common lemons. They are hardier also, growing well in home gardens in northern California or as potted plants in less forgiving climates.

The thin peel of a lemon, left in a jar of sugar, yields a lovely sugar for use in teas or as a coating for crystallized fruits or flowers.

The leaves have some use (see CITRUS LEAVES).

In Morocco, the fruits (*msir* or *citrons confits*) are preserved in salt and a mixture of spices that may include bay leaves, black pepper, cinnamon, and cloves. Moroccan Jews add olive oil. Preserved lemons are an indispensable element of the many-layered flavors of Moroccan food. Dried limes, called *limoo amoni* (Oman lemons), are a popular seasoning in Iran. In Iraq, they are known as *noumi basra*.

The juice of underripe djeruk limau, *Citrus × amblycarpa,* is used in Indonesia as a condiment. The leaves, like citrus leaves, are an ingredient in meat curries.

Juice and zest of yuzu, *Citrus × junos,* are used in Japan to flavor various soybean products, including *kinugoshi tofu, miso,* and *shoyu,* and made into a lemony vinegar that perfumes dishes like *chirinabé,* a soupy stew made with fish and tofu, simmered in a soy sauce and a citrus-flavored broth of *dashi* (the standard Japanese broth, flavored with dried bonito flakes and seaweed).

Lime zest is used in the Philippines to make a candy with milk and coconut. In India, pickled limes and lemons are made, using salt, chiles, mustard oil, and asafoetida; they are extremely sour, salty, and hot but are a delicious component of an Indian meal. Lime syrup (Rose's Lime Juice) adds an intriguing tartness to gin drinks such as gimlets.

Most of the limes seen in the United States are Bearss, Tahitian, or Persian limes (*Citrus latifolia*). The native limes, known as bartender's limes, key limes, Mexican limes, or West Indian limes, are smaller, with thinner skins and much less green color. Their flavor, however is much finer. It is unthinkable to use anything else for a key lime pie. *Please:* no green food coloring; true key lime pie is never green.

Lemon juice has little character besides sourness, derived from fruit acids and a bit of sugar; the characteristic flavors and scents of lemons reside in the peel. Lemon peel contains α-terpineol, citral, citronellal, d-geranyl acetate, lemon oil, limonene, and linalyl acetate. Bitterness and a slight sweetness are provided by glycosides and coumarin. Italian lemon peel can contain up to twice the citral of domestic lemon peel.

Limes are similar to lemons in their components, but they add bisabolene, fenchone, and terpineol and substitute dipentene and lime oil for the d-limonene and lemon oil.

OTHER USES

The commercial flavoring and scent industry uses the cedro oil derived from the peels in items such as soaps and air fresheners.

Lemon Aspen: *Acronychia acidula*

GROWTH HABITS
    Shrubby tree
    Origin: Australia
    Range: Australia, Indonesia, Pacific islands

Lemon aspen is somewhat misnamed, as the subtle citrus notes that characterize it are reminiscent of grapefruit and lime, not lemon. Like lemon myrtle and other citrus-scented herbs, this plant offers the freshness of citrus without the sour acidity of the fruits themselves. Lemon aspen combines well with cilantro.

Rue: *Ruta graveolens*

OTHER COMMON, ETHNIC, OR SCIENTIFIC NAMES

Herb-of-grace, herbygrass, mother-of-pearl herb. *Herba Rutae* is its old apothecary name.

China: Chow-cho, yun hsiang ts'ao
Costa Rica: Ruda
Denmark: Almindelig rude, rude
East Indies: Godong mungu
East Timor: Aruda
Estonia: Aedruud, ruud
Ethiopia: Tena adam
Finland: Ruuta, tuoksuruuta
France: Herbe d'grâce, la rue, rue des jardins, rue fétide, rue odorante
Germany: Raute, Weinkraut, Weinraute
Greece: Píganon
Holland: Wijnruit
Iceland: Rturunni
India: Aruda, arvada, ermul, maruya, sadabu, satapa, satari, sudah
Indonesia: Ubat atal
Iraq: Sdab
Italy: Ruta
Japan: Henruda
Malaysia: Aroda, aruda, sadal
Mexico: Ruda
Netherlands: Wijnruit
Norway: Ruta, vinrute
Poland: Ruta zwyczajna
Portugal: Arruda
Spain: Ruda
Sweden: Vinruta
Turkey: Bahce sedefotu (garden rue)
Wales: Gorddon, llysyr echryshaint, rhutain, rhyw, torwenwyn

CULTIVARS

'Divaricata', 'Variegata'

Ruta chalepensis: Egyptian rue
Ruta montana: Mountain rue

GROWTH HABITS
Evergreen shrubby perennial
Origin: Mediterranean region
Range: Cultivated in southern United States and Europe

CULINARY USES
Rue seeds have been used in cooking since at least the first century CE. They combine well with lovage and mint (q.v.). The seeds are often used in Ethiopian cookery.

The foliage has a bitter, somewhat musty taste, but that does not prevent its use, in minute quantities, with soft cheeses, chicken, eggs, fish, mushrooms, and potatoes. It is used in Scandinavian cooking, where the smallest imaginable amount adds a wild taste to marinades for beef, game, or lamb. Balancing the bitterness of rue with sweet fruit flavors, such as plum or apricot preserves, can yield a delicious glaze or sauce for rich meats, such as duck, goose, or pork.

Rue flavors vinegars and sometimes salads and vegetable stews. The leaves have been used in herbal teas.

In North Africa, a kind of palm wine called *laqmí,* or *legmi,* is flavored with the seeds (see DATE PALM). Rue seeds and/or leaves also flavor the Italian brandy called grappa alla ruta.

Egyptian rue, *Ruta chalepensis,* and mountain rue, *Ruta montana,* are rumored to have been used as condiments.

Rue contains rutin (up to 20,000 ppm), rutarin (up to 9,000 ppm), 2-undecalactone (up to 6,300 ppm), carotene (up to 950 ppm), and traces of many other flavoring compounds, as well as quercetin and quinoline alkaloids.

OTHER USES
Natural insecticide

COMMENTS
Some people develop an allergic reaction to rue merely by handling it. It can be toxic in large quantities, causing internal hemorrhaging. Its bitterness discourages overindulgence, but pregnant women should avoid eating even small amounts of rue.

"Wild rue" is a name used for *Peganum harmala,* which is also known as Syrian rue, esphand, harmal, and isband. This wild Moroccan plant (totally unrelated; it's part of the *Zygophyllaceae* family) is used as incense and is a source for the dye "Turkish red."

Szechuan Pepper: *Zanthoxylum piperitum*

Aniseed stars, ash berries, badiana, brown peppercorns, Chinese anise, Chinese aromatic pepper, Chinese pepper, flower pepper, Japan pepper, Japanese pepper, Japanese prickly ash, prickly ash, Sichuan pepper, spice pepper. The genus is sometimes misspelled *Xanthoxylum*. In some texts, the species is listed as *Pericarpium zanthoxyli*. The genus *Zanthoxylum* was formerly known as *Fagara*.

China: Faa jiu, fagara, hua jiao
Colombia: Amamor
England: Anise pepper
Estonia: Koldpuu, pipra-koldpuu
Finland: Anispippuri, setsuanin pippuri
Germany: Anispfeffer, Blütenpfeffer, Chinesischer Pfeffer,
    Gelbholzbaum, Szechuan-Pfeffer
Iceland: Sichuanpipar
Japan: Kinome (leaves), sanshô
Mexico: Palo mulato
Nepal: Timur
Panama: Alcabu
Sweden: Sezchuanpeppar
Tibet: Emma

RELATED SPECIES

Zanthoxylum Americanum (sometimes listed as *Zanthoxylum fraxineum*):
    Clavalier (France); frassinospinosa (Italy); Zahnwehgelbholz
    (Germany); northern prickly ash, prickly ash, suterberry, toothache
    tree, yellow wood
Zanthoxylum armatum (sometimes listed as *Zanthoxylum alatum*): Chinese
    pepper, winged prickly ash
Zanthoxylum avicenne (sometimes listed as *Zanthoxylum piperitum*): Sanshô
    (berries, Japan), kinome (young leaves, Japan)
Zanthoxylum beechianum (sometimes listed as *Zanthoxylum arnottianum*):
    Hire-sanshô (Japan); sanshô, sensu, sensuru-gii (Okinawa); prickly
    ash
Zanthoxylum fagara (sometimes listed as *Fagara rhetsa*): Correosa, Indian
    pepper, wild lime
Zanthoxylum rhetsa: Chirphal, kaatmurikku, kamte kai, teppal, tilfda,
    tirphal, tippal (India); timur (Nepal); Indian pepper, lemon pepper
Zanthoxylum sanshô: Japanischer Pfeffer (Germany); sanshô (Japan);
    English prickly ash, Japanese pepper, Japanese prickly ash

Small evergreen tree
Origin: Northern China, Korea, and Japan
Range: Frost-free regions

CULINARY USES

Before the discovery of the New World and its chiles, Szechuan pepper and black pepper, *Piper nigrum* (q.v.), were the only sources of heat in Szechuan cooking. An intriguing aspect of this "lack" is that both of the indigenous peppers possess rich, complex, aromatic qualities that are absent in members of the *Capsicum* genus.

Szechuan pepper has a minty, resinous quality and induces a curious, slight numbing of the tongue. It is interesting that English has no words that distinguish between "hot" (temperature) and "hot" (spicy). Chinese has words not only for these two qualities, but also for the numbing heat of Szechuan peppercorns. The absence of this pepper in Szechuan cooking leaves the food flat and lifeless, even if its heat level is maintained with chile.

The Chinese use the brown peppercorns in five spice, a mixture that adds a characteristic sweetness to many red-cooked dishes and to roast pork. Another Chinese spice mixture deletes cinnamon from five spice and adds cassia, chile, pepper, coriander seed, nutmeg, and turmeric. It sounds like a curry mixture, which suggests its use in southeastern China.

Sanshô, or the foliage of Szechuan pepper, is also known as pepper leaf. In Japan, the bark is used as a substitute for black pepper. Szechuan pepper is an ingredient in *shichimi* (seven spice mixture), along with black hemp seeds, chile (q.v.), Mandarin orange peel, nori (seaweed), poppy seeds (q.v.), and sesame seeds (q.v.), although some recipes substitute rape seed for poppy seed.

Szechuan pepper's aromatic qualities are found only in the reddish brown husk of the peppercorns. The fresher, better grades of Szechuan pepper are markedly brighter and redder than the cheaper grades. Some recipes call for the removal of the shiny dark seeds found inside the peppercorn, as they are said to impart an undesirable bitter taste to the finished dish.

Szechuan pepper is sometimes used as one of the ingredients in the Moroccan spice mixture called *ras el hanout.*

The young flowers and leaves, called *kinome,* are used as a garnish in Japan, either fresh or pickled in soy sauce. They are added to rice dishes, soba (buckwheat noodles), and soups. The leaves have a grassy citrus aroma due to their citronellal, citronellol, and z-3-hexanal content. *Tsukudani* are sanshô seeds that are pickled by cooking in shoyu and mirin (soy sauce and sweet rice wine).

The bark of Indian pepper, *Zanthoxylum fagara,* is used as a seasoning in Southeast Asia. It is said to have a peppery lime-like flavor. The leaves of that species flavor rice beer in Vietnam. The zest of its unripe fruit, with its orange-like aroma, is used as a spice, as are the ripened seeds, which have a hot, peppery lemon flavor.

Szechuan peppercorns derive their scent, at once flowery, lemony, and resinous, from cineol, citronellal, dipentene, geraniol, and linalool. Hydroxy-a-sanshool provides the numbing heat.

The closely related *Zanthoxylum rhetsa* is used in Indian dishes containing fish, appearing, like Szechuan pepper, as a condiment or last-minute garnish. Its flavor and scent are more resinous than the other species, however, due to the presence of limonene, *p*-cymene, pinene, sabinene, terpenene, and terpineols.

OTHER USES
Bark is used as incense in Japan.

COMMENTS
Zanthoxylum avicenne is not listed in *Hortus Third,* and sanshô and kinome are sometimes listed there as *Zanthoxylum piperitum.*

The common names and uses of plants named "ash" are sometimes confusing (see also PRICKLY ASH, *Aralia spinosa;* ASH, *Fraxinus excelsior;* and EUROPEAN MOUNTAIN ASH, *Sorbus aucuparia*).

85. Santalaceae: The Sandalwood Family

Sandalwood: *Santalum album*

OTHER COMMON, ETHNIC, OR SCIENTIFIC NAMES
Amyris, saunders. *Lignum santali album* is the name that flavor chemists use for sandalwood.
France: Bois de santal
Germany: Sandelholz
Italy: Sandalo, sandalo delle Inde Occidentale
Mexico: Sandalo
Spain: Sandalo

RELATED SPECIES
Fusanus acuminatus: Quandong nut
Osyrius tenuifolia: Sandalwood
Pterocarpus indicus: Burmese rosewood
Pterocarpus santalinus: Rotes Sandelholz (Germany); sandalo rosso (Italy); santalia (Spain); santal rouge (France); red sandalwood, red sanders, red saunders
Santalum spicatum: Sandalwood

GROWTH HABITS
Evergreen tree

Origin: India
Range: Cultivated in tropics, including Hawaii

CULINARY USES

The bitter-tasting but sweetly aromatic oil from the wood is used in India. It hints at the presence of cinnamon and vanilla. A small piece of the wood is put in a sachet with other flavorings and then infused in the syrup used with some desserts. It is said to be used in some liqueurs.

Sandalwood is a good coloring material, especially the red variety. It contains β-caryophellene, d-cadinene, santalin, santal, and pteracarpin. White sandalwood (*Santalum album*) contains santalol, borneol, citronellol, eugenol, and geraniol. It has a more resinous, cedar-like aroma than the red sandalwood.

OTHER USES

Sandalwood oil is used in candles, incense, perfumes, and soaps. *Osyrius tenuifolia* is an African source of sandalwood oil, while *Santalum spicatum* is its Australian equivalent.

This oil is also extracted from unrelated plants, such as *Amyris balsamifera,* in the order *Rutaceae.* This sandalwood substitute comes from Venezuela and the West Indies. Another sandalwood substitute, *Erythroxylum,* also from the order *Rutaceae,* grows in India.

The wood itself is used to make small chests, such as jewelry boxes. Sandalwood chips are used in potpourri.

COMMENTS

Another tropical tree is sometimes called sandalwood tree, as well as Barbados-pride, coral pea, coralwood, redwood, peacock flower fence, and red sandalwood tree. It is *Adenanthera pavonia,* a member of the *Leguminosae.* It has no culinary uses, though it does yield the dye called Indian red.

86. Sapindaceae: The Soapberry Family

Akee: *Blighia sapida*

OTHER COMMON, ETHNIC, OR SCIENTIFIC NAMES

Ishin, seso vegetal, vegetable brain. Sometimes listed botanically as *Cupania sapida.*
Brazil: Castanha, castanheiro de Africa
Colombia: Bien me sabe, pan y quesito
Costa Rica: Akí
Côte d'Ivoire: Finzan, kaka

Cuba: Arbol de seso, palo de seso
Guatemala: Fruto de huevo, huevo vegetal
Haiti: Arbre à fricasser, arbre fricassé
Martinique: Ris de veau, yeux de crabe
Mexico: Arbor del huevo, pera roja
Sudan: Finza
Venezuela: Merey del diablo

RELATED SPECIES
Blighia welwitscii: Ankyewobiri

GROWTH HABITS
Evergreen tree
Origin: Tropical west Africa
Range: Africa, Caribbean, India, Philippines, South America

CULINARY USES
African cooks fry the arils (the mace-like covering of the seeds) and then add them to soups as a garnish. In the Caribbean, the arils are first par-boiled, then sautéed in butter, and served either on their own, as part of a seafood stew, curried with rice, or with braised beef or pork when flavored with thyme or culantro (q.v.).

COMMENTS
The membranes that attach the arils to the fruit contain dangerous toxins before the fruit ripens. Only when the fruit is fully ripe does it split open, revealing the edible aril. Unripe fruits are not permitted to be imported into the United States.

Balloon Vine: *Cardiospermum grandiflorum*

OTHER COMMON, ETHNIC, OR SCIENTIFIC NAMES
Heart seed

RELATED SPECIES
Cardiospermum halicacabum: Farolito (Colombia); balloonvine

GROWTH HABITS
Perennial vine
Origin: Tropical Asia, Africa, and America
Range: Invasive weed in Australia and the Pacific Islands

CULINARY USES
The seeds are used as a seasoning and the pods are eaten as a cooked vegetable. Young leaves are prepared as potherbs.

Guaraná: *Paullinia cupana*

OTHER COMMON, ETHNIC, OR SCIENTIFIC NAMES
Brazilian cocoa, panela supana, uabano, uaranzeiro. An outdated scientific name for guaraná is *Paullinia Sorbilis*.
France: Quarane
Italy: Cupana guarana
Mexico: Guaraná
Panama: Barbasco, hierba de alacran

GROWTH HABITS
Climbing shrub (liana)
Origin: South America
Range: Cultivated in Brazil, Uruguay, and Venezuela

CULINARY USES
In South America, ground roasted seeds are used to produce a coffee-like drink, at one time called "Brazilian cocoa." Guaraná has a slightly woody, bitter, and chocolate- or tobacco-like flavor. It is usually found in sweetened form and is used in soft drinks, liqueurs, and cordials.

The commercially marketed soft drink Guaraná is sold in some Brazilian markets in the United States, but it is available everywhere in Brazil, where it is traditionally garnished with a slice of orange. The amber-colored cream soda–like soft drink is quite sweet and packs a caffeine wallop to rival that of Jolt Cola. The seeds of guaraná contain about three times as much caffeine as an equivalent weight of coffee, as much as 76,000 ppm. Guaraná seeds also contain theophyllene (up to 570 ppm), theobromine (up to 330 ppm), and an essential oil called guaranin. Like tea, it derives a certain astringent quality from its tannin (up to 120,000 ppm).

COMMENTS
Excessive use can be harmful; insomnia is to be expected with a substance like guaraná (in fact, that is almost its raison d'être).

87. Sapotaceae: The Sapodilla Family

Argan: *Argania spinosa*

OTHER COMMON, ETHNIC, OR SCIENTIFIC NAMES
Argan tree, Morocco ironwood. Sometimes listed as *Argania sideroxylon*.

Achras zapota (also listed as *Manilkara zapota*): Sapodilla, chicozapote, naseberry, nispero
Calocarpum mammosum: Marmalade tree, sapote, zapote

GROWTH HABITS
Small evergreen, sometimes spiny, tree
Origin: Morocco
Range: Grown in Chile; can be grown in southern California

CULINARY USES
Argan oil is pressed from the hard seeds inside the oblong fruits. It is popular in the Souss region of southwestern Morocco. *Amalou* is a smooth creamy paste that is spread on Moroccan breads, especially fried breads. It contains toasted almonds, honey, argan oil, and a little salt. *Zematar* is a porridge-like cereal dish made of wheatgerm, honey, and argan oil. A similar porridge, made from toasted barley, is also flavored with argan oil.

Argan oil is sprinkled on the top of tagines, just before serving, or poured over goat cheeses. The oil, like sesame oil (q.v.), comes in two forms: raw and toasted. Either one can be used in lemon-based vinaigrettes or in combination with preserved lemon.

The oil tastes a bit like walnut oil, but with a slightly resinous, cedar-like finish due to traces of kaempferol, myricetin, and quercetin.

Sapodilla's edible fruits are tawny colored and honey flavored. The tree produces a latex-like sap that is the source of chiclé. The zapote's fruit has spicy red flesh.

COMMENTS
The leaves, fruit, and oil cake left after pressing are often fed to farm animals. Ruminants, such as cows and goats, are unaffected by saponin in argan, but some of the saponin is passed on in their milk. Children drinking the milk can suffer an attack of diarrhea as a result.

Elengi: *Mimusops elengi*

OTHER COMMON, ETHNIC, OR SCIENTIFIC NAMES
Medlar, Spanish cherry, tanjong tree
Malaysia: Bunga tanjung

GROWTH HABITS
Evergreen tropical tree
Origin: India, Malaysia, Sri Lanka
Range: Florida

The bark is astringently bitter and adds a tonic quality to arrack, a rum-like alcoholic beverage used in Asia. The tree yields edible fruit.

OTHER USES

The flowers are used in perfumes.

88. Saururaceae:
The Lizard's Tail Family

Rau Diep Ca: *Houttuynia cordata*

OTHER COMMON, ETHNIC, OR SCIENTIFIC NAMES

Chameleon plant, Chinese lizard tail, fish mint, fishwort, houttuynia. Sometimes listed as *Houthuynia cordata*.
China: Chu tsai, tsi, yu xing cao
Germany: Chamäleonpflanze, Chinesischer Eidechsenschwanz
Hmong: Kio kau
Japan: Dokudami, jyuyaku, zyuyaku
Thailand: Phak khao thong, phluu kae
Vietnam: Kio kau (Hmong); diep ca, giâp cá, rau giap ca, vap ca

GROWTH HABITS

Perennial
Origin: Temperate east Asia
Range: Moist areas, from Japan to Nepal and mountainous parts of Java

CULINARY USES

The heart-shaped leaves have a resinous, slightly sorrel-like sourness, but they also have an exaggerated *Pelargonium* quality that can only be described as "fishy." First-time tasters often find it difficult to accept the fishiness, but native Vietnamese eat the herb by the handful with their meals.

Fresh leaves are eaten in salads, soups, and stews. Their aromatic quality is a fine counterpoint to the richness of boiled, fertilized duck eggs. Chinese varieties are said to smell of fish or cilantro, while Japanese varieties are supposed to smell like oranges.

Giâp cá contains afzerin, decanoyl acetaldedehyde, isoquercitrin, methyl nonyl ketone, and lauryl aldehyde.

89. Schisandraceae:
The Schisandra Family

Schisandra: *Schisandra chinensis*

OTHER COMMON, ETHNIC, OR SCIENTIFIC NAMES
Five flavors, magnolia vine, schizanthus. The old scientific name for this plant was *Schizandra sinensis*.
Germany: Spaltblume

GROWTH HABITS
Twining shrub
Origin: Temperate eastern Asia
Range: Temperate zones anywhere

CULINARY USES
The sour berries are used in herbal teas.

90. Scrophulariaceae:
The Figwort Family

Eyebright: *Euphrasia rostkoviana*

OTHER COMMON, ETHNIC, OR SCIENTIFIC NAMES
Casse lunette, euphrasy. Eyebright is sometimes listed as *Euphrasia officinalis*.

RELATED SPECIES
Euphrasia americana: Eyebright

GROWTH HABITS
Annual
Origin: England, Europe
Range: Temperate regions

CULINARY USES
The bitter leaves have been eaten in salads.

Indian Paintbrush: *Castilleja lanata*

OTHER COMMON, ETHNIC, OR SCIENTIFIC NAMES
  Mexico: Hierba de conejo

GROWTH HABITS
  Perennial
  Origin: Southwestern United States and Mexico
  Range: California to Mexico

RELATED SPECIES
  Castilleja affinis subs. *Neglecta:* Tiburon Indian paintbrush
  Castilleja grisea: San Clemente Island Indian paintbrush
  Castilleja mollis: Soft-leaved Indian paintbrush

CULINARY USES
  Flowers are used as a flavoring for beans or rice, among the Utes and Zapotecs.

Mullein: *Verbascum thapsus*

OTHER COMMON, ETHNIC, OR SCIENTIFIC NAMES
  Aaron's rod, Adam's flannel, beggar's blanket, beggar's stalk, blanket herb, bullock's lungwort, candlewick plant, clot, clown's lungwort, cow's lungwort, cuddy's lungs, duffle, feltwort, flannel plant, fluffweed, goldenrod, hag's taper, hare's beard, Jacob's staff, Jupiter's staff, mullein dock, old man's flannel, our lady's flannel, Peter's staff, rag paper, torches, shepherd's clubs, shepherd's staff, velvet dock, velvet leaf, velvet plant, verbascum flowers, wild ice leaf, woolen blanket herb. The apothecary's name for mullein is *Flores Verbasci.*
  France: Molène commune
  Germany: Kleinblütige Königkerze, Wollkraut
  Italy: Verbasco
  Mexico: Gordo loco, verbasco
  Russia: Koroviak viosky
  Spain: Verbasco

RELATED SPECIES
  Verbascum phlomoides (sometimes listed as *Verbascum phlomoidea*):
    Grossblütige Königkerze (Germany); gordolobo, guaragnasco,
    tassobarbasso (Italy); molène medicinale (France); mullein
  Verbascum sinuatum: Gewellblättrige Königkerze (Germany); sigir
    kuyrugu (Turkey)
  Verbascum thapsiforme: Königkerze (Germany)

  Biennial
  Origin: Europe and Asia
  Range: Naturalized in the United States

CULINARY USES

  Teas are brewed from the dried leaves or from fresh leaves and flowers. Baerenfang, a German honey-based liqueur, is flavored with linden blossoms and mullein flowers.

  Sweet and slightly bitter, mullein is used in some commercial flavorings. It contains 43 ppm of β-carotene, plus a trace of coumarin.

COMMENTS

  The FDA restricts its use to alcoholic beverages.

  "Goldenrod" is much better known as a name for members of the *Solidago* genus. Sweet goldenrod, *Solidago odora,* has been used as an herbal tea.

Rice Paddy Herb: *Limnophilia chinensis*

OTHER COMMON, ETHNIC, OR SCIENTIFIC NAMES

  Ambulia, finger grass. Also known as *Limnophilia aromatica.*
  China: Shui fu rong
  Estonia: Järvelemb
  Germany: Reisfeldpflanze
  Japan: Shiso kusa
  Thailand: Phak khayaeng
  Vietnam: Ngò Ôm, rau ngo, rau om

GROWTH HABITS

  Aquatic perennial
  Origin: South Asia to Northern Australia
  Range: South Asia to Hawaii

CULINARY USES

  The plant is visually similar to mint (without the characteristic square stems), but it has a distinctive lemony flavor reminiscent of cumin and celery. Fresh leaves are used in sweet-sour Vietnamese dishes, and chopped stems and leaves garnish sour soups containing seafood.

Veronica: *Veronica officinalis*

OTHER COMMON, ETHNIC, OR SCIENTIFIC NAMES

  Bird's eye, speedwell
  France: Véronique

Germany: Echter Ehrenpreis, Wald Ehrenpreis
Italy: Veronica
Mexico: Tonalxihuitl, veronica
Spain: Veronica macho
Sweden: Ärepris

GROWTH HABITS
Perennial
Origin: Europe
Range: Eurasia, North America, Azores

CULINARY USES
Veronica's mildly bitter flavor, used in limited commercial flavoring applications, is derived mainly from glucosides, mannitol, and tannin.

COMMENTS
The FDA restricts the use of veronica to alcoholic beverages.

Water Hyssop: *Bacopa monnieria*

OTHER COMMON, ETHNIC, OR SCIENTIFIC NAMES
Bacopa. Water hyssop is sometimes listed as *Herpestis Mouniera.*
Vietnam: Rau dâng

RELATED SPECIES
Limnophila aromatica: Keukeuhan, rau om (Vietnam); swamp leaf
Limnophila indica (sometimes listed as *Limnophila gratioliodes*): Ambuli
  water plant

GROWTH HABITS
Aquatic perennial
Origin: Tropical Americas
Range: Wild in waterways south of Virginia, and west as far as Texas

CULINARY USES
This purslane-like herb is used raw in salads or cooked in soups or as a vegetable. The succulent leaves are sometimes pickled.
Limnophila aromatica is used in Vietnamese sweet-sour dishes, especially cantaloupe and tamarind soup. The leaves and stalks are eaten as an aromatic accompaniment for rice.

OTHER USES
All of these plants are used as aquarium plants.

COMMENTS
This "water hyssop" has nothing whatever to do with hyssop, *Hyssopus officinalis* (q.v.).

91. Solanaceae: The Nightshade Family

Belladonna: *Atropa belladonna*

OTHER COMMON, ETHNIC, OR SCIENTIFIC NAMES
Deadly nightshade, dwale, English belladonna, poison black cherry, sleeping nightshade
Germany: Tollkirsche
Morocco: Zbibet el laidour

GROWTH HABITS
Perennial
Origin: Mediterranean region
Range: Naturalized in North America

CULINARY USES
Belladonna is sometimes found among the ingredients in the Moroccan spice mixture *ras el hanout* (see Comments, below).

COMMENTS
The only culinary use I've found for belladonna is in *ras el hanout*. Of course, some of these Moroccan formulations also contain Spanish fly and hashish.

Belladonna is a poison, containing atropine. All parts of the plant are poisonous to humans, although not to all other animals. People have been poisoned by eating the meat of animals that have fed on the plant, especially rabbits and birds. Skin irritation in humans can result from contact with even dried plant material.

Boxthorn: *Lycium chinense*

OTHER COMMON, ETHNIC, OR SCIENTIFIC NAMES
Chinese matrimony vine, wolfberries. Formerly known as *Lycium carnosum*.
China: Gau gei choi (leaf); gau gei jee (berry)

RELATED SPECIES
Lycium halimifolium: Common matrimony vine, matrimony vine, wolfberry.
It is so similar to *Lycium chinense* that the two species may be the same.

GROWTH HABITS
Shrub
Origin: Asia
Range: Naturalized in Europe and eastern United States

Leaves of boxthorn have a slightly bitter, mint-like taste and are added, just before service, to soups in China, usually those containing ginger, white pepper, and sugar.

Wolfberries are sometimes used to flavor red-cooked (braised) meat dishes, especially chicken and pork. Although duck and goose are not cooked this way in China, they seem likely candidates for this process. The berries have a sweet-sour, anise-like taste.

COMMENTS

Do not confuse these wolfberries with another wolfberry, *Symphoricarpos occidentalis,* part of the *Caprifoliaceae* or honeysuckle family.

All *Lyciums* spread by suckers and extended root systems. Treat like mint (q.v.) in the garden.

Chile Pepper: *Capsicum* spp.

OTHER COMMON, ETHNIC, OR SCIENTIFIC NAMES

Red pepper. An old apothecary's term for chile is *Fructus Capsici Acer.*
Afganistan: Murgh
Algeria: Felflel driss
Arabic: Ahmur, bisbas, felfel, filfilianhar
Bali: Tabia
Brazil: Auija, pimenta malagueta (bird pepper), pimenta da cheiro (habanero), quiya
Burma/Myanmar: Nayu-si, na yop, nga yut thee, nil thee
Chile: Thapi
China: Fan chiew, lat tsiao
Costa Rica: Dipá-boró-boró, tiesh
Denmark: Paprika
East Timor: Ai-manas
Egypt: Filfil-achdar
England: Chilli
Estonia: Harilik paprika, kibe paprika
Ethiopia: Berbere, mit'mita
Finland: Chilipippuri, paprika, ruokapaprika
France: Paprica de Hongrie, piment, piment annuel, piment-aiseau, piment de Guinée, piment fort, piment doux, piment doux d'Espagne, piment enragé, poivre de Brézil, piment sec (fort et rouge), poivre de cayenne, poivre d'Inde, poivre rouge
French Guiana: Furtu
Germany: Cayenne-Pfeffer, Chili-Pfeffer, Gewürtzpaprika, Paprika, Pfefferschote, Roter Pfeffer, Spanischer Pfeffer

Gold Coast: Mako
Greece: Pipería
Haiti: Achí, agí, ají, axí
Hungary: Csilipaprika, paprika
Iceland: Cayennepipar, chilipipar, paprikuduft
India: Achar, deghi mirch, gachmirich, gujrati, jolokia, marathi, lanka, marichiphala, merapu kai, menashinakayi, mirapakaya, mirchi, mulagu, rathu miris, ujjvala
Indonesia: Cabé hijau (green), cabé merah (red), cabe rawit (cayenne), cabai, lombok, tjabé
Iran: Filfile srkh
Iraq: Felfel ahmar har, felfel ahmar helou (paprika), filfil ahmar (cayenne), filfil hiloo (paprika)
Israel: Pilpel adom
Italy: Diavoletto, paprica, pepe, pepe di Caienne, pepe rosso picante, peperone, peperoncini, pepe di Cayenna
Japan: Togarashi
Java: Cabé, lombok
Kenya: Piri-piri
Korea: Gochu
Laos: Mak phe kunsi
Liberia: Mano
Malaysia: Chabai, cili, lada hijau, lada merah, lombok
Mexico: Chac-ic, chilli, max-ic, itz, ng-i
Morocco: Felfa hlouwa (paprika), felfa soudaniya (cayenne), felfa harra (a mixture of cayenne, paprika, and other chiles)
Netherlands: Bzefilie peper, Cayennepeper, paprika, Spaanse peper
Netherlands Antilles: promenton, promèntòn
Nigeria: Ata-jije, barkono
Peru: Huayca, uchu
Philippines: Pa sitis, sili, siling haba, siling labyo
Poland: Papryka roczna
Portugal: Malagueta, pimenta de Caiena, pimentão, pimentão doce, pimento, piri-piri
Romania: Ardei
Russia: Krasny peretz, struchkovy peppar
Saudi Arabia: Filfile ahmur, filfilianhar
Senegal: Foronto
Sierra Leone: Pujei
Spain: Ají, Cayena Inglesa, guindilla, paprika, pimienta de Cayena, pimienta picante, pimiento dulce, pimiento morrón, pimientón, pimientos verdes
Sri Lanka: Amu miris, kochchi miris, mulagay, rathu miris
Sumatra: Chabai

Swahili: Pilipili hoho
Sweden: Chilipeppar, paprika, spansk peppar
Thailand: Pisi hui, prik chee fa, prik kee noo suan, prik khee, prik e noo, prik leung, prik yuak
Turkey: Aci kirmizi biber
Vietnam: Ot
Yemen: Dar feller

Virtually all hot and sweet peppers (except habaneros, rocotos, and tabascos) commonly encountered in the United States are *Capsicum annuum*. There are five groups of peppers in this species:

Cerasiform: Cherry peppers

Coniodes: Cone peppers

Fasciculatum (all cluster peppers belong to this group): bird's beak, chilli pin, mad pepper, Nepal pepper. These are incredibly thin red peppers, very hot, with a dry, earthy taste when fresh. Popular in Thailand.

Grossum: Prik yuak (Thailand); bell peppers, sweet peppers, green peppers, pimentos. Only the Grossum group is mild, but it freely hybridizes with other, hotter *Capsicum annuum* varieties, often producing hot offspring. This does not affect the first generation's peppers. However, if you save seeds from year to year, you will eventually grow nothing *but* hot peppers.

Longum: Capsicum peppers, chile peppers, cayenne, long pepper, prik chee fa (Thailand), red pepper

RELATED SPECIES

Capsicum baccatum: Sambal, a South American species useful in hybridization with other *Capsicums*

Capsicum chinense: Bonney peppers, datil chilis, habanero, Mayan peppers, savinas, Scotch bonnets

Capsicum frutescens (sometimes listed as *Capsicum annuum* subs. *conoides*): Aji (Panama); aji picante (Spain); cabai burong (Malaysia); cabé rawit or lombok rawitt (Indonesia); prik e noo (Thailand); rocoto (Colombia); tabasco, tabasco sauce pepper

Capsicum pubescens: Rocoto, unlike most other domesticated peppers, has purple flowers and dark seeds.

Solanum nigra: Yerba mora (Mexico); wild spinach

Solanum torvum: Ca phao (Vietnam); ma khuea phuang (Thailand); seiban nasubi (Okinawa); talong na ligaw, tandang-aso (Philippines); nightshade, pea aubergine, turkeyberry. The firm, bitter fruits are used in Southeast Asian curries.

GROWTH HABITS

Perennial, cultivated as an annual in areas that have frost

Origin: Tropical America
Range: Grown virtually everywhere

CULINARY USES

The primary principle of all the chiles is capsaicin, a slightly bitter but incredibly powerful oil-soluble oleoresin that burns whatever it touches. Humans can detect its presence in minute quantities, sometimes as low as a few parts per million. Contrary to the opinion of many chile-phobes, the chile aficionado is not merely a deranged masochist. Once past the pain—a state easy to achieve, since the body quickly develops a tolerance for the drug— one can experience an incredible range of flavors. Some chile fanciers find as much complexity in the taste of *Capsicum annuum* as a wine enthusiast finds in *Vitis vinifera*.

Much of the flavor, but none of the heat, of chiles is related to the presence of pigments in the fleshy wall of the fruit (see Other Uses, below). When dried chiles' colors fade with age, the peppers also lose their flavor. They may still be hot, but the complex fruity or wine-like flavors that made them so appealing will have dissipated, never to return. When buying dried chiles, choose pods that are free of bleached, crumbly spots. They should have a good rich smell and be slightly flexible, not brittle.

Mexican and Southwestern cuisine is unimaginable without chile peppers. The "chile powder" that is sold in supermarkets is practically never pure ground chile. It is usually a mixture of chile, cumin, garlic, and oregano, along with some silicon dioxide (fine sand) to prevent caking. Some blends include ground coriander seed. In most cases, serious cooks prefer to make their own chile powder, varying the components to suit the needs of the moment.

Chile is an ingredient in *shichimi* (a Japanese seven-spice mixture), along with black hemp seeds, Mandarin orange peel, nori (seaweed), poppy seeds, sesame seeds, and Szechuan pepper (q.v.). The mixture is also known as *shichimi togarashi. Ichimi togarashi,* on the other hand, is just finely crushed red pepper.

"Italian Seasoning" is a name for several different mixtures of herbs and spices that are sold commercially. They often contain paprika.

Chile peppers are part of the complex mix of seasonings that are used in *niter kebbeh,* the clarified butter that is the preferred fat used in the preparation of Ethiopian food.

In Tunisia, a condiment composed of chiles ground together with salt and cumin is known as *brisa*. Chopped fresh green chiles are the basis for the Yemenite relish called *shuq*. Paprika appears in the Moroccan version of the classic French seasoning *quatre épices,* although it is not included in the original French mixture.

Chile pepper is used in the Amazonian cassava-based condiment called *tucupi. Molho brasiliero,* "Brazilian sauce," is a kind of green salsa made with melegueta pepper, lime juice, and other spices and herbs. "Melegueta pepper" in Brazil refers to chiles, usually pickled in vinegar. Piri piri is a chile-laced olive oil that is used in Portugal. Iraqi Jews make a condiment called 'amba from chiles and pickled mango.

Many different chile pastes are used around the world. For example, chili paste with garlic (*lat jiu din, lat jiu keung yau*) and Szechuan hot bean sauce are Chinese standbys, available anywhere Chinese groceries are sold. *Gochu jang* is the heat of preference in Korea. It is made with chiles, fermented tofu, malt syrup, short-grain rice, and salt. It is the defining taste in Korean cooking, although the Koreans also exhibit a certain fondness for *silgochu* (which is dried red pepper, sliced into filament-like shreds, looking like slightly matted, henna-dyed hair) and *gochu karu* (ground dried chiles, without seeds, similar to cayenne).

Returning to pepper pastes: *Harissa* is chile, cumin, garlic, salt, coriander seed, and caraway seed, ground to a paste in oil. Cinnamon is added to some formulations. Popular all over North Africa, it is the classic accompaniment to couscous. *Berberé* is similar, but more complex; it provides the accent that defines a dish as Ethiopian.

In Indonesia, *sambal ulek* (or *oelek*) is made from chile, shrimp paste, salt, and tamarind (*sambal* is known as *achar* or *chatui* in India, *sambol* or *sambola* in Sri Lanka). *Sambal nasi goreng* is similar, but with added garlic and onions, slowly cooked until it becomes a fiery confit.

Jamaican jerk seasoning tastes very similar, but it adds the zip of allspice and large quantities of ginger root. Jerk can contain many different spices, depending on the cook, the location, and the intended use. Among the other approved ingredients are bay leaves, black pepper, cinnamon, garlic, nutmeg, and, of course, Scotch bonnet peppers. West Indians don't really think of jerk seasoning as hot; they treat it more as a kind of aromatic. For real heat, choose hot sauces made with a greater emphasis on Scotch bonnets (or bonney peppers, varieties of habaneros). These sauces typically contain yellow prepared mustard and are thickened with tropical fruits, such as mangoes, and/or cooked carrots. A favorite commercial product, from Barbados, is S Bend Hot Pepper Sauce. So thick as to be a paste in all but name, it is yellow from ripe Scotch bonnets and mustard. Habaneros have a tropical sweetness and an omnipresent ethereal heat that borders on rapture for chile addicts. Inner Beauty is a sauce with a similar formula from the East Coast Grill in Cambridge, Massachusetts.

Thailand, not to be outdone in culinary pyrotechnics, has several pastes based on hot chiles. *Nam prik* is composed of chiles, pungent dried shrimp, garlic, *nam pla* (fish sauce), lime juice, and sour pea eggplant. *Nam prik pan-ang* combines chiles, dried shrimp, garlic, onion, and salt. *Nam prik pao* is composed of chiles, dried shrimp, garlic, onion, tamarind pulp, peanuts, and brown sugar (or palm sugar).

Thais love their curry pastes, most of which belong in this section because the main ingredient is chile. Thai cooks usually make the pastes fresh, but they are also available in tiny flat cans and small plastic pouches. Green curry paste, known as *krung gaeng keo wan, gaeng keo wan gai,* or *kang kiew warn,* contains fresh green chiles, coriander seeds and roots, onion, garlic, galingal, lemongrass, caraway, white pepper, and shrimp paste. Red curry paste, *krung gaeng ped daeng* or *kang pet dang,* is not as hot as green, but it still packs a powerful chile punch. It uses dried red chiles instead of green, contains all the other ingredients of green curry paste, but adds Kaffir lime leaves. Yellow curry paste, *nam prik kang karie,* uses dried red chiles, coriander seeds, caraway seeds, cinnamon, cloves, red onion or shallots, lemongrass, and garlic. Masman, Muslim or *gaeng mussaman,* curry paste contains dried red chiles, curry leaves, galingal, coriander seeds, caraway seeds, cardamom, cinnamon, cloves, red onion or shallots, lemongrass, garlic, and shrimp paste. Orange curry paste, *krung gaeng som,* is simpler, containing only dried red chiles, salt, vinegar, red onion or shallots, and shrimp paste.

Thais use chiles in forms other than paste, of course. *Nam som* is a chile-spiked vinegar used as commonly as other people use salt. Where some cooks would use black pepper, Thais sprinkle on *prik kee nu bon,* which is just dried crushed red pepper (much like the jarred stuff found on the tables of every pizza parlor in America).

In Laos, the preferred chile paste is called *tieo.*

And what about the *rouille* of Marseilles? It contains chiles, garlic, and olive oil, thickened with a few bread crumbs and pounded to paste. In the Middle Ages, all sauces were thickened with either bread or ground nuts. Of the latter category, the leading survivors (in Western cuisine, anyway) are the *pipians* of Mexico, made of chiles with ground, roasted pumpkinseeds (pepitas), and the classic *sauce romesco,* puréed red chiles thickened with ground almonds. There is *pesto alla genovese,* of course, but that's another story altogether (see PINE NUTS).

A few cheeses make use of chile's culinary charms. Pepper Jack is an American chile-spangled descendant of English Cheddars. Roundtower, from County Cork, is a garlic-laced Gouda-like cheese that also contains red pepper. The Hungarian soft cheese known as Liptói, or in Slovakia, Liptovká Bryndza, is occasionally colored with paprika. Spanish cheeses, notably Sierra de Zulteros and Mahón, are usually colored and flavored with paprika. As American palates have developed (or pain thresholds raised), cheeses containing habaneros have begun to appear on market shelves.

Extracts of capsaicin are used in some ginger beers. Italian chile-laced spirits are known as *grappa al peperoncino. Pertsovka* is vodka (a form of nastoika) flavored with a few chiles and some cubeb pepper. The Ukrainian version is called *ukrainskaya s pertsem.* Russian okhotnichya, or hunter's brandy, is a heady, warming concoction consisting of alcohol, chiles, and other flavorings (see glossary).

My own firewater consists of five Scotch bonnets and the zest of one lemon, placed in a liter of vodka, steeped for a month, then strained and kept icy cold in the freezer. It is not a drink for the timid.

Finally, the leaves of chile plants are eaten in the Philippines and Papua, New Guinea, as a potherb. The leaves contain no capsaicin, hence there is no heat. They are described as having a taste similar to that of spinach, with basil overtones.

OTHER USES

The main pigment in chiles, red capsanthin, is often used as a food colorant. Chiles contain a number of other pigments, including β-carotene, capsorubin, lutein, neoxanthin, violaxanthin, and zeaxanthin.

COMMENTS

Some of these peppers are *seriously hot*. When handling them, it is essential to wear rubber gloves and to carefully clean your kitchen tools and surfaces. If you have skipped this advice and find that your hands are burning from exposure to the wrath of capsaicin, there is a remedy. Try soaking your hands with a mild solution of household bleach. Your hands will stink of chlorine, but the pain will subside.

Resist the temptation to surprise people with capsicum-loaded dishes. Some people like to think that they are macho enough to eat *any* pepper, but as any sailor can tell you, for every boat there is a wave that can capsize it. Be sure to issue ample warnings to inexperienced but adventurous mouth surfers, and provide plenty of milk or bread to absorb the fiery oils from a shocked victim's tongue.

Anyone who has begun the study of chiles has found that the names are extremely misleading. For example, the name "bird pepper" refers to peppers of the chile de arbol type in Thailand. It is long and as thin as a nail. In the American Southwest, "bird pepper" means a small, pea-shaped chile called chiltepin. Elsewhere the name has been used to describe the small, cone-shaped pepper called chile pequin. The only thing they share, besides the name, is a tendency to grow wild, especially from seeds passed by birds. The name *pasilla* refers to one variety in Mexico and the American Southwest, but to a totally different chile in California.

A word about the spelling. The English-speaking world seems divided between "chile," "chili," and "chilli." Chile is the only accepted spelling in New Mexico, where people are quite adamant on the subject; since everyone else seems flexible about it, let the New Mexicans win this one.

Dozens of books are devoted to the subject of chiles, but I warmly recommend *The Whole Chile Pepper Book,* by Dave DeWitt and Nancy Gerlach; *Peppers,* by Amal Naj; and anything written by Jean Andrews, Diana Kennedy, or Mark Miller.

Henbane: *Hyoscyamus* spp.

OTHER COMMON, ETHNIC, OR SCIENTIFIC NAMES

Arabic: Bang
China: Lang tang (ancient)
Germany: Bilsenkraut, Pilsenerkrut
Mexico: Beleno

RELATED SPECIES

Hyoscyamus falelez: No common name found. The seeds are added to coffee in Arabic countries.
Hyoscyamus niger: Henbane
Hyoscyamus physaloides: No common name found. The seeds are used as a coffee substitute in Siberia.

GROWTH HABITS

Annuals and biennials
Origin: Mediterranean Region
Range: Naturalized in United States

CULINARY USES

Henbane, and the related species *Hyoscyamus falelez* and *Hyoscyamus physaloides,* has been added to beers, mead, and coffee (or even substituted for

Henbane
Hyoscyamus niger

From Köhler, *Köhler's Medizinal-Pflanzen*, vol. 1

coffee). In the New World, it has spiked alcoholic beverages based on corn (*chicha*) and agave (*pulque*). See Comments, below, before trying any of these potent and potentially dangerous potables.

COMMENTS

All parts of henbane plants contain dangerous alkaloids: atropine, hyoscyamine, and scopalomine. While these compounds are the reasons the plants are used in rituals around the world, they are also responsible for many serious poisonings. Hamlet's father, you may recall, became a significant otherworldly figure with the help of henbane.

92. Sterculiaceae: The Chocolate Family

Cacao: *Theobroma cacao*

OTHER COMMON, ETHNIC, OR SCIENTIFIC NAMES
Chocolate tree, cocoa
Germany: Kakao

RELATED SPECIES
Sterculia foetida: Gurapa badam chettu, peenaree marum (India); Java olive. Roasted seeds are eaten.
Sterculia quinqueloba: Mhuja (Tanzania). Roasted seeds are eaten.

SUBSPECIES AND HYBRID
Theobroma cacao subs. *cacao:* Criollo lines
Theobroma cacao subs. *sphaerocarpum:* Forestero lines
Cacao × sphaerocarpum: Trinitarios

GROWTH HABITS
Tropical tree
Origin: Central and South America
Range: Africa, Central and South America, Indonesia, and New Guinea

CULINARY USES
The seeds (nibs) of cacao are, of course, the source of cocoa and chocolate. Much of chocolate's charm lies in the cocoa butter; when crystallized properly, it is hard, almost brittle, but it melts at body temperature. This gives it a creamily luscious mouthfeel that we can get only from fats. That very unctuousness, however, can become cloying, especially if the substance is oversweetened. Consequently, chocolate is often paired with ingredients that either cut through the fat (fruit acids, such as those found in citrus fruits,

and the tarter varieties of berries, such as raspberries and strawberries) or add complexity to it (coffee, mint, vanilla, and roasted nut flavors are typical examples).

Not all uses for chocolate are to provide sweetness, at least, not in the sense that desserts are sweet. The classic Oaxacan dish mole poblano combines both these strategies described: fruit acids (from raisins), a number of spices, toasted almonds and sesame seeds, and several different chiles add depth and complexity. Mole negro is less complex than mole poblano, but it still plays the hot fruitiness of chiles against the rich bittersweet chocolate flavor and mouthfeel.

The roasted seeds of *Sterculia foetida* and *Sterculia quinqueloba* are eaten in tropical Central and South America.

Chocolate's captivating flavor is due primarily to linalool and aliphatic acids, while its stimulating effects are a result of caffeine, theobromine, and theophylline. The complex flavor and aroma develop only after the beans are separated from the sweet fruit pulp and are allowed to ferment, then dry. The natural product is so bitter that even so-called bitter chocolate requires as much as 40 percent sugar in order to be palatable.

OTHER USES

The lowest-quality beans, those that have been affected by mold or other impurities, cannot be made into acceptable chocolate products. Such beans are pressed for their cocoa butter, which is then used in the cosmetics industry.

COMMENTS

Some taxonomists list the *Sterculiaceae* as a subfamily of the *Malvaceae*.

The names "cacao" and "cocoa" are derived from the Mayan *ka-ka-wa* and the Náhuatl *xocoatl*.

The criollo line of cacao, originally from Mexico and Central America, produces the finest grade of chocolate, called *fine* or *flavor*. These trees are very rare and their product is used only in the very finest products.

The forestero line, originally from South America, is hardier and provides greater yields, but the nibs yield a lower-quality product called bulk cocoa. Bulk cocoa is used when flavor is less important, for example, in filled or milk chocolates, baked goods, and beverages, including breakfast cocoa. There are several varieties of forestero: cacao nacional (Ecuador); Ceylan, matina (Costa Rica and Mexico); comum (Brazil); and West African amelonado (Camaroon to Côte d'Ivoire). Africa produces nearly 70 percent of the world supply of cacao.

Normally included in the forestero line are the hybrid trinitarios. Trinitarios have the hardiness of the forestero line, while improving the quality of the product to near-criollo standards. The first trinitarios were grown in Trinidad, but they are now planted almost everywhere cacao is grown.

The first crisp snap of the best chocolate, which then yields a creamy mouthfeel as the flavors are revealed, is a result of careful tempering—a process that determines the crystalline structure of the cocoa butter in the chocolate—which, in turn, determines physical properties of the chocolate (such as its melting point).

Kola Nut: *Cola nitida*

OTHER COMMON, ETHNIC, OR SCIENTIFIC NAMES
Bissy nuts, guru nuts. Formerly known botanically as *Cola vera*.
France: Cola
Germany: Kola
Italy: Cola

RELATED SPECIES
Cola acuminata (sometimes seen as *Sterculia acuminata*): Cola nuts, female cola, guru nuts

GROWTH HABITS
Tropical tree
Origin: Africa
Range: Africa and South America

CULINARY USES
The seeds of kola nuts were, of course, the basis of many popular soft drinks. Most major soft drink companies no longer use natural kola nuts, however, substituting synthetic compounds that have similar flavor profiles. The distinctive bitter flavor of kola nuts is still found, however, in aperitifs and bitters.

Kola nuts' stimulating effects are a result of their caffeine, theobromine, and theophylline content. Caffeine content varies with freshness. The nuts' characteristic astringency is provided by phenols: catechin, chlorogenic acid, epicatechin, tannins, and kola red, a glucoside. *Cola nitida* has higher levels of these phenols than *Cola acuminata;* hence, it is the preferred species in flavoring.

COMMENTS
Kola nuts are sometimes adulterated with the unrelated male kola (*Garcinia kola*).

The original recipe for Coca-Cola must have provided a bigger jolt than today's specially caffeinated beverages. It contained caffeine citrate, in addition to extracts of *Cola nitida* and *Erythroxylon coca*.

Do not confuse the kola nut with gotu kola, *Hydrocotyle asiatica* subs. *minor;* cola de caballo, *Spartium junceum;* or genda-kola, *Portulaca oloraceae*.

93. Taxaceae: The Yew Family

California Nutmeg: *Torreya californica*

OTHER COMMON, ETHNIC, OR SCIENTIFIC NAMES
Stinking nutmeg

RELATED SPECIES
Torreya nucifera: Kaya, Japanese torreya

GROWTH HABITS
Evergreen tree
Origin: California
Range: Temperate, frost-free regions

CULINARY USES
Not surprisingly, California nutmeg is said to smell and taste of turpentine. *Torreya nucifera* is said to have edible seeds.

COMMENTS
I know of no useful culinary properties for this oddly named relative of the pines. It is included here because its common name might suggest use in the kitchen, and because "California nutmeg" is another name for California laurel, *Umbellularia californica* (q.v.).

94. Theaceae: The Tea Family

Tea: *Camellia sinensis*

OTHER COMMON, ETHNIC, OR SCIENTIFIC NAMES
Tea used to be known scientifically as *Camellia Thea, Camellia theifera, Thea Bohea, Thea sinensis, Thea Viridis,* or *Thea stricta* subs. *Jassmica*
Burma/Myanmar: Lephet or leppet-so (used as vegetable)
Denmark: Te
Finland: Tee
France: Thé
Germany: Tee
Greece: Tsaï
India: Cha, char
Italy: Tè
Japan: Cha

Netherlands: Thee
Norway: Te
Russia: Chay
Spain: Té
Sweden: Te
Thailand: Miang (used as vegetable)

GROWTH HABITS

Evergreen shrub

Origin: Southeast Asia

Range: Warm temperate regions, especially India, the Himalayan region, Vietnam, China, Japan, and Taiwan

CULINARY USES

More tea is consumed than any other caffeinated beverage in the world. It has a following that is as dedicated and sophisticated as that of wine. Discussion of the subtlety of tea, in its usual form, is well beyond the scope of this book, so I will just mention some of its other culinary attributes.

When tea was first used as a beverage, it was only one ingredient in a kind of invigorating soup that might have included fatty meats (like mutton), vegetables, other herbs, and even such unlikely substances as yak butter and salt. The idea of combining energy-packed nutrients with a magical plant that banished sleepiness must have been very appealing, even if the combination seems disgusting to modern palates. In China, in the fifth century, tea was prepared with ginger, lemons, milk, orange peel, rice, salt, scallions, and other spices. Three hundred years later, most of these additives had been deleted, but the salt was still de rigueur.

In the United States, people tend to think of tea as something that should be "enhanced" only by flowers (such as jasmine) or fruit flavors (such as orange peel with cloves), perhaps a little sugar, honey, lemon, or milk. They are slightly repulsed by the notion of using several of these enhancers at the same time.

Other cultures have been open to greater experimentation. In Afghanistan, cardamom is added to black tea. A similar drink, boiled with condensed milk in addition to cardamom and other spices, is known as *chai* and is enjoyed in India. Chai-like beverages have become popular in the United States, in—of all places—coffee bars. Indians also flavor tea with mangoes, while some Chinese teas contain lichees. In Kashmir, sweet spices and almonds perfume steaming green tea. *Masala cha* is a sweet spicy brew consumed in India and Sri Lanka. It is flavored with cardamom, cinnamon, cloves, fresh ginger, and mint. *Genmaicha* is a Japanese green tea flavored with toasted rice.

Herbs of all sorts are combined with tea, of course. Mint is popular in hot tea, especially in Muslim areas of Africa. Moroccans, for example, prefer their tea minted, and very sweet. Islam, of course, forbids the use of alcohol (even though the very word "alcohol" is derived from Arabic words having to do with the chemical process of sublimation), so tea and coffee are the beverages of choice among Muslims. The Japanese are not bound by such restrictions. They have created a green tea liqueur that is flavored with a blend of rolled and powdered varieties of tea.

Beyond beverages, this camellia has other culinary uses. Tea leaves, known as *lephet* or *leppet-so,* are eaten as a pickled vegetable in Burma/Myanmar and Thailand, accompanied by fried garlic, dried shrimp, toasted peanuts, and sesame seeds.

In China, tea eggs are made by lightly cracking hard-boiled eggs and then simmering them for hours in a mixture of tea, star anise, and soy sauce. They are cooled and peeled to reveal glossy, slightly licorice-scented orbs, crazed like antique ironstone. Serve them with scallion brushes, sweet-salty radish fans, and Chinese sausage or ham or even brown bean curd slices (moistened with a little sesame oil).

Jasmine tea is used as a "broth" to accompany stir-fried squid in Shanghai. Longjin teas leaves are used as a seasoning and garnish for stir-fried shrimp in Handzhow. Tea leaves are also used in China to smoke fish (such as trout) and in the recipe for the famous camphorated duck.

OTHER USES
Tea has been used in the formulation of some perfumes.

Tilia: *Ternstroemia* spp.

OTHER COMMON, ETHNIC, OR SCIENTIFIC NAMES
Ternstroemia. The genus was formerly known as *Adinandrella.*

GROWTH HABITS
Broadleaf evergreen shrub
Origin: Asia
Range: Mexico

CULINARY USES
Blossoms and fruits are combined with fennel and orange blossoms in Mexican herbal teas.

OTHER USES
Pods are used in potpourri.

COMMENTS
This plant is not related to the lindens (*Tilia* spp.).

95. Tiliaceae: The Linden or Basswood Family

Linden: *Tilia cordata*

OTHER COMMON, ETHNIC, OR SCIENTIFIC NAMES
American basswood, common lime, lime tree
France: Tilleul
Germany: Linde, Lindenblutten
Italy: Tiglio
Mexico: Flor de tilo, tila, tilia, tilo
Russia: Lippa
Spain: Tilo
Turkey: Ihlamur

RELATED SPECIES
Tilia americana: American basswood
Tilia grandiflora: Linde (Germany)
Tilia mexicana: Tila (Mexico)
Tilia tomentosum: Linden, lime tree

HYBRID
Tilia × europaea: ihlamur (Turkey); common lime, lime tree, linn flowers
(*Tilia intermedia, Tilia vulgaris, Tilia platyphylla*), tilleul (*Tilia cordata ×
Tilia platyphyllos*)

GROWTH HABITS
Deciduous tree
Origin: Europe
Range: Temperate Northern Hemisphere

CULINARY USES
Blossoms are steeped in sweet herbal teas; linden blossoms and peppermint make a classic combination. The blossoms are also used to flavor wines. An excellent aromatic honey is derived, with some help from bees, from the flowers of the linden tree. The honey, in turn, is used in making liqueurs. Baerenfang is a German honey-based liqueur that is flavored with linden blossoms and mullein flowers.

In Europe, linden is sometimes added to black tea blends. *Tilleul* is the French word for the flowers and the tea that is made from them. This is the tea that liberated *le temps perdu* from Proust's madeleine. The dried leaves and flowers are available in places that sell ingredients for Hispanic cooking.

The dried flowers of *Tilia mexicana* are brewed into a soothing tea in Mexico. The dried flowers and leaves smell of coumarin (see Comments, below).

Tilia tomentosum has been used to adulterate dried marjoram.

COMMENTS

There is no connection—other than linguistic—between this species and the better-known members of the Citrus family.

Linden honey is sometimes contaminated by honeydew, a secretion of the aphids that feed on linden leaves. More annoying is the honeydew that drops from the trees to whatever is parked below. It forms a sticky coating that adheres to cars, then turns black as a result of fungi that feed upon it.

Because of linden's coumarin content, the FDA restricts the use of the leaves to alcoholic beverages. The leaves are said to have mild sedative properties. Old flowers are thought to be slightly intoxicating.

Mulukhiyya: *Corchorus olitorius*

OTHER COMMON, ETHNIC, OR SCIENTIFIC NAMES

Bush okra, Jew's mallow, nalta, nalte jute, tussa jute. Has appeared, in error, as *Carchorus olitorius*.
Turkey: Ip otu

GROWTH HABITS

Annual in temperate regions; perennial in the tropics
Origin: Possibly Egypt
Range: Africa, Hawaii, India, Malaysia, Philippines, Puerto Rico, and
    the Virgin Islands

CULINARY USES

Young shoots and leaves are eaten as a potherb, and occasionally as salad greens. They are also cooked in soups and stews containing chicken, lamb, or rabbit. In West Africa, the shoots are used, like true okra, to thicken soups and stews. In Tunisia, dried and ground leaves serve the same purpose.

OTHER USES

Source of fibers for rope (jute)

COMMENTS

Jew's mallow is also a name for *Kerria japonica,* or bachelor's button, which is a member of the *Rosaceae* family.

96. Tropaeolaceae: The Nasturtium Family

Nasturtium: *Tropaeolum majus*

OTHER COMMON, ETHNIC, OR SCIENTIFIC NAMES
Bitter Indian, Indian cress

Denmark: Baerkarse, blomsterkarse, kapuciner karse, landloeber, nasturtie
Estonia: Suur mungalill
Finland: Koristekrassi, köynnöskrassi
France: Capucine, cresson d'Inde
Germany: Indische Kresse, Kapuzinerkresse, Kresse
Hungary: Sarkantyka
Iceland: Skjaldflétta
Italy: Cappuccina, nasturzio, nasturzio indiano, nasturzio del Perù, tropeolo
Mexico: Capuchina, mastuerzo
Netherlands: Oostindische kers
Norway: Blomkarse
Poland: Nasturcja wieksza
Portugal: Chaga seca
Russia: Nasturtsiya
Spain: Capuchina, espuela de galán, nasturcia
Sweden: Indiankrasse

CULTIVARS
'Empress of India', 'Gourmet Brand Salad Mixture', 'Whirlybird'

Nasturtium
Tropaeolum majus

From Woodville, *A supplement to Medical botany*, vol. 4

Tropaeolum minus: Dwarf nasturtium
Tropaeolum perigrinum: Canary creeper
Tropaeolum tuberosum: Añu, anyu, mashua, ysañu

GROWTH HABITS
Annual
Origin: Andes, north to Mexico
Range: Temperate regions

CULINARY USES

All parts of these plants contain a form of mustard oil that is more volatile than acrinyl isothiocyanate or allyl isothiocyanate, hence their quick-
acting, but short-lived, heat. The flowers have a hint of honey in the scent.

Leaves and flowers are used in salads. Flowers appear as garnishes. Minced
leaves can be added to soft cheeses for use in canapés. Flowers and leaves
produce a delicately peppery vinegar. The unopened flower buds are pickled
in China. The seeds have been roasted and used like pepper.

Some herbalists suggest that nasturtiums can be used as a substitute for
capers. It is unlikely that pickled nasturtiums could resemble capers, and
those who have tried the pickled buds confirm my suspicion. The product is
said to be deliciously peppery and not a bit like capers.

Nasturtium leaves contain glucotropaeolin, which becomes benzyl isothiocyanate in an enzymatic reaction like that of mustard (q.v.). A similar
reaction in the seeds yields isopropyl isothiocyanate.

OTHER USES
Naturtiums are a willing and splashy annual for the garden.

97. Turneraceae: The Turnera Family

Damiana: *Turnera diffusa* var. *aphrodisiaca*

OTHER COMMON, ETHNIC, OR SCIENTIFIC NAMES
Sometimes listed as *Damiana Messicana.*
Mexico: Hierba de la pastoria
Spain: Escobilla

RELATED SPECIES
Turnera afrodisiaca: Damiana (Mexico)
Turnera ulmifolia: Damiana

GROWTH HABITS
  Shrub
  Origin: Tropical and subtropical Americas
  Range: California to Brazil and the islands of the Caribbean

CULINARY USES
  Both species have seen some use in teas and aromatic liqueurs. The leaves have a bitter, tonic quality that results from the presence of tannins and some unspecified essential oils.

COMMENTS
  False damiana, *Aplopappus discoideus,* has been sold as damiana.

98. Urticaceae: The Nettle Family

Nettle: *Urtica dioica*

OTHER COMMON, ETHNIC, OR SCIENTIFIC NAMES
  Stinging nettle
  Germany: Brennessel, Nessel
  India: Bichu, chicru
  Mexico: Ortiga, ortiguilla
  Netherlands: Netel
  Russia: Krapiva

GROWTH HABITS
  Perennial
  Origin: Europe and Asia
  Range: Naturalized in the United States

CULINARY USES
  Young nettles are used as potherbs, especially in France, Ireland, and Scotland (and in areas of the United States inhabited by the descendants of immigrants from those countries). They are similarly popular in the Middle East, where they are found in savory pastries, soups, and rice dishes. Their subtle edge is a complement to dairy products and grains.

  Herbal beers have been made from the leaves, usually in combination with other wild herbs, such as burdock, chamomile, dandelion, herb bennet, and meadowsweet.

  Supposedly, nettles have been used in place of rennet in cheese making. They also add flavor to Kerry Farmhouse, a Cheddar-like cheese from Ireland's County Kerry; England's Single Gloucester is sometimes nettled, as are some Dutch Goudas.

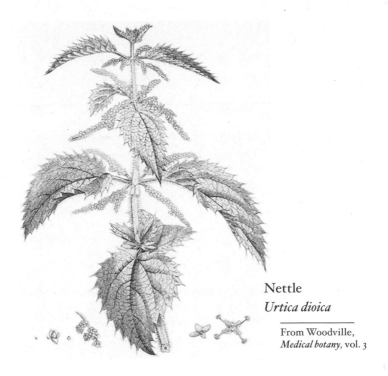

Nettle
Urtica dioica

From Woodville,
Medical botany, vol. 3

The leaves of nettles contain 2-methylhepten-(2)-on-(6), butyric acid, and *p*-coumaric acid.

OTHER USES

Nettles have been used as a source of fibers, for cloth and cordage. The plants also yield several useful vegetable dyes.

COMMENTS

Always wear gloves and a long-sleeved shirt when picking nettles. Before the plants are cooked, the tiny hairs that cover the stems and leaves will raise burning, stinging welts on any skin that brushes against them.

99. Valerianaceae: The Valerian Family

Corn Salad: *Valerianella Locusta* subs. *olitoria*

OTHER COMMON, ETHNIC, OR SCIENTIFIC NAMES

Field salad, fetticus, lamb's lettuce, nut lettuce, white potherb. *Lactuca Agnina* and *Valerianella olitoria* are outdated scientific names for corn salad.

France: Doucette, loblollie, mâche, salade de chanoine, salade de prêtre

'Coquille', 'D'Etampes', 'Dutch Corn Salad', 'Elan', 'Etampes Corn Salad', 'Mâche à Grosse Graine', 'Mâche Veinée' or 'Vert d'Étampes', 'Piedmont', 'Rosette Corn Salad' or 'Vert Coquille de Louviers'. In seventeenth-century France, there was a popular round-leaved cultivar known as 'Mâche Ronde' or 'Mâche à Feuille Ronde Maraîchère'.

RELATED SPECIES
Valerianella eriocarpa: Greese mâche, Italian corn salad, mâche d'Italie or mâche d'Italie à feuille de laitue (France)

GROWTH HABITS
Annual
Origin: Europe, North Africa and western Asia
Range: Temperate regions

CULINARY USES
Corn salad is used (obviously) in salads, but also as a garnish and as cooked greens.

Valerian: *Valeriana officinalis*

OTHER COMMON, ETHNIC, OR SCIENTIFIC NAMES
All heal, amantilla, capon's tail, common valerian, garden helioptrope, phu, setwall, setwell, setewale. Occasionally seen as *Valeriana officinale*. In old herbals, the name of the herb is preceded by *Radix,* for "root."
France: Valeriane
Germany: Baldrian
Italy: Valeriana
Mexico: Valeriana
Spain: Valeriana

RELATED SPECIES
Nardostachys Jatamansi (also known as *Valeriana Jatamansi*): Spikenard
Valeriana Wallichii: Indian nard, spikenard, Syrian nard

GROWTH HABITS
Shrubby perennial
Origin: Eurasia
Range: Naturalized in Canada and northern United States

CULINARY USES
During the Middle Ages, valerian's balsamic warmth made it useful as a seasoning in Europe. It has a honey-like scent that is musky and not entirely pleasant. Other members of the genus (possibly including *Valeriana Wallichii,*

above) are said to be more pleasantly scented and are used in cooking in the Himalayas.

Extracts of valerian are used in the commercial flavorings industry, primarily in beers, candies, ice cream, liqueurs, and soft drinks. Valerian contains β-carotene, β-elemene, borneol, caryophyllene, and *p*-cymol, among over a hundred aromatic compounds, plus many salts and esters of valeric acid.

OTHER USES

Valerian is used to flavor tobacco. It is said to be as attractive as catnip to our feline friends.

COMMENTS

Valeriana Wallichii is not found in *Hortus Third*. Do not confuse these spikenards with the better-known spikenard, *Aralia racemosa*.

100. Verbenaceae:
The Verbena or Vervain Family

Lemon Verbena: *Aloysia triphylla*

OTHER COMMON, ETHNIC, OR SCIENTIFIC NAMES

Gray verbena, lemon-scented verbena, limonetta, yerba louisa, vervain. Some outdated scientific names for lemon verbena include *Aloysia citriodora, Lippia citrodore, Lippia triphylla, Verbena citriodore,* and *Verbena triphylla.* Some ancient Latin names for it include *Verbenaca* and *Veneris Herba.*

Colombia: Alousia
France: Verveine, verveine citronelle, verveine odorante
Germany: Echtes Verberenkraut, Zitronenverbene
Italy: Verbena
Mexico: Cedron, lipia, oregano
Morocco: Louisa
Spain: Hierba louisa

RELATED SPECIES

Aloysia gratissima: Quebradora (Mexico); bee bush
Lippia alba: Jaunilama (Costa Rica); mastranto, orozul (Panama); pitiona (Mexico); anise verbena, lemon verbena, licorice verbena
Lippia dulcis: Tzopelic xlhuitl (Mexico)
Lippia graveolens (formerly listed as *Aloysia lyciodes*): Oregano cimarron (Costa Rica); oreganillo, yerba dulce (Mexico); bee bush, hierba dulce, lippia, Mexican lippia, Mexican oregano, red brush, wild marjoram
Lippia micromeria: Dominican oregano

Lippia nodiflora: Yerba de la Santa Maria (Chile); buccar, ratolia, vakhar (India)

Lippia oreganoides: Mexican oregano (Hawaii); culantro cimarron, oregano de burro (Venezuela)

Lippia scaberrima: Benkas boas (South Africa)

Verbena hastata: Blue vervain, Indian hyssop, simpler's joy, wild hyssop

Phyla scaberrima: Aztec sweetherb

GROWTH HABITS

Shrub

Origin: South America (Chile and Peru)

Range: Greenhouses anywhere. It does well outdoors if it is potted so it can be moved indoors for the winter.

CULINARY USES

Lemon verbena is commonly brewed as an herbal tea. It is also used as a seasoning for drinks, fish, fruits and fruit puddings, jellies, poultry, salads, soups, and stuffings. The leaves are eaten as potherbs and included in omelets.

Perhaps a dozen *Lippia* species are called "oregano" in Mexico, each the object of local preferences. For example, Oaxacan oregano, prized for its grassy-lemony flavor, is never confused with ordinary Mexican oregano.

Tzopelic xlhuitl, *Lippia dulcis,* contains hernadulin, a compound that is ten times sweeter than sucrose. Bee bush, *Lippia graveolens,* contains carvacrol.

Lemon verbena extracts are used in liqueurs. They contain citral (up to 40 percent of the essential oil), cineol, dipentene, limonene, and several floral-scented alcohols.

OTHER USES

Colognes, perfumes, potpourri, and sachets

COMMENTS

According to one source, excessive use may be harmful, and the FDA restricts the use of lemon verbena to alcoholic beverages.

Tzopelic xlhuitl, *Lippia dulcis,* is not listed in *Hortus Third.* Most of that genus seems to have moved to *Aloysia.* Considering some of the common names for *Lippia graveolens,* above, they may very well be the same species.

This is not the same species as verbena, *Verbena officinalis* (q.v.).

Indian hyssop and wild hyssop should not be confused with true hyssop, *Hyssopus officinalis,* or any of the other herbs that include "hyssop" in their names.

According to *Hortus Third,* no members of the genus *Lippia* are cultivated in North America. Nonetheless, Mexican oregano from a local nursery thrived in my little herb garden.

Monk's Pepper: *Vitex agnus-castus*

OTHER COMMON, ETHNIC, OR SCIENTIFIC NAMES

Chaste tree, hemp tree, Indian spice, sage tree, vitex, wild lavender, wild pepper. Monk's pepper is sometimes listed scientifically as *Agnus castus* and pharmaceutically as *Fructus Agni-casti*.

China: Huang jing zi, mai ya

Denmark: Kykshedstrae

Estonia: Harilik mungapipar

France: Arbre au poivre

Germany: Keuschbaum, Mönchspfeffer

Italy: Agnocasto

Morocco: Kheroua

Portugal: Agno casto, árvore da castidade, flor da castidade, pimenteiro silvestre

Sweden: Munkpeppar

Turkey: Hayit

Monk's Pepper
Vitex agnus-castus

From Woodville,
A supplement to Medical botany, vol. 4

  Shrubby tree
  Origin: Eurasia
  Range: Naturalized in North America

CULINARY USES
  The leaves of monk's pepper are used as a seasoning. The seeds are ground
like black pepper. Dried red berries are an ingredient in some recipes for
Moroccan *ras el hanout.*
  The fruits of *Vitex cienkowskii* are eaten in tropical Africa.
  Leaves of the chaste tree contain 1,8-cineole (up to 3,800 ppm), sabinene
(up to 815 ppm), α-pinene (up to 685 ppm), terpinen-4-ol (up to 360 ppm),
and *p*-cymene (up to 325 ppm). Fruits of the chaste tree contain cineole and
pinene.

Verbena: *Verbena officinalis*

OTHER COMMON, ETHNIC, OR SCIENTIFIC NAMES
  Druid's weed, European vervain, herb of grace, herb of the cross, herba
veneris, holy wort, kuma tsuzura, vervain. The old apothecary's names for
verbena were *Herba Verbenae, Venieris Herba,* and *Herb of Venus.*
  France: Herbe sacrée, verveine officinale
  Germany: Eigenkraut, Eisenkraut
  Spain: Yerba sacra
  Turkey: Tibbi mine çiçegi

GROWTH HABITS
  Annual
  Origin: Mediterranean Europe
  Range: Temperate regions

CULINARY USES
  An herbal liqueur, Verveine de Velay, comes from the Auvergne region
of France. Like Chartreuse, it is made with a number of herbs and comes in
green and yellow forms, with the green having the higher alcoholic content.
Its primary flavoring is a wild verbena. A local treat, *bonbons à la Verveine de
Velay,* are flavored with the liqueur.
  In Turkey a condiment is made by combining the blossoms of verbena
with salt.
  The tart, lemony taste of verbena is furnished by citral; its aroma, by terpenene; its bitterness, by glycosides (verbenalin and verbenin) and tannins.

COMMENTS
  The FDA restricts the use of verbena to alcoholic beverages.

This is not the same species as lemon verbena, *Aloysia triphylla* (q.v.).
Verbena oil is also extracted from lemon verbena, *Lippia citriodore* (q.v.).

101. Violaceae: The Violet Family

Sweet Violet: *Viola odorata*

OTHER COMMON, ETHNIC, OR SCIENTIFIC NAMES
English violets, little faces
France: Violette
Germany: März-Veilchen, Veilchen
India: Banaf shah
Italy: Viola, violetta, violetta mammola
Russia: Fialka polevaya
Spain: Violeta odorosa

RELATED SPECIES
Viola cornuta: Prince Henry petite violas
Viola tricolor: Anutini glazki (Russia); flor de la Trinidad (Spain);
    pensamiento (Mexico); Steifmütterchen (Germany); viola tricolore
    (Italy); violette tricolore (France); pansy, johnny jump-ups, violeta
Viola calcarata: Swiss violet

HYBRID
Viola × *Wittrockiana:* Pansy

GROWTH HABITS
Perennial
Origin: Asia, Europe, North America
Range: Temperate regions

CULINARY USES
Flowers are used as garnishes, in salads, or candied on desserts. A sweet
syrup made from violet petals (minus the bitter white base of the flower) can
be turned into an elegant sorbet. The petals can also be used to color and
perfume vinegars.

Crème de Violettes, or Crème Yvette, is a French liqueur that is made
with violet petals. Krambambuli is a German angelica-based liqueur that is
also flavored with violets.

Violet leaves have been eaten in salads, battered and fried like tempura,
or steeped as herbal teas. Extracts from the leaves are used in commercial
flavorings for candies, baked goods, and ice cream.

Violet flowers' sweet, slightly spicy taste comes from a number of aldehydes (up to 50,000 ppm), rutin (up to 20,000 ppm), and eugenol (up to 350 ppm), plus many other trace ingredients. Violet leaves contain 2,6-nonadien-1-ol, eugenol, octadienol, quercetin and rutin. Violet roots contain methyl salicylate, n-2-octen-1-ol and quercetin.

Viola tricolor contains methyl salicilate, myricetin, and *p*-coumaric acid, with bitterness provided by quercetin, rutin, and tannin.

COMMENTS

The FDA restricts the use of *Viola calcarata* and *Viola tricolor* to alcoholic beverages.

102. Vitaceae: The Grape or Vine Family

Grapes: *Vitis vinifera* (and other species)

OTHER COMMON, ETHNIC, OR SCIENTIFIC NAMES
Arabic: 'Inah
Bulgaria: Growde
China: Pu tao
Finland: Viinirypäle
France: Raisin
Germany: Traube, Weinreb
Greece: Trapezou
Iran: Angur
Israel: 'Enav
Italy: Chicco d'uva, uva
Japan: Budo
Netherlands: Druif
Norway: Drue
Poland: Winogrona
Portugal: Uva
Romania: Boaba de strugare
Russia: Vinograd
Spain: Uva
Sweden: Druva
Thailand: A-ngung
Turkey: Asma, üzüm

GROWTH HABITS
Perennial vine
Origin: Caucasus
Range: Grown everywhere except in the Antarctic and Arctic regions

Grapes are, of course, used as fresh fruit, raisins, wine, and brandy. The juice of unripe grapes has been used to acidify sauces; it was known as *verjuice* in the past, and as *agresto,* in Italy today. Verjuice is still used in traditional French cooking, but only in the area around Tours, just west of the center of France. It has recently been rediscovered and has begun to be produced in California. In Iran, verjuice is known as *abghooreh,* while in Lebanon it is called *hosrum.*

At the opposite end of the flavor spectrum is grape molasses. The sweet, unfermented juice of wine grapes is reduced to a spicy, sweet syrup called *dibs* or *pekmez,* in Turkey and the Middle East. Italy has two forms of grape molasses: *mosto,* which is similar to other types already mentioned, and *saba,* which is reduced even further and used in place of sugar in baking.

A number of French cheeses have some kind of interaction with grapes, aside from the obvious pairing of wine and cheese. Some cheeses are macerated in grape products. Picodon is a form of *fromage fort,* that is, a cheese that is pickled by sealing it in a jar with herbs, spices, and alcohol, usually wine, and allowing it to ferment. These "strong cheeses" are sometimes fortified with stronger spirits, such as eau-de-vie. Foudjou is a goat cheese that is made in Vivarais. It is flavored with garlic, salt, pepper, and eau-de-vie—flavored, not fermented as in fromage fort. L'Ami du Chambertin is a handmade cheese that is rinsed with Marc du Bourgogne, a grappa-like spirit. Tomme au Marc actually ripens in a vat of fermenting must.

A high level of tannin gives stuffed grape leaves, or *dolmas,* a pleasant tang.

Grape seeds yield a fine cooking oil with a high smoke point. It is used as the cooking medium in fondue bourguignonne.

103. Zingiberaceae: The Ginger Family

Cardamom: *Elettaria cardamomum*

OTHER COMMON, ETHNIC, OR SCIENTIFIC NAMES

Ailum, capalaga, ebil, kakelah seghar. In medieval Europe, cardamom was called "grains of paradise." It was formerly known scientifically as *Amomum Cardamomum.* When old herbals and apothecaries used the Latin names *Fructus Carvi* or *Cardamomi Semina,* they referred to the fruit (what we think of as seeds) of the plant. Cardamom has had an absurdly large number of "scientific" names, including *Alpinia Cardamomum, Matonia Cardamomum, Cardamomum Minus,* and *Amomum Repens.*

Afghanistan: Hale
Arabic: Hab-hal, hail, hal
Burma/Myanmar: Phalazee

China: Pai-tou-k'ou, sha jen, wok lok uvat
Denmark: Cardamomme
Estonia: Kardemon
Finland: Kardemumma
France: Cardamome, cardamome vert
Germany: Cardamon, Grüner Cardamom, Grüner Kardamom, Kardamom
Iceland: Kardimomma
India: Choti elaichi, elachi, elaichi, elam, enasal, illaichi, velchi, wailchi,
    yalukalu
Indonesia: Kepillaga, kapulaga
Iran: Hel
Iraq: Hail, hale
Israel: Hel
Italy: Cardamomo, cardamomo verde
Japan: Karudamom
Malaysia: Buah pelaga
Morocco: Qaqula
Netherlands: Kardemom
Norway: Kardemomme
Portugal: Cardamomo
South Africa: Caramong (name used mainly by Malaysian emigrés, the
    "Cape Malays")
Spain: Cardamomo
Sri Lanka: Enasal
Sweden: Kardemumma
Thailand: Kravan, krawaan thet
Turkey: Hername, kakule
Vietnam: Ka chong kai, kau blong (Hmong)

CULTIVAR
'Major': Abachi (Morocco); bitter black cardamom, wild cardamom

RELATED SPECIES
Aframomum korarima: Kewrerima (Ethiopia); Ethiopian cardamom, falls
    (false) cardamom, korarima cardamom
Afromomum angustifolium: Madagascar cardamom, wild cardamom
Afromomum elliotii: Alligator cardamom
Amomum compactum: Kepulaga, round cardamom
Amomum subulatum: Badi elaichi, bigillachi, boro alach, kali elaichi,
    upakunchika, veldode (India); cardamome noir, cardamome du Népal
    (France); cardamomo negro (Spain); cardamomo nero (Italy); fekete
    kardamomum (Hungary); mustakardemumma (Finland); Nepal-
    Cardamom, Schwarzer Cardamom (Germany); zwarte kardemom
    (Netherlands); black cardamom, brown cardamom, false cardamom,

greater Indian cardamom, India cardamom, Indian cardamom, large
cardamom, Nepal cardamom

Amomum xanthioides: Bastard cardamom, wild Siamese cardamom

GROWTH HABITS

Perennial

Origin: India and Ceylon

Range: Frost-free areas. It grows wild in Java but it is cultivated there
as well. Commercially raised in Indonesia, India, Sri Lanka, and
Thailand.

CULINARY USES

Cardamom seeds are the familiar spice. The sweetly aromatic pods contain
up to twelve hard, brownish seeds that are used in savory dishes like meats,
poultry, and sausages, and in pickling, soups, and stews. When combined
with enough sugar to counter their bitterness, the seeds also make tasty additions to pastries and other baked goods, such as breads and cookies.

Cardamom has caraway-like warmth and bitterness in the taste, but also
a charming scent that is reminiscent of violets. A fairly expensive spice
(though not as expensive as saffron), it is included only in the better curry
powder blends.

The seeds are good in baked goods, with meats and poultry, in pickling,
and in soups and stews. They combine well with caraway, cinnamon, cloves,
and orange.

In Arabic-speaking areas of the Middle East and Africa, *ras el hanout* is a
mainstay of every kitchen. It can be made from any number of spices and
herbs, but it almost always contains both black and green cardamom. *Baharat* is a Turkish spice blend that includes cardamom; the Iraqi version is
called *boharat*. In Persian cooking, cardamom is an ingredient in the spice
mixture called *advieh*.

Cardamom is a minor ingredient in amaretto, Angostura Bitters, anisette,
some gin recipes, Grand Marnier, and both yellow and green Chartreuse.
Steep the seed pods in sweetened hot white wine for a surprising winter
tonic. Cardamom is said to be an ingredient in Benedictine; of course, the
secret recipe is rumored to include almost every plant that was ever used for
culinary or medical purposes in the sixteenth century.

The toasted seeds are an essential ingredient in garam masala. They are
also used to flavor black tea in Afghanistan, Africa, and India. In Muslim
homes, in parts of Africa and the Middle East, they are used to flavor coffee.
In India, the fermented milk drink *lassi* is often garnished with roasted and
ground cardamom.

Cardamom seed pods come in two common varieties. The large dark ones
have a coarser, smokier flavor and are used in Indian sweet pickles. The lighter
ones (sometimes called white cardamom or green cardamom) are thought to

be of better quality. The only difference between white cardamom or green cardamom is that white cardamom is bleached with sulfur dioxide.

The seeds and leaves are used in Indonesian and Thai curries based on Indian recipes.

Cardamom's essential oil consist of α-terpineol (45 percent), 1,8-cineol (40 percent), myrcene (27 percent), limonene (10 percent), and other terpinoids.

Afromomum elliotii is used to lend a warming bite to alcoholic beverages and to soft drinks like ginger beer. Madagascar cardamom, *Afromomum angustifolium,* is one of many *Afromomums* used as pepper. *Afromomum* seeds have also been used as a flavoring for coffee. Ethiopian cardamom, *Aframomum korarima,* has a harsh, camphoraceous flavor. India cardamom, *Amomum subulatum,* has a smoky, camphoraceous flavor, the smokiness of which disappears upon cooking. It contains, primarily, 1,8-cineol, along with traces of other terpinoids.

COMMENTS

A number of other spices are named (or sold as) cardamom. Kepulaga, *Amomum compactum,* is sometimes sold as a substitute for true cardamom.

In Greece, the word *kárdamon* refers to watercress.

"Wild cardamom" or "Camaroon cardamom" are names for a plant of the *Amomum* genus that is closely related to melegueta pepper (q.v.).

There is allegedly an orange cardamom that is not available in the United States because of its supposed narcotic properties. This may or may not be true. After all, nutmeg is readily available in spite of its potential for illicit use as a hallucinogen.

Chinese Key: *Boesenbergia pandurata*

OTHER COMMON, ETHNIC, OR SCIENTIFIC NAMES
Chinese ginger, fingerroot, fragrant ginger
Also known scientifically as *Boesenbergia rotunda* and *Gastrochilus panduratum.*
China: Suo shi
Germany: Chinesischer Ingwer, Gewürzlilie, Fingerwurz
Indonesia: Temu kunci
Malaysia: Temu kunci
Netherlands: Temoe koentji
Thailand: Krachai, temoo kuntji
Vietnam: Ngai num kho

RELATED SPECIES
Curcuma xanthorrhiza: Tem lawak

Perennial
Origin: Java and Sumatra
Range: Throughout Southeast Asia

CULINARY USES

The ginger-like rhizomes are used in Southeast Asian pickles and *sambals*. Thais use it in salads, raw, as well as in fish curries.

COMMENTS

The name *krachai* is used by Thais for this species as well as for lesser galingal, *Kaemferia galanga* (q.v.).

Costus: *Costus* spp.

OTHER COMMON, ETHNIC, OR SCIENTIFIC NAMES

Kuth, spiral flag. Costus is sometimes listed as *Saussurea lappa* in old botanical texts (see Comments, below).

RELATED SPECIES

Costus speciosus: Wild ginger

GROWTH HABITS
Perennial
Origin: Himalayas
Range: Cultivated in Nepal

CULINARY USES

Roots used in the flavorings industry for baked goods, beverages, candy, ice cream, and puddings. Its aroma—similar to that of orris, vetiver, or violets—is derived from myrcene, *p*-cymene, *l*-linalool, β-ionone, and various sesquiterpenes.

Costus speciosus grows wild in Jamaica, but it is cultivated in the East Indies and Malaysia.

COMMENTS

The genus *Costus* is part of the Zingiberaceae family, while *Saussurea* is part of the Asteraceae, closely related to the thistles. Both are likely sources of flavorings, but neither has led to any positive identification. The species *Saussurea lappa* does not show up in *Hortus Third*.

Do not confuse *Costus speciosus* with wild ginger, *Asarum canadense* (q.v.).

Galingal: *Alpinia galanga*

OTHER COMMON, ETHNIC, OR SCIENTIFIC NAMES

Ginger lily, Laos ginger, Thai ginger, shellflower, Siamese ginger, Java root. Some old herbals and apothecaries used the Latin name *Rhizoma Galangae*. Galingal is listed in some botanical texts as *Languas galanga*.

Arabic: Adkham, galangal
Burma/Myanmar: Pa-de-gaw-gyi
Cambodia: Romdeng
China: Gao liang jiang, hang dou kou, lam keong, lam kieu
Denmark: Grote galanga, stor galanga
Estonia: Kalganirohi
France: Souchet long, souchet odorant
Germany: Galangant, Großer Galgant, Siamesischer Ingwer, Siam Ingwer
India: Arattai, kachoramu, kolinja, kosht-kulinjan, kulanja, pear-rattai, punnagchampa, rasmi
Indonesia: Laos, lengkuas
Iran: Djus rishe
Italy: Galanga maggiore
Japan: Naukyo
Malaysia: Langkuas, lengkuas, lenkuas
Morocco: Kedilsham
Netherlands: Galgant, galigaan, lengoewas
Portugal: Gengibre do Laos, gengibre tailandés, junça ordinária
Spain: Galang, galangal
Sweden: Galangarot
Thailand: Kha
Vietnam: Gieng, rieng

RELATED SPECIES

Alpinia caerula: Native ginger
Alpinia galanga: Liang tiang
Alpinia speciosa (also known as *Alpinia zerumbet*): Shell ginger

GROWTH HABITS

Perennial rhizome
Origin: Asia and Oceania
Range: Frost-free areas or in greenhouses. Cultivated in China and Thailand.

CULINARY USES

The flavor of galingal is similar to that of fresh ginger, only hotter, and with a resinous, vaguely mint-like finish. It is similar to Szechuan pepper in slightly numbing the tongue. Galingal has a sweet, almost floral muskiness in the scent, a little like old roses.

The plant is supposedly one of the warming flavors in Angostura Bitters. Galingal root provides essences used in the manufacture of some aromatic bitter liqueurs made in Czechoslovakia. According to one source, galingal is used in some formulations of Chartreuse and the Russian vodka-based liqueurs known as nastoikas, and in okhotnichya (hunter's brandy), a warming concoction consisting of alcohol, galingal, and other flavorings. Gorny doubnyak is another bitter Russian liqueur that includes galingal among its ingredients (see glossary for these Russian beverages).

Unlike ginger, galingal does not lose its heat when the roots are dried. It may even increase in strength. While powdered dry ginger cannot be substituted in recipes calling for fresh ginger root, dried galingal does work in the place of the fresh root. This is fortunate, since the fresh roots are difficult to obtain outside of Southeast Asia.

If you are not familiar with this seasoning, it is well worth a trip to a Thai market. Sometimes Chinese markets also carry it. It is available as sliced dried roots, called galanga, or as a powdered spice, called Laos. The powdered root is good in sausages. Its ginger-like qualities make it useful in pudding desserts and in jellies used to accompany or glaze meats.

The Moroccan spice mixture *ras el hanout* usually contains galingal.

Galingal
Alpinia galanga

From Köhler, *Köhler's Medizinal-Pflanzen,* vol. 2

The flowers and buds of galingal are used in a highly spiced Indonesian version of tempura. The root is used in Thai curry pastes. It is added to soups in Indonesia and Thailand. It might add a beguiling accent to consommé. It is used in sweet drinks all over Southeast Asia. It is also part of *blachan,* a salted shrimp paste that is the foundation of much Southeast Asian cooking. Blachan is known as *blachang* in India, *blatjan* or *trasi* in Indonesia, or *kapi* in Thailand. Aside from the uses mentioned above, it is used with baked chicken in Guang-dong Province on the southern coast of China.

Once popular in Europe, galingal is now seen primarily in the cuisines of Southeast Asia and of the Arabic countries along the spice route that supplied Europe with exotic flavors of the East.

The hot, fresh-ginger flavor comes from methyl cinnamate (up to 40 percent of the essential oil), cineol (up to 30 percent of the essential oil), camphor, d-pinene, galangin, and many other compounds. When the rhizomes are dried, some of the volatile compounds are lost, leaving a still-hot but rounder-tasting mixture of cineol and farnesene.

OTHER USES

The active flavoring ingredient (flavonoid) is galangin. Flavonoids are the whole class of (mainly vegetable) pigments that give our food its color and often its taste and scent. Galangin is not especially powerful as a pigment (see LESSER GALINGAL).

Essence d'amali is extracted from the galingal rhizomes for use in the perfume industry.

COMMENTS

Another galingal, *Cyperus longus,* is not related but has starchy edible roots with a similar flavor. *Cyperus* is the same genus as papyrus. I have found old references to other galingales, *Dulichium arundinaceum* (1822) and *Dulichium spathecum* (1892), but I have not found that genus mentioned in any modern texts.

Indian galingal, Java root, kha, Laos, and Thai galingal are names that are sometimes used for lesser galingal, *Kaempferia galanga* (q.v.). Commercial extracts of "galingale" are usually lesser galingal.

The FDA restricts the use of galingal to alcoholic beverages.

Ginger: *Zingiber officinale*

OTHER COMMON, ETHNIC, OR SCIENTIFIC NAMES

Adrak, adu, Canton ginger. *Rhizoma Zingiberis* was the old apothecary name for ginger root.

Algeria: Skandjbir
Arabic: Zanjabil
Burma/Myanmar: Gin, gyin sein, khyen-seing
Cambodia: Khnehey, knei

China: Jiang
Colombia: Ajenjibre
Denmark: Ingefaer
Estonia: Harilik ingver
Ethiopia: Zinjibil
Finland: Inivääri, inkivääri
France: Gingembre
Germany: Ingwer
Iceland: Engifer
India: Sonti, sukku (dried); adrak, allam, ingee, inji, shoonti (fresh);
    murraba (preserved); ada, adraka, alha, inchi, inguru, shringaran,
    Sunthi
Indonesia: Aliah, djahe, jahé
Iran: Jamveel, zanjabil
Iraq: Zanjafeel
Italy: Zenzero
Japan: Mioga (shoots only); shoga
Korea: Saenggang
Malaysia: Halia
Mexico: Ajenjibre
Morocco: Skinjbir; skinjbir bied (bleached or limed)
Netherlands: Gember
Nigeria: Atale, chittafo
Norway: Ingefaer
Okinawa: Sõ gã
Philippines: Laya, luya
Poland: Imbir
Portugal: Gengibre
Russia: Imbir
Spain: Jengibre
Sri Lanka: Inguru
Swahili: Tangawizi
Sweden: Ingfära
Thailand: Khing
Turkey: Zencefil
Vietnam: Gung

RELATED SPECIES

Curcuma amada (also known as *Curcuma mangga*): Manga injee (India);
    mango ginger
Nicolaia elatior (also known as *Nicolaia atropurpea* and *Etlingera elatior,*
    formerly known as *Phaeomeria speciosa*): Bunga kantan or bunga siantan
    (Malaysia); myoga (Japan); honje, kecombrang (Indonesia); ginger
    bud, pink ginger buds

437

Zingiber mioga: Hajikama-shoji "blushing ginger," mioga, myōga, myohga (Japan); xiang he (China); mioga ginger

Zingiber zerubet: Ginger (another species, same uses)

GROWTH HABITS

Perennial

Origin: Tropical Southeast Asia

Range: Greenhouses or frost-free areas. Grown commercially in China, Hawaii, southern Florida, Fiji, Tonga, Jamaica, northern Australia, West Africa

CULINARY USES

Ginger loses much of its fire when dried, but it becomes deeper, rounder, and more comforting in its warmth. It is available in a number of forms: green (fresh), powdered, candied, in syrup, and pickled or preserved. Brown ginger is made from roots that were dried without peeling, while white ginger is peeled before drying. Dried ginger should be ground fresh, like pepper, for best flavor.

The best-quality ginger is grown in the West Indies (Jamaica), although most fresh ginger in the United States comes from Hawaii. Indian ginger, also known as cochin ginger, is of lesser quality and is generally used in spice mixtures. African ginger is of lower quality still; it is pungent but does not have West Indian ginger's elegant perfume.

Dried ginger is used in baked goods, candies, and condiments. Guatemalan brown sugar cookies, *bulé,* are unusual in that they are made with fresh grated ginger.

Ginger is an essential ingredient in most Asian cuisines. Thai, Chinese, and Indian food would be unthinkable without the bite of ginger. Ginger's tropical origin explains its appearance in cuisines as far-flung as the Caribbean and Indonesia. Jerk seasoning and some *sambals* use ginger; perhaps Dutch traders have something to do with the use in both. Typically, Chinese dipping sauces use ginger and scallions, especially in Shanghai, where instead of soy sauce, Chianking black vinegar is preferred.

Beni shoga is the sweet, delicate-pink, aromatic young ginger that is cut in almost transparently thin slices and placed on plates of sushi and sashimi. Along with a dab of deceptively cool green wasabi, beni shoga is the perfect accompaniment to the subtly briny flavors of raw seafood.

While the Chinese flavor-principle (to use Elizabeth Rozin's excellent term) is comprised of soy sauce, garlic, ginger, and scallion, an Indian flavor-principle must be made up of chile, garlic, ginger, and turmeric. Ethiopia's flavor-principle includes *berberé* and *niter kebbeh,* complex mixtures of spices and herbs that invariably include ginger. In Persian cooking, ground dried ginger is an ingredient in the spice mixture called *advieh.* It is one of the ingredients in the Iraqi spice blend *boharat.*

Ginger is not much used in Italian cooking, except in Calabria. When a Calabrian describes a dish as "strong," it is understood that ginger is the primary seasoning.

Qishr is a Yemeni coffee-like beverage made from the husks of coffee beans and flavored with ground dried ginger.

Ginger's warmth is essential to ginger ale, ginger beer (*gengbirra* in Brazil) and root beer, as well as higher-powered liquids such as Grand Marnier and Angostura Bitters. The Russian okhotnichya, a concoction consisting of alcohol, ginger, and other flavorings, is calculated to ease the sting of the seemingly endless Russian winters. Gorny doubnyak is a bitter Russian liqueur flavored with ginger and other ingredients. Krupnikas is a Czech liqueur containing dried ginger in addition to allspice, caraway, cinnamon, cloves, honey, lemon zest, orange zest, nutmeg, saffron, turmeric, and vanilla. Stone's Ginger Wine is actually a sweet currant wine infused with ginger. Try using it, reduced to a syrup, over vanilla ice cream, or use paper-thin slices of ginger preserved in syrup in the same way.

Chinese liqueurs are flavored with the ginger-like wild Siamese cardamom, *Amomum xanthioides*.

The dried ground ginger root is used, in combination with other spices and salt, in the French seasoning called *sel épice*. *Quatre épices* is the same thing without the salt. *Épice parisienne* is similar, but it includes marjoram, rosemary, and sage. The three mixtures are used in French charcuterie.

The Arabic spice mixture *ras el hanout* usually contains ginger. In Morocco, ginger is used in curry-like tagines, as well as in *chermoula,* a vinaigrette-like marinade that usually contains cumin and other herbs and spices.

Zingiber mioga is indigenous to Japan and can be grown in cooler regions than any other *Zingiber* species.

As our tastes mature, we find that the most satisfying flavors are those that offer the most complexity, continuously opening up to reveal new subtleties, new layers of culinary allusions, and new hints of exotic realms previously unexplored. Perhaps more than any other spice, ginger, with its characteristic spicy, aromatic pungency, tropical floral overtones, and veiled muskiness, most rewards a revisit. The dried ground version on supermarket shelves, while perfectly usable in its own narrow way, cannot begin to rival the freshly grated root. The drying process and a lingering death on the shelf tend to eliminate most of the rhizome's most fascinating and ethereal volatile oils.

One look at the list of compounds found in fresh ginger explains why the spice has such powers; it reads like a who's who of the flavorings industry. The chemical makeup of ginger takes up over a dozen pages of Paul Schulick's book on ginger. Among ginger's 300-plus chemical constituents, it contains geranial (up to 20,000 ppm), zingiberenes (up to 17,800 ppm), citral (up to 13,500 ppm), several gingerols (up to 13,000 ppm), and neral (up to 13,000 ppm), along with a host of other compounds specific to the genus, such as α-zingiberene, β-zingiberene, zingerberone, zingerone, zingibain, several zingiberenols, zingiberol, and zingiberone.

Lesser Galingal: *Kaempferia galanga*

OTHER COMMON, ETHNIC, OR SCIENTIFIC NAMES

Aromatic ginger, Chinese ginger, colic root, East India catarrh root, finger-root, galingal, gargaut, India root, Indian galingal, Java root, kha, Laos, kachai, kra chaai, maraba, Thai galingal. Former scientific names include *Alpinia officinarum*. The old apothecary's name was *Rhizoma Galangae*. Lesser galingal is sometimes listed botanically as *Bosenbergia rotunda*.

China: Saa jiang, sa leung geung, san bai, sha geung fun
Estonia: Väike kalganirohi
France: Petit galanga
Germany: Kleiner Galanant, Kleiner Galgant
India: Chandramula, kachri, kacholam, kechulu-kalangu
Indonesia: Kencur, kentjoer
Italy: Galanga
Malaysia: Cekuh, cekur, kecil galanga, Kunchor
Netherlands: Kentjoer
Spain: Galangal
Sri Lanka: Hingurupiyali, ingurupiyali
Thailand: Krachai, proh hom, waan teendin

RELATED SPECIES

Kaemferia aethiopica (also known as *Siphonochilus aethiopicus*): No common name found.
Kaemferia rotunda: Himalayan ginger lily, resurrection lily, tropical crocus

GROWTH HABITS

Perennial
Origin: Southeast Asia
Range: Frost-free areas or in greenhouse

CULINARY USES

Lesser galingal is a popular spice in Lithuania and Estonia. It is used in Russia for flavoring vinegars and also in the high-powered drink nastoika.

It is similar to galingal (q.v.), only hotter. It is used as a spice in curry mixtures, especially with fish, in Southeast Asia. In Thailand, where intensely spicy foods are a way of life, it is eaten as a vegetable. For people with relatively timid palates, this would be the incendiary equivalent of sitting down to a salad of jalapeños.

The roots of Himalayan ginger lily, *Kaemferia rotunda,* are chewed in southern Asia, the way sugarcane is chewed in the Caribbean. They are also used as a condiment.

In Ghana, *Kaemferia aethiopica* is used as a spice.

Lesser galingal lends its aromatic, or camphoraceous, presence to vermouth and bitters. Its fragrance is due to pinenes, cineol, linalool, sequiterpenes, and zingiberene. Its pungency comes from gingeroles, shoagoles, and zingerone.

COMMENTS

Like turmeric (q.v.), lesser galingal is a powerful dyestuff. Its deep yellow color will stain anything it touches.

Indian galingal, Java root, kha, Laos galingal, and Thai galingal are names that are sometimes used for galingal (q.v.).

The name *krachai* is used by Thais to mean this species as well as Chinese key, *Boesenbergia pandurata* (q.v.).

Melegueta Pepper: *Afromomum Melegueta*

OTHER COMMON, ETHNIC, OR SCIENTIFIC NAMES

African pepper, cardamom seed, grains of paradise, guinea grains, guinea seed, Hungarian pepper. Melegueta pepper was formerly known scientifically as *Aframomum granum-paradisi, Aframomum melagueta, Aframomum melegueta, Amelopsis Grana Paradisi, Amelopsis Habzeli,* and *Amomum grana paradisi.*
Dominica: Poivre guinée
Estonia: Melegeti aframon
Ethiopia: Kenang, kewrerima
France: Graines de paradis, malaguette, poivre de guinée
Germany: Guineapfeffer, Meleguetapfeffer, Paradieskörner
Italy: Grani de meleguetta, grana paradisi
Morocco: Gooza sahraweea
Netherlands: Paradijskorrels
Russia: Malagvet, rajskiye zyorna
Spain: Malagueta

RELATED SPECIES

Afromomum danielii: Bastard melegueta, Camaroon cardamom (or *Afromomum hanburyi*)

GROWTH HABITS

Perennial
Origin: Tropical West Africa
Range: Cultivated in a number of tropical countries, especially Sierra Leone and Nigeria

Melegueta pepper is sometimes used as a substitute for the more expensive cardamom (q.v.). It was brought to Morocco by spice traders from Mauritania and Senegal. It is used in Brazilian cooking, probably as a result of slave trade between West Africa and South America. Berbers use it to season meats and as a flavoring for breads. The shiny brown husk, or shell, of the seeds is used as a spice by sub-Saharan peoples, especially the Khoisan. Melegueta pepper is an ingredient in *ras el hanout,* the ever-present, ever-changing blend of spices found in North Africa.

Gâlat dagga is a similar Tunisian spice blend consisting of cinnamon, cloves, melegueta pepper, nutmeg, and black pepper. It is typically added to braised dishes.

In Louisiana, melegueta pepper is combined with lemon, red vinegar, and hot pepper sauce for use as a condiment.

Hippocras is a wine flavored with cinnamon, ginger, and melegueta pepper. The herb's clove-like taste, appearing in candies, ice cream, and soft drinks, is supplied by eugenol. Alligator cardamom tea is made from the leaves. Melegueta pepper's aromatic, slightly bitter pungency comes from (6)-paradole, (7)-paradole, (6)-shoagole, and (6)-gingerole.

COMMENTS

Many beers and wines have been adulterated with this "pepper." Its warmth is intended to give the illusion of higher alcoholic strength. Elizabeth I loved the taste of melegueta pepper in drinks, but George III banned its use in the brewing trades because its "heat" could be used to disguise a quaff with lower alcoholic content. It is used today, without larcenous intent, in some liqueurs.

This plant is no relation to true pepper or chile pepper (q.v.). "Hungarian pepper" is much better known as the name of the chile that is the source of paprika.

In Brazil, the terms *pimenta malagueta* or *melegueta pepper* do not refer to this species, but to a small chile that is generally sold pickled in vinegar.

While it is related to cardamom, and sometimes sold as "cardamom seed," melegueta pepper is not the same spice.

"Melegueta pepper" is used as a name for the berries of bay rum, *Pimenta racemosa,* in the Caribbean.

Turmeric: *Curcuma domestica*

OTHER COMMON, ETHNIC, OR SCIENTIFIC NAMES

Besar, Indian saffron, yellow ginger. The flavorings industry knows turmeric as *Rhizoma curcumae.* It used to be known botanically as *Curcuma longa* or *Curcuma xanthorrhiza*. Other old scientific names for the plant include *Curuma rotunda* and *Amomum curcuma*.

Afghanistan: Zarchoba

Burma/Myanmar: Hsanwen, sanae, sa nwin

Cambodia: Romiet

China: Huang jiang, ng-kiew, wong geung, yu-chin

Colombia: Achirilla, azafran, batatilla, camotillo, raiz americana

Costa Rica: Yuquilla

Denmark: Gurkemeje

Swahili: Manjano

East Timor: Kinur

Estonia: Harilik kurkuma

Ethiopia: Ird

Finland: Keltajuuri

France: Curcuma longue, safran des Indes, souchet des Indes, terre-mérite

Germany: Gelbwurz, Indischer Safran, Kurkuma

Hawaii: 'Olena

Iceland: Trmerik

India: Arsina, haldi, huva, kaha, marmarii, munjal, pasupu

Indonesia: Daun kuning (leaves), kunjit

Iran: Zard choobeh

Iraq: Kurkum

Italy: Curcuma, zaffarano Indiano

Japan: Ukon

Java: Kunir

Malaysia: Daun kunyit, kunyit basah

Morocco: Quekoum

Netherlands: Geelwortel, kurkuma

Nigeria: Gangamau

Norway: Gurkemeie

Okinawa: Uccin

Philippines: Dilao, kulyao, kunig

Poland: Klacze kurkumy

Portugal: Açafrão da Índia, curcuma

Russia: Zholty imbir

South Africa: Borrie (term used by Malayan immigrants, the so-called Cape Malays)

Spain: Azafrán arabe, curcuma, cúrcuma

Sri Lanka: Kaha, saffron

Sweden: Gurkmeja

Thailand: Kha min

Vietnam: Cu nghe, nghe kuong huynh

Perennial
Origin: Tropical Asia
Range: China, India, and Southeast Asia

RELATED SPECIES
Curcuma xanthorrhiza: Temu lawak (Indonesia)

CULINARY USES

Turmeric has a musky scent and a slightly bitter taste, a little like ginger without the heat and flowery overtones. It is used primarily for its intense, somewhat muddied yellow color (a result of the pigment curcumin). It does not offer the exquisite perfume of saffron (q.v.), but there is a hint of citric sweetness in the scent. It does have the advantage of low cost. It has a more assertive presence than annatto (q.v.), which is also used for its yellow color. Turmeric is most commonly used in curries. It is good with eggs, in pickling, and in condiments. Turmeric gives ordinary prepared mustard (the kind my family calls "baby mustard") its almost frighteningly radiant yellowness.

Commercial curry powder is a rather insipid blend of turmeric, red pepper, fenugreek (q.v.), ginger (q.v.), cardamom (q.v.), cumin (q.v.), nutmeg (q.v.), cloves (q.v.), cinnamon (q.v.), and other spices. Madras curry powder is a little better, encouraged by the addition of more hot chile powder. In India, hundreds of variations on these spice mixtures, called masalas, are prepared everyday. Everyone has his or her own favorites, carefully roasted and ground fresh to complement specific foods.

In Thailand, flowers and young shoots are eaten as cooked vegetables. The leaves are used as a seasoning in Indonesia, especially for fish dishes.

Turmeric contains turmerone (up to 40,000 ppm), curcumin (up to 38,000 ppm), cineole (up to 29,000 ppm), curcumenol (up to 21,000 ppm), zingiberene (up to 18,000 ppm), and other pigments and flavoring compounds.

OTHER USES
Dyestuffs

COMMENTS

Turmeric stains anything with which it comes in contact.

"White turmeric" is actually zedoary (q.v.).

Golden seal orange root, sometimes called "turmeric," *Hydrastis canadensis,* a relative of buttercups, is not related to this turmeric, *Curcuma domestica.* About the only thing the two plants have in common is their yellow roots.

Indiscriminate use of generic curry powder to make food taste "Indian" is as ridiculous as pouring ketchup on any dish to make it taste "American." Granted, some people use a lot of ketchup, but even the most gastronomically backward individual would gag at the thought of ketchup on ice cream or pancakes. While there is nothing inherently wrong with these combinations, some pretty compelling cultural biases dissuade us from trying them.

Zedoary: *Curcuma zedoaria*

OTHER COMMON, ETHNIC, OR SCIENTIFIC NAMES

Indian arrowroot, kunchor, turmeric, white turmeric. *Rhizoma Zedoariae* and *Zedoariae Rhizoma* were terms used in old herbals and apothecary books. Two names were used for the root, but they distinguished between the angles at which the root was cut, prior to drying. *Radix Zedoaria Longae* was cut at an oblique angle, while *Radix Zedoaria Rotundae* was cut straight across the root.

France: Rhizom de zédoaire
Germany: Zitterwurzel, Zitwer
India: Amb halad, gandhmul, kachur
Indonesia: Temu putih
Italy: Zettovario
Malaysia: Temu putih

Zedoary
Curcuma zedoaria

From Köhler, *Köhler's Medizinal-Pflanzen,* vol. 2

Netherlands: Maagwortel, zedoarwortel
Spain: Cedoaria
Thailand: Khamin khao

GROWTH HABITS
Perennial
Origin: India
Range: Warm temperate regions

CULINARY USES
Zedoary's edible leaves have a bitter, camphoraceous, ginger-like flavor.
The finely shredded roots have been used in condiments, salads, and some
curries. They are said to taste like a more resinous version of green mango.

Zedoary provides a small portion of the "bitter" of Angostura Bitters and
Fernet Branca. It contains camphor and several sesquiterpenes specific to
zedoary.

OTHER USES
Aromatic oil, extracted from roots, is used in industrial flavorings, especially in pharmaceuticals.

COMMENTS
Kunchor is also the name used for lesser galingal (q.v.) in Malaysia.

104. Zygophyllaceae: The Caltrop Family

Guaiac Wood: *Guaiacum officinalis*

OTHER COMMON, ETHNIC, OR SCIENTIFIC NAMES
Guaiacum, guajacan negro, lignum sanctum, lignum vitae. Has been seen
listed botanically as *Guaiacum officinale*.
Colombia: Guayaco
France: Gaiac
Germany: Guajachol
Italy: Guaico
Mexico: Guayacan, huaxacan, palo santo
Spain: Guayacan, guajaco

RELATED SPECIES
Peganum harmala (also listed as *Peganum harmela* and *Peganum hermala*):
    Besasa (ancient term), zit el harmel (refers to oil, in Egypt); üzerlik (oil,

in Turkey); churma (South Africa); epnubu (Egypt); peganon (Greece); Syrian rue, wild rue

GROWTH HABITS
Tropical evergreen tree
Origin: Caribbean, South America
Range: Central America, northern South America and the West Indies. Can be grown in Southern California and Florida

CULINARY USES
The wood has an aromatic scent reminiscent of anise, clove, and rose that appears only when the wood is heated. Guaiac wood and sawdust are the source of extracts used in candy, chewing gum, and soft drinks. They contain the sesquiterpene alcohol called guaiaol.

OTHER USES
Guaiac wood is known commercially as lignum-vitae. Turkish red is a dyestuff made from the seeds of *Peganum harmela*.

COMMENTS
California and several other states list Syrian rue as a noxious weed. Seeds are said to be toxic, causing hallucinations and vomiting. This culinarily useless plant is included here only because its name might imply possible use in cooking.

105. Fungi and Lichens

Angola Weed: *Rocella fuciformes*

GROWTH HABITS
Lichen
Origin: Netherlands
Range: Temperate to subarctic

CULINARY USES
Angola weed is a bitter addition to commercially produced beverages.

COMMENTS
Rocella is not listed in *Hortus Third*. This is not surprising, since not many gardeners plant lichens.
The FDA restricts the use of angola weed to alcoholic beverages.

Cordyceps: *Cordyceps sinensis* or *Cordyceps robertii*

OTHER COMMON, ETHNIC, OR SCIENTIFIC NAMES
Chinese caterpillar fungus
China: Dong chong xiacao, tung chong ha cho

GROWTH HABITS
Fungus
Origin: Qinghai Province, China
Range: China

CULINARY USES
Used as a sweet and warm flavoring in Singapore. Cordyceps-flavored liquid chicken extract is marketed by a company called Brand's. It is used as people would use bouillon cubes.

COMMENTS
Cordyceps is actually a fungus that exists as a parasite on a kind of worm. For part of its life cycle, it *looks* like a plant, and it is used like a plant part (herb or spice) in China and Tibet. Cordyceps provides an odd place to end this catalog of herbs, spices, and flavorings, since it's not really an herb but serves as one in the kitchen.

Glossary

Most of the chemical names that appear in the text are defined here, at least the most important ones. The glossary is meant as a supplement to, not a substitute for, an organic chemistry text. The formulas are written in the simplest, most condensed forms. They do not reveal important structural details of interest to chemists, but they should be sufficient for our purposes.

Synonyms are provided for the same reason that multiple common names for plants are provided in the text: to help serious herbalists who may encounter these unfamiliar terms in their reading. In the entries below, the synonyms are given, preceded by the italicized abbreviation *Syn.* or *Syns.*

Readers who require more detailed information on the science of flavorings should consult standard texts, such as *Fenaroli's Handbook of Flavor Ingredients.*

1-octen-3-ol: $C_8H_{16}O$. *Syn.* octenol. Herbal scent.

1,4-cineole: $C_{10}H_{18}O$. *Syns.* 1,4-epoxy-*p*-menthane; monoterpene epoxide. A terpene with a cool, soothing, slightly spicy taste and vaguely camphoraceous scent.

1,8-cineole: $C_{10}H_{18}O$. *Syns.* 1,8-epoxy-*p*-menthane; cajuoutol; cineol; cineole; eucalyptol; limonene oxide; *p*-cineol; zedoary oil. Chemically the same as previous item but structually different, with a spicy camphoraceous scent and pungent taste.

2-nonanone: $C_9H_{18}O$. *Syns.* methyl heptyl ketone; nonan-2-one; n-heptyl methyl ketone. Sweet, earthy, herbal or weedy scent.

2-undecanone: *See* methyl nonyl ketone.

2,6-nonadienal: *Syns.* cucumber aldehyde; *trans,cis*-2,6-nonadienal. Cucumber scent, with a hint of violet.

3-octanol: *See* octenol.

3-*p*-cymenol: *See* thymol.

4-allylveratrole: *See* methyl eugenol.

4-terpineol: $C_{10}H_{18}O$ *Syns.* 1-*p*-menthen-4-ol; 1-methyl-4-isopropyl-1-cyclohexen-4-ol; origanol. Chemically the same as 1,4-cineole, but structurally different, with sweet, peppery, earthy scent.

α-cadinene: $C_{15}H_{24}$. Chemically identical to β-cadinene, but structurally different; found in citronella.

α-ionone: $C_{13}H_{20}O$. *Syns*. α-cyclocitrylidenacetone; 4-(2,6,6-trimethyl-2-cyclohexen-2-yl). Sweet tasting with violet/raspberry scent.

α-phellandrene: $C_{10}H_{16}$. *Syns*. 1-isopropyl-4-methyl-2,4-cyclohexadiene; 4-isopropyl-1-methyl-1,5-cyclohexadiene; 5-Isopropyl-2-methyl-1,3-cyclohexadiene; *p*-mentha-1,5-diene; 1-methyl-4-isopropyl-1.5-cyclohexadiene; 2-methyl-5-isopropyl-1.3-cyclohexadiene. Monocyclic monoterpene with an herbaceous, mint-like scent, with hints of citrus and pepper.

α-pinene: *See* pinene.

α-santalol: *See* santalol.

α-terpineol: $C_{10}H_{16}$. *Syns*. 1,4-*p*-menthadiene; 1-methyl-4-isopropyl-1,4-cyclohexadiene; α-terpinene; β-terpineol. An oxygenated monoterpene with an herbaceous lemon-like scent and slightly bitter flavor. A different chemical, also called α-terpineol, smells like lilacs and peaches. *See* α-terpinyl acetate.

α-terpinyl acetate: $C_{12}H_{20}O_2$. *Syns*. α-terpineol; α-terpinyl propionate; alpha terpineol. Sweet tasting, with a bergamot-lavender scent suggesting lilac.

α-thujone: $C_{10}H_{16}O$. *Syn*. isothujone. Bitter taste and aromatic scent.

absinthol: *See* thujone.

acetaldehyde: C_2H_4O. *Syn*. ethanal. Pungent-tasting, naturally occurring or synthetic compound with a fruity aroma.

acetic acid: $C_2H_4O_2$. *Syn*. ethanoic acid. An aliphatic acid with the familiar biting flavor and scent of vinegars.

acetophenone: C_6H_8O. *Syns*. acetyl benzene; hypnone; phenyl methyl ketone. Ketone with a peppermint-like scent and bitter taste.

achilleic acid: $C_6H_6O_6$. *Syns*. 1-propene-1.2.3-tricarboxylic acid; aconitic acid; citridic acid; equisetic acid. Bitter tonic taste.

acrinyl isothiocyanate: Provides the quick tongue-burning heat of Chinese mustard. *See* allyl isothiocyanate.

advieh: Iranian spice mixture usually containing cardamom, cinnamon, cloves, dried ginger, and sometimes black pepper.

adzhika: Russian spice mixture containing bay leaves, dried chiles, salt, and black pepper.

alantin: *See* inulin.

alcohols: Organic compounds with this generalized structure: one or more hydrocarbon chains attached to one or more hydroxyl radicals (OH). The number of hydroxyl radicals determines the sweetness (the more, the sweeter). Alcohols containing eight to twelve carbon atoms tend to have floral scents, while alcohols containing twelve or more carbon atoms are odorless.

aldehydes and ketones: Organic compounds with this generalized structure: two aromatic rings (such as benzene), aliphatic hydrocarbons (compounds in which the atoms are not arranged in rings), or hydrogen atoms are connected by a carbonyl group (>C=O). Acetaldehyde is a typical aldehyde, while ethyl acetoacetate is a typical ketone.

allicin: $C_6H_{10}OS_2$. *Syns*. 2-propene-1-sulfinothioic acid S-2-propenyl ester; diallyl disulfide oxide. Short-lived raw garlic flavor created when enzymes in the cells react with alliin.

alliin: S-2-propenyl-l-cysteine sulfoxide; see above.

allyl disulfide: *See* diallyl disulfide.

allyl isothiocyanate: C_4H_5NS. *Syn*. mustard oil. Formed when sinigrin ($C_{10}H_{16}NO_8S_2$, allyl glucosinolate) is exposed to moisture in the presence of enzyme myrosinase.

Gives brown mustard, horseradish, and watercress their bite. It attacks the nose and eyes with a long-lasting, stinging burn. Pure mustard oil is extremely irritating; don't even think of smelling or tasting it, except in very dilute form.

aloin: $C_{21}H_{22}O_9$. *Syn.* barbaloin. Glycoside with bitter flavor.

ambrettolide: $C_{16}H_{28}O_2$. *Syns.* ambrette oil; ω-6-hexadecenolactone; musk ambrette. Commercial flavoring ingredient with a musky scent and sweet blackberry/cherry/peach flavor.

amyl acetate: *See* isoamyl acetate.

amyris oil: *Syn.* West Indian sandalwood oil. A naturally occurring mixture of β-caryophylline, d-cadinene, furfural, and methanol derived primarily from *Amyris balsamifera,* with a sweet scent and hot, burning taste.

anethol: $C_{10}H_{12}O$. *Syns.* 1-methoxy-4-propenyl benzene; anethole; *p*-propenylanisole; isoestragole; *p*-propenylphenyl methyl ether; *trans*-anethol. Naturally occurring, or synthetically produced, compound responsible for sweet anise, fennel, or licorice flavor and aroma. Sold as oil of anise, oil of star anise, or oil of badian.

angelic acid: $C_3H_6O_{20}$. *Syns.* angelica acid; dimethyl acrylic acid. Warm, pungent scent and bittersweet flavor.

angelica aldehyde: C_3H_8O (derived from angelic acid). Aromatic, balsamic scent found in the essential oil of chamomile.

angelicin: $C_{11}H_6O_3$. *Syns.* furo[2,3-h]benzopyran-2-one; isopsoralen. A furocoumarin with a musky scent, reminiscent of celery and iris.

anisic acid: $C_8H_{10}O_2$. *Syns.* 4-methoxybenzyl alcohol; anisyl acid. An aromatic acid with a peach-like flavor and a floral scent.

anisic aldehyde: $C_7H_8O_2$. *Syns.* 4-methoxybenzaldehyde; aubepine; *p*-anisic aldehyde. Aromatic carbonyl with hawthorn scent and a bitter, hot licorice taste.

anisaldehyde: $C_8H_8O_2$. *Syns.* 4-methoxybenzaldehyde; *p*-anisaldehyde. Chemically similar to anisic aldehyde, but structural differences and an additional carbon atom result in less anise and more floral scent.

anisol: C_7H_8O. *Syns.* anisole; methoxybenzene; methyl phenyl ether. Naturally occurring, or synthetically produced, compound with a floral, fruity aroma and slightly pungent sweet taste.

apiole: $C_{12}H_{14}O_4$. *Syns.* 1-allyl-2,5-dimethoxy-3,4-(methylendioxy)-benzol; 2,5-dimethoxy safrole; 5-allyl-4,7-dimethoxa-1,3-benzodioxol; apiol; *p*-apiol. Parsley-camphor scent.

asarone: $C_{12}H_{16}O_3$. *Syns.* 1,2,4-trimethoxy-5-(e)-1-propenylbenzol; trans-1-propenyl-2,4,5-trimethoxybenzol; asarin; asarabacca camphor. Pungent camphoraceous scent.

ascaridol: $C_{10}H_{16}O_2$. *Syns.* 1,4-epidioxy-*p*-menthen-(2); 1,4-epodioxy-*p*-menth-2-en. Unpleasant-smelling monoterpene peroxide, reminiscent of kerosene, found in boldo leaves and epazote.

β-bisabolene: $C_{15}H_{24}$. *Syns.* 1-methyl-4-(5-methyl-1-methylene-4-hexanyl)-1-cyclohexene, β-bisbolene; limene. Sesquiterpene hydrocarbon with a balsamic scent.

β-cadinene: $C_{15}H_{24}$. Chemically identical to α-cadinene, but structurally different. Found in cedar and juniper.

β-caryophyllene: $C_{15}H_{24}$. *Syn.* caryophyllene. Naturally occuring bicyclic sesquiterpene, chemically identical to β-cadinene, but structurally different, with a resinous, slightly clove-like aroma.

β-citral: $C_{10}H_{16}O$. Terpene, chemically identical to α-citral, but structurally different. Lemon scent and bittersweet flavor. *See also* neral.

β-ionone: $C_{13}H_{20}O$. *Syns.* β-cyclocitrylidenacetone; 4-(2,6,6-trimethyl-1-cyclohexen-1-yl) o-3-buten-2-one; beta ionone. Sweet, fruity, woody, violet scent. *See also* α-ionone.

β-pinene: *See* pinene.

β-santalol: *See* santalol.

β-terpineol: $C_{10}H_{18}O$. *Syns. p*-menth-8-en-1-ol. Woody, earthy or humus-like scent, slightly pungent. *See also* α-terpineol.

β-thujone: $C_{10}H_{16}O$. Aromatic monoterpene with a bitter taste.

baharat: Turkish spice blend. See *boharat*.

barbaloin: *See* aloin.

benzaldehyde: C_7H_6O. *Syns.* benzenecarbonal; benzene carboxaldehyde; benzene methylal; benzoic aldehyde; benzoyl hydride; bitter almond oil. Aromatic with a strong, bitter-almond and cherry scent.

benzoic acid: $C_7H_6O_2$. *Syns.* benzencarboxylic acid; dracylic acid; phenylformic acid. Aromatic, with a slight balsamic scent and sweet-sour taste.

benzyl acetate: $C_9H_{10}O_2$. *Syn.* benzyl ethanoate. Aromatic ester with a floral, jasmine scent and a bitter, burning taste.

benzyl acetoacetate: $C_{11}H_{12}O_3$. *Syns.* benzyl acetyl acetate; benzyl β-ketobutyrate; benzyl 3-oxobutanoate. Ester with a winey, pineapple-like scent.

benzyl alcohol: C_7H_8O. *Syns.* α-hydroxy toluene; phenyl carbinol; phenyl methanol. Aromatic alcohol with a floral (rose), fruity, slightly aromatic scent and a sweet, burning taste.

benzyl benzoate: $C_{14}H_{12}O_2$. *Syns.* benzyl benzene carboxylate; benzyl phenyl formate. Ester with a slightly aromatic, balsamic, almond-like scent and a sharply burning taste.

benzyl butyrate: $C_{11}H_{14}O_2$. *Syn.* benzyl butanoate. Sweet-tasting aromatic ester with the aroma of ripe apricots, pears, plums, and jasmine.

benzyl cinnamate: *Syns.* benzyl alcohol cinnamic ester; cinnamein. Aromatic ester with sweet honey flavor and a fruity balsamic scent.

benzyl formate: $C_8H_8O_2$. *Syn.* benzyl methanoate. Sweet-tasting aromatic ester with a floral pineapple or apricot scent.

benzyl isothiocyanate: C_8H_7NS. Pungent peppery taste in nasturtium leaves and flowers; formed when enzymes in the cells react with glucotropaeolin (benzyl glucosinolate).

berberé: A pepper paste used as a condiment and a seasoning ingredient in North Africa, especially Ethiopia. Primarily composed of hot and sweet chiles, it also contains a great, and varying, number of other herbs and spices, such as allspice, basil, bishop's weed, black pepper, cardamom, cinnamon, cloves, coriander, cumin, fenugreek leaves and seeds, garlic, ginger, onions, nutmeg, rue seeds, salt, and turmeric.

bisabolol: $C_{15}H_{26}O$. *Syns.* 1-methyl-4(1,5-dimethyl-1-hydroxyhex-4(5)-enyl)-cyclo-hexen-1; 6-methyl-2-(4-methyl-3-cyclohexen-1-yl)-5-hepten-2-ol; α-bisabolol. Woody balsamic scent.

bixin: $C_{25}H_{30}O_4$. *Syns.* 9'Z-6,6'-diapocarotene-6,6'-dioate; arnotta; carotenedioic acid. Red-orange pigment in annatto, with a slightly musty, nutty flavor.

boharat: Iraqi spice mixture, as variable as *ras el hanout,* but usually containing allspice, black pepper, cardamom, cinnamon, cloves, dried ginger, nutmeg, and dried rose petals. Sometimes listed as *abazir, afawi, baharat, bharat, bjar,* or *bohar.*

borneol: $C_{16}H_{18}O$. *Syn.* borneo camphor. Bicyclic monoterpene alcohol with characteristic peppery camphoraceous scent, somewhat less pungent than camphor.

butyric acid: $C_4H_8O_2$. *Syns.* butanoic acid; ethylacetic acid. An aliphatic acid with a sharp rancid-butter smell.

cadinene: $C_{15}H_{24}$. *Syns.* α-cadinene; β-cadinene. Naturally occuring mixture of bicyclic sesquiterpenes: α-cadinene and β-cadinene.

caffeine: $C_8H_{10}N_4O_2$. *Syns.* 1,3,7-trimethyl-1-2-6,-dioxopurine; 1,3,7-trimethylxanthine; coffeine; guaramine; methylbromine; theine; trimethylxanthine. Odorless, somewhat bitter alkaloid stimulant found in chocolate, coffee, guaraná, maté, and tea. Caffeine, as its chemical name indicates, has three methyl groups attached to its xanthine component. Theophylline and theobromine contain only two methyl groups.

cajuputene: *See* limonene.

camphene: $C_{10}H_{16}$. *Syns.* 3,3-dimethyl-2-methylene norcamphane; 2,2-dimethyl-3-methylene norbornane, adamantane; d-camphene; l-camphene; terebene. Combined monocyclic monoterpenes (d-camphene and l-camphene) with a camphoraceous scent and taste.

camphor: $C_{10}H_{16}O$. Bicyclic monoterpene ketone with a pungent, aromatic scent and burning taste.

capraldehyde: *See* capric aldehyde.

capric acid: $C_{10}H_{20}O_2$. *Syns.* decanoic acid; rutic acid. An aliphatic acid with a sweaty, rancid odor, reminiscent of goats.

capric aldehyde: $C_9H_{20}O$. *Syns.* capraldehyde; decanal; decyl aldehyde; n-octanal. Fruity orange-peel scent and pungent taste.

caproic acid: $C_6H_{12}O_2$. *Syns.* capronic acid; hexanoic acid; hexoic acid. An aliphatic acid with a pungently sour, sweaty-goat smell.

caprylic acid: $C_8H_{16}O_2$. *Syns.* caprinic acid; octanoic acid. An aliphatic acid, often associated with saturated fats, with a fruity scent and mildly sour flavor.

carotol: $C_{15}H_{26}O$. *Syn.* carrot seed oil. Essential oil from carrot seeds, with a warm, woody and spicy scent, suggesting cumin and caraway.

capsaicin: $C_{18}H_{27}NO_3$. *Syns.* N-vanillyl-8-methyl-6-(E)-nonenamide; *trans*-N-vanillyl-8-methyl-6-nonenamide; n-(4-hydroxy-3-methoxybenzyl)-8-methylnon-trans-6-enamide. Hot component of chile peppers. The hotness of chiles is not controlled solely by the amount of capsaicin they contain. There are many different forms of capsaicin, with varying molecular shapes and lengths. *See* capsaicinoids.

capsaicinoids: *Syns.* dihydrocapsaicin; nordihydrocapsaicin; homodihydrocapsaicin; homocapsaicin; nonanoic acid vanillylamide; decanoic acid vanillylamide. Close chemical relatives of capsaicin, with varying degrees of hotness, rate of attack, duration, and location where burn is felt. The forms with shorter molecular lengths are supposed to be hotter, but the hotness lasts for a shorter time. Structural differences might explain some otherwise inexplicable effects, such as some chiles "attacking" the mouth; some, the throat; and some, the sinuses.

carvacrol: $C_{10}H_{14}O$. *Syns.* 5-isopropyl-2-methylphenol; cymophenol; 2-p-cymenol; isothymol. An oxygenated monoterpene with a spicy, oregano/thyme-like scent and a slight smokiness. Can be synthesized from p-cymene.

carvene: *See* d-limonene.

carveol: $C_{10}H_{16}O$. *Syn.* p-mentha-6,8-Dien-2-ol. Pungent monocyclic monoterpene alcohol with caraway-spearmint scent.

carvone: $C_{10}H_{14}O$. *Syn.* carvol. *See also* d-carvone; l-carvone. Naturally occurring mixture of monocyclic monoterpene ketones d-carvone and l-carvone with a warm aromatic caraway scent and taste.

caryophellene: *See* β-caryophellene.

cascarillin: $C_{12}H_{18}O_4$. *Syns.* cascarilla oil; eleuthera bark; sweetwood bark oil. Bitter oil with a spicy scent.

cassie aldehyde: *Syns.* cassia aldehyde; cassia oil; cinnamaldehyde; oil of cinnamon; phenyl acrolein. Typical sweet flavor and scent of cinnamon. Derived from leaves and twigs of *Cinnamomum cassia.*

cayenne oil: *See* linalool.

charmoula: Syn. chermoula. Middle Eastern marinade consisting of honey, slow-cooked onions, vinegar, and *ras el hanout.*

cineol: *See* 1,8-cineole.

cinnamic acid: $C_9H_8O_2$. *Syn.* 3-phenylpropenoic acid. Aromatic acid with the scent of apricots, flowers, and honey with a sweet/hot taste.

cinnamic alcohol: C_9H_9O. *Syns.* cinnamyl alcohol; phenylallylic alcohol; styryl carbinol. Naturally occurring nine-carbon alcohol, providing the floral component of the scents of several esters found in spices such as allspice and cinnamon.

cinnaminic aldehyde: C_9H_8O. *Syns.* 3-phenylpropenal; 3-phenyl-acrolein; 3-phenyl-2-propenal; α-amylcinnamaldehyde; alpha-amylcinnamaldehyde; β-phenylacrolein; cassia aldehyde; cinnamal; cinnamaldehyde. Natural or synthetic source of the balsamic/floral scent and spicy, hot taste of cinnamon.

cinnamyl acetate: $C_{11}H_{12}O_2$. *Syns.* 3-phenyl-2-propen-1-yl acetate; 3-phenyl allyl acetate; phenyl-2-propen-1-yl acetate; phenyl allyl acetate. Aromatic ester with a sweet floral, pineapple, or woody scent and a hot, sweet taste.

citral: $C_{10}H_{16}O$. *Syns.* 3,7-dimethyl-2,6-octadienal; geranial; neral. Naturally occurring or synthetic mixture of monoterpene aldehydes α-citral and β-citral; responsible for lemon's scent; has a bittersweet flavor.

citric acid: $C_7H_8O_7$. *Syn.* sour salt. Fruit acid with characteristic tart, sour taste.

citronellal: $C_{10}H_{18}O$. *Syns.* 3,7-dimethyl-6-octen-1-al; d-rhodinal. Naturally occurring (in lemongrass) or synthetic monoterpene aldehyde with a waxy lemon-rose aroma.

citronellol: $C_{10}H_{20}O$. *Syns.* cephrol; dimethyl-6-octen-1-ol; d-citronellol; l-citronellol. Aliphatic monoterpene alcohol with a musty leather, rose scent and a sweet taste, like peaches. Naturally occurring in lemongrass or synthesized from citronellal or geraniol.

citronellyl acetate: $C_{12}H_{22}O_2$. *Syns.* 3,7-dimethyl-6-octen-1-yl ethanoate; 3,7-dimethyl-6-octen-1-yl acetate. Fruity, apricot-rose, scent, with a hint of bergamot, lime, and lavender. Its initial pungent taste is gradually replaced by sweetness in the finish.

ciu britsa: Romanian herb/spice blend (*tschubritza* in Polish) containing savory, lovage, celery, fenugreek, and salt. Tarragon-like scent with a hint of hay (coumarin).

colombo: A curry-like spice mixture from the French Antilles. Contains allspice, cinnamon, coriander, garlic, and saffron, and soured with either green mango or tamarind.

coriandrol: *See* linalool.

coumarin: $C_9H_6O_2$. Bitter, naturally occurring phenolic compound characterized by a fresh-mown-hay scent, with a hint of vanilla. First synthesized in 1868. Somewhat toxic, it is used in medicine; its use is prohibited in food products in the United States. Coumarin is extracted from tonka beans and woodruff by alcohol, hence its use in vanilla extracts and may wine.

cultivar: A more narrowly defined category than species. Cultivars are usually produced by careful selection of plants with desired characteristics. They are sometimes produced by inducing genetic "damage" with radiation or compounds such as colchicine, or by crossing two or more species (*see* hybrids). Newer methods include gene-splicing and other forms of genetic engineering.

cuminic aldehyde: $C_{10}H_{12}O$. *Syns.* cuminaldehyde; cuminal; cumaldehyde; *p*-isopropyl-benzaldehyde. Aromatic monoterpene with a pungently spicy, woody, and fruity scent.

cuminyl alcohol: $C_{10}H_{14}O$. *Syns.* cumic alcohol; cuminic alcohol; cuminol; *p*-cymen-1-ol. Strong caraway scent; pungent burning taste.

cymol: $C_{10}H_{14}$. *Syns.* cymene; *p*-methyl cumene; *p*-cymene; para-cymene; 4-methyl-1-isopropyl benzene. Aromatic monoterpene hydrocarbon with a strong carrot scent.

d-carvone: $C_{10}H_{14}O$. *Syns.* 2-methyl-5-(1-methylethenyl)-2-cyclohexene-1-one; dextro-carvone. Chemically identical to carvone and l-carvone, but structurally different. Naturally occurring compound responsible for the slightly mint-like scent and characteristic warm flavor of cumin and caraway.

d-limonene: $C_{10}H_{16}$. *Syns.* D-1,8-p-menthadiene; carvene; citrene; dextro-limonene. Chemically identical to limonene and l-limonene, but structurally different. Naturally occurring terpene found in caraway seeds, with a sweet lemon scent.

d-linalool: *See* linalool.

damascenone: *Syns.* 4-(2,6,6-trimethyl cyclohexa-1,3-dienyl)but-2-en-4-one; β-damascenone. Sweet fruity rose scent.

decanal: *See* capric aldehyde.

decoction: A kind of solvent extraction in which material such as barks, roots, or twigs are simmered for over an hour in order to release their essential oils and other flavoring compounds in the hot water.

diacetyl: $C_4H_6O_2$. *Syns.* 2,3-butanedione, 2,3-diketobutane; dimethyl glyoxal. When dilute, it has a buttery caramel flavor and scent. Pungent in more concentrated form. Usually synthetic, but can be derived from some fermentations of glucose.

diallyl disulfide: $C_6H_{10}S_2$. *Syn.* allyl disulfide. Typical garlic scent. *See also* allicin.

dihydrocarveol: $C_{10}H_{18}O$. *Syns.* 6-menthen-3-isopropenylcyclohexanol; 8-*p*-menthen-2-ol; tuberyl alcohol. Monocyclic monoterpene alcohol with a warm, sweet taste and a floral scent.

dihydrocarvone: $C_{10}H_{16}O$. *Syns.* cis-l-dihydrocarvone; 8-*p*-menthen-2-one; *cis-p*-menthen-4-isopropenyl cyclohexan-2-one. Monocyclic monoterpene alcohol with a mint-like herbaceous taste.

dihydrocarvyl acetate: $C_{12}H_{20}O_2$. *Syns.* 8-*p*-menthen-2-yl acetate; *p*-menth-8-(9)-en-2-yl acetate. Ester with a minty, floral scent.

dipentene: *See* limonene.

distillation: Method of flavor extraction in which a material is heated, driving off its volatile essential oils. The resulting vapor is collected and then cooled, condensing the essential oils.

dukka: Egyptian spice mixture, similar to *ras el hanout,* but having a base consisting of ground chickpeas or hazelnuts. Typical spices included are black pepper and the seeds of coriander, cumin, and sesame. Sometimes spelled *dukkah* or *duqqa.*

elecampane camphor: *See* helenin.

épice parisienne: Literally "Parisian spice," a blend of bay leaves, cinnamon, cloves, ginger, nutmeg, mace, marjoram, rosemary, sage, and white pepper. Also known as *épice fines.* See also *quatres épices.*

ester: Compound formed by the reaction between an alcohol and an acid.

estragole: *See* methyl chavicol.

ethers: Compounds whose structures consist of two or more hydrocarbon chains attached to an oxygen atom.

ethyl acetate: $C_4H_7O_2$. *Syns.* acetic ether; ethyl ethanoate. Bittersweet ester of ethanol and acetic acid, with a musty wine or pineapple scent.

ethyl acetoacetate: $C_6H_{10}O_3$. *Syns.* acetoacetic ester; ethyl β-ketobutyrate; ethyl-3-oxobutanate. Ester with fruity, ether-like scent.

ethyl butyrate: $C_6H_{12}O_2$. *Syn.* butanoic acid ethyl ester. Sweet ester of ethanol and butyric acid, smelling and tasting like banana, pineapple, and orange, used in the synthesis of artificial rum flavor.

ethyl formate: $C_3H_6O_2$. *Syns.* ethyl methanoate; formic ether. Sweet ester of ethanol and formic acid, with a fruity rose and pineapple/rum scent.

eucalyptol: *See* 1,8-cineole.

eugenol: $C_{10}H_{12}O_2$. *Syns.* 2-methoxy-4-(2-propenyl)pheol; 4-(1-propene-3-yl)-2-methoxy-phenol. Bitter, naturally occurring phenylether compound responsible for typical clove flavor and scent.

eugenol acetate: $C_{12}H_{14}O_3$. *Syns.* 2-4-allyl-2-methoxyphenyl acetate; acetyl eugenol; allyl-2-4-methoxyphenyl acetate; eugenyl acetate; methoxy-4,2-propen-1-yl phenyl acetate. Ester with a sweet, floral, fruity, spicy, balsamic scent characteristic of cloves.

exaltolide: $C_{15}H_{28}O_2$. Trademark for ω-pentadecalactone; 15-hydroxypentadecanoic acid, angelica lactone, ω-lactone. Strong, long-lasting, musky scent.

expression: A method of flavor extraction in which a material is pressed or crushed, breaking cells and releasing their essential oils and other compounds, such as esters, acids, and alcohols.

farnesol: $C_{15}H_{26}O$. Aliphatic sesquiterpene alcohol with a musky scent reminiscent of nutmeg and/or lily of the valley.

fenchone: $C_{10}H_{16}O$. *Syns.* d-1,3,3-trimethyl-2-norbornanone; d-fenchone; dextro-fenchone. Bicyclic monoterpene ketone with a warm herbal scent carrying a hint of camphor and cedar; has a bitter, hot flavor.

five spice: Chinese mixture of cinnamon, cloves, fennel seed, star anise, and Szechuan peppercorns, ground together.

fructosin: *See* levulin.

furfural: $C_5H_4O_2$. *Syns.* 2-furaldehyde; α-furfuraldehyde; pyromucic aldehyde. Intense, sweet, caramel-almond scent.

γ-terpinene: $C_{10}H_{16}$. *Syns.* 1-methyl-4-isopropyl-1,4-cyclohexadiene; 1-methyl-4-propyl iso-1,4-cyclohexadiene; gamma-terpinene; moslene. Terpene with an oily or woody lemon-lime scent.

γ-undecalactone: $C_{11}H_{20}O$. *Syns.* 4-hydroxyundecanoic acid; γ-heptyl butyrolactone; γ-lactone. Musty peach scent.

galangin: $C_{15}H_{10}O_5$. Yellow pigment found in galingal.

galipoline: $C_{15}H_{26}O$. Bitter sesquiterpene alcohol found in angostura.

gaultheria oil: *See* methyl salicylate.

geranial: $C_{10}H_{16}O$. *Syn.* 2-trans-3.7-dimethyl-2,6-octadien-1-al. Lemon-scented terpene with a bittersweet flavor.

geraniol: $C_{10}H_{18}O$. *Syn.* 2-trans-3,7-dimethyl-2,6-octadien-1-ol. Bitter, naturally occurring aliphatic monoterpene alcohol, smelling of roses and wax. An isomer of nerol.

geranyl acetate: $C_{12}H_{20}O_2$. *Syns.* geraniol acetate; *trans*-3,7-dimethyl-2,6-octadien-1-yl acetate; *trans*-3,7-dimethyl-2,6-octadien-1-yl ethanoate. Floral-scented ester with a fresh, fruity, lavender and rose scent. A synthetic version can be derived from carrot oil and eucalyptus oil.

geranyl tiglate: $C_{15}H_{24}O_2$. Bitter ester with herbaceous geranium scent.

glucosides: Bitter compounds consisting of a carbohydrate (sugar) and an aldehyde or ketone.

gomasio: Japanese condiment made by toasting sesame seeds together with sea salt, then grinding them coarsely.

gorny doubnyak: Bitter Russian liqueur flavored with angelica, cloves, galingal, ginger, and oak tastes derived from acorns and wood chips.

green fairy: A nickname for absinthe. *See* thujone.

guaiacol: $C_7H_8O_2$. *Syns.* *o*-methoxyphenol; *o*-hydroxyanisole; methylcatechol; *o*-1-hydroxy-2-methoxybenzene; pyrocatechol monomethyl ether. Phenolic compound with a sweet woody or smoky balsamic odor and slightly biting taste.

guaranin: Alkaloid that is similar to caffeine (q.v.).

harissa: North African pepper paste containing, typically, chiles, cilantro, coriander seed, caraway seed, garlic, olive oil, mint, and salt. Also the name of some unrelated dishes in several Arabic-speaking countries.

helenin: C_6H_8O. *Syns.* elecampane camphor; inula camphor. Aromatic scent and bitter taste.

heliotropine: *See* piperonal.

herbes de Provence: Blend of basil, fennel, marjoram, rosemary, sage, summer savory, and thyme; sometimes includes lavender.

hexadecenolactone: *See* ambrettolide.

hierbas de olor: Mexican equivalent of a French *bouquet de fines herbes,* but contains bay leaves, marjoram, Mexican oregano, and thyme.

hror: Hot Algerian spice blend, similar to, but less complex than, *ras el hanout.* Typically contains black pepper, cinnamon, cloves, coriander seed, and nutmeg.

hybrid: A sterile cross between two or more genera or species; procedure is intended to create desirable characteristics in the offspring.

imperatorin: $C_{12}H_{12}O_3$. *Syns.* imperatrin; peucedanin. Aromatic tonic scent.

indole: C_8H_7N. *Syns.* 1-benzazole, 1-benzol β pyrrol; benzopyrrole. Musky naptha scent, reminiscent of mothballs.

inosite: $C_4H_{12}O_6$. Unfermentable sugar, with a sweet taste and no discernable odor. Chemically identical to glucose, but structurally different.

inula camphor: *See* helenin.

inulin: $C_6H_{10}O_5$. *Syns.* alantin; alant starch; dahlin. Starchy (polysaccharide) substance used in bread substitutes for people with diabetes.

ionone: $C_{13}H_{20}O$. *Syns.* α-cyclocitrylidenacetone; 4-(2,6,6-trimethyl-2-cyclohexen-1-yl)-3-buten-2-one. Sweet-tasting sesquiterpene ketone found in the essential oils of many flowers. *See also* α-ionone; β-ionone.

irone: $C_{14}H_{22}O$. *Syns.* *cis*-α-irone; trans-α-irone; mixture of α-irone, β-irone, and γ-irone. Sesquiterpene ketone with violet or orris scent.

isoamyl acetate: $C_7H_{14}O_2$. *Syns.* 3-methyl-1-butanol; amyl acetate; β-methylbutyl acetate; isoamyl ethanoate; isopentyl acetate. Naturally occurring or synthetic ester with a banana scent and bitter-sweet taste.

isoamyl alcohol: $C_5H_{12}O$. *Syns.* isobutyl carbinol; isopentyl alcohol; 3-methyl-1-butanol. Ester contributing a fruity, whiskey-like note to the scents of chamomile, strawberries, raspberries, and rum.

isoeugenol: $C_{10}H_{12}O_2$. *Syns.* 1-hydroxy-2-meythoxy-4-propenylbenzene; 2-methoxy-4-propenylphenol; 4-propenyl guaicol. Phenolic compound with a woody, floral, slightly spicy clove scent.

isopentyl acetate: *See* isoamyl acetate.

isopulegone: $C_{10}H_{18}O$. *Syns.* 1-methyl-4-isopropenyl cyclohexan-3-ol; *p*-8,9-menthen-3-ol. Monocyclic monoterpene alcohol with a strong woody or medicinal mint scent.

isovaleraldehyde: $C_5H_{10}O$. *Syns.* 3-methylbutanal; 3-methylbutyraldehyde. Nutty or fruity scent when dilute; penetratingly sharp when concentrated.

jasmone: $C_{11}H_{16}O$. *Syns. cis*-jasmone; ectocarpene. Ketone found in jasmine oil and orange blossoms, with a long-lasting fruity, floral scent.

kekik: Turkish name for a number of herbs of the Lamiaceae family. *See* marjoram; oregano; thryba; thyme; savory; za'atar.

ketones: *See* aldehydes and ketones.

kmeli suneli: Russian spice mixture containing basil, bay leaves, celery seed, coriander seed, dill, fenugreek, mint, parsley, saffron, and thyme.

l-carvone: $C_{10}H_{14}O$. *Syns.* 2-methyl-5-(1-methylethenyl)-2-cyclohexene-1-one; laevo-carvone. Chemically identical to carvone and d-carvone, but structurally different. Produces spearmint odor and flavor of caraway seeds. Derived from *Mentha spicata* or synthesized from d-limonene.

l-citronellol: $C_{10}H_{20}O$. *Syns.* laevo-citronellol; rhodinol. Bitter tasting, with a cool rose scent. Occurs naturally in geranium oil.

l-limonene: $C_{10}H_{16}$. *Syn.* laevo-limonene. Chemically identical to limonene and d-limonene, but structurally different. Naturally occurring monocyclic monoterpene found in pine needles and cones, with a sweet lemon-mint, piney scent.

l-menthol: $C_{10}H_{20}O$. *Syn.* laevo-menthol. Chemically identical to menthol, but structural differences are responsible for its uniquely cool taste. *See also* menthol.

l-menthone: $C_{10}H_{18}O$. *Syns.* 5-methyl-2-(1-methylethyl) cyclohexanone; laevo-menthone. An oxygenated monoterpene with a cool mint scent.

l-menthyl acetate: $C_3H_6O_2$. *Syn.* laevo-menthyl acetate. Milder mint taste than menthol, with a hint of fruit or rose in the scent.

la kama: Moroccan spice mixture containing black pepper, cinnamon, ginger, nutmeg, and turmeric.

lauric aldehyde: $C_2H_{21}O$. *Syns.* aldehyde C-12 lauric; lauraldehyde; dodecanal; dodecyl aldehyde; lauryl aldehyde. Fresh, soapy scent.

lemon oil: Naturally occurring compound with the odor and flavor of the outer, pith-free peel of lemon.

limonene: $C_{10}H_{16}$. *Syns.* cajuputene; dl-limonene; dipentene. Mixture of d-limonene and l-limonene. Naturally occurring terpene found in turpentine, characterized by a sweet, fresh, lemon scent.

linalool: $C_{10}H_{18}O$. *Syns.* 2,6-dimethyl-2,7-octadien-6-ol; 3,7-dimethyl-1,6-octadien-3-ol; coriandrol; d-linalool. Naturally occurring or synthetic aliphatic monoterpene alcohol with a sweet citrus-blossom scent, very much like lavender. Cayenne oil is derived from linalool; it has a sweet, floral, woody scent and is used in the perfume industry.

linalyl acetate: $C_{12}H_{20}O_2$. *Syns.* 3,7-dimethyl-1,6-octadien-3-yl acetate; bergamol; linalool acetate. Sweet, naturally occurring or synthetic ester (oxygenated monoterpene) with a pleasant fruity, floral scent, like lavender and black currants with a hint of bergamot, wax, and wood.

malic acid: $C_4H_6O_3$. *Syns.* hydroxy dicarboxylic acid; hydroxysuccinic acid. Fruit acid responsible for the tart flavor of green apples.

mandelonitrile glucoside: *See* sambunigrin.

mannite: $C_6H_{14}O_6$. *Syn.* mannitol. Sweet, odorless nutrient, used as replacement for sugar.

menthol: $C_{10}H_{20}O$. *Syns.* oil of mint, peppermint camphor. Naturally occurring or synthetic monocyclic monoterpene alcohol with odor of peppermint.

menthone: $C_{10}H_{18}O$. *Syns.* 5-methyl-2-(1-methylethyl)-cyclohexanone; *p*-menthan-3-one. Monocyclic monoterpene ketone with a slightly woody, peppermint scent.

methyl anthranilate: $C_8H_9NO_2$. *Syns.* methyl 2-amino benzoate; methyl o-amino benzoate; o-amino methyl benzoate. Bitter-tasting ester, smelling primarily of orange blossoms and grapes. Can be derived from neroli oil and citrus oil.

methyl benzoate: $C_8H_8O_2$. *Syns.* methyl benzene carboxylate; niobe oil. Ester with a sharp wintergreen scent.

methyl butyrate: $C_5H_{10}O_2$. *Syn.* methyl butanoate. Sweet-tasting ester with apple-banana-pineapple scent.

methyl chavicol: $C_{10}H_{12}O$. *Syns.* estragole; iso-anethol; paramethoxyallylphenol. Naturally occurring compound responsible for anise or licorice flavor of fresh tarragon, but sweeter than anisol (q.v.).

methyl cinnamate: $C_{10}H_{10}O_2$. *Syn.* methyl 3-phenyl propenoate. Sweet-tasting, naturally occurring aromatic ester with a fruity, balsamic scent, smelling faintly of cherries and strawberries.

methyl eugenol: $C_{11}H_{14}O_2$. 1,2-dimethyl-4-allylbenzene, methyleugenol; 4-allylveratrole. Phenylether with a clove scent and a hot, bitter taste.

methyl nonyl ketone: $C_{11}H_{22}O$. *Syns.* 2-hendecanon; 2-undecanone. Bitter rue scent with a sweet peach-like taste.

methyl salicylate: $C_8H_8O_3$. *Syns.* gaultheria oil; methyl 2-hydroxybenzoate; oil of wintergreen; sweet birch oil; synthetic wintergreen oil; synthetic sweet birch oil; synthetic teaberry oil. Aromatic ester with typical wintergreen flavor and scent.

mirepoix: A mixture of chopped aromatic vegetables used as flavoring for sauces, soups, and stocks. The classic French version is comprised of two parts onion to one part each of carrots and celery. Cajun mirepoix (known as "trinity") substitutes green peppers for the carrots.

mixed spice: A mixture commonly called for in old English cookbooks. Depending on the commercial brand chosen, it *can* contain allspice, cassia, cinnamon, coriander, cloves, ginger, nutmeg, and sometimes even dill, although allspice, cinnamon, cloves, ginger, and nutmeg are the most common ingredients. In the United States, it is marketed as "Pumpkin Pie Spice."

mustard oil: *See* allyl isothiocyanate. Descriptive term, often applied to any of several burning or irritating isothiocyanates.

myrcene: $C_{10}H_{16}$. *Syn.* 7-methyl-3-methylene-1,6-octadiene. Acyclic monoterpene with a pleasant spicy, peppery balsamic scent and a pungent flavor.

myrtenol: $C_{10}H_{16}O$. *Syns.* 2-pinene-2-ol; 6,6-dimethyl-2-oxymethyl bicyclo 1,1,3 hept-2-ene. Bicyclic monoterpene alcohol with a slightly medicinal, sweet, woody pine/balsam scent.

n-octanal: *See* capric aldehyde.

n-valeric acid: $C_5H_{10}O_2$. *Syns.* ethyl propanoate; pentanoic acid; propyl acetic acid; valerianic acid; valeric acid. Pungent, rancid-butter odor, disgustingly reminiscent of feces.

nastoika: *Syns.* vodka *nastoyennye* or *nastoyki*. Any of a number of herb- or spice-infused vodkas used in Russia. The distinctions between social and medical uses are a bit hazy. *Zel'e* is a generic term for herbs and hops that are added to vodkas.

neral: $C_{10}H_{16}O$. *Syn.* β-citral. Terpene that is chemically identical to α-citral, but structurally different. Lemon scent and bittersweet flavor, sweeter than geranial. *See also* geranial.

nerol: $C_{10}H_{18}O$. *Syns.* (2-*cis*-3,7-dimethyl-2,6-octadien-1-ol); neroli. Aliphatic monoterpene alcohol with a sweet rose-like scent. Bitter fruit flavor. An isomer of geraniol.

nerolidol: $C_{15}H_{26}O$. Aliphatic sesquiterpene alcohol with a flowery citrus, slightly woody scent.

niter kebbeh (*nit'ir qibe*): Ethiopian ghee-like fat, seasoned with a number of spices and herbs, such as basil, bishop's weed, cardamom, garlic, ginger, nutmeg, and turmeric.

nonadienal: $C_9H_{14}O$. *Syns.* 2,6-nonadien-1-al; trans-2,cis-6 nonadienal. Cucumber-like scent.

nonadienol: $C_9H_{16}O$. *Syns.* 2,6-nonadien-1-ol; *trans*-2,*cis*-6 nonadienol. Strong cucumber aroma with a hint of violet.

o-pentadecalactone: *See* exaltolide.

ω-pentadecalactone: $C_{15}H_{28}O_2$. Musk/fruit/berry scent.

ocimene: An acyclic monoterpene with a scent that is fruity, woody, sweetly citrus-like, and floral. Characteristic for basil but occasionally found in other species.

octanoic acid: *See* caprylic acid.

octenol: $C_8H_{18}O$. *Syns.* 3-octanol; n-amyl ethyl carbinol. Sweet herbal-spicy scent, suggesting citrus, melon, and mint, with an organic woodsy hint of wild mushrooms.

oil infusion: A method of flavor extraction in which a material is soaked in fat, capturing fat-soluble essences from the material in the fat. *Enfleurage* is done in cold oil, while *maceration* is done in hot oil or melted fat. Maceration can also be done using alcohol instead of fat and sometimes refers to cold infusion in water.

oil of mint: *See* menthol.

oil of quassia: *See* quassine.

oil of thyme: *See* thymol.

oil of vetiver: *See* vetiverol.

oil of wintergreen: *See* methyl salicylate.

okhotnichya: *Syn.* hunter's brandy. Russian alcoholic beverage flavored with anise seeds, chiles, citrus peel, coffee, cloves, galingal, ginger, and juniper berries.

oxalic acid: $C_2O_4H_2$. Sour component of rhubarb, sorrel, and spinach.

oxylates: Sour salts of oxalic acid.

p-cresol: C_7H_8O. Phenolic compound, chemically identical to anisole and m-cresol, but structurally different. Sweet tasting, with a honey-like scent.

p-cresyl methyl ether: $C_8H_{10}O$. *Syns. p*-methyl anisole; *p*-methoxy toluene; methyl *p*-cresol. Pungent phenolic scent, reminiscent of ylang-ylang.

p-cymene: *See* cymol.

panch phoron: Syn. Bengali five spice. Indian spice mixture typically consisting of the seeds of cumin, fennel, fenugreek, brown mustard, and nigella, roasted and ground together. Aniseed, cassia leaves, or dried red chiles are occasional substitutions for some of the traditional ingredients.

paramethoxyallylphenol: *See* methyl chavicol.

patchouli alcohol: $C_{15}H_{26}O$. Sesquiterpene with a strong, persistent, moldy/musky scent.

pebre: Mexican pesto-like mixture containing cilantro, lemon juice, olive oil, onion, parsley, garlic, jalapeño, salt, and black pepper.

pentanoic acid: *See* n-valeric acid.

perillic aldehyde: $C_{10}H_{14}O$. *Syns.* dihydrocuminic alcohol; iso-carveol; *p*-mentha-1,8-dien-7-ol; *p*-menthadien-1,8(9)-al(7). Terpineol smelling like linalool (q.v.).

perillyl alcohol: $C_{10}H_{16}O$. *Syn.* 1-hydroxymethyl-4-isopropenyl-1-cyclohexene. Monocyclic monoterpene alcohol with a floral scent reminiscent of lilacs and lavender.

phellandrene: *See* α-phellandrene.

phenols: Organic compounds containing one or more aromatic rings (such as benzene) attached to one or more hydroxyl radicals (OH). The organoleptic differences between them are determined by any additional attached radicals and their positions on the benzene ring (indicated by a prefix consisting of a Greek letter, such as α, β, and γ). Phenols tend to have pungent, peppery tastes. While most have leather-like scents, those with relatively few hydroxyl radicals are fairly sweet smelling; as more hydroxyl radicals are added, the scent becomes increasingly hot and spicy.

phenyl ethyl alcohol: $C_8H_{10}O$. *Syns.* 2-phenylethanol; β-phenethyl alcohol; benzyl carbinol; phenethyl alcohol. Bitter aromatic, with a dried-rose scent suggestive of peaches.

phenylethylene isothiocyanate: C_9H_8NS. *Syns.* 2-phenylethyl isothiocyanate; phenyl ethyl isothiocyanate. Characteristic horseradish pungency.

phenyl methyl ketone: *See* acetophenone.

picrocrocin: *See* safranal.

pinene: $C_{10}H_{16}$. *Syns.* 6,6-dimethyl-2-methylene norpinane; β-pinene; beta pinene. Monocyclic monoterpene with a piney, resinous, turpentine-like scent.

piperidine: $C_{10}H_{16}O$. *Syns.* hexazane; hexahydropyridine; pentamethylenimine. Sweet, floral-scented alkaloid that gives black pepper its characteristic scent and contributes to its hot taste.

piperine: $C_{17}H_{19}NO_3$. *Syn.* l-piperoylpiperidine. Primary hot component of black pepper. No scent; practically no taste other than heat.

piperitone: $C_{10}H_{16}O$. *Syns.* 4-isopropyl-1-methyl-1-cyclohexen-3-one; *p*-menth-1-en-one. Monocyclic monoterpene ketone; d-form has peppermint scent, l-form smells like spruce, i.e., minty and camphoraceous.

piperonal: $C_8H_6O_3$. *Syns.* 3,4-methylene dioxybenzaldehyde; dioxymethylene procatechuic aldehyde heliotropine; heliotropine; protocatechuic aldehyde methylene ether. Aromatic carbinyl with a sweet almond, floral, heliotrope-like scent and a bittersweet taste.

propenyl sulfenic acid: C_3H_6SO. Chemically equivalent to thiopropanal-S-oxide, but structurally different. Eye irritant formed when S-1-propenyl-L-cysteine sulfoxide, found in the cells of onions, is exposed to air through cutting or chopping. The formation is a mechanism similar to that of allyl isothiocyanate (q.v.).

pulegone: $C_{10}H_{16}O$. *Syns.* 1-isopropylidene-4-methyl-2-cyclohexanone; d-4,8-*p*-menthen-3-one; delta-4,8-P-menthen-3-one; pulegon. Monocyclic monoterpene ketone with a strong camphor/peppermint scent.

quatre épices: Literally "four spices," but the selection varies depending on the country in which the term is used. France uses cloves, ginger, nutmeg, and white pepper. In Egypt it's cinnamon, clove, nutmeg, and pepper. Cinnamon, paprika, pepper, and rosebuds are combined in Tunisia. In Morocco people use clove, ginger, nutmeg, and pepper. See also *épice parisienne.*

quinine: $C_{20}H_{24}N_2O$. Odorless but very bitter alkaloid.

ras el hanout or *raz el hanout:* A blend of spices, widely variable and popular all across the Maghreb—Morocco, Algeria, Tunisia, and Libya. It is known as *kama* in Tangier. Some recipes require as few as eleven spices, while others call for twenty-five or more.

recardo: Belizean seasoning paste based on annatto. Red version includes black pepper, cumin, garlic, onion, and vinegar. Black version uses the same, plus cloves and burned corn tortillas.

rhodinol: *See* l-citronellol.

sabinol: $C_{10}H_{16}$. *Syns.* dextro-thujene; dextro-thujane; dihydrosabinene; tanacetane; thuj-4(10)-ene; thujane; sabinane; sabine; sabinene. Monocyclic monoterpene with a woody, pine-like, spicy citrus scent.

safranal: $C_{10}H_{14}O$. *Syns.* 1,1,3-trimethyl-2-formyl cyclohexa-2,4-diene; 2,6,6-trimethyl cyclohexa-1,3-dienyl methanal; dehydro-beta-cyclocitral. Bitter glucoside with the perfumed, slightly iodine-like scent and taste typical of saffron.

safrol: $C_{10}H_{10}O_2$. *Syns.* 3-4-methylenedioxyallylbenzene; 4-allyl-1,2-methylenedioxybenzene; m-allylpyrocatechin methylene ester; safrole. Phenyl ether with a sassafras scent.

santalol: $C_{15}H_{24}O$. *Syns.* 2-methyl-5-(2,3-dimethyltricyclo[2.2.1.0(2,6)]hept-3-yl)-pent-2-en-1-ol; 2-methyl-5-(2-methyl-3-methylenebicyclo[2.2.1]hept-2-yl)pent-2-en-1-ol; argeol; α-santalol; β-santalol. Bicyclic sesquiterpene alcohol with a spicy sweet taste and a woody/raspberry scent, characteristic of sandalwood.

santalyl acetate: Isomer of santalol with bittersweet taste and apricot scent.

sel épice: French seasoning mixture, consisting of allspice, cassia, cinnamon, cloves, coriander seed, ginger, nutmeg, salt, and white pepper.

sofrito: A green seasoning paste of cilantro, culantro, and small mild chiles that are closely related to the infinitely hotter Scotch bonnets. Used mainly in Puerto Rican cooking. Available in jars.

suwanda kudu: Sri Lankan spice mixture containing black cumin, cardamom, cinnamon, cloves, cumin, and fenugreek.

syrup: In modern recipes, a simple syrup is composed of equal amounts of sugar and water. A heavy syrup contains twice the amount of sugar. When older herbal books or flavoring texts refer to a "syrup," they mean equal amounts of a decoction or infusion with honey or sugar.

tabil: Tunisian seasoning paste composed of caraway seed, cilantro or coriander seed, chiles, and garlic.

tadka: Ghee (clarified butter) in which a mixture of spices has been fried. Spices usually include seeds of ajowan, cumin, and dill. Sometimes asafoetida, garlic, and ginger are added near the end of the frying so they do not burn.

tanacetin: *See* thujone.

tannins: Bitter, astringent group of phenolic compounds responsible for the "bracing" quality of tea and the dry mouthfeel of red wines.

tea: Not just hot water flavored with *Camellia sinensis*. Any dried herb, soaked in freshly boiled water, yields an infusion (a kind of solvent extraction). Herbal teas that do not contain *Camellia sinensis* are called tisanes.

tenacetone: *See* thujone.

terpenes: Type of hydrocarbon found in essential oils, such as neroli.

terpinen-4-ol: $C_{10}H_{18}O$. *Syns.* 1-methyl-4-isopropyl-1-cyclohexen-4-ol; 4-carvomenthenol; 4-terpinenol; terpinene-4-ol. Warm, earthy, peppery flavor and scent.

terpineol: $C_{10}H_{18}O$. *Syns.* 1-methyl-4-isopropyl-1-cyclohexen-8-ol; terpineol, α-terpineol; α-terpilenol. Bittersweet monocyclic monoterpene alcohol with a lilac-peach scent.

theobromine: Tasteless alkaloid stimulant, found together with caffeine, in chocolate and some other plant products. *See also* caffeine.

theophyllene: Faintly bitter alkaloid stimulant, found together with caffeine, in maté, tea, and some other plant products. *See also* caffeine.

thiopropanal-S-oxide: *See* propenyl sulfenic acid.

thujone: $C_{10}H_{16}O$. *Syns.* absinthol; tenacetone. Bitter bicyclic monoterpene ketone typical of arborvitae, feverfew, hyssop, sage, and wormwood. *See also* sabinol.

thyme camphor: *See* thymol.

thymol: $C_{10}H_{14}O$. *Syns.* 5-methyl-2-isopropyl-1-phenol; oil of thyme; thyme camphor; 3-*p*-cymenol. Naturally occurring aromatic compound (phenol) responsible for thyme's resinous, smoky, almost carbolic scent and flavor.

tiglic acid: $C_5H_8O_2$. *Syns. trans*-2-methyl crotonic acid; *trans*-2-methyl-2-butenoic acid. Spicy, woody scent with a hint of caramel.

tincture: A kind of solvent extraction in which a material is steeped in a mixture containing alcohol, dissolving its flavoring components in the liquid. Alcohol is needed because many flavoring compounds contain resins or other substances that do not readily dissolve in water.

tucupi: Amazonian cassava-based condiment consisting of agriao do para (a chicory-like plant), garlic, melegueta pepper, and other spices and herbs.

USDA: United States Department of Agriculture

valerianates: Salts of valerianic acid.

valerianic acid: *See* n-valeric acid.

valeric acid: *See* n-valeric acid.

valeric aldehyde: $C_5H_{10}O$. *Syns.* amyl aldehyde; cyclopentanol; pentanal; valeral; valeraldehyde. Woody, nutty scent with fruity or vanilla overtones.

vanillin: $C_8H_8O_3$. *Syns.* 4-hydroxy-3-methoxy-benzaldehyde; vanillaldehyde. Bitter-tasting natural or synthetic phenolic compound largely responsible for characteristic vanilla flavor and scent.

vanillyl acetone: *See* zingerone.

variety: A more narrowly defined category than species. Varieties can be naturally occurring or artificially induced. Varieties will show true in succeeding generations. *See* hybrids.

verbenol: $C_{10}H_{16}O$. *Syn.* 2-pinen-4-ol. Pine/balsam scent.

verbenone: $C_{10}H_{14}O$. *Syn.* 2-pinen-4-on. Minty, camphoraceous, celery-like scent.

vetivone: $C_{15}H_{22}O$. *Syns.* α-vetivone; β-vetivone. Sweet, earthy, woody, vegetal scent.

za'atar: Generic name for a number of Middle Eastern herbs of the Lamiaceae family (including plants of the *Origanum, Satureja, Thymbra,* and *Thymus* genera), used interchangeably as a condiment. They all contain thymol and carvacrol, but those possessing the highest levels of carvacrol are preferred.

zhug (also *s'khug*): Yemeni seasoning paste consisting of black pepper, caraway (or cumin), cardamom, chiles, cilantro, garlic, salt, and sometimes cloves.

zingerone: $C_{11}H_{14}O_3$. *Syns.* 4-(4-hydroxy-3-methoxyphenyl)-2-butanone; vanillyl acetone. Ketone with characteristically pungent, woody ginger scent and burning taste.

Sources

Numbers in parentheses indicate products or services available: (1) source of additional information; (2) source of seeds and plants; (3) source of herbs and spices. All of the URLs were accessed on October 5, 2006.

Alfrey Seeds (2)
   Post Office Box 415
   Knoxville, TN 37901
Aloha Seed and Herb (2)
   http://www.alohaseed.com/
American Herb Association (1)
   http://www.ahaherb.com/
American Herbalists Guild (1)
   http://www.americanherbalistsguild
   .com/
American Indian Ethnobotany
   Database (1)
   http://www.kstrom.net/isk/Food/
   plants.html
Anzen Japanese Foods and Imports (3)
   736 Northeast Martin Luther King
   Boulevard
   Portland, OR 97232
   Telephone: (503) 233-5111
Aphrodisia Products, Inc. (3)
   282 Bleeker Street
   New York, NY 10014
   Telephone: (212) 989-6440
Applewood Seed Company (2)
   http://www.applewoodseed.com/
Arizona Herb Association (1)
   http://www.azherb.org/
Arnold Arboretum (1)
   http://www.arboretum.harvard.edu/
Baker Creek Heirloom Seeds (2)
   http://www.rareseeds.com/

Baltimore Herb Club (1)
   http://www.herbsearch.com/
   BHClub/BaltimoreHerbClub.htm
Bee Rock Herb Farm (2)
   5807 Sawyer Road
   Signal Mountain, TN 37377
Bezjian's Grocery, Inc. (3)
   4725 Santa Monica Boulevard
   Los Angeles, CA 90029
   Telephone: (323) 663-1503
Blossom Farm (1, 2, 3)
   http://www.blossomfarm.com/
Botany Libraries/Gray Herbarium
   Libraries/Economic Botany (1)
   http://www.huh.harvard.edu/
   libraries/index.html
Bountiful Gardens/Ecology Action (2)
   18001 Shafer Ranch Road
   Willets, CA 95490-9626
   Telephone: (707) 459-6410
California School of Herbal Studies (1)
   http://www.cshs.com/
Canadian Herb Society (1)
   http://www.herbsociety.ca/
Caprilands Herb Farm (1, 3)
   http://www.caprilands.com/
Cross Country Nurseries (2)
   http://www.chileplants.com/
Crownsville Nursery (2)
   http://www.crownsvillenursery
   .com/

Dabney Herbs (2)
http://www.dabneyherbs.com/

Da Gift Basket Chile Products of New Mexico (3)
http://www.dagiftbasket.com/

Dat'l Do It (3)
http://www.datildoit.com/

Earl May Seed and Nursery Company (2)
http://www.earlmay.com/

Elixir Farm (2)
http://www.elixirfarm.com/

Evergreen Y.H. Enterprises (2)
http://www.evergreenseeds.com/

Fernwood Botanic Garden (1)
http://www.fernwoodbotanical.org/

Fragrant Garden (1, 2)
Portsmouth Road
Erina 2250, New South Wales
Australia
Telephone: (15) 02-4367-7322
Fax: (15) 02-4365-1979
e-mail: frgntgar@worldgrp.fastlink.com.au

Fruit and Spice Park (1)
http://www.floridaplants.com/fruit&spice/index.html

Garden Medicinals and Culinaries (1, 2)
http://www.gardenmedicinals.com/

Geo. W. Park Seed Company (2)
http://www.parkseed.com/

Gernot Katzer's Spice Pages (1)
http://www-ang.kfunigraz.ac.at/-katzer/engl/

Goodwin Creek Gardens (1, 2)
http://www.goodwincreekgardens.com/

Gourmet Gardener (1, 2)
http://www.gourmetgardener.com/

Green Dealer Exotic Seeds (2)
http://www.GreenDealer-Exotic-Seeds.com/seeds/Index.html

Gurney's Seed & Nursery (2)
http://www.gurneys.com

Hartman's Herb Farm (2)
http://www.petershamcommon.com/hartman.htm

Hatch Chile Express (3)
http://www.hatch-chile.com/

Heirloom Herbals (3)
122 Spring Run Road
Butler, PA 16001-8432
Telephone: (724) 282-2940

Henry Fields Seed and Nursery Company (2)
http://www.henryfields.com/

Herb Companion (1)
http://www.herbcompanion.com/

Herb Quarterly (1)
http://www.herbquarterly.com/

Herb Research News (1)
http://www.herbs.org/index.html

Herb Shop (3)
http://www.bulkherbshop.com/

Herb Society (1)
http://www.herbsociety.co.uk/index.html

Herb Society of America (1)
http://www.herbsociety.org/

Herb Society of Southwestern Virginia (1)
http://dir.gardenweb.com/directory/hssv/

HerbalCroft Gardens (2, 3)
http://www.herbalcroft.com/

HerbalGram (1)
http://www.herbalgram.org/

Herbal Safety (1)
http://www.herbalsafety.utep.edu/

Herbie's Spices (3)
http://www.herbies.com.au/

Herbs Australia (1)
http://www.screamingseeds.com.au/

Herbs-Liscious (2)
1702 South Sixth Street
Marshalltown, IA 50158
Telephone: (515) 752-4976

Heritage Herb Garden (1)
http://www.ozarkfolkcenter.com/crafts-herbs-music/

Hidden Springs Nursery (2)
170 Hidden Springs Lane
Cookeville, TN 38501
Telephone: (931) 268-2592
http://hiddenspringsnursery.com

Hobson Gardens (3)
    Route 2, 3656 East Hobson Road
    Roswell, NM 88201
    Telephone: (505) 622-7289
House of Spices (3)
    http://pages.princegeorges.com/
    dining/spices.htm
Hurov's Seeds & Botanicals (1, 2)
    Post Office Box 1596
    Chula Vista, CA 91912
    Telephone: (619) 291-4969
India House of Spices (3)
    http://www.hosindia.com/
International Herb Association (1, 2)
    http://www.iherb.org/
J.L. Hudson, Seedsman (2)
    http://www.jlhudsonseeds.net/
Johnny's Selected Seeds (2)
    http://www.johnnyseeds.com/
Kalustyan's (1,3)
    http://www.kalustyan.com/
Kings Herb Heaven (2)
    1660 Great North Road
    Avondale, Auckland
    New Zealand
Kitazawa Seed Company (2)
    http://www.kitazawaseed.com/
Kräuterlexikon (2)
    http://www.heilkraeuter.de/lexikon/
Las Hierbas de Cocina (2)
    http://mexconnect.com/mex_/
    recipes/puebla/kgyerbas.html
Latin Wordlist of Assorted Herbs,
    Spices, Plants & Miscellaneous
    Foodstuffs (1)
    http://www.chebucto.ns.ca/~ag151/
    latin/herb_index.html
Le Jardin du Gourmet (2)
    http://www.artisticgardens.com/
    catalog/
Lhasa Karnak Herbs (1)
    http://www.herb-inc.com/
Lily of the Valley Herb Farm (2)
    3969 Fox Avenue
    Minerva, OH 44657
    Telephone: (330) 862-3920
Lingle's Herbs (1, 2)
    http://www.linglesherbs.com/

Logee's Greenhouses, Ltd. (2)
    http://www.logees.com/
Mary Flagler Carey Arboretum (1)
    Route 44a
    Millbrook, NY 12545
    Telephone: (845) 677-5358, 5359
Massachusetts Horticultural
    Society (1)
    http://www.masshort.org/
McCrory's Sunny Hill Herb Farm (2)
    35152 LaPlace Court
    Eustis, FL 32726
    Telephone: (352) 357-9876
Meyer Seed Company (2)
    http://home.1stpage.com/1stlook/
    pages/standard.cfm?url
    =meyerseedco
Mild to Wild Pepper & Herb
    Company (2, 3)
    http://www.wildpepper.com/
Missouri Botanical Garden (1)
    http://www.mobot.org/
Mountain Gardens (1, 2, 3)
    http://www.mountaingardensherbs
    .com/
Mountain Valley Growers, Inc. (1, 2)
    http://www.mountainvalleygrowers
    .com/
Mulberry Creek Herb Farm (1, 2)
    http://www.mulberrycreek.com/
Native American Seed (2)
    http://www.seedsource.com/
Native Seeds/SEARCH (1, 2)
    http://www.nativeseeds.org/
New York Botanical Garden (1)
    http://www.nybg.org/
Nichol's Garden Nursery (2)
    http://www.nicholsgardennursery
    .com/
Nickel and Thyme Herb Shoppe (2)
    http://www.theherbshop.com/
No Thyme Productions (1, 2)
    http://www.nothyme.com/
Orol Ledden and Sons (2)
    Post Office Box 7
    Sewell, NJ 08080-0007
    Telephone: (609) 468-1000
    Fax: (609) 464-0947

Otis Twilley Seed Company (2)
121 Gary Road
Post Office Box 4000
Hodges, SC 29653
Telephone: (215) 639-8800
Fax: (215) 245-9043

Papa Geno's Herb Farm & Prairie
Perennials, Ltd. (1, 2)
http://www.papagenos.com/

Pendery's (3)
http://www.penderys.com/

Pepper Fool (1, 2, 3)
http://www.PepperFool.com/

Pepper Gal (2)
http://www.peppergal.com/

Pinetree Garden Seeds (2, 3)
http://www.superseeds.com/

Plants of the Southwest (2)
http://www.plantsofthesouthwest
.com/

R.H. Shumway Seedsman (2)
http://www.rhshumway.com/

Rabbit Shadow Farm (2, 3)
2880 East Highway 402
Loveland, CO 80537
Telephone: (303) 667-5531

Redwood City Seed Company (2)
http://www.ecoseeds.com/

Richter's Herb Specialists (2, 3)
http://www.richters.com/

Robins Bush Foods (3)
http://www.robins.net.au/
bush_foods.html

Rosemary House and Gardens, Inc.
(1, 2, 3)
http://www.therosemaryhouse.com/
home.html

Sage Garden Herb Farm (1, 2, 3)
http://www.herbs.mb.ca/

Sandy Mush Herbs (2)
http://www.brwm.org/
sandymushherbs/

Scott Arboretum at Swarthmore
College (1)
http://www.scottarboretum.org/

Secret Garden Herb Farm (3)
http://www.a-secretgarden.com/
sg-home.html

Seed Savers Exchange (1, 2)
http://www.seedsavers.org/

Seeds Blüm (2)
27 Idaho City Stage Road
Boise, ID 83716
Telephone: (800) 742-1423
Fax: (208) 338-5658

Seeds of Change (2)
http:// www.seedsofchange.com/

Seeds of Texas Seed Exchange (2)
Post Office Box 9882
College Station, TX 77842

Shady Acres Herb Farm (1, 2)
http://www.shadyacres.com/

Shady Oaks Ginseng Co. (2)
http://www.shadyoaksginseng.net/

Spice Barn (3)
http://www.spicebarn.com/

Stokes Seeds Company (2)
http://www.stokeseeds.com/

Stream Cliff Herb Farm (3)
http://www.streamclifffarm.com/

Sunshine Farm and Garden (2)
http://www.sunfarm.com/

Technisem Seeds Company (2)
http://www.technisem.com/

Territorial Seed Company (2)
http://www.territorial-seed.com/

Thai Herbs & Spices (3)
http://www.thaiherbs.com/

Thompson and Morgan (2)
http://www.thompson-morgan.com/

Thyme Cookbooks (1)
c/o Marge Clark
6242 West State Route 28
West Lebanon, IN 47991-8054
Telephone: (800) 930-3899
or (317) 893-4270

Thyme Garden Herb Company (2)
http://www.thymegarden.com/

Tinmouth Channel Farm (2)
Town Road 19
Wallingford, VT 05773
Telephone: (802) 446-2812

Tomato Grower's Supply Company (2)
http://www.tomatogrowers.com/

University of Florida Herbarium
Library (1)

http://www.flmnh.ufl.edu/natsci/
herbarium/
Uwajimaya Inc. (3)
http://www.uwajimaya.com/
Vaughn's Seed Company (2)
5300 Katrine Avenue
Downer's Grove, IL 60515
Telephone: (708) 969-6300
Fax: (708) 969-6373
Vermont Bean Seed Company (2)
http://www.vermontbean.com/
Vileniki, An Herb Farm (1)
http://www.vilenikiherbfarm.com/
Vineyard Sound Herbs (1, 2, 3)
Union Street
Vineyard Haven, MA 02568
Telephone: (508) 696-7574
W. Atlee Burpee & Company (1, 2)
http://www.burpee.com/
Well-Sweep Herb Farm (2, 3)
http://www.wellsweep.com/
White Flower Farm (2)
http://www.whiteflowerfarm.com/
Wholeherb (2)
http://www.wholeherb.com/
Whole Spice (3)
http://www.wholespice.com/

Wild Earth Native Plant Nursery (2)
Post Office Box 7258
Freehold, NJ 07728
Telephone: (732) 308-9777
Fax: (732) 308-9777
e-mail: wildearthnpn@compuserve
.com
Wildseed Tasmania (2)
http://www.wildseedtasmania
.com.au/
Willhite Seed (2)
http://www.willhiteseed.com/
William Dam Seeds (2)
http://www.damseeds.com/
Woodlanders (1, 2)
http://www.woodlanders.net/
World Seed (1)
http://www.worldseed.org/
W. P. Cody (2)
635 Millswood Drive
Mooresville, NC 28115
Telephone: (704) 662-6957
Fax: (704) 660-5897
Wrenwood of Berkeley Springs (2)
Route 4, Box 361
Berkeley Springs, WV 25411
Telephone/Fax: (304) 258-3071

Bibliography

Algar, Ayla. *Classical Turkish Cooking.* New York: HarperCollins, 1991.

Allen, Gary. *The Resource Guide for Food Writers.* New York: Routledge, 1999.

Andrews, Jean. *Peppers, the Domesticated Species.* Austin: University of Texas Press, 1984.

Anthonio, H. D., and M. Isoun. *Nigerian Cookbook.* London: Macmillan, 1982.

Arndt, Alice. *Seasoning Savvy: How to Cook with Herbs, Spices, and Other Flavorings.* New York: Haworth Press, 1999.

Arnott, Margaret L., ed. *Gastronomy: The Anthropology of Food and Food Habits.* The Hague: Mouton, 1979.

Authentic Chinese Cuisine. 9 vols. Tokyo: Shufunotomo Company, 1984.

Bailey, L. H. *Hortus Third: A Concise Dictionary of Plants Cultivated in the United States and Canada.* New York: Macmillan, 1976.

Behr, Edward. *The Artful Eater.* New York: Atlantic Monthly Press, 1992.

Bennett, H. *Concise Chemical and Technical Dictionary.* Brooklyn, N.Y.: Chemical Publishing Company, 1947.

Blackwell, Elizabeth. *A curious herbal, containing five hundred cuts, of the most useful plants, which are now used in the practice of physick; engraved on folio copper plates, after drawings taken from the life / by Elizabeth Blackwell. To which is added a short description of ye plants and their common uses in physick.* Vol. 2. London: Printed for Samuel Harding, 1737–39.

———. *Herbarium Blackwellianum emendatum et auctum, id est, Elisabethae Blackwell collectio stirpium: quae in pharmacopoliis ad medicum usum asserauntur, quarum descriptio et vires ex Anglico idiomate in Latinum conversae sistuntu figurae maximam partem ad naturale exemplar emendantur floris fructusque partium repraesentationem augentur et probatis botanicorum nominibus illustrentur.* Vol. 3. Nuremburg: Fleischmann, 1750–73.

Bonpland, Aimé. *Description des plantes rares cultivées à Malmaison et à Navarre.* Paris: P. Didot l'aîne, 1813 [1812–17].

Bown, Deni. *Encyclopedia of Herbs and Their Uses.* London: Dorling Kindersley, 1995.

Boxer, Arabella, et al. *The Encyclopædia of Herbs, Spices, and Flavorings.* London: Octopus Books, 1984.

Bremness, Lesley. *Herbs.* New York: Dorling Kindersley, 1994.

Brissenden, Rosemary. *Asia's Undiscovered Cuisine.* New York: Pantheon, 1981.

Brouk, B. *Plants Consumed by Man.* New York: Academic Press, 1975.

Brown, Alice Cooke. *Early American Herb Recipes.* New York: Bonanza, 1966.

Carr, Sandy. *The Simon and Schuster Pocket Guide to Cheese.* New York: Simon and Schuster, 1992.

Claiborne, Craig. *An Herb and Spice Cookbook.* New York: Harper and Row, 1963.

Clevely, Andi, Katherine Richmond, Sallie Morris, and Lesley Mackley. *The Encyclopedia of Herbs and Spices: The Ultimate Guide to Herbs and Spices, with over 200 Recipes.* New York: Hermes House, 1997.

Columbia University College of Physicians and Surgeons. *Complete Home Medical Guide.* New York: Crown, 1985.

Conrad, Barnaby III. *Absinthe, History in a Bottle.* San Francisco: Chronicle, 1988.

Cordero-Fernando, Gilda, ed. *The Culinary Culture of the Philippines.* Hong Kong: Bancom Audiovisual, 1976.

Corn, Charles. *The Scents of Eden: A Narrative of the Spice Trade.* New York: Kodansha International, 1998.

Cost, Bruce. *Ginger, East to West.* Berkeley, Calif.: Aris, 1984.

Crane, Eva. *Honey: A Comprehensive Survey.* London: Heinemann, 1975.

Davidson, Alan. *A Kipper with My Tea.* London: Macmillan, 1988.

———. *The Oxford Companion to Food.* Oxford: Oxford University Press, 1999.

Delessert, Benjamin. *Icones selectae plantarum quas in systemate universali: ex herbariis parisiensibus, praesertim ex Lessertiano.* Vol. 1. Paris, [Fortin Masson et Sociorum], 1820–46.

Desfontaines, Renato L. *Flora Atlantica, sive Historia plantarum quae in Atlante, Agro Tunetano et Algeriensi Crescunt.* Vol. 2. Paris: L. G. Desgranges, [1798–99?].

Devi, Yamuna. *The Art of Indian Vegetarian Cooking.* Old Westbury, N.Y.: Bala, 1987.

DeWitt, Dave, and Nancy Gerlach. *The Whole Chile Pepper Book.* Boston: Little, Brown, 1990.

Elias, Thomas S., and Peter A. Dykeman, eds. *Edible Wild Plants: A North American Field Guide.* New York: Sterling, 1990.

Facciola, Stephen. *Cornucopia II: A Sourcebook of Edible Plants.* 2nd ed.. Vista, Calif.: Kampong, 1999.

Fenaroli, Giovanni. *Fenaroli's Handbook of Flavor Ingredients.* 2 vols. Cleveland: Chemical Rubber Company, 1971.

Fernald, Merritt Lyndon. *Gray's Manual of Botany: A Handbook of the Flowering Plants and Ferns of the Central and Northeastern United States and Adjacent Canada.* 8th ed. New York: American Book Company, 1950.

Fleisher, Alexander, and Zhenia Fleisher. "Identification of Biblical Hyssop and Origin of the Traditional Use of Oregano-group Herbs in the Mediterreanean Region." *Economic Botany* 42 (1988): 232–41.

Food Chemicals Codex. 2nd ed. Washington, D.C.: National Academy of Sciences, 1972.

Freeman, Margaret B. *Herbs for the Medieval Household, for Cooking, Healing, and Divers Uses.* New York: Metropolitan Museum of Art, 1943.

Gerber, Hilda. *Traditional Cookery of the Cape Malays.* Capetown: A. A. Balkema, 1954.

Gordon, Jean. *The Art of Cooking with Roses.* New York: Walker, 1968.

Gray, Patience. *Honey from a Weed.* Berkeley, Calif.: North Point Press, 1986.

Grieve, Mrs. M. *A Modern Herbal.* 1931. Revised. London: Dorset Press, 1992.

Halgarten, Peter. *Liqueurs.* London: Wine and Spirit Publications, 1967.

Hamady, Mary Laird. *Lebanese Mountain Cookery.* Boston: David R. Godine, 1987.

Hampstead, Marilyn. *The Basil Book.* New York: Pocket Books, 1984.

Harris, Jessica B. *Tasting Brazil.* New York: Macmillan, 1992.

Harrop, Renny, ed. *Encyclopedia of Herbs.* London: Marshall Cavendish, 1977.

Heath, H. B. *Flavor Technology: Profiles, Products, Applications.* Westport, Conn.: AVI, 1978.

Hedrick, U. P., ed. *Sturtevant's Edible Plants of the World.* 1919. Reprint, New York: Dover, 1972.

Holland, B., I. D. Unwin, and D. H. Buss. *Vegetables, Herbs, and Spices.* 5th Supplement to McCance and Widdowson, *The Composition of Foods.* Cambridge: Royal Society of Chemistry and the Ministry of Agriculture, Fisheries, and Food, 1991.

Host, Nikolaus Thomas. *Icones et descriptiones Graminum austriacorum.* Vol. 3. Vienna: A. Schmidt, 1801–9.

Hui, Y. H., ed.. *Encyclopedia of Food Science and Technology.* New York: Wiley, 1992.

Hutchins, Alma. *A Handbook of Native American Herbs.* Boston: Shambala, 1992.

———. *Indian Herbology of North America.* Boston: Shambala, 1991.

Hutton, Wendy. *Tropical Herbs and Spices.* Singapore: Periplus, 1997.

Jacquin, Nikolaus Joseph. *Fragmenta botanica, figuris coloratis illustrata: ab anno 1800 ad annum 1809 per sex fasciculos edita.* Vienna: A. Schmidt, 1809.

———. *Icones plantarum rariorum.* Vol. 2. Vienna: C. F. Wappler, 1781–93.

———. *Plantarum rariorum horti caesarei Schoenbrunnensis descriptiones et icones.* Vol. 4. Vienna: C. F. Wappler, 1797–1804.

Jamil-Garbutt, Nina. *The Baghdad Kitchen.* Kingswood, Tadworth, Surrey, Eng.: Kingswood Press, 1985.

Janzen, Daniel H., ed. *Costa Rican Natural History.* Chicago: University of Chicago Press, 1983.

Jaume Saint-Hilaire, Jean Henri. *La flore et la pomone françaises: historie et figure en couleur, des fleurs et des fruits de France ou naturalisés sur le sol français.* Vol. 5. Paris: by the author, 1828–33.

———. *Traité des arbres forestiers: ou historie et description des arbre indigènes ou naturalisées.* Paris: Firmin Didot, 1824.

———. *Traité des arbrisseaux et des arbustes cultivés en France et en pleine.* Paris: by the author, 1825.

Johns, Timothy. *With Bitter Herbs They Shall Eat It: Chemical Ecology and the Origins of Human Diet and Medicine.* Tucson: University of Arizona Press, 1960.

Keville, Kathi. *The Illustrated Herb Encyclopedia.* New York: Mallard Press, 1991.

Köhler, F. E. *Köhler's Medizinal-Pflanzen in naturgetreuen Abbildungen mit kurz erläuterndem Texte: Atlas zur Pharmacopoea germanica.* Vol. 1. Gera-Untermhaus: F. E. Köhler, [1883–1914].

Kowalchik, Claire, and William H. Hylton, eds. *Rodale's Illustrated Encyclopedia of Herbs.* Emmaus, Pa.: Rodale Press, c. 1987.

Krochmal, Connie and Arnold. *The West Indies Cookbook: Classic Recipes from the Spicy Caribbean.* Albuquerque: Border Books, 1992.

Larkom, Joy. *Oriental Vegetables, Complete Guide for Garden and Kitchen.* Tokyo: Kodansha, 1991.

LaTorre, Dolores L. *Cooking and Curing with Mexican Herbs.* Austin, Tex.: Encino Press, 1977.

Laudan, Rachel. *The Food of Paradise: Exploring Hawaii's Culinary Heritage.* Honolulu: University of Hawai'i Press, 1996.

Linares, Edelmira, and Judith Aguirre, eds. *Los Quelites, un Tesoro Culinario.* Mexico: UNAM, 1992.

Marcin, Marietta. *The Herbal Tea Garden: Planning, Planting, Harvesting, and Brewing.* Pownal, Vt.: Storey, 1993.

Marks, Copeland. *False Tongues and Sunday Bread.* New York: M. Evans, 1985.

Marks, Copeland, and Manjo Kim. *The Korean Kitchen: Recipes from the Land of the Morning Calm.* San Francisco: Chronicle, 1993.

McGee, Harold. *On Food and Cooking.* New York: Scribners, 2004.

McRae, Bobbi A. *The Herb Companion Wishbook and Resource Guide.* Loveland, Colo.: Interweave Press, 1992.

Meerburgh, Nicolaas. *Plantarum selectarum icones pictae.* Leiden: J. Meerburg, 1798.

Merory, Joseph. *Food Flavorings: Composition, Manufacture, and Use.* 2nd ed. Westport, Conn.: AVI, 1968.

Mesfin, Daniel J. *Exotic Ethiopian Cooking.* Falls Church, Va.: Ethiopian Cookbook Enterprise, 1987.

Miller, Richard Alan. *The Magical and Ritual Use of Aphrodisiacs.* Rochester, Vt.: Destiny Books, 1985.

Millspaugh, Charles F. *American Medicinal Plants.* 1892. Reprint, New York: Dover, 1974.

Morton, Julia F. *Major Medicinal Plants: Botany, Culture, and Uses.* Springfield, Ill.: Charles C. Thomas, 1977.

Murai, M., F. Pen, and C. D. Miller. *Some Tropical South Pacific Island Foods: Description, History, Use, Composition, and Nutritive Value.* Honolulu: University of Hawai'i Press, 1958.

Naj, Amal. *Peppers.* New York: Knopf, 1992.

Northcote, Rosalind Lucy. *The Book of Herb Lore.* Reprint, New York: Dover, 1971. Published in 1912 as *The Book of Herbs.*

Ortiz, Elisabeth Lambert. *The Encyclopedia of Herbs, Spices, and Flavorings.* New York: Dorling Kindersley, 1992.

Parry, J. W. *Spices.* New York: Chemical Publishing Company, 1969.

Passmore, Jacki. *The Encyclopedia of Asian Foods and Cooking.* New York: Hearst, 1991.

Pokhlebkin, William. *A History of Vodka.* Trans. Renfrey Clarke. London: Verso, 1991.

Poundstone, William. *Big Secrets.* New York: Quill, 1983.

Purseglove, J. W., et al. *Spices.* 2 vols. London: Longman, 1981.

Rätsch, Christian. *The Dictionary of Sacred and Magical Plants.* Dorset, Eng.: Prism Press, 1992.

Reilly, Ann, ed. *Taylor's Pocket Guide to Herbs and Edible Flowers.* Boston: Houghton Mifflin, 1990.

Roden, Claudia. *A New Book of Middle Eastern Food.* New York: Viking, 1985.

Rohde, Eleanor Sinclair. *Culinary and Salad Herbs: Their Cultivation and Food Values with Recipes.* London: Country Life, 1940. Reprint, New York: Dover, 1972.

Root, Waverley, ed. *Herbs and Spices: The Pursuit of Flavor.* New York: McGraw-Hill, 1980.

Rousseau, Jean-Jacques. *Recueil de plantes coloriees, pour servir a l'intelligence des lettres elementaires sur la botanique.* Paris: Poincot, Libraire, 1789.

Salloum, Mary. *A Taste of Lebanon.* Essex, Eng.: Scorpion, 1989.

Schauneberg, Paul, and Ferdinand Paris. *Guide to Medicinal Plants.* New Canaan, Conn.: Keats, 1977.

Schivelbusch, Wolfgang. *Tastes of Paradise, A Social History of Spices, Stimulants and Intoxicants.* Trans. David Jacobson. New York: Vintage, 1993.

Schneider, Elizabeth. *Uncommon Fruits and Vegetables.* New York: Harper and Row, 1986.

Schulick, Paul. *Ginger: Common Spice and Wonder Drug.* 3rd ed. Brattleboro, Vt.: Herbal Free Press, 1996.

Shaudys, Phyllis V. *Herbal Treasures.* Pownal, Vt.: Storey, 1990.

Simmons, Adelma Grenier. *Herb Gardening in Five Seasons.* New York: Hawthorne Dutton, 1964.

Smith, C. Earle, Jr., ed. *Man and His Foods: Studies in the Ethnobotany of Nutrition; Contemporary, Primitive, and Prehistoric Non-European Diets; Papers.* Eleventh International Botanical Congress. Tuscaloosa: University of Alabama Press, 1973.

Sokolov, Raymond. *Why We Eat What We Eat.* New York: Summit, 1991.

Solomon, Charmaine, and Nina Solomon. *Charmaine Solomon's Encyclopedia of Asian Food.* Boston: Periplus, 1991.

Staples, George W., and Michael S. Kristiansen. *Ethnic Culinary Herbs: A Guide to Identification and Cultivation in Hawai'i.* Honolulu: University of Hawai'i Press, 1999.

Stuart, Malcolm, ed. *The Encyclopedia of Herbs and Herbalism.* New York: Crescent Books, 1979.

Tannahill, Reay. *Food in History.* 2nd ed. New York: Crown, 1988.

Tolley, Emelie, and Chris Mead. *The Herbal Pantry.* New York: Clarkson N. Potter, 1992.

Vallet, Pierre. *Le jardin du Roy tres chrestien, Loys XIII, Roy de France et de Navare . . .* Paris: by the author, 1623.

Von Reis, Siri. *Drugs and Foods from Little-Known Plants: Notes in Harvard University Herbaria.* Cambridge, Mass.: Harvard University Press, 1973.

———. "Exploring the Herbarium." *Scientific American,* May 1977, 96–104.

Weatherford, Jack. *Indian Givers: How the Indians of the Americas Transformed the World.* New York: Fawcett Columbine, 1988.

Weinmann, Johann Wilhelm. *Phytanthoza iconographia . . .* 4 vols. Regensburg: Hieronymum Lentzium, 1737-45.

Winter, Ruth. *A Consumer's Dictionary of Food Additives; Definitions for the Layman of Ingredients Harmful and Desirable Found in Packaged Foods, with Complete Information for the Consumer.* 4th ed. New York: Three Rivers Press, 1994.

Witty, Helen, ed. *Billy Joe Tatum's Wild Foods Cookbook and Field Guide.* New York: Workman, 1976.

Wolfert, Paula. *The Cooking of the Eastern Mediterranean.* New York: HarperCollins, 1994.

———. *Couscous and Other Good Food from Morocco.* New York: Harper and Row, 1973.

———. *Mediterranean Grains and Greens.* New York: HarperCollins, 1998.

Woodville, William. *Medical botany: containing systematic and general descriptions, with plates, of all the medicinal plants, indigenous and exotic, comprehended in the catalogues of the materia medica, as published by the Royal Colleges of Physicians of London and Edinburgh.* 4 vols. London: James Phillips, 1790–93.

———. *A supplement to Medical botany, or, Part of the second: containing plates with descriptions of most of the principal medicinal plants not included in the materia medica of the collegiate pharmacopoeias of London and Edinburgh.* Vol. 4. London: James Phillips, 1794.

Zee, A. *Swallowing Clouds.* New York: Simon and Schuster, 1990.

Index

For the sake of brevity, synonyms for the herbs and spices themselves (which are included in the entries) are not listed in this index, nor are items that are defined in the glossary.

Mahón, 407
maître d'hôtel butter, 64
Majocchino, 330
majoun, 146
mapouchari, 147
margarita, 11
marrowbone pie, 67
masala, 444
masala cha, 414
Mascarpone, 41
masho-hara, 331
Masman curry. *See* gaeng mussaman
Mastic (or Masticha, Mastika), 37, 253
mata-bicho. *See* cachaça
maubi (or mauby), 357
ma ward. *See* my warid
ma yau, 320
may wine, 369, 374
mead, 178
Mentucca, 213
mescal, 11
mezes, 321
mignonette, 332
mimea (or momea), 147
mirin, 390
miso, 264, 352, 356, 386
misticanza, 135
Mohn, 316
mojo criollo, 377
mokan, 314
mole negro, 411
mole poblano, 320, 411
mole verde, 322
molho brasiliero, 48, 64, 328, 405
momiji-oroshi, 134
Monte Aguila, 239
moon cakes, 302
Morello Ratafia, 249, 366
mortadella, 48
mostarda di frutti di Cremona, 132
mosto, 429
Moxie, 174
Moyarra, 118
mozzarella, 41, 53
msir. *See* preserved lemon
Mull of Kintyre, 118
Muslim curry. *See* gaeng mussaman
my warid, 365

Nagelkaas (or Friese Nagelkaas), 53, 294

nam pla, 335, 406
nam prik, 406
nam prik kang karie. *See* yellow curry paste
nam som, 407
Narbonne honey, 223
nar eksisi. *See* dibs riman
nasi kunyit, 314
navaitai, 167
netetou. *See* kinda
Newbury, 19
nimono, 302
Ninkasi, 312
noumi basra. *See* limoo amoni
nyonya kuey, 315
nyponsoppa, 366

Ojen. *See* absinthe; Pastis
oleo do urucum, 117
olivette, 317
orange curry paste, 407
ouzo, 37
Oxygenée. *See* absinthe

pachadis. *See* ranas
pacorza, 312
paella, 88, 184
pai kua. *See* gingko
palma de vino, 312
palm oil. *See* dendê oil
Pant-Ys-Gawn, 15, 19, 328
Parfait Amour, 366
Passaia, 318
Pastis, 37
pekmez, 429
Pélardon, 328
Pepper Jack, 407
Pernod, 35, 104, 161, 187, 200, 204, 289
Perroche, 55, 109
Perry, 362
persillé, 64
pertsovka, 328, 407
pescara, 37
pesto alla genovese, 190, 322, 407
petitgrain, 377
pho, 341
Picodon, 429
Pierre-qui-Vire, 118
pignoli, 322
piki, 22

GARY ALLEN is a food writer in New York's Hudson Valley.
He is the author of *The Resource Guide for Food Writers*
and coauthor of *Remarkable Service: A Guide to Keeping
Customers for Restaurant Owners, Managers, and Servers*.
His articles on foods and cooking have appeared in
Flavor and Fortune, The Valley Table, and several
encyclopedias. He is webmaster of the
Association for the Study of Food
and Society (ASFS) and an
adjunct professor at
Empire State
College.

THE FOOD SERIES

A History of Cooks and Cooking
Michael Symons

Peanuts: The Illustrious History
of the Goober Pea
Andrew F. Smith

Marketing Nutrition: Soy, Functional Foods,
Biotechnology, and Obesity
Brian Wansink

The Banquet: Dining in the Great Courts
of Late Renaissance Europe
Ken Albala

The Turkey: An American Story
Andrew F. Smith

The Herbalist in the Kitchen
Gary Allen

The University of Illinois Press
is a founding member of the
Association of American University Presses.

Composed in 10/12.5 Hoefler Text,
designed by Jonathan Hoefler,
with Hoefler Titling display
by BookComp, Inc.
for the University of Illinois Press
Designed by Copenhaver Cumpston
Manufactured by Thomson-Shore, Inc.

UNIVERSITY OF ILLINOIS PRESS
1325 South Oak Street   Champaign, IL 61820-6903
www.press.uillinois.edu